GÜNTER BEER · PATRIK JAROS

THE COOK'S ENCYCLOPEDIA

GÜNTER BEER · PATRIK JAROS

THE COOK'S ENCYCLOPEDIA
THE ULTIMATE GUIDE FOR ALL COOKS

LOVE FOOD is an imprint of Parragon Books Ltd

LOVE FOOD and the accompanying heart device is a registered trade mark of Parragon Books Ltd in Australia, the UK and the EU.

Parragon Books Ltd
Queen Street House
4 Queen Street
Bath BA1 1HE, UK

ISBN: 978-1-4054-9576-9

Printed in China

Concept: Patrik Jaros & Günter Beer

The visual media is on file at the OHIM as a registered design of Buenavista Studio S.L. under the number 000252796-001.

Original German edition

Photography: Günter Beer I www.beerfoto.com
Written by: Günter Beer, Gerhard von Richthofen, Patrik Jaros, Jörg Zipprick
Photography assistants: Sigurd Buchberger, Aranxa Alvarez
Kitchen assistants: Magnus Thelen, Johannes von Bemberg
Design by: Estudio Merino I www.estudiomerino.com
Produced by: Buenavista Studio S.L. I www.buenavistastudio.com

English-language edition produced by Cambridge Publishing Management Ltd

Translators: Elisabeth Moser, Rónat O'Neill, Cathryn Siegal-Bergman

Photo credits: All photographs taken by Günter Beer, Barcelona

Except: p. 303, Gettyimages – 3rd row middle; p. 423, Davies + Starr – 2nd row middle, Eising – 3rd row left and middle, Foodcollection – 3rd row right.

Notes for the Reader:

This book uses both metric and imperial measurements. Follow the same units of measurement throughout; do not mix metric and imperial. All spoon measurements are level: teaspoons are assumed to be 5 ml, and tablespoons are assumed to be 15 ml. Unless otherwise stated, milk is assumed to be full fat, eggs and individual vegetables are medium, and pepper is freshly ground black pepper.

The times given are an approximate guide only. Preparation times differ according to the techniques used by different people and the cooking times may also vary from those given. Optional ingredients, variations or serving suggestions have not been included in the calculations.

Recipes using raw or very lightly cooked eggs should be avoided by infants, the elderly, pregnant women, convalescents and anyone suffering from an illness. Pregnant and breastfeeding women are advised to avoid eating peanuts and peanut products. Sufferers from nut allergies should be aware that some of the ready-made ingredients used in the recipes in this book may contain nuts. Always check the packaging before use.

Contents

How to Use This Cookbook

The list of ingredients with their images at the top left side of the page is like a flipbook that can be used as an index. Without having to read the book, you can quickly flip through and find recipes according to the ingredients you wish to use.

↓

  100 ml (3½ fl oz) white wine

 5 eggs

  1 pinch of salt

 350 g (12 oz) butter

Juice of ½ lemon

1 tbsp tarragon vinegar

1 pinch of cayenne pepper

 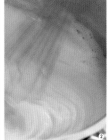

This sauce is too runny either because the butter was too hot when it was added, or it was added too quickly.

Hollandaise Sauce

1. Bring 3 cm (1¼ inches) water to the boil in a pan as a bain-marie. Pour the white wine in a bowl with a rounded bottom. Separate the eggs, putting the yolk in the bowl, and the egg white in a sealed container for later use, storing it in the refrigerator. Now place the bowl over the bain-marie, add salt, and mix together using a whisk.

Beat the egg yolk vigorously with the whisk until it is thick and pale.

Melt the butter in a small pan until it is warm, not hot, then carefully drizzle it into the foamy egg yolk using a ladle. Keep stirring all the time with the whisk so that the butter blends with the yolk, resulting in a thick and creamy consistency. The preparation is exactly as for mayonnaise, except this sauce is warm. Finally, add salt, lemon juice, tarragon vinegar and cayenne pepper to taste.

Makes about 600 g (1 lb 5 oz) or 1 litre (1¾ pints).

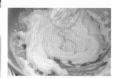

The egg has curdled because it was beaten over boiling water. It wouldn't be possible to stir in more butter to smooth it.

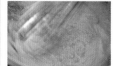

Kitchen doctor: The sauce is runny here too. Add 1 tbsp of hot water and try stirring it again using small movements in one spot, then stir in more and more of the rest of the sauce.

25

   ■ To whip up a really good Hollandaise sauce, 5 eggs yolks are best. Never use fewer than 3 egg yolks, otherwise the sauce will not reach the correct consistency. Place the finished sauce over a pan of water, not letting it touch the cooker, and cover with baking paper. This allows the sauce to stay warm for up to an hour. This sauce goes best with steamed asparagus or poached fish.

152 | Sauces & Stocks

↑ ↑

↑ **Preparation time:** The number on the lower left side of the page gives the approximate preparation time in minutes.

↑ **Tips:** Substitutions and variations for the recipe, useful suggestions or possible menu combinations.

↑ ✳ **Kitchen doctor:** The kitchen doctor helps to troubleshoot if something goes wrong.

↑

↑ **Level of difficulty:** The stars indicate the level of difficulty. One star is for easy, two stars are for intermediate and three stars are for advanced.

The **recipes** will generally serve four people using the amounts given, unless otherwise specified.

A teaspoon equals 5 ml; a tablespoon equals 15 ml. If milk is called for and nothing else is specified, use full-fat milk. The amounts specified for potatoes, vegetables and eggs refer to medium sizes. Pepper always means freshly ground pepper.

You've been here before: you want to make something delicious. You look for the perfect recipe, one that delivers the goods. You shop for the ingredients and get going in the kitchen. And soon the problems begin, perhaps while cutting a classic ingredient like an onion. It looked so easy: dice the onion – but how do you do that?

This is exactly where this book comes in. Words and pictures clearly explain the essential steps of preparing basic ingredients. How do I peel tomatoes correctly? How do I deseed a pepper? When do I slice artichokes, and when do I leave them whole? It will soon be clear that 'cut into small pieces' is not always going to mean the same thing: mushrooms are cut differently for sauces and omelettes than they are for ragouts. And that goes for all vegetables.

Problems also arise while carrying out a recipe. Who hasn't cooked rice that got sticky while boiling, when it was supposed to be light and fluffy? It may have been because partially polished brown rice is not cooked in the same way as basmati rice, for example. The same goes for potatoes. Why do mashed potatoes get gluey and heavy? This book finally explains how to make light, creamy mashed potatoes. You will find basic recipes that clearly explain how to make pasta, gnocchi, bread, dumplings, pizza and shortcrust pastries successfully. Basic recipes for stocks and sauces, required for many dishes, are also included.

This book offers numerous recipes with clear step-by-step photography – recipes that have been expanded to include additional ingredients, as well as techniques for preparation and methods.

So you need no longer fret that your onion will get soggy with tears as you cut it, or have the oh-so-promising dish literally leave a bitter taste in your mouth. You will not just *plan* to cook something delicious, you *will* cook something delicious!

Consumer
Guide

Contents

General Consumer Guide

Good kitchens need good ingredients. Even an amateur can create a special menu with a free-range chicken or a freshly caught sea bass – with good-quality food, a simple recipe is all you need for a most enjoyable meal. It's true that a little precision is required, especially with cooking times. If mediocre ingredients are all that's available, it'll take an outstanding cook to make them taste good.

Despite the abundance of ingredients, it is getting more and more difficult to pick out really good food from the range being offered. When was the last time you ate a tomato, for example, that didn't taste like water with food colouring in it? Most people judge food purely in terms of how it looks. Meat and fish counters have the right lighting, and vegetables look spotless, as though torn from a picture book – no one talks about flavour any more.

In every chapter of this book, we will take a closer look at the most important ingredients. However, there are some ground rules for shopping:

Even experts find it hard to tell if a fish has been properly scaled, gutted and filleted without examining it further. The flesh in a fillet should be firm and (other than 'red' fish such as salmon) have a nice white shimmer without looking dull. At the end of the day, you will taste the difference.

Whole fish should always have glossy, clear eyes, with flesh that is firm to the touch and, depending on the species, the gills should have a reddish shimmer. Fillets should always be purchased fresh and, if possible, eaten within two hours or, at the very least, on the same day. Otherwise the fish oxidises and loses its flavour.

Cheap meat is often pale, flabby and watery. It shrivels up in the pan. Visible signs of quality are not easy to discern as the lighting at the meat counter can be deceptive. Do not generally spurn meat for having rims of fat, because fat is an important flavour carrier.

You cannot recognise definitive quality based on the regional origin or breed either. There is both superior and inferior Angus beef, yet they are sold under the same name.

No one can really determine the quality of packaged chicken either. The skin should not be spotty, and visible damage should ring an alarm bell. Unlike with other meats, chicken labels can give reliable indications of quality. A free-range chicken always tastes much better than a caged one. And a free-range chicken with certification of its origins is even better.

Looking at vegetables alone does not tell you which ones have the best flavour. Note: dehydration is the vegetable's natural enemy. Spots on skins and cracked stalks are, therefore, signs of poor quality. Choose smaller or medium-size vegetables over larger ones, which often contain a lot of water that will just end up in the pan.

Fruit is almost always nice to look at these days – all shiny, glossy and crisp-looking in its display. Organic foods are better: organic apples may be either lightly wrinkled or completely worm-eaten, but they simply have more flavour. And that is the bottom line.

Staples

Many cookbook readers make the same mistake: they look for a particularly attractive recipe, and the first thing they do is buy each and every ingredient on the list. Then, after complaining all the way home about how much it cost, they decide that cooking at home may be too expensive.

The truth is, cooking for yourself is not expensive. But you should avoid shopping for each individual recipe.

To have a sensible kitchen you can work in, you need some basic non-perishable ingredients. Fill your kitchen cabinets with, for example:

1. Rice (basmati and jasmine (Thai))
2. Flour
3. Spaghetti and tagliatelle
4. Lentils, bulgur, other dried legumes
5. Cocoa powder
6. Dark chocolate with a high cocoa content (above 70 per cent)
7. Sliced almonds
8. Currants
9. Dried fruit, e.g. apricots
10. Dried mushrooms, e.g. porcini
11. Tomato purée
12. Sugar
13. Salt
14. Pepper, black and white, whole corns
15. Groundnut oil
16. Olive oil
17. Balsamic vinegar
18. Cinnamon sticks
19. Nutmeg
20. Thyme
21. Rosemary
22. Sesame seeds
23. Bay leaves
24. Peas (dried or frozen)
25. Tinned fish (e.g. tuna)
26. Alcohol such as cognac, port, rum or Cointreau

Groceries that need to be stored in a refrigerator spoil more quickly. To start cooking, you need:

27. Butter
28. Cream
29. Natural yogurt
30. Milk
31. Eggs
32. Fresh lemons

■ Warning: Nothing lasts forever. Always check the use-by date on the item before using.

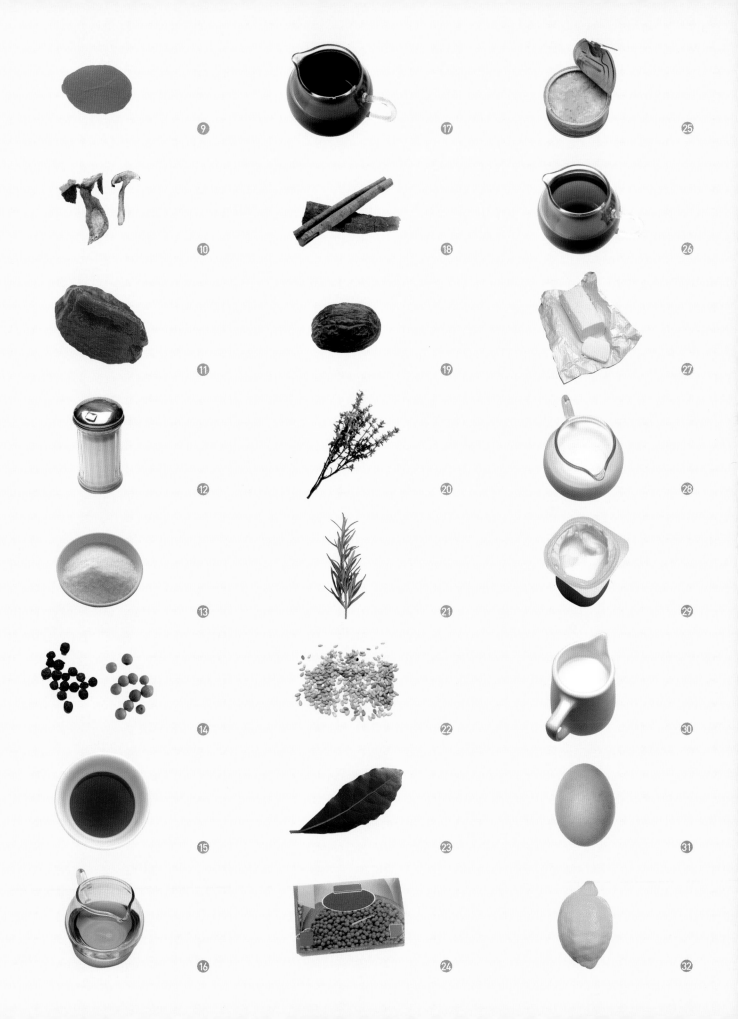

Basic Tools and Equipment

Kitchen foil (1): To cover cooked foods. It protects food surfaces from overbrowning.

Baking powder (2): This helps dough and mixtures rise and stay fluffy while baking.

Bamboo mat (3): To roll sushi or other rolls.

Cotton tea towel (4): To dry potatoes and uncut vegetables.

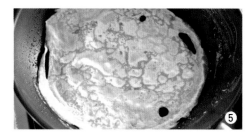

Round nonstick frying pan (5): To make pancakes and for frying potatoes, vegetables, meat, poultry and fish.

Colander (6): For rinsing and draining lettuce, vegetables, fruit or cooked foods.

Steamer (7): Relatively flat dish with a cover for steaming vegetables and fish.

Meat fork (8): For removing roasts and poultry from dishes, or for turning meat over in a dish.

Ricer (9): Used to press through potatoes, vegetables, or chunky vegetable sauces.

Stock (10): Always a good base for soups, stews, sauces and risottos.

Easy-blend yeast (11): Important ingredient in bread, pastries and dough. Only mix into lukewarm liquids.

Gelatine (12): To bind creams, desserts, savoury and sweet mousses. Soak in cold water first, then let it dissolve in a hot liquid.

Paring knife (13): Curved slightly from the front end downwards, this knife is used for peeling, or for cutting and cleaning vegetables and fruit.

Vegetable bouquet I. (14): Comprising root vegetables and herbs for fish soups and sauces.

Vegetable bouquet II. (15): Comprising root vegetables, except carrots, with lemon peel and herbs for fish soups and sauces.

Gratin dish (16): For dishes topped with cheese like vegetable casseroles, stuffed vegetables or lasagne.

Griddle pan (17): Cast-iron grill pan for cooking meats, fish, vegetables or side dishes. The pan has to be brushed with oil first, then heated well, otherwise the food will stick to it.

Coarse grater (18): For grating vegetables and fruit.

Large salad bowl (19): For making and mixing salads, for making fillings, or for keeping cooked ingredients.

Fishbone tongs (20): Important for getting the smaller bones out of fish fillets so you can make a fish dish clear of any bones.

Terrine mould (21): Able to hold 1.8 litres (3¼ pints) for pâtés, meat loaf, aspic, vegetables and fish loaf.

Stainless steel frying pan (22): Pan for frying all foods and for heating up sauces.

Loaf tin (23): For baking bread and cakes – first grease with butter and sprinkle with a little flour so that the contents slide out of the tin better after baking.

Ceramic casserole dish (24): For baking fish in the oven, and for making casseroles and some desserts.

Ceramic roasting dish (25): For roasting poultry, fish or vegetables in the oven.

Cling film (26): For keeping cooked food or prepared, marinated meats or fish in the refrigerator. This prevents them from taking on the taste and odour of other foods, and vice versa.

Small stainless steel roasting tin (27): For roasting smaller dishes in the oven.

Small ladle (28): For removing foam from soups or stocks.

Small whisk (29): For stirring salad dressings, warm sauces, cake mixes and soups.

Rubber spatula (30): For spreading fillings or stuffings, or scraping sauces out of dishes or bowls.

Garlic press (31): To press peeled garlic for marinades or salad dressings.

Springform pan (32): Normally nonstick and 28 cm (11 inches) in diameter. For cakes and tortes.

Melon baller (33): With its sharp edges, the melon baller is also good for scraping out pumpkins, cucumbers or courgettes.

Kitchen brush (34): For brushing off and cleaning shellfish.

Kitchen twine I. (35): For trussing bacon, herbs, roasts, or even two different kinds of meat together, so that they hold their shape while cooking.

Kitchen twine II. (36): For fixing one ingredient to another one, such as a lemon slice to a piece of artichoke, or bacon to meat or poultry.

Blender (37): For mixing sauces, soups, milkshakes, smoothies or vegetable purées.

Kitchen paper (38): For blotting fried foods to soak up the extra oil or fat.

Kitchen shears (39): For cutting shellfish shells to be used in sauces or poultry bones used in stocks and sauces.

Measuring cup (40): For measuring liquids and creams.

Nutmeg grater (41): For grating whole nutmeg. Important for clear soups and mashed potatoes.

Oval nonstick pan (42): For frying fish or shellfish.

Baking paper (43): For covering delicate foods in the oven, so they don't come in direct contact with the heat.

Parsley bouquet (44): Tie up any leftover parsley stems into a bouquet with kitchen twine and cook it in sauces, soups or stews – it adds a nice, fresh flavour.

Plastic chopping board (45): A board on which to cut foods. Always use a separate board for cutting raw meat to avoid cross-contamination.

Round cutters (46): You can buy sets in different sizes. For cutting dough, and making potato or carrot scales for fish.

Round, heatproof mixing bowl (47): For whipping Hollandaise or egg yolks over a bain-marie.

Slotted spoon (48): For removing cooked foods from soups or stocks.

Soda siphon (49): For foaming cream or cream-like liquids while adding it to gelatins.

Soufflé dish (50): Round ceramic dishes varying in diameter for sweet and savoury soufflés.

Piping bags and decorating tips (51): For decorative egg fillings or decorating small buns, cakes and tortes.

Steel saucepan (52): For cooking and heating up sauces, soups or stews.

Pastry or cookie cutter (53): For working with biscuit, pastry and puff pastry doughs.

Truffle slicer (54): For slicing truffles over dishes, of course, but also for shaving Parmesan cheese over pasta and other dishes.

Wok (55): Large pan with high, sloping sides used for stir-frying.

Cocktail picks (56): For sealing poultry cavities closed and for fixing ham or bacon to small cuts of meat.

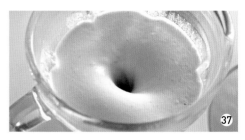

The Food Pyramid

The food pyramid is supposed to help you eat healthily.

It shows the proportions of servings of the different foods we should consume.

The bottom section shows foods that should be consumed frequently; for example, starchy foods like pasta, bread or rice.

The foods at the top, such as fats and sugar, should be eaten in smaller quantities.

However, the pyramid has been disputed for years. There are alternatives, for example, that use a glycaemic index measure. Some scientists believe red meat, cheese and white bread should be closer to the top of the pyramid.

The food pyramid can be a guide to healthy eating, but it should not be taken as gospel. Most food models fall short because they assume the human body works like a machine. A diesel engine always needs diesel gas, whether it's driven with a light foot or a heavy one. Our bodies, however, are not machines. Our food requirements depend on how we live our lives – on whether we lead active or sedentary lifestyles. Do we exercise during our free time, or sit in front of the TV?

Genetic factors also play a role. It's a fact that some people can eat whatever they like and still stay thin their whole lives.

Others can eat just a small amount yet put on weight. Everyone metabolises food differently.

Regular exercise,
a minimum of
2–3 times a week
(20–30 minutes)
Alcohol in moderation

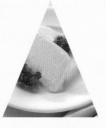

Animal fats, sweets, salt

Meat 2–3 times per week   **Eggs** 2–3 per week

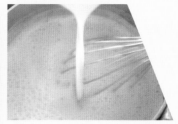

Fish 1–2 portions per week   **Milk & dairy products** min. 2 portions per day

Vegetables min. 2–3 portions per day   **Fruit** min. 2–3 portions per day

Carbohydrates several portions per day, e.g. bread, potatoes, pasta, legumes

Drink min. 8 glasses of water a day

Cooking for Yourself Is the First Step to Better Eating

When you cook, you know what is going into the pan. You can decide between fatty and lean meats; you can choose between cooking with butter or with olive oil. And you can spare your body all the additives hiding in junk foods; for example, substances that preserve junk foods, make them look nicer, or just give them flavour. The last group, flavour enhancers, are especially controversial.

Energy Density

Even though calories have asserted themselves in the public eye, many experts in food-energy density see a better option for healthy eating. Energy density is the energy content of food in relation to weight (Calorie/30 g/1 oz). That sounds abstract, but it has concrete implications. Foods with less energy density are more filling with lower calorie intakes.

Food-Energy Density Cal/30 g (1 oz)

Wheat rye bread	63
Wholemeal roll	66
Croissant	129
Cheesecake	111
Biscuits	147
Gingerbread	120
Cow's milk, 1.5% fat	12
Cow's milk, 3.5% fat	12
Fruit yogurt, added sugar, 1.5% fat	24
Fruit yogurt, added sugar, 3.5% fat	27
Soured cream	36
Whipped cream	93
Jam	81
Honey	99
Hazelnut spread	156
Low-fat butter/margarine	111
Light margarine	240
Butter	240
Ham, cooked (lean)	39
Meatloaf	90
Salami	111
Bratwurst	93
Tuna (no oil)	33
Pickled herring	63
Emmental/Gruyère cheese, 45% fat	120
Apple, grapefruit, honeydew melon, cherries, kiwi fruit, mandarins, nectarines, plums	15
Gummibears	102
Granola bars	33–126
Full-fat chocolate milk	162
Beef, lean	30
Veal, lean	30
Pork cutlet	33
Pork cutlet, breaded (cooked)	96
Chicken breast	30
Trout	30
Fish, breaded (cooked)	96

Potatoes	21
White rice, cooked	30
Fried potatoes	39
Pasta, cooked	42
Chips	63
Eggs	45
Beans, broccoli, cress, pumpkin, carrots, leeks, Savoy cabbage, onion	9
Fruit sorbet	24–36
Ice cream, scoop	30–117

The ideal average is about 45 Cal/30 g (1 oz). Turning to cheesecakes and pizza is perfectly allowable on occasion, but using the energy density table cleverly ensures you'll be able to put together palatable meals on your own. So it might be better to limit bread consumption at breakfast and eat a little more cooked ham instead. Potatoes have a lower energy density than rice or pasta, and avoiding pasta means you can dish up a little more meat. And don't forget, the energy density table guarantees less hunger; after all, it directly relates to how filling each food is.

- Under 45 Cal/30 g (1 oz)
- 45–75 Cal/30 g (1 oz)
- Above 75 Cal/30 g (1 oz)

Excerpted from the energy density table from the Else Kröner Fresenius Centre at the Technical University of Munich.

Calories

Calories are a measure of energy:
1 calorie is the amount of energy needed to heat 1 kg (2 lb 4 oz) water by 1°C (1.8°F). The term calorie comes directly from the era of steam engines. To make one work, it was important to know how wood or coal could be used to heat water, and thereby create energy. The human body, however, does not burn food like a steam engine – and it does not work as consistently either. Despite all the tables in women's and fitness magazines, human energy conversion depends heavily on your individual constitution. The brain is considered the largest energy user. By weight, it equals about 2 per cent of total body mass, but monopolises about 20 per cent of the body's own converted energy.

Caloric content of each item for every 100 g (3½ oz) unless otherwise specified:

Hare	105
Venison	94
Veal	94
Calf's liver	115
Rabbit	121
Lamb	178
Venison saddle	94
Beef fillet	115
Minced beef	212
Beef, fatty	281
Beef, lean	164
Beef, top round	162
Pork fillet	171
Pork knuckle	189
Pork, fatty	311
Pork, lean	143
Pork cutlet	105
Roast chicken	99
Chicken leg	80
Chicken breast	75
Duck	192
Goose	227
Turkey	122
Frankfurter sausage	257
Wiener sausage	249
Ham, cooked	264
Sole	59
Tuna	239
Turbot	42
Hamburger, 105 g (¼ lb)	273
Cheeseburger, 120 g (¼ lb)	324
Fish burger, 150 g (5½ oz)	380
Chips, 120 g (4 oz)	420
Spicy sausage with ketchup, 150 g (5½ oz)	516
Veal patties, 150 g (5½ oz)	280
Sausage, 150 g (5½ oz)	460
Mayonnaise (80% fat)	765

Milk chocolate	569
Plain chocolate	521
Potatoes with skins	70
Potatoes without skins	86
Crisps	598
Mushrooms	12
Carrots	29
Aubergines	21
Tomatoes	16
Butter	776
Margarine	748
Apricots	49
Apricots, dried	308
Bananas	70
Olive oil	930
White wine	69
Red wine	67
Beer	43
Apple turnover, approx. 80 g (3 oz)	220
Doughnut, approx. 60 g (2 oz)	310
Croissant, approx. 60 g (2 oz)	280

Picnic Menu Suggestions

Generally speaking, recipes do not follow the rules of mathematics. You will not often find a recipe serving four that allows you to neatly divide all the ingredients and cooking times in half to serve two people. And, likewise, you can't just double the time and all the ingredients in a recipe for four to serve eight people. For example, the cooking time for a piece of meat for eight people is not double the cooking time for a piece of meat for four – there is a formula for working out cooking times based on weight after an initial fixed cooking period. The same goes for fish, too. But there are exceptions. You can, in fact, multiply the ingredients needed for a cold salad. In most cases, multiplying the ingredient quantities will work for soups as well. However, you should be especially careful with cakes and home-made breads.

You can have a picnic with a variety of smaller dishes. Simply make several different recipes for four people and serve them as finger foods. The only important thing is to calculate the total amount of food you'll need. Most adults eat a main dish equal to about 300–500 g (10½–18 oz), including side dishes. People take in closer to 500 g (18 oz) at a restaurant, where there are multiple courses served over several hours. For eight people, you have to figure on filling about a 2.4 to 4 kg (6–9 lb) picnic basket, depending on the occasion and cost.

1. **Tomato Basil Butter and Herb Butter** (see p. 36)

2. **Tomato Pesto with Black Olives and Genovese Pesto** (see p. 60) – For a cold salad, or as a spread for bread.

3. **Fresh Chicken Liver Pâté** (see p. 80) – Slice and serve on brioche or toast and pair with a sweet wine.

4. **Waldorf Salad** (see p. 84)

5. **Potato and Cucumber Salad with Bacon Strips** (see p. 86) – Always a success with cold veal patties (see p. 590), cold chicken or cold cuts.

6. **Pasta Salad with Tuna and Boiled Egg** (see p. 94)

7. **Spanish Tortilla** (see p. 117) – Cut into pieces and serve in ciabatta buns, with aioli and green olives on the side.

8. **Nigiri Sushi** (see p. 242) – Also a delicious picnic snack with other sauces and wasabi filling.

9. **Quiche Lorraine with Leeks** (see p. 394) – Bake and bring to the picnic in the dish: it will avoid damage that way.

10. **Cornish Hen Roasted with Lemon and Garlic** (see p. 540) – Roast the day before and serve it cold. Don't forget napkins.

11. **Exotic Fruit Salad** (see p. 657) – Fresh and easy to eat.

12. **Chocolate Brownies** (see p. 710) – These stay moist, are easy to bake, and make everyone happy (as chocolate is known to do!).

Party Time

Good preparation is everything. After all, you want to spend the evening with your guests and not in the kitchen. As with picnic recipes, if you have a recipe serving four people, you can't always convert it for eight or sixteen people using multiplication. It's easier to stick with the recipes as they are in the book and prepare a nice buffet for your guests with several delicious little dishes; it's difficult with warm dishes; it definitely can be a lot of work to get everything on the table at the right temperature if you have a lot of guests. But there is one exception that is appropriate for parties – and that's a barbecue.

Simply cooking meat or fish over an open fire – it doesn't get much more natural and authentic than that. For the meat to turn out well, you should pay attention to a few easy tips.

— The grill should not be too hot. Otherwise, it won't take long for the outside to char and for the meat to become tough. So it's better to reduce the heat by spreading the coals apart, to place the grill a little higher over the flame and allow the food to cook for a few more minutes. You can test the heat by holding your hand about 12 cm (5 inches) above it. If you have to move it after only one or two seconds, the flame is too high. About five seconds means it's a medium heat.

— Grilled meat should sit for one to two minutes on a plate, covered with foil. Doing this keeps the juices from running out of the meat with the first cut.

— Marinades or spice mixtures taste even better when they're home-made. Ready-made grilling spices often contain flavour enhancers like monosodium glutamate.

Beef and pork are great without a marinade as long as there is fat marbled through them. Chicken breasts can simply be brushed with a mixture of the juice of 1 lemon, ½ bunch chopped parsley, 3 tbsp olive oil and one pressed garlic clove. Let them rest for two hours before putting them on the grill.

Fish like salmon, herring, bream or mackerel also taste good on the grill. On the other hand, prawn and shellfish should only be grilled in the shell. Grilling time is only two or three minutes.

1. **Tartar Sauce** (see p. 52), Cocktail Sauce (see p. 53) and Aioli (see p. 53) for dipping bread and vegetables.

2. **BBQ Sauce** (see p. 56) – For steaks and grilled pork chops.

3. **Ham Aspic with Radishes** (see p. 74)

4. **Tomato Mousse with Pesto** (see p. 76)

5. **Lobster Cocktail with Mushrooms** (see p. 82) – Serve in glasses.

6. **Potato and Cucumber Salad with Bacon Strips** (see p. 86) – Always a hit with cold meat patties, chicken or cold cuts.

7. **Italian Frittata** (see p. 116) – Prepare this in the morning and serve it lukewarm.

8. **Devilled Eggs** (see p. 118) – A classic must-have for any 'retro' party! These decorative eggs also work well as a garnish for salads.

9. **Fried Quail Eggs on Beef Tartare Canapés** (see p. 120) – The beef tartare is prepared beforehand, and the quail eggs are fried only at the last minute so you can serve the canapés with beer right at the beginning of the party.

10. **Gazpacho** (see p. 162) – Prepare the day before and allow it to settle overnight. Then serve it in large bowls.

11. **Penne Bolognese** (see p. 202) – Precook and just bake in the oven later to finish. Pasta is a real winner at parties and with the exception of spaghetti, can be eaten while standing.

12. **Indian Chickpea Curry with Cinnamon Yogurt and Mint** (see p. 290) – Easily prepared, it tastes nice and spicy and it's also vegetarian.

13. **Stuffed Aubergines with Goat's Cheese and Oregano** (see p. 366) – Bake ahead of time, warm it up quickly when your first guests arrive, and bring it to the table practically freshly cooked.

14. **Mussels Served Cold in a Herb Marinade** (see p. 506) – Can also be made the day before.

15. **Chicken Legs in BBQ Sauce** (see p. 522) – Easy to prepare in large portions, marinated the day before. The chicken pieces can also be baked slowly at 140°C (275°F/Gas Mark 1). The low temperature extends the cooking time, allowing the chicken legs to stay in the oven longer without browning.

16. **Chilli con Carne** (see p. 554) – Especially popular at later hours, or warmed up with a sunny-side up egg the next day – your guests will thank you for it!

17. **Bavarian Cream** (see p. 658) – Easily multiplied. Either serve it in individual glass bowls, or fill a large bowl and serve with various fruit sauces (see p. 695).

18. **Panna Cotta** (see p. 674) – So easy, you can hardly go wrong, and it's also a favourite dessert at every party.

Salt
Butter
Oil
Vinegar

Contents

Salt

Not all salts are the same. The most important kinds are table salt with or without iodine supplements. Then you have sea salt and coarse salt. Sea salt comes from the salt mines in Guérande (Brittany), Aigues-Mortes (Languedoc-Roussillon), the Camargue, the French Atlantic coast or Maldon (Essex). The size and shape of the crystals and their flavour can vary slightly. The light grey 'fleur de sel' ('salt flower') from Guérande, which is harvested by hand from June to September, apparently only forms if the wind blows from the east. People say that the 'salt rose' from the 'Salins du Midi' has a mild peppery note, while the coarse salt from the Atlantic coast, on the other hand, has slightly sour notes.

Salt should always be stored dry. Metal boxes are not good for storing salt, because salt crystals contain chlorine.

Coarse salt is often used for soups and vegetable dishes. Smaller salt granules season fish, meat and sauces. Meat should be salted as it begins to cook, because the salt releases the flavours drawing the natural juices to the surface. Likewise, salt fish inside and out before cooking. Then place it immediately in the pan or on the grill.

Salt should be used sparingly but it does bring out the flavour in dishes.

Some reference books count monosodium glutamate as a culinary salt. But it's really a flavour enhancer and it can cause nausea. If you cook with good ingredients, you won't need such flavour enhancers.

An increasing number of 'lifestyle salts' have appeared in the last few years – red wine-infused salts are included among them, as are Hawaiian salts, available in green, red and black; Himalayan salt; and Korean bamboo salt. They can add colour accents to certain dishes and are a unique gift idea. But if you use only a little salt, you'll barely notice a difference in taste. These are not kitchen must-haves; generations of cooks have created first-class dishes without using these 'lifestyle salts'.

English Maldon salt is a very nice salt that tastes great on a boiled egg or on roasted meat.

Coarse white sea salt from Mallorca and lavender-coloured Hibiscus salt, also from Mallorca. Hibiscus flowers mixed with the salt lend it a fruity flavour.

Butter

Butter is made from the fat, or cream, that comes from milk. It's rarely made in a traditional butter churn any more. Most of the time the cream is put in a centrifuge, where the fat separates from the rest of the liquid. Roughly 10–15 litres (2½–4 gallons) milk goes into just over 500 g (1 lb 2 oz) butter. In theory, butter can be made from the milk of all animals such as yaks for example; yak butter is served with tea in Tibet.

All types of butter differ in salt and moisture content. But other factors affect the quality, too. For example, a cow's diet affects the taste of her milk.

Butter browns and burns easily when heated because of its high water content. This is why some people start with a little oil in the pan, then add the butter to it.

Soft, slightly warm butter can be mixed easily with other ingredients. These include shallots, parsley, garlic and horseradish. Anyone can create his or her own herb butter. You can also add almonds, sardines or mustard to it.

'Beurre noisette' (literally, 'hazelnut butter') is a term for lightly browned butter. The name refers to the colour and taste, not the ingredients. There are no nuts in beurre noisette, but rather caramelised milk sugars. It is traditionally served with fish.

Butter goes rancid quickly and should only be kept up to three weeks at most in the refrigerator.

Low-fat butter contains 50 per cent less fat than normal. Emulsifiers, food dyes, stabilisers and preservatives are added to make it look like real butter.

The traditional way of making butter is very different. Only a few companies still follow it today – it takes about three days to produce butter this way. These small producers allow the customer to specify the salt and moisture content, as well as the shape. The milk spins in a horizontal metal drum for 90 minutes and turns into flakes in a kind of white mash. When cooled with iced water, the flakes draw together. The butter is allowed to set for three days, and is then kneaded on a wooden surface.

When salt is added, the butter has to sit for at least two hours while the salt sets in. Salt content in traditional butter varies according to what the customer wants, but usually lies between 1.8 and 7 per cent.

Traditionally made butter will keep for three weeks, but it begins to lose its natural flavour after seven days.

Whipped Butter

Bring **250 g (9 oz) butter** to room temperature and beat with a whisk for as long as it takes to increase the volume by a third, and for the butter to take on a creamy consistency. This butter can be worked into other butter mixtures or used in baking recipes.

To serve butter on the dining table, cut thin slices of a little less than 5 mm (¼ inch) and then cut the slices in half. Then put the slices in a bowl with ice and water. The butter won't melt and you can take one piece at a time.

Store opened butter in a well-sealed container. Uncovered butter can take on various odours from other foods in the refrigerator.

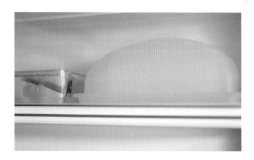

It's best to keep the butter container on a separate shelf in the refrigerator door. It's not too cold there, and the butter will be easier to spread or work with.

Butter from Around the World

1. Buffalo milk butter – for baking over pasta and for roasting Italian meat dishes, on bread or baked goods, or for binding pasta sauces.

2. Cultured butter from Italy – on bread, or for binding pasta sauces.

3. French butter, semi-salted – works well for roasting meats, for binding sauces, and for spreading on fresh baguettes.

4. French sweet cream butter – works well in butter or cream sauces, French cakes and fine pastries.

5. German farmer's butter – for baking and cooking.

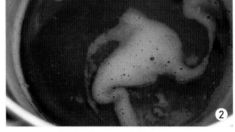

Melted Butter

Melt **250 g (9 oz) butter** in a small pan over medium heat, then pour over boiled potatoes or steamed white asparagus.

Beurre Noisette

1. Melt **250 g (9 oz) butter** in a small pan over medium heat, until the liquid takes on a light brown colour.

2. As soon as it reaches the desired colour, remove the pan from the heat, as the butter will continue to brown in the pan. For best results, immediately place the pan on a wet tea towel. This cools the pan somewhat so the butter doesn't brown too much and burn.

Clarified Butter

Run **250 ml (8½ fl oz) beurre noisette** through a muslin cloth or fine-mesh conical sieve, to separate the browned liquid from the butterfat.

■ **Clarified butter is used for roasting or baking different dishes. It's known as 'ghee' in Indian cooking. Clarified butter can be heated to higher temperatures more easily because it contains no whey, which can burn.**

125 g (4½ oz) butter

 3 tsp tomato purée

 1 bunch fresh basil

 ½ garlic clove

 1 pinch of salt
1 pinch of black pepper

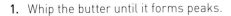

Tomato Basil Butter

1. Whip the butter until it forms peaks.

2. Add the tomato purée. Chop the basil into thin ribbons, finely chop the garlic, and then add both to the tomato and butter mixture. Add the salt and pepper, then stir.

3. Fill small bowls with the tomato basil butter, cover, and keep cool in the refrigerator until needed.

Serve with grilled or roasted meat or fish. Another option is to spread it on oven-toasted bread and serve as a starter with a rosé wine.

20

 125 g (4½ oz) butter

 1 bunch fresh chives
1 bunch fresh parsley

 ½ garlic clove

 3 shallots

 1 tsp hot mustard

 1 pinch of salt

 1 pinch of nutmeg, freshly grated

 ½ tsp Worcestershire sauce

Herb Butter

1. Whip the butter until it forms peaks.

2. Rinse the chives and chop them finely. Pick the parsley leaves from the stems, rinse, and chop finely. Peel the garlic and the shallots and chop them finely. Add the herbs, mustard, salt, nutmeg and the Worcestershire sauce to the butter.

3. Mix everything well with a whisk. Fill small bowls with the herb butter, cover, and keep cool in the refrigerator until needed.

Serve this butter with grilled steaks or with reheated potato dishes.

10

Oils

There's oil for cooking, frying and seasoning, but an oil that does everything – that doesn't exist.

You need at least two oils in your kitchen, and usually they are olive and sunflower or groundnut oils.

A relatively neutral-tasting oil, like peanut, is ideal for frying. It starts to smoke when it reaches 220°C (425°F), and then it can catch fire. A deep fryer with a temperature display can prevent that from happening.

Even with something simple like chips, throwing them in hot oil is not enough. They have to be fried first at 150°C (300°F), drained, then allowed to sit. Next, fry them at 190°C (375°F) briefly, until golden brown, and then remove the grease.

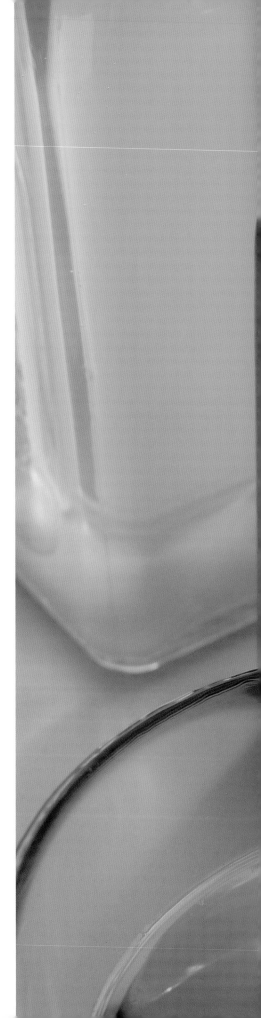

Oil Lexicon

On the Label

Extra virgin olive oil, olio extra virgine, or huile vierge extra: Oil from the first pressing. It contains a portion of free oleic acids, less than 0.8 per cent.

Virgin olive oil: 'Second-class' oil, with less than 2 per cent free oleic acids.

Olive oil: The 'third class'. These oils can be extracted and refined using chemical solvents. A blend of virgin and refined olive oil is suitable for cooking and frying in most cases.

Olive pomace oil: Oil that has been chemically extracted from olive pomace (the residue of pressed olives).

100 per cent pure oil: The contents of the bottle were obtained from a single oil; blending is prohibited.

Cold press: A gentle press done at 17°C (63°F), often carried out using hydraulic presses.

The designations 'first pressing' and 'cold pressed' are outdated. Virgin olive oil is always cold pressed; the second pressing, which once served to increase the yield, is not common any more. In addition, the acidity levels say very little about the taste of the oil itself.

The label should show the year the oil was pressed, the name of the mill and the name of the 'cultivation area'. This is how inferior oil blends from different countries can be avoided. Different labels such as Appellation d'Origine Contrôlée (AOC), Appellation d'Origine Protégée (AOP) or Identification Géographique Protégée (IGP) point to the care taken in production.

Olive oil should be stored upright and in a cool (10–16°C/50–61°F), dark place. Do not put oils in the refrigerator, as they will get cloudy.

1. Hazelnut oil
2. Walnut oil
3. Grapeseed oil
4. Pumpkin seed oil
5. Argan oil
6. Sunflower oil

Infused Oils

Almond is considered ideal with raw mussels, pistachio tastes good with lobster or rock lobster, and hazelnut can make fish more refined or refresh the taste of cold chicken or turkey. We mean the oils, of course, not the nuts.

Apart from the simple, all-purpose oils for the deep-fryer or pan, there is also a cult that has built up around speciality oils. Oils that have their own flavour and can spice other dishes or refine them, like Styrian pumpkin seed oil, which is sometimes enjoyed straight on a piece of boiled beef in Austria. Hazelnut and almond oil from the Perigord region of France tastes outstanding on salads. A strong sesame seed oil lends a simple vegetable salad an exotic flavour. These oils are only as good as the mills that pressed them though. Purists do not buy oils in a shop, but have them shipped from remote farms, where the fruits are milled between two large stone blocks according to centuries-old tradition.

Nutty argan oil comes from the fruit of the argan tree, which only grows in southwest Morocco, not far from the Atlantic. Moroccan women consider it a beauty secret. They use the rare liquid as a natural moisturiser, as a body gel, against dry hair or for strong fingernails. The outer flesh becomes animal feed, and the extremely hard kernel beneath is crushed between two stones. A nut is stored inside. Once gathered, these nuts are toasted in an oven, their shells a useful source of 'fuel'. Then the Berber women mill the toasted nuts – a process that takes hours by hand.

Gourmet shops carry, among other things, diverse infused oils for pepping up salads or fresh seafood – sometimes with just a little caraway added, sometimes enriched with sophisticated spice blends from the most distinct herbs and exotic spices. Oils like this can be made easily at home. Just put a little basil or lemon in a bottle of neutral oil and wait. After a week, a new scent comes storming through the bottle, and it can be served after a good six weeks of infusion. Try it first with just half a vanilla pod (cut it open and scrape out the seeds with the tip of a knife) in a small bottle of groundnut oil – it works wonders with a simple tomato salad.

Infused oils, like a chilli-garlic oil, can easily be made at home.

1. Truffle Vinegar

Slice about **50 g (1¾ oz) black truffles**, then cut the slices into strips and put them in a container with **6 blackberries**. Pour **50 ml (1⅔ fl oz) red port wine** and **250 ml (8½ fl oz) sherry vinegar** over them, seal the container and place it in the refrigerator for about one week. Use this vinegar for strong vinaigrettes, to season mayonnaise, or for deglazing kidneys or sweetbreads.

2. Chilli Pepper Vinegar

Put **250 ml (8½ fl oz) white wine vinegar**, **10 dried red chillies**, **1 tbsp black peppercorns** and **1 tsp coriander seed** in a bottle and seal. Leave to stand for about one week. Use on summer salads with tomatoes and cheese, for poaching eggs or for seasoning sauce reductions. The spiced vinegar lends the dish a strong, piquant note.

3. Garlic Coriander Vinegar

Pour **125 ml (4 fl oz) white wine vinegar** and **125 ml (4 fl oz) rice wine vinegar** into a bottle. Add **5 pressed garlic cloves** with **½ bunch fresh coriander** and **2 galangal slices** to the vinegar. Seal and place in the refrigerator for a few days. Use for salad dressings, to accompany fish and shellfish with fruit, or when making Asian dips.

4. Vanilla Cardamom Vinegar

Pour **125 ml (4 fl oz) white wine**, **100 ml (3½ fl oz) red wine vinegar** and **1 tbsp balsamic vinegar** into a bottle. Cut **2 vanilla pods** in half, and scrape out the insides. Along with the vanilla scrapings, add **3 star anise seeds** and **5 black cardamom seeds** to the vinegar. Seal and shake well to mix the vanilla thoroughly. Use on winter salads with red cabbage and oranges, or in stewed quince with venison.

5. Lemon Rosemary Vinegar

Pour **250 ml (8½ fl oz) white wine vinegar** into a container. Press together **3 bay leaves**, **1 sprig fresh rosemary** (removing the needles from the stem), **½ a lemon** (cut in slices) and **10 white peppercorns**. Add everything to the vinegar and place in the refrigerator for a few days. Use in salad dressings or for seasoning mayonnaises.

■ Since these vinegars aren't cooked, they won't keep as long, but they'll be far tastier.

Cold Sauces

Contents

6 eggs

 1 tsp hot mustard

 1½ tsp salt

 800 ml (1½ pints) sunflower oil

 Juice of ½ lemon

 1 large pinch cayenne pepper

Mayonnaise

Important: All ingredients must be used at the same temperature; that means oil and eggs should either both come out of the refrigerator, or both be at room temperature.

1. Separate the eggs. Put the egg yolks in a bowl and put the egg whites in the refrigerator for later use.

2. Add the mustard and the salt to the egg yolks and stir.

3. Add half of the oil a little at a time and beat vigorously using a whisk.

4. Then add the lemon juice and the cayenne pepper. Beat in the rest of the oil now that there is enough to bind it.

Makes 1 litre (1¾ pints).

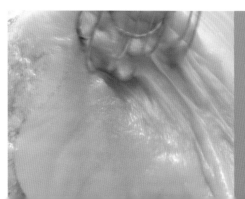

■ Lay a damp tea towel under the bowl so it doesn't slide while you stir the oil. If the mayonnaise gets runny, you can save it by carefully beating the mayonnaise on the side of the bowl. The runny part will get mixed in a little at a time and the mayonnaise will bind again.

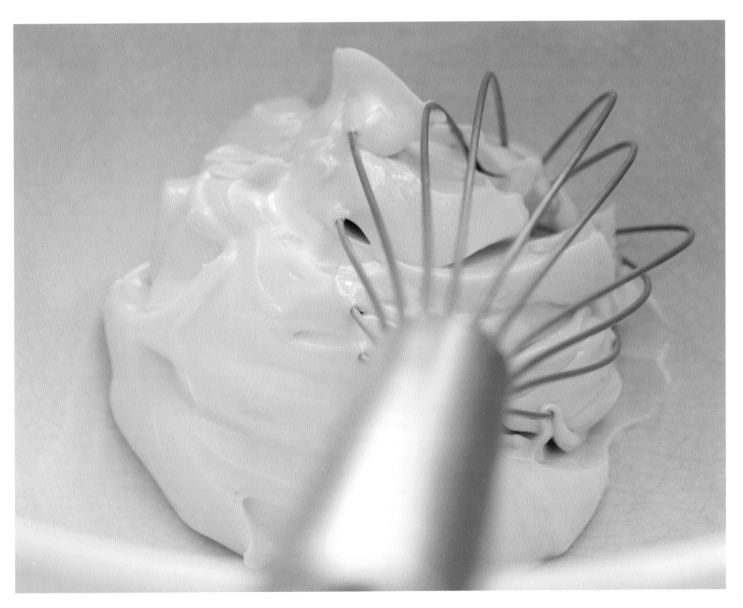

Tartar Sauce

Boil **2 eggs** for 10 minutes. Rinse the eggs under cold water and peel them. Peel **1 shallot**, cut it in half and chop it finely. Rinse **1 bunch fresh chives**, removing any damaged parts, and snip into small rings. Grate the hard-boiled eggs on the finest grate. Mix the ingredients with **200 g (7 oz) mayonnaise**. Next, add **1 tsp hot mustard**, the juice of ½ a lemon and **½ tbsp Worcestershire sauce**. Finish it by seasoning with **salt** and **pepper** to taste.

Makes about 400 g (14 oz).

■ To make the sauce a little lighter, add 1 tbsp soured cream. Serve with sliced, cold roast beef, beef aspic, or warm or cold fish dishes.

Remoulade

Peel **3 shallots**, cut them in half and chop finely. Cut **3 small pickles** into thin slices, then into strips, then dice finely. Rinse **½ bunch fresh parsley** and **½ bunch fresh chervil**, removing any damaged leaves, and chop finely. Chop **3 anchovies** and **1 tbsp capers** finely. Stir all ingredients into **200 g (7 oz) mayonnaise**. Add **1 tsp hot mustard** and **½ tsp Worcestershire sauce**, stir and add **1 pinch of salt** and **pepper**.

To make the sauce a little lighter, add **1 tbsp soured cream**.

Makes about 400 g (14 oz).

■ Serve with cooked, warm meat, cold roast beef, baked vegetables or egg dishes.

Rouille Sauce

Peel **3 garlic cloves** and slice them. Peel **1 small, starchy cooked potato** and dice finely. Add everything to a small pan with **1 tbsp extra virgin olive oil** and sweat lightly. Add **6 saffron threads**, **½ tsp paprika** and **½ tsp salt**. Pour **200 ml (7 fl oz) water** in and let it simmer slowly for 10 minutes. Crush the potato pieces with a fork and stir into the liquid. Let it cool until the mixture is only lukewarm. Then mix with **200 g (7 oz) mayonnaise**.

Makes about 400 g (14 oz).

■ Rouille sauce is an important part of bouillabaisse, but it also tastes good with cold poached fish or shellfish, or simply with a fresh baguette and a glass of wine.

Cocktail Sauce

Add **3 tbsp tomato ketchup**, **2 tsp grated horseradish**, **3 tbsp cognac**, and the juice of **½ an orange** to **200 g (7 oz) mayonnaise**. Blend with a whisk until smooth. Add **1 pinch of salt**, **1 pinch of cayenne pepper** and **3 drops of Worcestershire sauce** to taste.

Makes about 400 g (14 oz).

■ Great as a dressing on shellfish salads or as a dip with cold or baked vegetables and tastes really good with fondue.

Dill Mustard Sauce

Rinse **1 bunch fresh dill**, remove the stems and chop finely. Stir **2 tbsp coarse mustard**, **2 tbsp hot mustard** and **5 tbsp honey** with **200 g (7 oz) mayonnaise**. Finish it by seasoning with **salt** and **pepper** to taste.

Makes about 400 g (14 oz).

■ Goes best with marinated fish such as salmon, halibut or trout – but it can also be served with fresh steamed prawns or crayfish.

Aioli

Peel **3 garlic cloves**, slice them, then grind them together with **½ tsp salt** in a mortar and add to **200 g (7 oz) mayonnaise**. Squeeze the juice of **½ a lemon** and mix with the mayonnaise. For best results, let it marinate for half an hour so the flavour of the garlic is evenly distributed and the sauce doesn't taste too hot.

Makes about 250 g (9 oz).

■ Serve with cooked fish, or cold fried fish or shellfish. Also great as a dip with raw vegetable sticks. For a Spanish themed evening, it makes an essential starter with a lot of white bread and ice-cold Chablis.

Preparing Herbs

1. Rinse the chives, removing any damaged pieces, and chop them into fine rings.

2. Rinse the basil, pick the leaves from the stems, removing any damaged pieces, and cut into thin strips.

3. Rinse the tarragon, pick the leaves from the stems, removing any damaged pieces, and cut into thin strips.

4. Rinse the chervil, pick the leaves from the stems, removing any damaged pieces, and chop finely.

5. Rinse the parsley, pick the leaves from the stems, removing any damaged pieces, and chop finely. Hold the herbs together with your left hand to chop them more finely.

6. A food processor naturally works faster, but the herbs can become bitter, diminishing in quality. The best thing is to cut gently through the herbs with a knife, rather than hacking them. Use the knife like a mezzaluna.

Yogurt Sauce with Herbs

Rinse **1 bunch fresh chervil**, **½ bunch fresh basil**, **1 bunch fresh parsley**, **1 bunch fresh chives** and **½ bunch fresh tarragon** and chop them finely. Peel **2 shallots**, cut them in half and chop them finely. Add **250 g (9 oz) yogurt** and **200 g (7 oz) crème fraîche** to a bowl, then add the chopped herbs and the garlic. Add **1 tsp sugar**, **1½ tsp salt**, **1 pinch of black pepper** and **4 tbsp extra virgin olive oil**, and mix well.

Makes about 600 g (1 lb 5 oz).

■ Serve this sauce as a dip for raw vegetables, cooked meat or fish, cold roast beef or roasted chicken or turkey – or simply with fresh white bread.

Green Chervil and Watercress Sauce

Rinse **1 bunch fresh chervil** and **1 bunch fresh watercress**, pick the leaves from the stems, removing any damaged pieces. Boil the herbs in salted water for 1 minute and refresh them immediately in a bowl of cold water. Fill a bowl with **200 g (7 oz) mayonnaise**, then add **1 tbsp extra virgin olive oil**, **100 g (3½ oz) crème fraîche**, **1 tsp salt** and **1 pinch of cayenne pepper**. Squeeze the juice of **½ a lemon** over a sieve to keep the seeds out of the bowl. Mix everything well with a whisk. Put the herbs and **3 tbsp water** in a food processor, and process until it is an evenly fine mass. Then mix it with the remaining sauce.

Makes about 500 g (1 lb).

■ Serve with shellfish, such as prawns or lobster, cold steamed salmon, warm veal or cold chicken.

Lingonberry Horseradish Sauce

Using a whisk, stir about **200 g (7 oz) natural yogurt** with **1 pinch of salt**, **1 pinch of white pepper** and the juice of **½ a lemon** until smooth. Add **1 tbsp lingonberry jam** and about **150 g (5½ oz) grated horseradish**, then mix together. Finish by mixing in about **100 g (3½ oz) whipped cream**.

Makes about 500 g (1 lb).

■ This lingonberry horseradish sauce goes very well with warm beef, cold roast venison and cold poultry such as turkey.

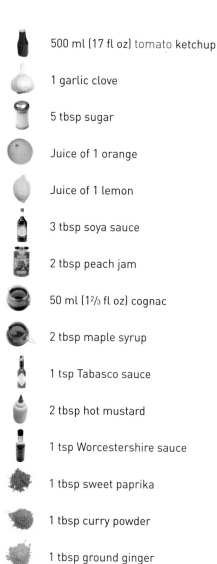

500 ml (17 fl oz) tomato ketchup

1 garlic clove

5 tbsp sugar

Juice of 1 orange

Juice of 1 lemon

3 tbsp soya sauce

2 tbsp peach jam

50 ml (1⅔ fl oz) cognac

2 tbsp maple syrup

1 tsp Tabasco sauce

2 tbsp hot mustard

1 tsp Worcestershire sauce

1 tbsp sweet paprika

1 tbsp curry powder

1 tbsp ground ginger

1 sprig fresh rosemary

1 tbsp dried thyme

①

BBQ Sauce

1. Put the tomato ketchup in a bowl. Peel the garlic cloves, chop them finely and add them to the bowl with the sugar, the orange and lemon juices and the soya sauce. Briefly stir everything with a whisk.

2. Then add the peach jam, cognac, maple syrup, Tabasco sauce, hot mustard, Worcestershire sauce, paprika, curry powder and ground ginger, and stir again.

3. Pick the rosemary needles from the stem, chop and add them to the sauce along with the thyme, and mix.

Use as a marinade for spare ribs, or serve with pork chops or steaks, grilled chicken wings or curry sausage.

Makes 1 litre (1¾ pints).

■ BBQ sauce will keep for up to three months in the refrigerator if it's kept in a sealed container. When grilling, check that the flames or oven temperature isn't too high: the sauce could darken and burn around the edges because of the honey and sugar in the peach jam.

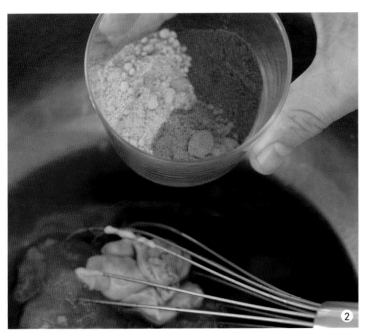

2 eggs

 4 tsp hot mustard

 2 tsp salt

 1 pinch of white pepper

 150 ml (5 fl oz) white wine vinegar

 1 pinch of nutmeg, freshly grated

 600 ml (1 pint) sunflower oil

 100 ml (3½ fl oz) water

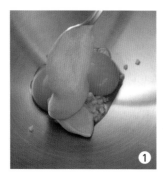  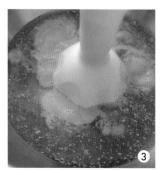

French Dressing

1. Separate the eggs, putting the yolks in a bowl. Put the egg whites in the refrigerator for later use. Add the mustard to the egg yolks.

2. Add the salt, pepper, white wine vinegar and nutmeg.

3. Mix everything with a hand-held blender and add the oil a little at a time.

Then add the water and stir. Season with white pepper and salt to taste.

Makes 1 litre (1¾ pints).

■ **This classic salad dressing goes with most leafy salads. It serves as a foundation for other dressings such as Thousand Island and Caesar dressings.**

Thousand Island Dressing

Caesar Dressing

Rinse ½ **green** and ½ **red pepper**, cut them in half, deseed, peel and dice finely. Peel **2 shallots**, cut them in half and chop finely. Then mix everything with **500 ml (17fl oz) French dressing**. Now add **2 tbsp tomato ketchup, 1 tbsp sugar** and **1 pinch of cayenne pepper** and stir everything well together. The diced peppers look like tiny islands in the sea – that's why it's called 'thousand island' dressing.

Makes about 800 ml (1½ pints).

■ As a simple variation, you can add a variety of pickles instead of peppers and shallots. Mix the pickles by chopping them in a food processor and add them to the dressing.

Grate **80 g (2¾ oz) Parmesan cheese** and finely chop **1 tsp capers** (without the brine). Finely chop **5 anchovies** and crush them with the flat side of a knife. Fill a bowl with **250 ml (8½ fl oz) French dressing**. Add about **200 g (7 oz) crème fraîche**, the capers, the anchovies and the Parmesan cheese to the dressing and mix. Season with **black pepper** to taste.

Makes about 550 ml (18 fl oz).

■ Mix in romaine lettuce and finish with a sprinkle of crisp bacon strips and Parmesan shavings on top. This one is a salad classic.

100 g (3½ oz) Parmesan cheese

 200 g (7 oz) sun-dried tomatoes, in oil

 1 tsp salt
1 pinch of black pepper

 125 g (4½ oz) almonds, blanched

 250 ml (8½ fl oz) extra virgin olive oil

 50 g (1¾ oz) black olives, pitted

Tomato Pesto with Black Olives

1. Grate the Parmesan cheese. Put the grated cheese, sun-dried tomatoes, salt and pepper, almonds and half the oil in a food processor and mix.

2. Now pour in the rest of the oil and mix for 3 minutes until the pesto displays a paste-like consistency.

3. Finish by adding the black olives and mixing again for just 30 seconds so the olives don't get too fine.

Makes about 750 g (1 lb 10 oz).

■ **Serve the tomato pesto with grilled fish or pasta dishes.**

 100 g (3½ oz) Parmesan cheese

 3 bunches fresh basil

 3 garlic cloves

 125 g (4½ oz) pine nuts

 1 tsp salt
1 pinch of black pepper

 1 pinch of nutmeg, freshly grated

 200 ml (7 fl oz) extra virgin olive oil

Genovese Pesto

1. Grate the Parmesan cheese. Rinse the basil and remove any damaged leaves. Peel the garlic and cut into thin slices. Put these ingredients in a food processor.

2. Add the pine nuts; season with the salt, black pepper and nutmeg.

3. Pour in half the oil and mix everything in the food processor.

4. Finally, add the remaining oil and process another 1 or 2 minutes, until the pesto displays a paste-like consistency.

Makes about 650g (1 lb 7 oz).

■ **Serve this classic basil pesto on pasta or grilled vegetables, or use it to marinate olives.**

1 garlic clove

 1½ tsp hot mustard

 1 pinch of white pepper

 1 tsp salt

 1 tbsp sugar

 4 tbsp white wine vinegar

 125 ml (4 fl oz) extra virgin olive oil

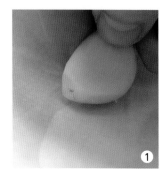  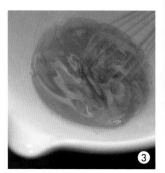

Classic Vinaigrette

1. Rub the inside of a bowl with the garlic clove. This is all it takes to lend the vinaigrette the necessary garlic flavour.

2. Add the mustard, pepper, salt and sugar to the bowl. Then pour in the white wine vinegar and stir until the salt and sugar have completely dissolved.

3. Next, pour in the olive oil. Stir well with a whisk until the vinaigrette takes on a creamy consistency. This is how to make a basic vinaigrette, a simple yet very tasty salad dressing.

Makes about 180 ml (6 fl oz).

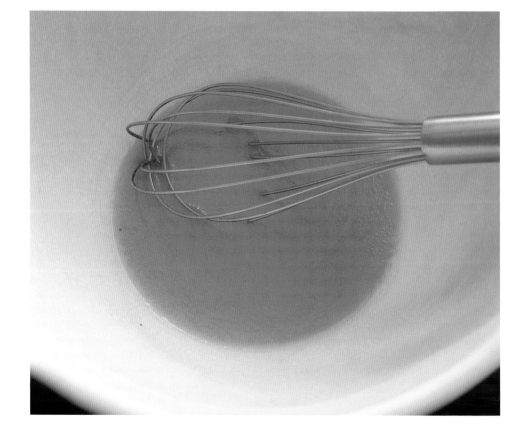

 15

Herb Mustard Vinaigrette

Rinse ½ **bunch parsley**, **1 bunch chives**, ½ **bunch basil** and ¼ **bunch tarragon**, removing any damaged pieces, and chop finely. Peel **2 shallots**, cut them in half and chop them finely. Mix all of the ingredients with **140 ml (4½ fl oz) classic vinaigrette** and **1 tsp mustard**.

Makes about 250 ml (8½ fl oz).

■ This herb mustard vinaigrette works as a marinade for roasted vegetables, such as artichokes, steamed asparagus or beans, or as a dressing on tomatoes, endive or mixed salad.

Tomato Vinaigrette

Skin **2 tomatoes**, deseed, and dice them finely. Peel **1 shallot** and ½ **garlic clove** and chop them finely. Rinse ½ **bunch fresh basil**, removing any damaged pieces, and chop into thin ribbons. Pour **4 tbsp balsamic vinegar** into a bowl. Add **1 pinch of salt**, **1 pinch of black pepper** and **1 tbsp sugar** to the vinegar and stir with a whisk until the sugar and salt have dissolved. Now stir in **125 ml (4 fl oz) oil** a little at a time. Add the tomatoes, garlic, shallots and basil and mix everything together.

Makes about 250 ml (8½ fl oz).

■ This vinaigrette tastes very good on roasted fish, calamari or steamed mussels. Fried mushrooms with tomato vinaigrette are a delicious side dish with anything grilled.

Soya Vinaigrette with Coriander

Rinse ½ **bunch fresh coriander**, removing any damaged pieces, and chop finely. Peel and finely grate a **2.5-cm (1-inch) piece of ginger**. Add the ginger, **4 tbsp brown rice vinegar**, **1 tbsp soya sauce**, **1 tbsp sesame seeds** and a **sprinkle of chili flakes**. Pour in **1 tbsp sesame oil** and **5 tbsp groundnut oil** and mix. Add the coriander last and stir it in.

Makes about 250 ml (8½ fl oz).

■ Serve mixed with cold Asian noodles, or as a dip with small pieces of raw vegetables such as carrots, fennel, celery sticks or Chinese cabbage.

Salads & Starters

Contents

Lettuce & Herbs

Lettuce should be eaten as soon as possible after picking, otherwise it can wither and rot. Wrapped in a damp tea towel, it will keep for two to four days in the salad drawer of the refrigerator, depending on how fresh it is.

Fresh herbs can be stored in half a glass of cool water. Herbs will also keep for up to five days in a plastic bag in the salad drawer. Dried herbs do not like light or heat.

Lollo rosso

Lollo biondo

Romaine

Curly endive

Green looseleaf lettuce

Yellow dandelion leaves

Oak leaf lettuce

Iceberg lettuce

Buttercrunch

Chicory

Radicchio

Red chicory

Rocket

Hijiki seaweed

Dulse seaweed

Bean sprouts

Watercress

Purslane

Chives

New Zealand spinach

Parsley

Iceberg Lettuce

1. Iceberg lettuce should have a crisp heart, and the stalk should not be too dried out.

2. Cut off the stalk.

3. Cut out any brown spots on the ribs of the outer leaves.

4. Rinse the whole iceberg head under running water. Then let it drain well.

5. Now cut the lettuce into pieces and marinate it in salad dressing, or wrap it in cling film and store it in the refrigerator.

6. The water helps keep the lettuce fresh for a good week in the refrigerator.

Green Batavia (Looseleaf) Lettuce

1. The lettuce should have a firm heart and the stalk should not be too dried out.

2. Cut off about 2 cm (¾ inch) of the stalk plus any wilted tips.

3. Place the lettuce in a large colander and separate the leaves under running water to remove any dirt.

4. Rinse the leaves well under running water, removing any rotten pieces at the same time. Let the leaves drip dry or shake them dry. Then toss with salad dressing or place in a bowl, cover with cling film and store in the refrigerator for later use.

Preparing Ginger

1. Ginger stays fresh longer if you store it in a plastic bag in the refrigerator, keeping it moist with a few drops of water.

2. Peel with a small paring knife.

3. Grate it with a fine grater.

Preparing Horseradish

1. Peel the horseradish.

2. Grate the amount needed with a grater.

3. Rub the remaining portion with lemon so the horseradish stays white while stored.

4. Then wrap it in plastic to keep it fresh.

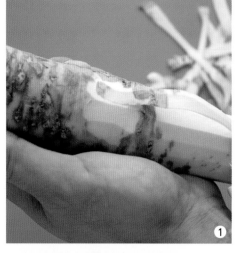

1. Ginger
2. Horseradish

400 g (14 oz) white asparagus

 400 g (14 oz) green asparagus

 2 shallots

 2 sprigs fresh mint

 ½ bunch fresh chives

 ½ bunch fresh parsley

 ½ bunch fresh chervil

 2 tbsp sugar

 2 tbsp salt

 Juice of ½ a lemon

 150 ml (5 fl oz) vinaigrette

 4 eggs

 2 tbsp water

2 tbsp cream

1½ tbsp mayonnaise

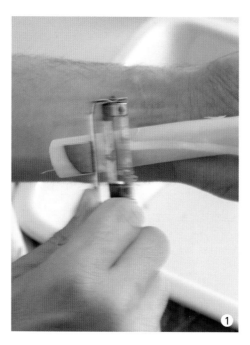

Green and White Asparagus Salad with Poached Egg

1. Peel the white and green asparagus. Peel the shallots, cut them in half and chop them finely. Rinse the mint, removing any damaged pieces, pick the leaves from the stems and cut them into thin ribbons. Rinse the chives, removing any damaged pieces, and snip them finely. Likewise, rinse the parsley and chervil, removing any damaged pieces, pick the leaves from the stems and cut them into ribbons.

2. In a pan, add the white asparagus, the sugar, half the water, half the salt, the lemon juice, and cook for about 8 minutes. In another pan, add the green asparagus, the rest of the water and the salt, and cook about 5 minutes. Remove both asparagus and briefly refresh them in cold water. The asparagus must remain warm to absorb the marinade better. Arrange the asparagus in a baking dish. Sprinkle the shallots and herbs over the asparagus stalks.

3. Pour the vinaigrette over the asparagus. Meanwhile, poach the eggs in vinegar water (see p. 110).

4. Mix the asparagus carefully with the marinade and leave to marinate for about 10 minutes. Then divide the asparagus onto plates and drizzle with the herb vinaigrette from the marinade. Lay one poached egg on top of the asparagus and garnish with a little of the cooking water and cream mixed with mayonnaise.

■ This salad tastes great with steamed crayfish, poached quail eggs, sautéed mushrooms (e.g. morels), roasted veal medallions or triangle steaks.

40

3

4

 1 tbsp salt

 350 g (12 oz) leeks

 150 g (5½ oz) celery

 140 g (5 oz) celeriac

 80 g (2¾ oz) parsnip

 300 g (10½ oz) carrots

 3 ham hocks

 250 g (9 oz) onions

 1 head of garlic

 3 sprigs fresh thyme

 3 bay leaves

 10 cloves

 10 juniper berries

 1 pinch of nutmeg, freshly grated

 1 tsp white peppercorns

 1 tsp black peppercorns

250 g (9 oz) onions

 3 sheets of gelatine

 500 ml (17 fl oz) beef stock

½ bunch fresh parsley

+ 2½ hours cooking time
+ 6 hours cooling time

Ham Aspic with Radishes

1. Bring a large pan with 5 litres (8¾ pints) of water to the boil and add the salt. Clean the vegetables and leave them whole. Reserve 150 g (5½ oz) of the carrots and 180 g (6 oz) of the leeks. Now put the ham hocks in the boiling water and add the unpeeled onions, leeks, celery, unpeeled head of garlic, thyme, bay leaves, cloves, juniper berries, nutmeg, as well as white and black peppercorns. Let it simmer 2¼ to 2½ hours, depending on the size of the ham hocks, adding more water when needed. Soak the gelatine in cold water.

2. Bring a pan of salted water to the boil, cook the carrots, leeks, parsnip and celeriac until very soft. As the cooking times for the vegetables are different, add them to the boiling water in the following order: the celeriac, which needs the longest time, followed by the carrots, the parsnip and the leeks. Dissolve the gelatine in the beef stock, adding salt to taste if necessary. Put the stock in the freezer, cooling it to room temperature. Cut the vegetables in wide strips.

3. Cut the ham hocks and remove any undesirable parts such as fat and skin. Using your hands, pull the meat apart into pieces about 2–3 cm (¾–1¼ inches). Pour a little stock into the dish so that the cling film doesn't stick to the bottom. Insert the cling film, pressing down in the corners so that it sits right and doesn't crease. Layer the vegetables, meat and the parsley, filling the dish with the gelatine dissolved in the beef stock in between layers.

■ Crisp fried potatoes and remoulade work well as side dishes with the aspic. The aspic shown here is served with radish slices and some classic vinaigrette, marinated with chives.

4. Continue to alternate the meat and vegetables, pressing on each layer so that no air pockets are left, otherwise the aspic will fall apart more easily when cut.

5. When the dish is completely filled, finish by pouring in the remaining dissolved gelatine and pressing down the aspic with your hand.

6. Take the overlapping film from the side, cover the aspic and seal it in.

7. Take a board the same size as the aspic and lay it on top, weighing it down to apply pressure. Place the aspic in the refrigerator for at least 6 hours (for best results, leave in overnight), so the gelatine can set until firm.

8. Remove the aspic from the dish and carefully unwrap. With a sharp knife, cut about 2-cm (¾-inch) thick slices, arrange on a plate and serve.

600 g (1 lb 5 oz) tomatoes

 2 garlic cloves

 3 shallots

 60 g (2¼ oz) celery

 1 sprig fresh rosemary

 2 sprigs fresh thyme

 3 tbsp water

 2 tbsp sugar

 3 tbsp tarragon vinegar

 4 tbsp extra virgin olive oil

 2½ tsp salt

 1 pinch of black pepper

 500 ml (17 fl oz) tomato juice

 4 sheets of gelatin

 500 g (1 lb 2 oz) cream, whipped

 4 tbsp pesto

Tomato Mousse with Pesto

1. Skin the tomatoes, cut them into eighths, remove the cores, and cut into about 1-cm (½-inch) pieces. Peel the garlic and cut it into thin slices. Peel the shallots and cut into rings. Dice the celery finely. Likewise, chop the rosemary and thyme finely.

2. Add water to a pan and dissolve 1 tbsp sugar in it. Heat until the sugar has a golden colour. Then add the tarragon vinegar.

3. Now add the olive oil, shallots, garlic and herbs and sweat for 1 minute over medium heat. Add the celery and let it sweat for 5 minutes.

4. Then add the tomatoes, salt and pepper to the pan. Pour in the tomato juice and simmer for 8–10 minutes over medium heat. Next, purée it with a hand-held blender and cool to room temperature. This makes 750 ml (1⅓ pints) of the tomato liquid.

5. Soak the gelatine for about 10 minutes in cold water. Squeeze the gelatin, put it into a pan and let it melt over heat.

6. In the meantime, beat the cream until stiff and put in the refrigerator to cool. Pour the tomato liquid into a bowl, stir in the melted gelatine and season once more with tarragon vinegar, salt and pepper to taste.

+ 3 hours cooling time

* * * 30

■ You can save time by putting 500 ml (17 fl oz) cream in a soda siphon and whipping the cream using two capsules.

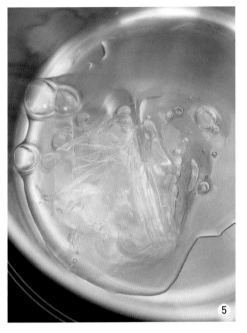

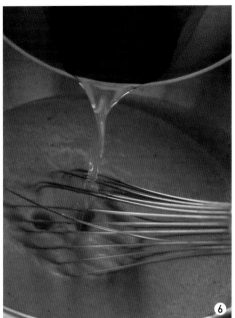

7. Add half the whipped cream and, using a whisk, fold it into the tomato liquid with one turn of the wrist.

8. Fold in the remaining cream carefully with a rubber spatula, then stir with a whisk to get rid of any lumps in the cream. Next, put some of the pesto in glasses, fill them with the tomato mousse, cover with cling film and leave to stand for 3 hours in the refrigerator to cool. Top with some pesto and serve with white bread.

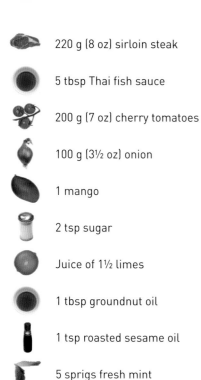

220 g (8 oz) sirloin steak

5 tbsp Thai fish sauce

200 g (7 oz) cherry tomatoes

100 g (3½ oz) onion

1 mango

2 tsp sugar

Juice of 1½ limes

1 tbsp groundnut oil

1 tsp roasted sesame oil

5 sprigs fresh mint

1 small head of lettuce

①

Beef Mango Salad with Cherry Tomatoes and Mint

1. Cut the steak into strips and marinate it in 2 tbsp Thai fish sauce. Cut the cherry tomatoes into quarters. Peel the onion, cut them in half, and dice finely.

2. Wash the mango and peel it, removing the stone, then cut the mango into strips.

3. Add the onion, tomatoes, mango and sugar to a medium-sized bowl and squeeze the lime juice over it.

4. Add both the peanut and sesame oils to a pan and set over a high heat. Sear the meat for 1 minute, turning frequently.

5. Rinse the mint, removing any damaged pieces, and pick the leaves from the stems. Remove the tips from the leaves and set them aside as a garnish, cutting the remaining leaves into ribbons. Add the meat and the mint to the bowl. Add the remaining 3 tbsp Thai fish sauce over the top and mix. Decorate with some lettuce leaves and the mint tips, and serve on plates.

■ Chopped, roasted peanuts or spelt berries could also lend this dish a special note.

* * *
45

700 g (1 lb 9 oz) chicken liver

250 ml (8½ fl oz) red port wine

250 ml (8½ fl oz) cognac

600 g (1 lb 5 oz) butter

250 g (9 oz) thin bacon rashers

3 eggs

1½ tsp salt
½ tsp black pepper

1 pinch of nutmeg, freshly grated

4 juniper berries

1 sprig fresh thyme

Fresh Chicken Liver Pâté

1. Clean the liver and, with a small kitchen knife, remove the skin, veins and any blood.

2. In a pan, boil the port and cognac down to a fifth of their original volume and let the reduction cool down to room temperature. Use the butter to prepare a beurre noisette (see p. 34) and cool it likewise to room temperature.

3. In the meantime, layer the terrine with the bacon rashers so that they overlap and go over the edges of the dish.

4. Put the chicken liver, eggs, salt, pepper and the boiled-down spirits into a mixer.

5. Grate the fresh nutmeg over it, pour in the beurre noisette, and mix everything

until it all looks like a smooth chocolate milkshake.

6. Add the mixed ingredients to the bacon layered dish with a ladle.

7. Cover the filled dish with the bacon.

8. Lay the juniper berries and the thyme over the bacon. Cover with kitchen foil and cook in the oven for 90 minutes at 100°C (210°F). Remove and leave to cool overnight in the refrigerator for best results. Then carefully remove it from the dish. With a long knife soaked in hot water, cut a 2-cm (¾-inch) thick slice and lay it on a plate. Serve with French stick, white bread or brioche. Garnish with pickles and/or orange chutney.

+ 6 hours cooling time

*
*   240
*

■ Alternatively, you can use ingredients such as pickled green peppercorns, sautéed mushrooms or morels, black truffle pieces or apple slices sautéed in sugar and butter. The ingredients should be only lukewarm at the most.

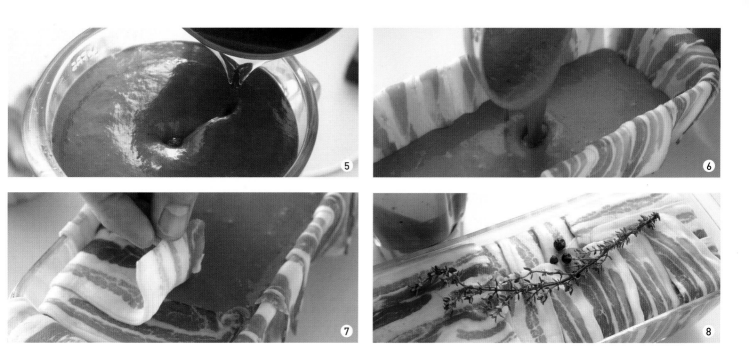

2 lobsters, cooked and shelled

 1 chicory

 200 g (7 oz) mushrooms

 50 ml (1²⁄₃ fl oz) white wine

Juice of ½ lemon

 120 g (4½ oz) cocktail sauce

1

Lobster Cocktail with Mushrooms

1. Remove the lobster meat from the shell and cut it in half (see p. 480). Using the tip of a knife, pull out the vein. Keep one claw per person as a garnish. Cut the lobster into 5-mm (¼-inch) cubes. Set aside four nice chicory leaves, cutting the rest into thin ribbons.

2. Clean and cut the mushrooms into quarters. Bring the white wine to the boil in a pan and add the mushrooms. Squeeze the lemon juice over a sieve so the seeds don't fall in the pan. Let everything simmer lightly for about a minute.

3. Drain the mushrooms in a sieve and let them cool. Keep the liquid as it can be used in a fish sauce or Hollandaise sauce.

4. Mix the mushrooms in a bowl with the lobster meat and cocktail sauce. Stick a few chicory ribbons and one leaf in a cocktail glass. Then fill with the lobster cocktail and decorate with the claws.

■ You can make this cocktail with crabmeat or prawns and garnish with different herbs.

250 g (9 oz) celeriac

 1 lemon

 12 walnuts

 3 apples

 ½ tsp salt

 1 tsp sugar

 1 pinch of black pepper

 100 g (3½ oz) crème fraîche

 100 g (3½ oz) mayonnaise

①

Waldorf Salad

1. Peel the celeriac and rub it with ½ the lemon to keep it from browning. Crack the walnuts and set them aside.

2. Peel the apples, removing the tops and bottoms. Remove the core from the fruit.

3. Grate the apple pieces and celery into strips using a fine grater.

4. Put the apple and celeriac strips in a bowl. Squeeze the other ½ lemon over a sieve so the seeds don't fall in the bowl. Add the sugar and salt and pepper to taste.

5. Add the crème fraîche and the mayonnaise, mixing everything together. Serve in a glass and garnish with walnuts.

30

■ You can cut the celeriac into thin, even slices using an automatic slicer. Celeriac strips can also be blanched to achieve an even more refined flavour. Walnuts are easier to peel if you boil them briefly in equal parts milk and water.

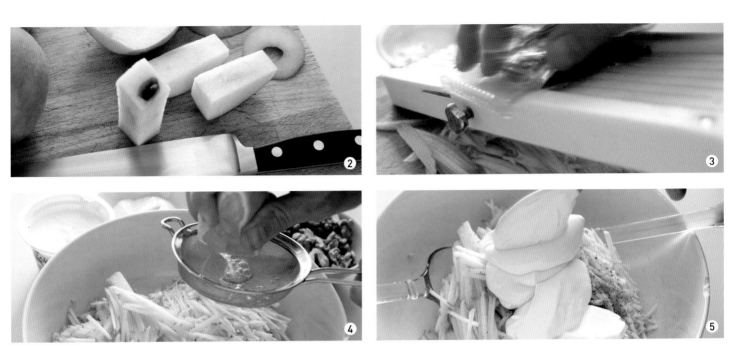

 1.5 kg (3 lb 5 oz) potatoes

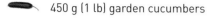 450 g (1 lb) garden cucumbers

 100 g (3½ oz) smoked bacon

2 onions

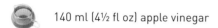 200 ml (7 fl oz) sunflower oil

3 tbsp hot mustard

250 ml (8½ fl oz) chicken stock

140 ml (4½ fl oz) apple vinegar

1½ tsp salt

1 large pinch of black pepper

Potato and Cucumber Salad with Bacon Strips

1. Boil and cool the potatoes, peel them and, while still warm, cut them into slices about 5 mm (¼ inch) thick.

2. Peel the cucumbers and grate them into thin slices.

3. Next, cut the bacon into slices, then into strips. Peel and dice the onions.

4. Add sunflower oil to a pan and fry the bacon until crisp. Then add the onions and sweat them. Add the mustard and stir. Pour the chicken stock and vinegar into the pan and season with salt and pepper to taste. Let everything marinate for 3 minutes.

5. Pour the hot dressing over the potatoes and stir carefully. Season again with salt and pepper to taste. Serve while still warm.

■ Cooking the potatoes with caraway seeds will give them a spicier flavour. The salad is even tastier served with mayonnaise and is a wonderful side dish with roast beef, baked fish or ham aspic, or with a variety of sausages.

200 g (7 oz) pinto beans, cooked weight

 200 g (7 oz) white beans, cooked weight

 200 g (7 oz) broad beans, cooked weight

 300 g (10½ oz) French beans

 1 tsp salt

 3 spring onions

 1 pinch of black pepper

 4 tbsp apple vinegar

 5 tbsp sunflower oil

 1 tbsp parsley

Mixed Bean Salad with Parsley

1. Boil the beans (see p. 282), drain them and put them in a bowl.

2. Cut the French beans into diagonal strips and cook in salted water until firm to the bite. Pour them into a sieve and refresh under cold running water.

3. Now add the lukewarm French beans to the other beans.

4. Cut the spring onions in half and cut into thin slices. Add to the beans.

5. Now season with salt and black pepper. Pour the apple vinegar and sunflower oil over the beans and mix well. Leave to marinate for 10 minutes. Next, rinse the parsley, pick the leaves from the stems and chop them finely, then mix in.

This dish goes well with grilled fish or veal patties.

■ You can tell if the beans are old if they break apart when soaking (left). Fresh beans stay whole (right).

2 packets dried seaweed mix

 6 tbsp soya sauce

 2 tbsp roasted sesame seeds

 2 tbsp roasted sesame oil

 300 g (10½ oz) spinach leaves

Seaweed Salad with Spinach Leaves and Sesame Dressing

1. Soak the seaweed in lukewarm water according to the package instructions – usually about 30 minutes.

2. Drain the soaked seaweed in a colander.

3. Mix the soya sauce with the roasted sesame seeds and the roasted sesame oil for the dressing.

4. Rinse the spinach leaves, shake them thoroughly dry and add them to the dressing.

5. Next, add the drained seaweed on top of the spinach and mix together.

Put in a bowl and serve.

■ Julienned carrots or radishes, small fried tofu squares, and small pieces of raw tuna or salmon can be mixed into the seaweed salad to give it more colour and substance. These ingredients make this salad a wholesome dish.

400 g (14 oz) cooked long grain rice

 200 g (7 oz) cooked ham

 200 g (7 oz) tinned fruit cocktail

 3 tbsp mayonnaise

 1 tbsp curry powder

 1 pinch of salt
1 pinch of black pepper

 Juice of 1 lemon

Rice Salad with Curry Mayonnaise and Fruit

1. Put the rice and diced ham into a bowl.

2. Strain the fruit salad and cut up the large pieces if necessary.

3. Add the fruit pieces and mayonnaise to the rice.

4. Sprinkle with curry powder; add salt, pepper and lemon juice to taste.

5. Mix everything together and let sit for about 30 minutes.

Serve in the bowl or in cocktail bowls and garnish with a lettuce leaf and lemon slice.

40

■ You can use simple fruit salad (see p. 656) instead of tinned fruit.

2 eggs

 400 g (14 oz) penne

 2 spring onions

 150 g (5½ oz) tuna in brine

 1 pinch of salt
1 pinch of black pepper

 2 tbsp mayonnaise

2 tbsp natural yogurt

 1 tbsp honey mustard

Pasta Salad with Tuna and Boiled Egg

1. Boil the eggs well (see p. 102). Cook the penne, drain, and let cool under cold running water (see p. 189). Peel the eggs and chop coarsely. Clean the spring onions and snip them into small rings.

2. Put the cold cooked pasta into a bowl. Add the eggs, spring onion and tuna.

3. Add the salt, pepper, mayonnaise and yogurt to the salad.

4. Add the honey mustard last and mix everything well.

Serve in bowls or on plates and garnish with herbs.

■ You can make this salad with other types of pasta as well, such as farfalle, rigatoni or spaghetti.

2 yams

 2 litres (3½ pints) vegetable oil for frying

 1 pinch of salt

 1 pinch of sugar

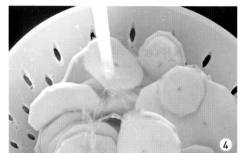

Home-made Yam Crisps

1. Using a knife, cut away the skin from the yam.

2. Cut the yams into thin slices.

3. Lay the slices in cold water for 15 minutes to draw the starches out.

4. Then rinse well under running water.

5. Dry the slices well in a tea towel.

6. Heat the oil in a deep pan to 170°C (340°F) and fry the yam slices until crisp.

7. Using a slotted spoon, take the crisps out of the oil when they are fried to a golden brown.

8. Spread them over kitchen paper to dry.

Sprinkle with salt or sugar according to taste, and serve in bowls.

■ Serve the home-made yam crisps with a light herb sauce or a piquant tomato salsa.

8 tbsp extra virgin olive oil

1 pinch of sea salt

1 pinch of black pepper

5 basil leaves

400 g (14 oz) beef fillet steak

Juice of 1 lemon

1 piece of Parmesan cheese

1

Beef Carpaccio with Parmesan Cheese and Lemon Juice

1. Brush four plates each with 1 tbsp olive oil, and sprinkle with salt, pepper and some thin ribbons of basil.

2. Using a long, sharp knife, cut the beef into very thin slices.

3. Lay the beef slices next to each other on the pre-seasoned plates and drizzle with 1 tbsp olive oil. Add salt and pepper to taste.

4. Sprinkle ribbons of basil and drizzle some lemon juice over the beef.

5. Grate the Parmesan cheese over the beef slices with a vegetable peeler and serve with fresh bread.

■ Instead of beef, you can use fresh, raw salmon, tuna, mussels, and fresh veal fillet steak or saddle of veal.

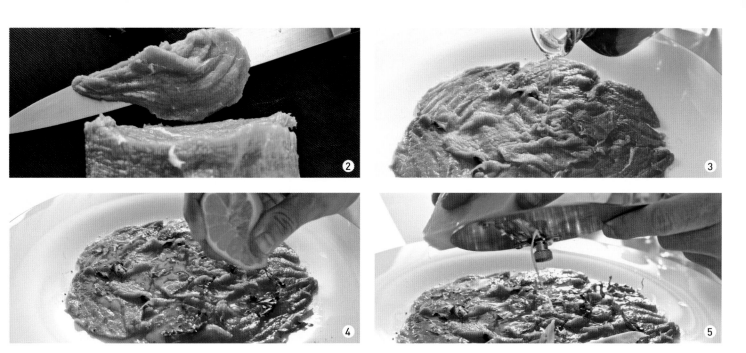

Egg Dishes

Contents

Boiled Egg

1. Five Minute Egg: The egg white is firm, the yolk is no longer runny but still soft.

2. Seven Minute Egg: The breakfast egg. The egg yolk is still quite soft.

3. Ten Minute Egg: The egg white and yolk are equally firm.

4. Overcooked egg: Has a green ring around the yolk – this happens when eggs are boiled for longer than 15 minutes, then not cooled in cold water.

5. A fresh egg: The egg white is very tight and compact, almost like a pudding.

6. An egg that is not very fresh: The egg white is no longer compactly framed around the egg yolk. Instead, it separates, and runs all over the plate.

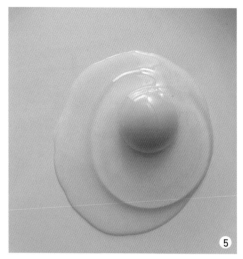

Duck, Chicken and Quail Eggs

1. A comparison of duck, chicken and quail egg sizes.

2. Duck, chicken and quail eggs cracked open.

3. To open a quail egg, use the tip of a knife to scratch the eggshell carefully so as not to damage the egg yolk.

4. Then cut a hole and let the egg run into a bowl. The delicacy of the shell makes it hard to simply crack it open.

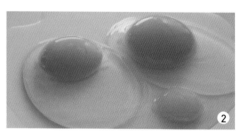

Thousand Year Egg

It is also called a century egg, but of course it's not that old. For this Chinese speciality, raw, fresh duck eggs are covered in a mixture of limestone, ashes from various woods, tea and salt. After a good three months, the eggs are washed. Because the shell is so porous, the lime mixture reacts with the egg inside. The egg becomes a yellowish green, gelatinous mass with a strong odour reminiscent of cheese. In China, it is served for breakfast.

Pickled Egg

Bring **1 litre (1¾ pints) water** to a boil with **4 tbsp salt, 1 tsp white peppercorns, 1 dried chilli, 3 garlic cloves** and **1 tsp mustard seeds**. Put **10 eggs** in the boiling water and cook them for 5 minutes. Remove them from the heat and pour the eggs and the liquids into a kilner jar.

The eggs will keep in cool storage for more than a month in the jar. Serve with vinegar and bread.

2 eggs

 1 tbsp cream

 1 pinch of salt
1 pinch of black pepper

 10 g (¼ oz) butter

Scrambled Eggs

1. Beat the eggs in a deep dish, because they will be easier to beat than if they are in a shallow bowl. Beat them using a quick circular movement with a fork.

2. Add the cream, season with salt and pepper to taste, and mix.

3. Put the butter in a pan and let it foam up over medium heat. Pour the eggs into the pan. Let the eggs become firm while you stir. They should be creamy, slightly shiny and moist.

 5

Scrambled Eggs with Herbs

In a deep dish, beat together **2 eggs, 2 tbsp chopped herbs, 1 tbsp cream** and **1 pinch each of salt** and **pepper**. As with the scrambled eggs (see p. 104), put **10 g (¼ oz) butter** in a pan. Good herbs for this dish are chives, basil and coriander.

Scrambled Eggs with Tomato

In a deep dish, beat together **2 eggs** with **1 tbsp cream** and **1 pinch each of salt** and **pepper**. Wash **1 tomato**, skin it, remove the core (see p. 346) and cut into small dice. Chop **5 basil leaves** into ribbons and, along with the tomato, mix them into the eggs. Heat **10 g (¼ oz) butter** in a small pan, pour in the egg mixture, letting it solidify as you stir it. This tastes delicious on toasted white bread, garnished with a few pieces of **mozzarella**.

Scrambled Eggs with Mushrooms

Clean **30 g (1 oz) mushrooms** (see p. 360) and cut into slices. Heat **10 g (¼ oz) butter** in a small pan, add the mushrooms and sweat them, then season with **1 pinch each of salt** and **pepper**. Beat together **2 eggs** with **1 tbsp crème fraîche** (see p. 106), and add to the mushrooms, allowing them to solidify as you stir them.

■ You can use button mushrooms, oyster mushrooms, chanterelles, porcini or shiitakes in this dish. Truffles go well with eggs too (see p. 106).

Scrambled Eggs with Cheese

In a deep dish, beat together **2 eggs, 40 g (1½ oz) grated cheese, 1 tbsp cream** and **1 pinch each of salt** and **pepper**. As with the scrambled eggs (see p. 104), put **10 g (¼ oz) butter** in a pan and add the egg mixture. The cheese should eventually become quite viscous.

■ For the cheese, use Gruyère, aged Gouda, Appenzell or raclette cheeses. For a milder choice, pick up some fresh goat's cheese, feta cheese or Brie.

4 eggs

 2 tbsp crème fraîche

 10 g (¼ oz) pickled black truffles from a jar

 20 g (⅔ oz) butter

 1 pinch of salt
1 pinch of black pepper

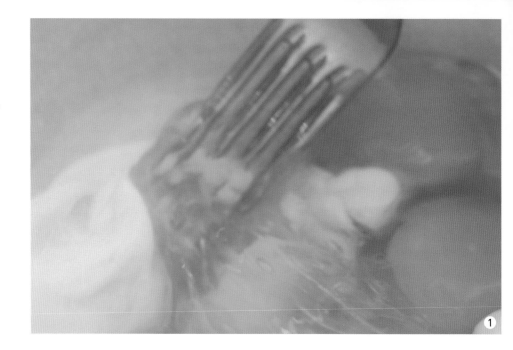

(1)

French Creamy Scrambled Eggs with Truffles

1. Beat the eggs in a bowl and stir in the crème fraîche.

2. Cut the truffles into thin slices – you can also use fresh or frozen truffles for this dish.

3. Add the truffle slices to the eggs, mix, cover, and leave to stand for 1 hour in the refrigerator so that the taste of the truffles develops better.

4. Put the butter in a pan over medium heat and let it foam up. Season the beaten eggs with salt and pepper and put them in the pan. Stir the scrambled eggs slowly and continuously so they solidify evenly.

5. Truffle-scrambled eggs are finished when they are consistently creamy and light. Put them on a plate and serve with white toast.

■ If you prefer to make this dish with white truffles, make the scrambled eggs first, then grate the white truffles over them with a truffle slicer. White truffles should not be cooked, otherwise they lose flavour.

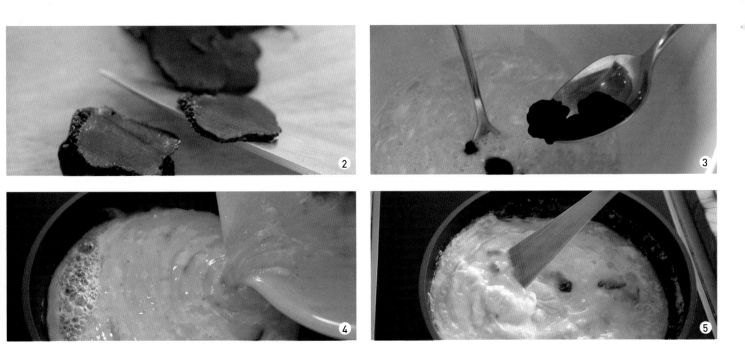

10 ml (2 tsp) vegetable oil

 2 eggs

 1 pinch of salt
1 pinch of pepper

 10 g (¼ oz) butter

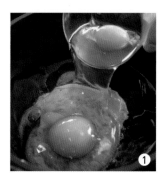

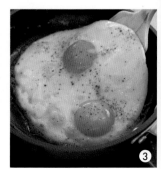

Sunny-Side Up Eggs

1. Add the vegetable oil to a nonstick frying pan and bring it to medium heat. Crack the eggs into a cup and slide them into the pan.

2. Add salt to the egg white only, avoiding the yolk – salt leaves white spots on the yolk. Pepper the whole egg. Using a fork, slide the butter along the sides of the pan, so the eggs maintain a more delicate flavour.

3. Then take the eggs out of the pan with a spatula and put them on a plate.

■ **Cracking the eggs into a cup is more hygienic than doing it directly into the pan. You can be sure that no eggshells or other impurities make it into the pan. The longer an egg is fried, the harder it is to digest!**

10

Strammer Max

Spread **10 g (¼ oz) butter** on **1 slice of mixed-grain toasted bread** and lay **2 slices of cooked ham** on top. Add **2 sunny-side up eggs** (see p. 108) to the toast using a spatula. Sprinkle with parsley leaves or watercress and serve. You can also make Strammer Max with cured ham.

■ For a fuller flavour, grate a little garlic over the toast first.

Spicy Sunny-Side Up Eggs

Crack **2 eggs** into a cup and slide them into a hot pan. Put **salt** only on the egg white, avoiding the yolk. **Pepper** the whole egg. Slice **2 hot green chilli peppers**, cut **1 tbsp spring onion rings**, and cut **1 tsp dried peppers** into strips, then add them over the eggs. Lift the eggs onto a plate with a spatula and finish by sprinkling with a **pinch of hot paprika**.

■ Serve with a fresh roll or a bagel. Spicy chilli beans also go well with this dish, as does crispy fried bacon.

2 litres (3½ pints) water

 50 ml (1⅔ fl oz) white wine vinegar

 1 egg

Poached Egg

1. Heat the water in a deep pan, then add the vinegar. The water should not boil. Crack the egg into a bowl and then carefully slide it into the vinegar water. Continue to turn the egg gently with a spoon, enclosing the yolk in the egg white. A medium-sized egg poaches in about 3–5 minutes, but the required cooking time also depends on personal taste.

2. Carefully lift the egg out of the pan with a slotted spoon and let it drain on a plate. If necessary, remove any overhanging strands of egg white with a knife. Then serve it on a salad, with toast, or just with butter and fresh herbs.

■ Eggs should be taken out of the refrigerator shortly before using them, so they maintain a better consistency while cooking and hold together. The vinegar helps the egg solidify better. Never add salt to the boiling water as that would have the opposite effect!

Fried Egg

Eggs Florentine

Put **200 ml (7 fl oz) vegetable oil** in a pan over medium heat. Crack **1 egg** into a bowl and carefully slide it into the oil. Turn the egg over in the pan and fry both sides, each for about 1 minute. Remove the egg from the pan with a slotted spoon and place on a **slice of white toast**. Season with a **pinch each of salt** and **pepper**.

■ Caution: When you put the eggs into the oil, some oil can splash up. Put the fried egg on white toast to soak up the excess grease. Serve the egg on toast with a piquant tomato sauce or on scaloppini.

Poach **2 eggs** as described on the preceding page. Put **10 g (¼ oz) butter** in a pan and let it foam up. Add **150 g (5½ oz) cleaned** and **rinsed spinach leaves**. Season with a **pinch each of salt, pepper** and **freshly grated nutmeg**. Let the spinach wilt in the pan. Toss it for about 1 minute. Divide the spinach between **2 slices of white toast**. Place a poached egg on top and pour **5 tbsp Hollandaise sauce** (see p. 152) over each one.

3 eggs

 1 pinch of salt
1 pinch of black pepper

 1 pinch of nutmeg, freshly grated

 1 tbsp cream

 10 g (¼ oz) butter

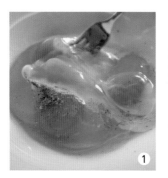
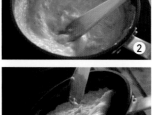
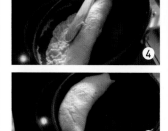

Classic French Omelette

1. Beat the eggs in a bowl and season with the salt, pepper and nutmeg to taste. Add the cream, and beat the eggs with a fork.

2. Add butter to a nonstick pan at least 20 cm (8 inches) in diameter, letting it foam up. Add the eggs to the pan, stirring continuously with a wooden spoon.

3. Reduce the heat and stop stirring the eggs so that they can solidify underneath. Hold the pan slightly diagonally.

4. Roll the omelettes into a half moon using the wooden spoon.

5. Spread a little butter over the finished omelette and slide it onto a plate.

Spread a little more butter over the top to make it glisten. It is important for the omelette to display a smooth, unfried surface and still be moist inside.

French Omelette with Creamed Mushrooms

Finely dice ½ **shallot**. Let **10 g (¼ oz) butter** foam up in a pan and sweat the shallot until it looks translucent. Cut about **80 g (2¾ oz) mushrooms** into slices and add them to the shallot. Cook for about 2 minutes, until the liquids have evaporated. Add **salt** and **pepper**, and drizzle with **10 drops of lemon juice**. This keeps the mushroom nice and white. Add **100 ml (3½ fl oz) cream** and leave to simmer another 2 minutes, until the sauce takes on a thick consistency. Cut the omelette lengthways. Fill the omelette with the creamed mushrooms and pour sauce over it. Garnish with **parsley leaves** and serve with **white toast**.

■ Fillings made with asparagus, crayfish, prawns, tomatoes and minced beef also go really well with omelettes.

50 g (1¾ oz) butter

 50 g (1¾ oz) breadcrumbs

 8 eggs

 1 pinch of salt
1 pinch of black pepper

 1 tsp cornflour

 1 pinch of nutmeg, freshly grated

 250 g (9 oz) raclette cheese

Cheese Soufflé

1. Preheat the oven to 190°C (375°F/Gas Mark 5), using bottom heat with no fan if possible. Grease 4 soufflé moulds, about 8 cm (3 inches) in diameter, with butter, and dust with fine breadcrumbs.

2. Separate the eggs. Add salt to the egg white. Beat the egg whites with a whisk until stiff, and fold in the cornflour. Add the egg yolks, pepper and a pinch of nutmeg.

3. Cut away and discard the rind and edges of the raclette and coarsely grate the cheese. Add 200 g (7 oz) of the grated raclette cheese and carefully fold it into the eggs with a rubber spatula. Don't stir it too much, otherwise the egg mixture will collapse and the soufflé will not rise properly.

4. Using a ladle, distribute the egg mixture into the soufflé moulds until they are three-quarters full.

5. Distribute the remaining cheese over the soufflés. Layer a porcelain casserole dish with baking paper and fill it with 2 cm (¾ inch) hot water. Place the soufflé moulds inside.

Put the dish in the oven. Bake for 20 to 25 minutes depending on the oven. The temperature can be increased to the highest temperature at the end so the tops of the cheese soufflés take on a golden colour. Then take out the soufflés immediately, serving either from the dish or on a plate. You can serve them with a light tomato butter sauce or a mushroom cream sauce.

■ It is important to grease the soufflé moulds all the way to the top edges. Otherwise while baking, the soufflé could stick to the areas that were missed and not take the desired shape. There is also a danger of the soufflé sticking when trying to get it out of the moulds. The eggs should be especially cold so they can be whipped to maximum volume.

5 eggs

 1 pinch of salt

 1 pinch of ground fennel seeds

 200 g (7 oz) courgettes

 1 garlic clove

 1 sprig fresh rosemary

 5 tbsp extra virgin olive oil

 4 tbsp aioli

 1 pinch of coarse black pepper

Italian Frittata

1. Preheat the oven to 180°C (350°F/ Gas Mark 4). Crack the eggs into a bowl. Season with the salt and ground fennel seeds. Then beat with a fork.

2. Cut the courgettes in half lengthways, then cut into thin slices. Peel the garlic and cut it into thin slices. Cut the rosemary needles coarsely. Heat the olive oil in a nonstick pan. Add the garlic and cook until golden. Add the courgette and rosemary to the pan as well and brown them for about 5 minutes. Add the eggs to the pan, covering the courgette slices. Heat the pan for about 30 seconds on the cooker.

3. Then put it in the oven and bake for 8–10 minutes. The frittata is finished when it has risen nicely and the surface takes on a golden yellow colour. Slide it out of the pan onto a chopping board, let it cool down, and cut it into 2-cm (¾-inch) thick slices. Serve on a plate with aioli (see p. 53) and garnish with the pepper.

■ You can use chopped fennel seeds instead of ground fennel seeds. Serve the frittata pieces on cocktail sticks as a finger food starter. Pesto or balsamic vinegar work nicely as a dip for this dish.

 25

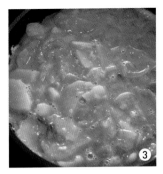

2 garlic cloves

400 g (14 oz) potatoes

4 tbsp extra virgin olive oil

1 pinch of salt
1 pinch of black pepper

130 g (4½ oz) onion

3 eggs

Spanish Tortilla

1. Press the garlic cloves in their skins. Peel the potatoes and cut them into thin slices. Heat 2 tbsp olive oil in a nonstick pan and add the garlic and potatoes. Add salt and pepper to taste. Cook the potatoes slowly over medium heat for about 15 minutes, without letting them brown.

2. Cut the onion in half and cut into thin slices. After 5 minutes, add the onion slices to the potatoes in the pan. Crack the eggs into a bowl and add salt and pepper to taste. Beat them with a fork, then add the cooked potatoes from the pan and mix.

3. Next, heat another 2 tbsp olive oil in a 30-cm (12-inch) diameter pan. Add the egg-potato mix to the pan and fry it over a low heat for 6–8 minutes. Then flip the tortilla out onto a plate and with the fried side on top, slide it back into the pan. Fry for another 5–7 minutes. Slide the finished tortilla onto a plate and serve.

■ Aioli (see p. 53) goes really well with this dish and so do pickled olives. The tortilla tastes best lukewarm.

35

6 eggs

 80 g (2¾ oz) butter

 1 pinch of salt

 1 pinch of cayenne pepper

 1 tbsp medium-hot mustard

 Juice of ½ a lemon

 10 drops of Worcestershire sauce

Devilled Eggs

1. Boil the eggs for 10 minutes. Then rinse them under cold water to cool. Peel and cut them lengthways. Carefully remove the egg yolks with a small spoon.

2. Beat the butter, at room temperature, in a bowl with salt and cayenne pepper until peaks form. Add the mustard and stir using a whisk.

3. Season with the lemon juice and Worcestershire sauce to taste. Add the egg yolks and stir until smooth.

4. Press the egg yolk mix through a fine sieve and then put it in a piping bag with a star decorating tip. Rinse the hard-boiled egg whites under running warm water. Place on a plate with kitchen paper to drain.

5. Pipe the egg yolk filling into the egg whites. Decorate them with cherry tomatoes, chillies, capers, anchovies or small parsley leaves.

■ Russian-style eggs: Cook 120 g (4½ oz) potatoes, 80 g (2¾ oz) parsnips and 80 g (2¾ oz) carrots whole, let them cool and then cut in 5-mm (¼-inch) dice. Place the diced vegetables and potatoes in a bowl. Toss them with 2 tbsp mayonnaise, 1 tsp medium-hot mustard, 1 tbsp white wine vinegar, salt and pepper. Arrange on plates and lay the filled eggs on top.

200 g (7 oz) lean beef mince

 1 shallot

 2 anchovies

 1 pinch of salt
1 pinch of black pepper

 1 tsp hot mustard

 1 tbsp tomato ketchup

 ½ tsp hot paprika

 1 egg, separated

 A few drops of Worcestershire sauce

 2 tbsp pickle or caper juice

 8 quail eggs

 2 tbsp vegetable oil

 4 slices of mixed-grain bread, toasted

 Parsley

(1)

Fried Quail Eggs on Beef Tartare Canapés

1. Put the minced beef in a bowl. Peel and finely dice the shallot. Finely chop the anchovies. Add both ingredients to the beef and, using a tablespoon, delicately toss the mix with the salt, pepper, mustard, tomato ketchup, paprika, egg yolk from the separated egg, Worcestershire sauce, and pickle or caper juice.

2. Carefully scratch the surface of the quail egg open with a small knife (see p. 102) and put it in a glass bowl.

3. Heat the vegetable oil in a nonstick pan over medium heat. Place each egg in the pan using a tablespoon, and ensure that the edges don't run together while frying. Season with black pepper.

4. Quail eggs are done when the egg white solidifies but the egg yolk glistens and is still runny. Generously spread the toasted mixed-grain bread with the beef tartare. Cut the bread slices in half and, with a fork, place a quail egg on each half. Garnish with parsley leaves and serve.

■ This dish should be served with a cold beer as an aperitif. 'Lean beef' refers to the low-fat content of the beef.

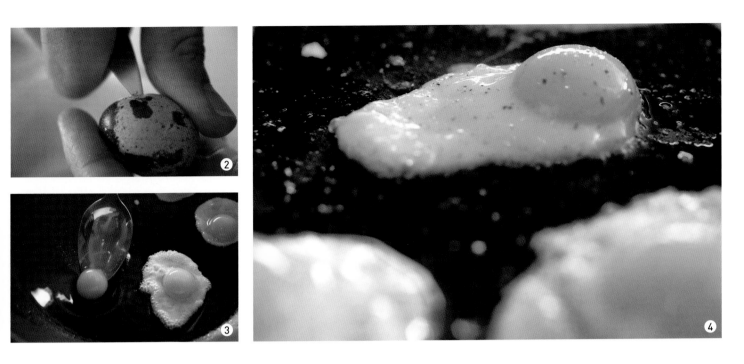

500 ml (17 fl oz) béchamel sauce (see p. 156)

 1 tbsp crème fraîche

 200 ml (7 fl oz) double cream

 2 tbsp medium-hot mustard
1 tsp hot mustard

 8 eggs, hard-boiled and peeled (see p. 102)

 600 g (1 lb 5 oz) boiled potatoes

½ bunch fresh parsley

10 g (¼ oz) butter

Boiled Egg in Mustard Sauce with Parsley Potatoes

1. Slowly bring the béchamel sauce to medium heat, stirring constantly. Add the crème fraîche and cream to the béchamel sauce.

2. Stir in both mustards using a whisk. In the meantime, mix the boiled potatoes with butter. Rinse the parsley, remove the leaves from the stems, reserving a few leaves for garnish. Finely chop the remaining parsley and add to the potatoes.

3. Lay the peeled hard-boiled eggs in the sauce. Arrange the parsley potatoes on a plate. Place two eggs on each plate with the mustard sauce and garnish with parsley leaves.

■ As soon as the mustard is added, stop cooking the sauce. Alternatively, this dish can be served with a cold green chervil and watercress sauce (see p. 55). In that case, the eggs should be freshly boiled, cut in half and placed over the sauce.

240 g (8½ oz) flour

 500 ml (17 fl oz) milk

 3 tbsp sugar

 3 eggs

 150 g (5½ oz) butter

 2 tbsp oil

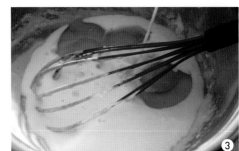

Sweet Pancake Batter

1. Put the flour in a mixing bowl. Add half the milk and the sugar.

2. Using a whisk, mix the batter until smooth. A thick batter is best.

3. Pour in the remaining milk and beat in the eggs.

4. Heat the butter in a small pan until the liquid is golden brown and a nutty odour arises – that's when you have beurre noisette.

5. Using the whisk, stir in the beurre noisette a little at a time – that makes the batter moist.

6. Put some oil in a pan and heat it. Using a ladle, pour some pancake batter and let it spread evenly thin by tilting the pan back and forth.

7. Using a spatula, loosen the batter from the edges and, with a skilled toss, flip the pancake! It takes some practice, but it really works!

8. Cook the pancake briefly after turning. Flip the pancakes onto a plate and let them cool.

■ Serve the pancakes according to taste by spreading them with fresh jam, or rolling them up and sprinkling with sugar. A combination of a fruit and cottage cheese filling with vanilla sauce is also delicious.

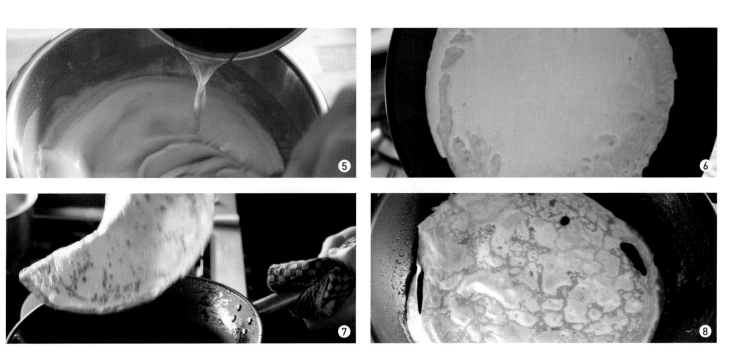

2 ripe apples (Golden Delicious)

 12 unsmoked bacon rashers

 1 tbsp vegetable oil

 400 ml (13½ fl oz) sweet pancake batter (see p. 124)

 4 tbsp sugar

 100 ml (3½ fl oz) maple syrup

Apple Pancakes with Crisp Bacon and Maple Syrup

1. Peel the apple, cut it in half and remove the core. Fry the bacon in a nonstick pan until slightly crisp.

2. Heat the vegetable oil in a pan. Pour in a quarter of the pancake batter.

3. Distribute the batter evenly by tilting the pan.

4. Cut the apple in thin slices and add a quarter of the slices into the wet pancake batter in the pan – they will cling to the pancake this way.

5. Sprinkle the pancake with about 1 tbsp sugar and flip. Cook for another 2 minutes on the apple side and let it caramelise until golden brown. Make three more pancakes this way.

Arrange on plates, pour maple syrup on top and lay the crispy bacon rashers on top. This is a very American breakfast!

■ Instead of apples, thin banana slices can be cooked into the pancakes. Plain fresh syrup rounds off this culinary delight.

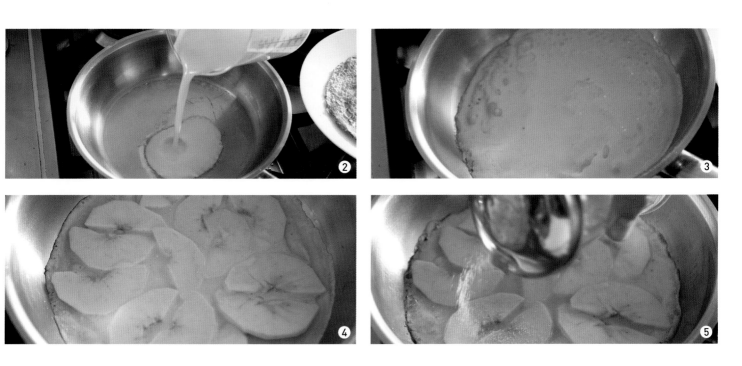

3 medium mirabelle plums

 1 tbsp butter

 2 tbsp soft brown sugar

 4 sweet pancakes (see p. 124)

Mirabelle Plum Pancakes

1. Preheat the oven to 200°C (400°F/Gas Mark 6). Using a knife, cut the mirabelle plums in half and remove the stones. Then cut the fruit in slices.

2. Let butter foam up in a pan. Add the sugar and let it melt.

3. Place the plums in the pan.

4. Cook the plum slices over a low heat until the sugar has completely dissolved and the slices begin to fall apart easily – about 5 minutes. Fold the pancakes into triangles and warm them up for 2 minutes in the oven.

Put two pancakes on each plate and distribute the mirabelle slices over them.

*
*
* **25**

■ Spread chocolate-hazelnut spread on the pancakes – and the chocolate pancakes are done!

Sauces & Stocks

Contents

½ fennel bulb

 1 leek

 3 carrots

 2 celery sticks

 1 tomato

 2 onions

 1 head of garlic

 1 sprig fresh rosemary

 1 bay leaf

 1 pinch of white pepper

½ tsp fennel seeds

Vegetable Stock

1. Remove any brown spots from the fennel and cut into large dice.

2. Clean the remaining vegetables, peel them and cut them into large dice. Cut the head of garlic in half along horizontally.

3. Pour 2.5 litres (4½ pints) cold water into a large pan and place all the vegetables in the pan carefully.

4. Now add the seasonings and slowly bring it to the boil.

5. Let the vegetable stock simmer for about 20 minutes. Then strain it through a sieve and let cool.

Place in the refrigerator until further use. Depending on the temperature inside your refrigerator, the stock will keep for up to 5–7 days.

Makes about 2.2 litres (3¾ pints).

■ The stock is good for stretching out or thinning substantial soups or sauces, for light soups, and for steaming vegetables.

1 chicken, about 1 kg (2 lb 4 oz)

 3 carrots

 5 shallots

 1 onion

 1 leek

 2 celery sticks

 4 litres (7 pints) water

 1 head of garlic

 1 sprig fresh rosemary

 2 sprigs fresh thyme

 2 bay leaves

 1 tsp white peppercorns

 5 cloves

 3 sprigs fresh parsley

Chicken Stock

1. Cut the chicken into large portions, i.e. disjoint the legs and cut the breast away from the backbone. Clean and peel the vegetables, then cut them in large pieces.

2. Pour the water into a large pan, add the chicken and salt. Slowly bring it to the boil. Add the vegetables, garlic, herbs and seasonings.

3. Cook the stock for about 45 minutes and remove the foam that builds up with a ladle – foam makes the stock cloudy.

4. Just before the stock is cooked, add the parsley and turn off the heat.

5. Take the chicken legs and breasts out and set them aside for later use.

Pass the stock through a sieve and let it cool.

Makes about 2.5 litres (4½ pints).

■ **The stock is good for stretching out or thinning thick soups or sauces, for light soups, and for steaming vegetables.**

✲ Kitchen doctor: Carefully skim the foam from the chicken stock continually, otherwise the foam cooks down into the stock and makes it cloudy.

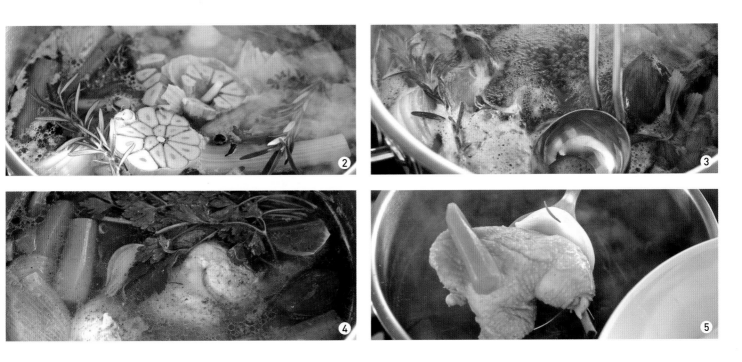

1 kg (2 lb 4 oz) fish carcasses

 1 onion

 3 shallots

 ½ fennel bulb

 3 celery sticks

 1 head of garlic

 3 tbsp vegetable oil

 10 white peppercorns

 ½ tsp fennel seeds

 20 g (²/₃ oz) sea salt

 2 bay leaves

 250 ml (8½ fl oz) white wine

 50 ml (1²/₃ fl oz) dry vermouth

 1.5 litres (2½ pints) water

2 lemon slices

1 sprig fresh basil

1 sprig fresh thyme

Fish Stock

1. Soak the fish carcasses for 30 minutes to completely wash out the blood, so that the stock doesn't get cloudy. Peel all the vegetables and cut them into medium-sized pieces (see pp. 348–55). Then sweat the vegetables in oil without browning. Add the spices, sea salt and bay leaves.

2. Now add the well-drained fish carcasses and likewise sweat briefly. Add white wine and dry vermouth. Then pour in the water and slowly bring it to a simmer.

3. Using a small ladle, remove any foam swimming on top. This is protein that has to be removed to keep it from cooking back into the stock and making it cloudy. Let it simmer gently for 15 minutes, and about 5 minutes before it's finished, add the lemon slices, basil leaves and the sprig of thyme. Next, pass the stock through a sieve to prepare it for sauces or soups.

Makes about 2.5 litres (4½ pints).

■ White fish carcasses are best for fish stock, for example sole, turbot, flounder, or cod and haddock. They give off the best flavour when boiled. Use this fish stock as a base for cream sauces and for fish soups.

80

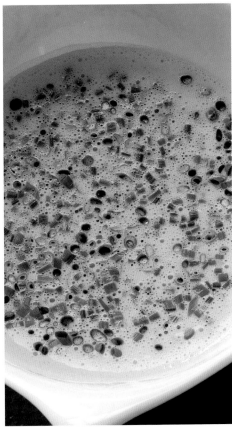

White Wine Sauce

Cut **1 small white mushroom** and **2 shallots** into thin slices. Let **30 g (1 oz) butter** foam up in a pan over medium heat. Add the shallots and mushroom, letting them sweat. Pour in **250 ml (8½ fl oz) white wine** and **100 ml (3½ fl oz) dry vermouth**. Let it reduce almost completely. This concentrates the flavour and evaporates the alcohol. Add **500 ml (17 fl oz) fish stock** and cook until it has a soup-like consistency, concentrating the flavour a second time. Pour in **300 ml (10 fl oz) cream** and **200 g (7 oz) crème fraîche**, and bring it to the boil just once. Remove it from the heat and season with a few drops of **lemon juice**, **1 pinch of salt** and a **pinch of cayenne pepper** to taste. Pass the sauce through a fine sieve, pushing the remnants through well and then vigorously purée using a hand-held blender. Round it off with **2 tbsp whipped cream** and serve.

Makes about 600 ml (1 pint).

■ White wine sauce goes well with steamed or lightly fried fish fillets.

Chive Sauce

Rinse **2 bunches chives**, removing any damaged parts, and snip into small rings. Mix **400 ml (13½ fl oz) whipped butter sauce** and add to it the chives along with **1 tbsp whipped cream**. Stir and serve.

Makes 450 ml (15 fl oz).

■ This sauce goes well with fried or steamed fish fillets such as sole, tilapia, or with lobster.

Whipped Butter Sauce

Dice **2 shallots** finely. Cut **200 g (7 oz) butter** into large cubes and chill immediately. Heat **20 g (²/₃ oz) butter** in a steel saucepan over medium heat until it foams, then add the shallots and sweat them. Then pour in **100 ml (3½ fl oz) white port wine** and **200 ml (7 fl oz) white wine** and let it reduce to a fifth of the volume. Add **400 ml (13½ fl oz) fish stock** and reduce to about half the volume. Add **1 tbsp cream** so the sauce binds better with the butter. Now add the cold butter cubes. Mix with a hand-held blender. The sauce should not be allowed to reduce any further. Season with salt and cayenne pepper to taste.

Makes about 400 ml (13½ fl oz).

■ The butter should be particularly cold, or the sauce won't bind. This is a classic with fish or shellfish – full bodied, but very delicate. Goes well with fried or poached white fish, but also with salmon and pasta dishes with large prawns and mussels.

3 kg (6 lb 8 oz) beef bones

 4 tbsp vegetable oil

 250 g (9 oz) carrots

 400 g (14 oz) onions

 120 g (4½ oz) celeriac

 120 g (4½ oz) celery, with young green leaves

 2 heads of garlic

 10 cloves

 1 tbsp white peppercorns

 1 tsp black peppercorns

 2 sprigs fresh thyme

 2 sprigs fresh rosemary

 5 bay leaves

 2 tsp salt

 2 tbsp tomato purée

 2 tbsp flour

 250 ml (8½ fl oz) red wine

+3 hours cooking time

①

②

Jus

1. For this recipe, the bones should be chopped into walnut-sized pieces but it's best to leave this work to the butcher. Put them into a wide pan with vegetable oil and fry all sides for about 30 minutes until golden brown. Keep stirring, continually scraping the residue from the bottom of the pan, otherwise it could burn, making the jus bitter.

2. Peel the carrots, onions and celeriac, then wash the celery. Set aside the green leaves from the celery. Cut the vegetables into 2-cm (¾-inch) dice and add them to the pan. Fry them for another 20 minutes, stirring continually.

3. Cut the heads of garlic in half horizontally and press all the spices into it with the flat side of the knife. This releases a more intense flavour. Rinse

the thyme and rosemary and cut through the stems twice. Add them and the bay leaves to the sauce. Sprinkle everything with salt.

4. Push the bones and vegetables to one side and add the tomato purée to the middle. Sauté the purée as well so it becomes milder and doesn't overpower the sauce.

5. Sprinkle with the flour and cook it another 10 minutes. The flour's taste disappears through cooking, while it binds the sauce.

6. Add the celery leaves, pour in half of the red wine and reduce completely. Pour in the remaining half of the wine and let it reduce again – this step is important for the intensity of the sauce. This cooks the flavours out, then back in!

■ Jus, the mother of all sauces, is necessary for nearly every beef sauce, and above all for seared beef cuts that don't produce enough juice while searing. Jus turns out well when enough meat is on the bones used to make it. Veal bones achieve a more refined flavour. The bones should come from the back or neck. Don't use a long bone – that works better for soups. Jus reserves may be frozen in small containers.

7. Pour in 3 litres (5¼ pints) cold water, or just enough water to just cover the bones – this will depend on the width of the pan. If you have veal stock available, use it instead of the water to add to the sauce. The sauce will be even more flavourful .

8. Let the sauce simmer slowly for at least 2 hours, though 3 hours would be better. Keep pouring in cold water so the bones stay just covered in liquid.

Keep removing any foam with a slotted spoon, otherwise it cooks into the sauce, making it cloudy. Finish by pouring the sauce through a large sieve. Press the bones and vegetables lightly. Then pour the sauce through a small sieve. Pour the jus back into the pan. Bring it back to the boil, removing the foam, and season it with salt and pepper to taste. This jus is an important base for other sauces.

Makes about 2.5 litres (4½ pints).

1 shallot

 60 g (2¼ oz) mushrooms

 30 g (1 oz) butter

 10 white peppercorns

 2 cloves

 200 ml (7 fl oz) white wine

 500 ml (17 fl oz) chicken stock

 300 ml (10 fl oz) cream

 150 g (5½ oz) crème fraîche

 1 pinch of salt

 1 pinch of cayenne pepper

 2 eggs

Thick Poultry Cream Sauce

1. Peel the shallot and dice it finely. Clean the mushrooms and slice them finely. Heat the butter in a steel saucepan until it foams. Add the shallot and mushroom slices and sweat. Crush the peppercorns and cloves with the flat side of a knife and add them to the pan.

2. Pour in the white wine and let it reduce down almost completely. Then pour in the chicken stock.

3. Again, let the chicken stock reduce almost completely, until a syrup-like residue remains.

4. Then pour in about 200 ml (7 fl oz) of the cream and the crème fraîche. Bring to the boil and season with salt and cayenne pepper to taste.

5. Mix with a hand-held blender and pass it through a sieve. Then use a ladle to push the remnants through. Return to the saucepan.

6. Separate the eggs, add the yolks to the remaining cream and stir with a whisk. Now add this egg yolk-cream combination (liaison, in technical terms) to the hot sauce so that it binds, or becomes thick. You should stop cooking the sauce at this stage, otherwise the egg yolk will curdle and the sauce will turn out thin and lumpy.

Makes about 500 ml (17 fl oz).

■ **This sauce goes well with fried chicken, fried turbot or flounder, and also with steamed artichokes, cooked asparagus, steamed chicory or crispy lettuce.**

40

Thick Tarragon Cream Sauce

Rinse ½ bunch fresh tarragon, pick the leaves from the stems and chop finely. Add the tarragon and 2 tbsp whipped cream to 500 ml (17 fl oz) completely thickened poultry cream sauce and serve.

Makes about 550 ml (18 fl oz).

■ This sauce tastes great on all types of poultry, whether stewed or roasted, and also with rabbit or veal medallions. If using with veal, you could substitute the chicken stock with a light veal stock. It goes best with roasted or stewed veal cutlets, poussin or chicken breasts, or other white meat from poultry.

Coarse Mustard Sauce

Using a whisk, stir together 2 tbsp hot mustard and 1 tbsp coarse mustard with 500 ml (17 fl oz) thickened poultry cream sauce. Then add 2 tbsp whipped cream and a pinch of cayenne pepper to taste, and stir.

Makes about 600 ml (1 pint).

■ Serve this sauce with stewed rabbit, cooked poussin or chicken, cooked calf's head, pork medallions, fillet of sole, or salmon and cucumber. The important thing is not to heat the mustard too high, otherwise it gets bitter quickly and the sauce tastes flat. It goes with veal medallions, with strong-flavoured poultry such as corn-fed chicken or guinea fowl, or with sweetbreads or calf's brain.

1 kg (2 lb 4 oz) shellfish shells

40 ml (1⅓ fl oz) olive oil

80 g (2¾ oz) butter

1 head of garlic

1 sprig fresh thyme

1 sprig fresh rosemary

2 bay leaves

150 g (5½ oz) carrots

300 g (10½ oz) onions

3 shallots

100 g (3½ oz) celery

100 g (3½ oz) fennel bulb

2 tsp tomato purée

20 ml (⅔ fl oz) cognac

30 ml (1 fl oz) red port wine

200 ml (7 fl oz) white wine

1.5 litres (2½ pints) water or vegetable stock

10 white peppercorns

2 cloves

1 sprig fresh basil

(1) (2) (3)

Shellfish Stock

1. Cut the shellfish shells into small pieces or crush them with the back of a heavy knife. Heat them in oil and butter gently in a wide pan, stirring constantly. Cut the garlic in half, and coarsely chop the thyme, rosemary and bay leaves.

2. Cut the vegetables in 1-cm (½-inch) dice and add them to the pan, along with the herbs and seasonings. Sauté everything until the vegetables become soft. Push the shells to the side and add the tomato purée, sautéing it lightly. This takes away the acidity. Next, mix it in with the shells and sauté it a little longer.

3. Finish by pouring in the cognac and port. Let the alcohol reduce and then add white wine to the mixture. Again, stir it as it reduces. Pour in water or vegetable stock. Add the peppercorns and cloves.

Let the stock simmer gently for about 30 minutes, and 10 minutes before it is finished, add the basil and let the stock simmer down. Keep removing the foam that builds up on the surface. Next, pass the stock through a sieve twice and store it for later use. It will keep in the refrigerator for up to a week, or can be frozen as well.

Makes about 1.2 litres (2 pints).

■ King prawn or langoustine shells and claws produce a nice, strong stock. You can cut them with kitchen shears, and in smaller pieces they roast better and are easier to press out. Use as a base for cream sauces or soups, for pasta sauces with shellfish or prawn risotto. It's also good for bouillabaisse or paella.

100

Ingredients for
shellfish stock, plus:

500 ml (17 fl oz) cream

5 basil leaves

10 tarragon leaves

1 pinch of salt

1 pinch of cayenne pepper

Shellfish Cream Sauce

1. Use the same ingredients and preparation as with the shellfish stock. As soon as the stock is reduced and the shells are only half-immersed, pour in the cream, add the basil and tarragon leaves, and simmer for 1 minute.

2. Using a hand-held blender, carefully mix the sauce on the lowest speed. This will mix in the now orange-coloured cream and make the flavour more intense.

3. Pour everything through a fine sieve and use a ladle to push it through. Since so much juice is contained in the shells, this ensures every possible drop is saved. Bring the sauce to the boil again, season with salt and a little cayenne pepper to taste and serve with steamed fish dishes or shellfish.

Makes about 1 litre (1¾ pints).

■ **When adding water, add 50 g (1¾ oz) short grain rice. It helps the sauce combine nicely.**

120 *
  **
  *

2 red onions

 2 garlic cloves

 6 tbsp olive oil

 A few fresh basil stems, chopped

 1 pinch of salt
1 pinch of black pepper

 1 pinch of sugar

 800 g (1 lb 12 oz) tinned, peeled tomatoes

1 tbsp tomato purée

Simple Tomato Sauce

1. Finely dice the onion, chop the garlic, and heat in olive oil. Add a few chopped basil leaves, and sweat them with the garlic and onion.

2. Season with salt, pepper, and a pinch of sugar.

3. Heat everything until the onions look translucent.

4. Drain the tomatoes in a sieve. Using a knife, dice the tomatoes and, while doing so, catch the running juices and add them to the juice from the tin.

5. Pour the tomato juice along with the tomato purée over the onions and garlic in the pan, and let it boil for about 20 minutes.

6. The tomato juice should reduce to about half of what you started with.

7. Now add the diced tomatoes and simmer for 5 minutes.

8. Season with salt, black pepper and sugar to taste and mix in a few large cut pieces of basil.

9. Fill storage jars with the warm tomato sauce, seal, and let it cool down.

Makes about 800 ml (1½ pints).

■ The sauce will keep for 1 to 2 weeks in the refrigerator. This sauce is absolutely essential in cooking, whether served simply on any kind of pasta or as a base for the various tomato sauces such as puttanesca, amatriciana, tomato mushroom sauce or aurora sauce. It also tastes great with cream over vegetable gratins or with aubergines, courgettes, fennel and chard, as well as with fried Mediterranean fish or calamari.

1. Green Curry Sauce

Heat **2 tbsp groundnut oil** in a pan, add **1 tsp green curry paste** and **1 tbsp soft brown sugar** and lightly sauté. Pour in **3 tbsp oyster sauce**, **1 tbsp soya sauce**, and a small portion of **600 ml (1 pint) coconut milk** and let it reduce. Add the remaining coconut milk and let it simmer gently for about 5 minutes. Lastly, add leaves picked from **half a bunch of coriander** to the sauce, mix with a hand-held blender and serve.

Makes about 600 ml (1 pint).

■ Green curry sauce tastes great as a vegetable curry and with beef dishes.

2. Red Curry Sauce

Heat **2 tbsp groundnut oil** in a pan, add **1 tsp green curry paste** and **1 tbsp soft brown sugar** and lightly sauté. Pour in **3 tbsp oyster sauce**, **2 tbsp soya sauce**, and a small portion of **600 ml (1 pint) coconut milk** and let it reduce. Add the remaining coconut milk and let it simmer gently for about 5 minutes. To make the curry sauce more aromatic, add **lemon leaves** chopped very finely shortly before serving.

Makes about 600 ml (1 pint).

■ Red curry sauce can be served with duck or beef, as well as with tofu.

3. Yellow Curry Sauce

Heat **2 tbsp groundnut oil** in a pan, add **1 tsp green curry paste**, **1 dash of turmeric**, **1 tbsp soft brown sugar** and lightly sauté. Pour in **3 tbsp oyster sauce**, **1 tbsp soya sauce**, and a small portion of **600 ml (1 pint) coconut milk** and let it reduce. Add the remaining coconut milk and let it simmer gently for about 5 minutes. To make the curry sauce more aromatic, add **fresh Thai basil** to it shortly before serving.

Makes about 600 ml (1 pint).

■ Yellow curry sauce goes best with chicken and vegetable or fruit curries.

2 shallots

 20 g (²/₃ oz) butter

 50 ml (1²/₃ fl oz) peppercorn brine

 100 ml (3½ fl oz) cognac

 500 ml (17 fl oz) chicken stock

 250 ml (8½ fl oz) cream

 150 g (5½ oz) crème fraîche

 2 tbsp green peppercorns in brine

Pepper Cream Sauce

1. Peel the shallots and finely dice them. Heat the butter in a small pan over medium heat until it foams, add the shallots and sweat them until they are translucent. Pour in the peppercorn brine and let the liquid reduce. Pour in the cognac and cook until the liquids are almost completely reduced.

2. Pour in the chicken stock and reduce to a fifth of the volume. Then pour in the cream, add the crème fraîche and bring it to the boil. Then remove it from the cooker and mix using a hand-held blender.

3. Pass the sauce through a fine sieve and, finally, add the green peppercorns to the sauce. If needed, add salt to taste.

Makes about 500 ml (17 fl oz).

■ This base can also be used to make a mushroom cream sauce, in which case the peppercorns and brine should be left out. After sweating the shallots in butter, add 200 g (7 oz) cleaned, sliced mushrooms and sweat them. Then follow step 2. Finally, pass the sauce through a sieve, mix and add the mushroom slices again. Serve with omelettes, pork medallions or roasted chicken breast. It tastes best with seared beef fillet steak, fillet steak tips, tournedos or filet mignon.

500 g (1 lb 2 oz) red peppers

 100g (3½ oz) onion

 2 garlic cloves

 4 tbsp extra virgin olive oil

 1 sprig fresh thyme

 2 bay leaves

 1 pinch of salt

 1 pinch of black pepper

 1 tbsp sugar

 150 ml (5 fl oz) white wine

 700 ml (1¼ pints) chicken stock

 200 g (7 oz) crème fraîche

 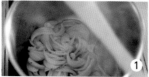 
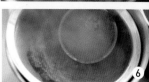  

Paprika Cream Sauce

1. Clean the peppers and dice into large pieces. Cut the onion in half and cut into thin slices. Peel the garlic cloves and cut them into thin slices as well. Warm up the olive oil in a pan, and slowly sweat the onion and garlic until translucent.

2. Add the thyme and bay leaves and sweat for about 1 minute. Then mix in the red pepper, add salt, pepper and sugar and sweat another 2–3 minutes.

3. Pour in the white wine and chicken stock and let it slowly simmer for about 15 minutes.

4. Add the crème fraîche and let it come to the boil.

5. Take out the thyme sprig and bay leaves and mix the sauce with a hand-held blender.

6. Then pass the sauce through a fine sieve. Using a ladle, push the pepper residue through the sieve so that the entire vegetable purée makes it into the sauce. This makes the sauce rich and thick.

Makes about 600 ml (1 pint).

■ **This sauce goes well with roast rabbit, stewed or roast chicken, cod or hake fillets, and also with stuffed peppers.**

1 2 3
4 5 6

Balsamic Vinegar Sauce

1. Put the water in a pan and dissolve the sugar in it, cooking until it is lightly caramelised and the water is boiled away. Pour in the balsamic vinegar and cook it until a syrup-like consistency is achieved.

2. Peel the shallots and cut them into thin slices. Press the garlic cloves in their skins. Cut the bay leaves, thyme and rosemary coarsely. Add the olive oil to the syrup first, then stir in the herbs, garlic cloves and shallots.

3. Add salt and pepper and sweat for about 5 minutes.

4. Pour in the chicken stock and let it reduce to about a fifth of the volume for

15 minutes. Then add the cream and crème fraîche.

5. Bring the sauce back to the boil. Then mix with a hand-held blender.

6. Pass the sauce through a fine sieve. Using a slotted spoon, push the remnants through well. Finally, stir in the whipped cream.

Makes about 600 ml (1 pint).

■ **This sauce goes well with fried cod or lentils, and with roasted young chicken or pigeon.**

100 ml (3½ fl oz) water

2 tbsp soft brown sugar

150 ml (5 fl oz) balsamic vinegar

3 shallots

4 garlic cloves

4 bay leaves

4 sprigs fresh thyme

1 sprig fresh rosemary

3 tbsp olive oil

1 pinch of salt
1 pinch of black pepper

500 ml (17 fl oz) chicken stock

350 ml (12 fl oz) cream

150 g (5½ oz) crème fraîche

2 tbsp whipped cream

45 ✳✳✳

100 ml (3½ fl oz) white wine

 5 eggs

 1 pinch of salt

 350 g (12 oz) butter

 Juice of ½ lemon

 1 tbsp tarragon vinegar

 1 pinch of cayenne pepper

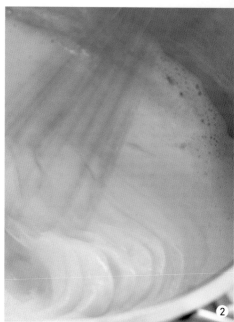

Hollandaise Sauce

1. Bring 3 cm (1¼ inches) water to the boil in a pan as a bain-marie. Pour the white wine in a bowl with a rounded bottom. Separate the eggs, putting the yolk in the bowl, and the egg white in a sealed container for later use, storing it in the refrigerator. Now place the bowl over the bain-marie, add salt, and mix together using a whisk.

2. Beat the egg yolk vigorously with the whisk until it is thick and pale.

3. Melt the butter in a small pan until it is warm, not hot, then carefully drizzle it into the foamy egg yolk using a ladle. Keep stirring all the time with the whisk so that the butter blends with the yolk, resulting in a thick and creamy consistency. The preparation is exactly as for mayonnaise, except this sauce is warm. Finally, add salt, lemon juice, tarragon vinegar and cayenne pepper to taste.

Makes about 600 g (1 lb 5 oz) or 1 litre (1¾ pints).

■ To whip up a really good Hollandaise sauce, 5 eggs yolks are best. Never use fewer than 3 egg yolks, otherwise the sauce will not reach the correct consistency. Place the finished sauce over a pan of water, not letting it touch the cooker, and cover with baking paper. This allows the sauce to stay warm for up to an hour. This sauce goes best with steamed asparagus or poached fish.

This sauce is too runny either because the butter was too hot when it was added, or it was added too quickly.

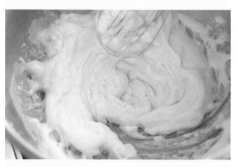

The egg has curdled because it was beaten over boiling water. It wouldn't be possible to stir in more butter to smooth it.

③

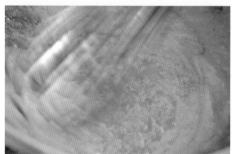

Kitchen doctor: The sauce is runny here too. Add 1 tbsp of hot water and try stirring it again using small movements in one spot, then stir in more and more of the rest of the sauce.

200 ml (7 fl oz) white wine

 1 tbsp tarragon vinegar

 1 tsp white peppercorns

 30 g (1 oz) mushrooms

 1 shallot

 ½ bunch fresh tarragon

 5 eggs

 350 g (12 oz) butter

 1 pinch of salt

 1 pinch of cayenne pepper

Juice of ½ lemon

½ bunch fresh chervil

½ bunch fresh parsley

½ bunch fresh chives

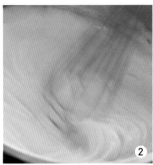

Béarnaise Sauce

1. Make a stock by putting the white wine, tarragon vinegar, peppercorns, mushrooms and shallot, sliced, and a tarragon sprig in a steel saucepan and reducing to half the volume. Then pass it through a fine sieve into a bowl with a round bottom.

2. The rest of the recipe follows the same steps as for Hollandaise sauce (see p. 152), except the egg yolks are beaten with stock. Stir in the butter just as for Hollandaise sauce and season the sauce with salt and cayenne pepper to taste.

3. Rinse the rest of the tarragon and chervil, removing any damaged leaves, pick the leaves from the stems and chop them finely. Prepare the parsley and chives the same way. Cut the parsley into thin ribbons and the chives into small rings. Finally, stir the herbs into the sauce.

Serve with chargrilled or roast beef, asparagus, boiled cauliflower, broccoli or fried fish.

Makes about 1 litre (1¾ pints).

Choron Sauce

Make the basic recipe described for Hollandaise sauce (see p. 152). Put **2 tbsp good-quality tomato purée** in a bowl. You can tell if it's good tomato purée as it will be nice and red, not brownish. Add **2 tbsp Hollandaise sauce** to the purée and mix them together. This step is called blending. Omitting it prevents the tomato purée from really mixing throughout the sauce, leaving large lumps in the Choron sauce. Add this to the Hollandaise sauce and mix together.

Makes about 1 litre (1¾ pints).

■ This nice, rich-flavoured sauce goes well with steamed fish, with cooked vegetables such as chard, spinach, or cauliflower, or with lightly fried chicken. Additionally, this sauce can be used in baked gratin dishes, or for a minestrone, which tastes particularly sophisticated with Choron sauce.

Foyot Sauce

Make the béarnaise sauce as described in the recipe on the preceding page. Heat **3 tbsp roast beef glaze** in a small pan and while continuously stirring, drizzle it slowly into the béarnaise sauce.

Makes about 1 litre (1¾ pints).

■ Foyot sauce is sometimes erroneously confused with béarnaise sauce. Foyot sauce, however, contains beef jus or beef extract; béarnaise sauce does not. Foyot sauce goes very well with large beef cuts such as roast and T-bone steaks as well as with baked oysters.

1 onion

 1 bay leaf

 2 cloves

 60 g (2¼ oz) butter

 30 g (1 oz) flour

 750 ml (1¼ pints) milk

 250 ml (8½ fl oz) cream

 1 pinch of salt

 1 pinch of white pepper

 1 pinch of nutmeg, freshly grated

  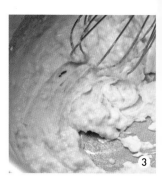

Béchamel Sauce

1. Peel the onion and tack the bay leaf to it using 2 cloves.

2. Melt the butter in the pan and sauté the flour in it lightly, making a roux.

3. Add a little bit of the milk to the pan and stir it immediately so the roux dissolves.

4. Pour in the remaining cold milk and the cream a little bit at a time and stir. Put the studded onion in the sauce.

5. Simmer gently for about 1 minute, stirring often. Season with salt, white pepper and nutmeg to taste.

6. Then pass the sauce through a fine sieve.

Cover with cling film to keep a skin from forming on the sauce. Use for lasagne or in other sauces.

Makes about 1 litre (1¾ pints).

■ **This is used as a base for other sauces – and it is certainly among the most important ingredients for a lasagne and for other baked gratin dishes.**

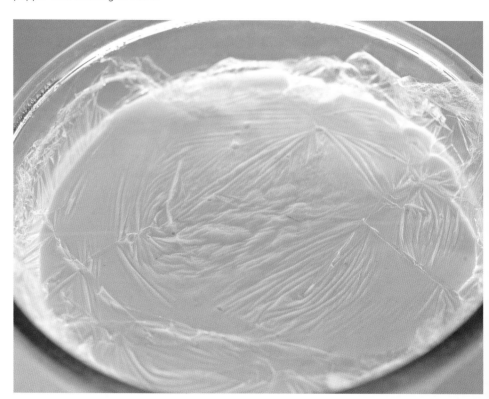

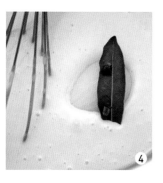

■ Thick béchamel sauce: Stir this sauce to bind soups or sauces until the desired consistency is reached. Cold, thick béchamel sauce can also be used as a binding agent for croquettes.

■ Creamy béchamel sauce: This serves as the base for many white sauces such as mustard sauce, for baking lasagne covered in cheese, or for horseradish sauce.

Horseradish Sauce

Bring **500 ml (17 fl oz) béchamel sauce** and **200 ml (7 fl oz) cream** to the boil and whisk until smooth. Next, remove it from the heat, add **50 g (1¾ oz) grated horseradish** and stir. Season with **2 tbsp sugar, 2 tbsp fruit vinegar**, a pinch of salt and a pinch of white pepper to taste, and serve.

Makes about 800 ml (1½ pints).

■ Horseradish sauce goes well with cooked beef, for example tri-tip. It also tastes good with boiled calf's tongue or calf's head, and with boiled potatoes or cauliflower.

✳ **Kitchen doctor:** This béchamel sauce is too thin. You should have another attempt at making the butter and flour roux and pour in the milk. Then simmer for another 10 minutes.

✳ **Kitchen doctor:** This sauce is lumpy. Pass it through a fine sieve again and then continue working.

Mustard Sauce

Bring **500 ml (17 fl oz) béchamel sauce** and **200 ml (7 fl oz) cream** to the boil and whisk until smooth, then remove it from the heat and stir in **2 tbsp good-quality medium-hot mustard**. Season with **1 pinch of salt** and **1 pinch of freshly milled white pepper** to taste, and serve.

Makes about 800 ml (1½ pints).

■ Serve this sauce with boiled eggs, boiled beef or steamed saltwater fish. It also goes well with poached shellfish, braised onions and boiled beef such as tri-tip.

3 tbsp olive oil

 600 g (1 lb 5 oz) beef mince

 1 tsp salt
1 pinch of black pepper

 1 onion

 2 carrots

 1 parsnip

 1 garlic clove

 2 tbsp tomato purée

 800 g (1 lb 12 oz) tinned peeled
tomatoes

 ½ bunch fresh basil

Simple Bolognese

1. Heat the olive oil in a shallow pan and fry the meat in it.

2. Add salt and pepper to the meat, stir and watch that it doesn't burn and stick to the bottom.

3. Peel the onion, carrots and parsnip, and grate them with a grater.

4. Add the grated vegetables, along with the peeled and finely chopped garlic, to the beef mince, and lightly sauté them.

5. Once juices are released with cooking, push the meat to the sides of the pan.

6. Put the tomato purée in the middle of the pan and sauté. This takes the acidity out. Then stir the tomato purée in with the meat.

7. Add the tomatoes to the meat and break down the tomato pieces with a wooden spoon.

8. Pour in 500 ml (17 fl oz) water and simmer gently for 45 minutes.

9. Finally, round off with cut ribbons of basil.

Mix with spaghetti, sprinkle with grated Parmesan cheese, and serve.

Makes about 2 litres (3½ pints).

■ Bolognese is an important ingredient for lasagne, and it tastes outstanding on other pasta.

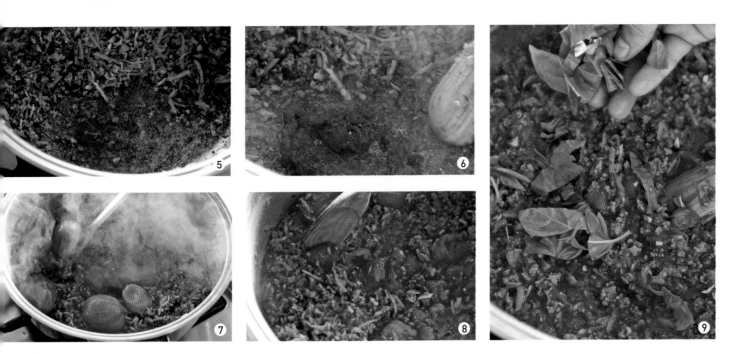

159

Soups

Contents

1 garlic clove

 9 tbsp extra virgin olive oil

 1 cucumber

 2 red peppers

 ½ onion

 750 ml (1¼ pints) tomato juice

 1 pinch of salt
1 pinch of black pepper

 2 tbsp red wine vinegar

Gazpacho

1. To make garlic oil, peel the garlic clove, press into 5 tbsp oil and stir.

2. Rinse the cucumber and peel coarsely. Deseed the peppers, rinse and cut them in quarters. Peel the onions and cut all the vegetables into 2-cm (¾-inch) dice.

3. Put the vegetables in a food processor.

4. Pour in the tomato juice.

5. Season with salt and black pepper, the red wine vinegar and 4 tbsp olive oil.

6. Now purée for about 1 minute in the food processor.

7. Pour into a bowl and place in the refrigerator for about 1 hour so the soup can cool completely. Drizzle a little of the garlic oil over the soup shortly before serving. Place a tall container of ice in the soup bowl, so the soup stays cool longer on the table.

■ During summer, use overripe, soft tomatoes instead of tomato juice.

163

60 ml (2 fl oz) olive oil

 2 tbsp sugar

 70 g (2½ oz) celery

 140 g (5 oz) carrots

 150 g (5½ oz) onion

 2 garlic cloves

 4 cloves

 1 lemon

 1 tsp white peppercorns

 1 sprig fresh rosemary

 1 sprig fresh thyme

 1 bay leaf

 1 tbsp tomato purée

 1.2 kg (2 lb 12 oz) tomatoes

 1 tsp salt

 750 ml (1¼ pints) chicken stock

Tomato Soup with Basil Croutons

1. Pour the olive oil into a large steel pan. Add the sugar and lightly sauté it, then add the finely diced vegetables (see p. 344). Sauté lightly for 5 minutes. Peel the garlic, cut it in half and sweat along with the cloves, 2 lemon peel strips (made using a vegetable peeler), the peppercorns crushed with the flat side of a knife, as well as the rosemary, thyme and bay leaf for another 5 minutes.

2. Now add the tomato purée and sauté for 1 minute. Then add the washed and quartered tomatoes and season them with salt.

3. Then pour in the chicken stock and bring it to the boil. Then reduce the heat to medium and let it simmer for 20 minutes.

4. Take out what is left of the sprigs of herbs and purée the ingredients of the pan for 1 minute using a hand-held blender.

5. Using a ladle, pour the soup through a fine sieve and use the bottom of the ladle to push it through firmly until the remnants are almost dry. This binds the soup and, more importantly, lends it flavour. Put the soup in a preheated bowl and serve with basil croutons.

 ✳ ✳ ✳ 60

■ For the basil croutons, melt 20 g (¾ oz) butter in a nonstick pan, add 50 g (1¾ oz) cubed white bread and fry, stirring continuously until golden brown. Add four basil leaves, cut into ribbons, lightly salt and mix together. Immediately remove croutons from the heat to keep them from overbrowning, and put aside in a bowl.

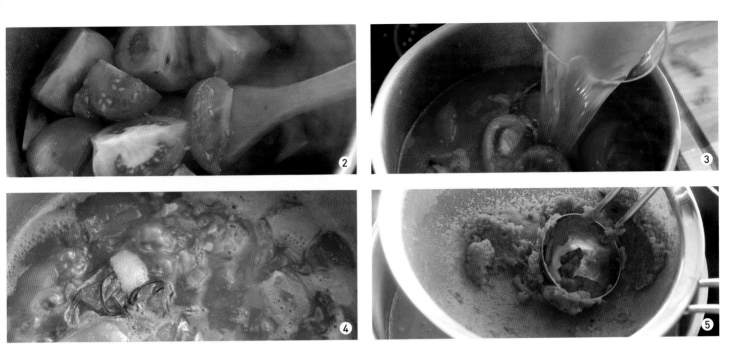

3 small carrots

 1 small leek

 2 celery sticks

 ½ courgette

 2 spring onions

 8 cherry tomatoes

 1 garlic clove

 4 tbsp olive oil

 1 pinch of salt
1 pinch of black pepper

 ½ tsp fennel seeds

 1.5 litres (2½ pints) vegetable stock

 1 tbsp fresh basil

 1 tsp fresh oregano

80 g (2¾ oz) Parmesan cheese

Italian Vegetable Soup

1. Clean and peel the vegetables, rinse and cut them into 5-mm (¼-inch) pieces. Cut the cherry tomatoes into quarters. Peel the garlic clove and mince.

2. Heat the olive oil in a pan and slightly brown the garlic. Add the spring onions and leek and sweat them lightly.

3. Now add the remaining vegetables, except the tomatoes, and likewise sweat them without browning. Season with salt, pepper and crushed fennel seeds.

4. Add the tomatoes and pour in the vegetable stock. Let it simmer gently for about 10 minutes.

5. Finally, add the torn basil and oregano leaves to the soup and serve immediately.

You can also add grated Parmesan cheese over the top of the soup according to taste.

✳ ✳ ✳ 40

■ If the garlic clove is already growing a green stem, take it out with a knife as it can taste bitter and sharp when cooked.

100 g (3½ oz) butter

 1 egg plus 1 egg yolk

 1 tsp parsley, chopped

 1 pinch of salt

 1 pinch of nutmeg, freshly grated

 60 g (2 oz) self-raising flour

 1 tbsp plain flour

 2 litres (3½ pints) chicken stock

Chicken Soup with Butter Dumplings and Nutmeg

1. Whip the butter, which should be at room temperature, until it forms peaks. Next, add the egg and egg yolk, parsley, salt and nutmeg. Beat until all the ingredients have blended.

2. Then, with a rubber spatula, work in the self-raising flour and leave the mixture to sit for 10 minutes.

3. Use two teaspoons to form the dumplings.

4. Put the dumplings on a board sprinkled with plain flour and put the board in the refrigerator for 30 minutes.

5. Bring the chicken stock to the boil and add the dumplings. Maintain a simmer until the dumplings float. Then cover and leave to steep for 25 minutes.

Serve in soup bowls and sprinkle with nutmeg.

■ Julienned root vegetables boiled in salted water and some chicken meat can be added to this dish.

400 g (14 oz) potatoes

 100 g (3½ oz) leeks

 50 g (1¾ oz) parsnip

 ½ garlic clove

 30 g (1 oz) butter

 1 pinch of salt

 1 pinch of white pepper

 1 pinch of nutmeg, freshly grated

 1 litre (1¾ pints) chicken stock

 ½ tsp dried marjoram

 200 ml (7 fl oz) cream

 150 g (5½ oz) crème fraîche

 1 tbsp oil

 30 g (1 oz) smoked bacon rashers

2 slices of white bread

Potato Soup with Marjoram

1. Peel the potatoes and cut them into 1-cm (½-inch) pieces. Put them in cold water until they're needed so they don't turn brown. Rinse and clean the leek, cut it in half lengthways, and then cut into half rings (see p. 350). Rinse the parsnip, peel it, and cut it like the potatoes. Peel the garlic and cut into thin slices. Melt the butter in a pan until it foams, and sweat the garlic, leeks, and parsnip in it without letting them take on any colour. Season with a pinch of salt and pepper.

2. Then add the potatoes, the nutmeg on top, and sweat them. Don't let the vegetables brown or the soup will turn grey.

3. Pour in the chicken stock, add the marjoram and bring to the boil. Then let it simmer gently over a low heat for about 20 minutes.

4. Now add the cream and crème fraîche to the soup. Bring it back to the boil and purée using a hand-held blender. Finally, cut the bacon into strips, heat the oil in a pan and fry the bacon until crisp. Cut the crusts off the slices of bread and cut into 1-cm (½-inch) pieces. Add the bread to the bacon and brown it until it turns golden. Serve the soup in deep bowls and sprinkle the bacon croutons on top.

■ Cold potato leek soup: Pass 500 ml (17 fl oz) potato soup through a fine sieve. Then wash the leeks, cut them into rings, and sweat in 1 tbsp olive oil. Add them to the soup. Let the soup cool then serve over another bowl filled with ice. This popular French summer soup is called vichyssoise.

45

2 onions

 4 bunches fresh chervil

 2 eggs

 40 g (1½ oz) butter

 750 ml (1¼ pints) chicken stock

 1 pinch of salt

 1 pinch of nutmeg, freshly grated

 400 ml (13½ fl oz) double cream

 100 g (3½ oz) crème fraîche

Chervil Cream Soup

1. Peel the onions, cut them in half and dice them finely. Rinse the chervil, pluck it, removing any damaged leaves. Set the leaves and stems aside. Boil the eggs for 6 minutes, rinse them in cold water, then peel them. Melt the butter in a pan and sweat the onions until they look translucent. Now add the chervil stems and cook them briefly.

2. Pour in the chicken stock and season with salt and nutmeg. Bring to the boil, then lower the heat and let it simmer for about 10 minutes.

3. Add the cream and crème fraîche and bring it briefly back to the boil.

4. Then pour the soup through a fine sieve and press it through with the bottom of a ladle.

5. Set aside a few chervil leaves as a garnish. Put the remaining leaves in a blender, pour in the soup, and mix it for 1 minute.

6. Season with the salt. Serve the foamy soup topped with the remaining chervil leaves and 2 quarters of an egg.

■ If you like it thicker, you can add 100 g (3½ oz) starchy potatoes to the recipe. Cut them into 1-cm (½-inch) pieces and add them to the soup before you add chervil stems.

※
※※ 45
※

Cream of Asparagus with Mint

Peel the lower third of **350 g (12 oz) green asparagus** and rinse. Then cut off the tips at a length of about 3 cm (1¼ inches) and set them aside. Cut the asparagus stalks into pieces about 1 cm (½ inch) long. Peel **60 g (2¼ oz) starchy cooking potatoes** and cut into 5-mm (¼-inch) pieces. Peel **1 shallot**, cut it in half and dice it finely. Cut a **courgette** in half lengthways, then into thin slices. Melt **20 g (⅔ oz) butter** in a pan until it foams. Add the **shallot** and potatoes and briefly sweat them. Add the asparagus stalk pieces and likewise sweat them, season with **1 pinch of salt, 1 pinch of white pepper** and **1 pinch of freshly grated nutmeg**. Pour in **750 ml (1¼ pints) chicken stock** and let it simmer for about 10 minutes. Boil the asparagus tips in salted water for 5 minutes and then refresh them under cool water. Pour **200 ml (7 fl oz) cream** into the soup, bring to the boil briefly and mix with a hand-held blender. Add **2 tbsp whipped cream** to the soup but don't let it boil again. Cut the leaves from a **sprig of fresh mint** into thin ribbons and sprinkle them over the soup. Warm the asparagus tips in **10 g (¼ oz) butter** and drop them into the soup.

Cream of Mushroom

Peel **1 shallot**, cut it in half, and dice finely. Peel **150 g (5½ oz) starchy cooking potatoes** and cut into 5-mm (¼-inch) pieces. Clean **300 g (10½ oz) mushrooms** (see p. 360) and cut into slices. Peel **½ a garlic clove** and cut it in thin slices. Let **20 g (⅔ oz) butter** foam up in a pan over medium heat. Add the shallots, garlic and potatoes and sweat them. After about 1 minute, add the mushrooms and season with **1 pinch of salt, 1 pinch of black pepper** and **1 pinch of freshly grated nutmeg**. Sprinkle with the juice from **½ a lemon** so the mushrooms don't darken too much while cooking. Pour in **750 ml (1¼ pints) chicken stock** and let it simmer for about 10 minutes. Pour in **200 ml (7 fl oz) cream** and mix well with a hand-held blender. Do not pass the soup through a sieve. Add **2 tbsp whipped cream** and remove from the heat. Divide the soup into preheated bowls and serve.

1.6 kg (3 lb 8 oz) butternut squash

 ½ bunch fresh dill

 15 g (½ oz) ginger

 1 garlic clove

 80 g (2¾ oz) carrots

 150 g (5½ oz) red pepper

 30 g (1 oz) celery

 80 g (2¾ oz) onion

 40 g (1½ oz) butter

 ½ tsp salt

 1 pinch of nutmeg, freshly grated

 3 cloves

 1 bay leaf

 1 tsp tomato ketchup

 ½ tsp curry powder

 1½ tsp sweet paprika

 1 litre (1¾ pints) chicken stock

 200 ml (7 fl oz) cream

 100 g (3½ oz) crème fraîche

American-style Squash Soup with Cheese Croutons

1. Cut the top off the squash from about 3 cm (1¼ inches) down. Scrape out the seeds with a soup spoon. Rinse the dill then pluck it, removing any damaged leaves, and finely chop.

2. Using a melon baller, scoop out the flesh from the squash and the top, without damaging the skin. Leave about a 1-cm (½-inch) thick wall. That yields about 225 g (8 oz) of flesh from the squash.

3. Peel the ginger and garlic and cut both into thin slices. Wash the vegetables, peel them and cut them, along with the onion, into 1-cm (½-inch) pieces. Melt the butter in a pan and sweat the garlic and onion together until they appear translucent. Then add the vegetables and the ginger and sweat them another 5 minutes.

4. Add the squash flesh. Season with salt and nutmeg, and add the cloves and bay leaf. Sweat over medium heat for about 10 minutes, until the squash begins to fall apart easily. Push it to the sides of the pan.

5. Lightly sauté the tomato ketchup, curry powder and paprika in the middle of the pan for 1 minute, then mix the squash in. This intensifies the flavour.

6. Pour in the chicken stock, bring it to the boil and let it lightly simmer over medium heat for 15 minutes. Add the cream and crème fraîche and bring it briefly back to a boil.

■ **Cheese croutons:** Cut half a baguette into 5-mm (¼-inch) thick slices, sprinkle 60 g (2¼ oz) grated aged Gouda cheese over them, and bake them in the oven at 200°C (400°F/Gas Mark 6) for 5 minutes.

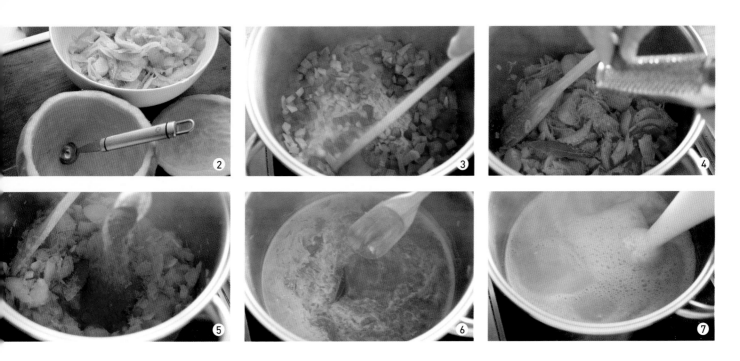

7. Then purée with a hand-held blender for 1 minute and pour it through a fine sieve. Use the bottom of a ladle to press the remaining liquid out of the remnants.

Pour the soup into the hollowed-out squash, sprinkle with the finely chopped dill and serve with the cheese croutons.

100g (3½ oz) onion

 3 shallots

 80 g (2¾ oz) carrots

 80 g (2¾ oz) celery

 3 garlic cloves

 10 black peppercorns

 1.2 kg (2 lb 12 oz) lobster

 3 tbsp olive oil

 50 g (1¾ oz) butter

 2 sprigs fresh thyme

 1 sprig fresh rosemary

 2 bay leaves

 4 tinned, peeled tomatoes

 15 g (½ oz) short grain rice

 50 ml (1²/₃ fl oz) dry vermouth
50 ml (1²/₃ fl oz) cognac

 150 ml (5 fl oz) white wine

 1 litre (1¾ pints) shellfish stock

 400 ml (13½ fl oz) cream

 2 basil leaves

 1 pinch of salt

 1 pinch of cayenne pepper

①

Lobster Bisque

1. Cut the onions, shallots, carrots and celery into 5-mm (¼-inch) pieces. Crush the garlic in its skin. Crush the peppercorns with a knife. Crack open the lobster (see p. 482) and store the flesh. Heat the olive oil in a wide pan, add the lobster carcasses (shells) and sauté them for about 5 minutes. Then add the butter and sauté the shells longer to remove their flavour.

2. Then add the vegetables, garlic, peppercorns and the coarsely chopped herbs, and sweat until translucent. Keep scraping any residue from the bottom of the pan so as not to let it burn, which will make the soup bitter.

3. Add the tomatoes, break them down and sauté them. Add the rice, pour in the vermouth, cognac and white wine and let it boil another 5 minutes so the alcohol evaporates.

4. Now pour in the shellfish stock (see p. 142) and let it slowly simmer for 20 minutes.

5. Pour in the cream, add the basil leaves and let it simmer for 1 more minute. Carefully mix the soup with a hand-held blender on the lowest speed – this gives the soup a more intense flavour. Then, using a ladle, pour the soup through a fine sieve into another pan, and squeeze out the carcasses well. Bring it back

■ This soup takes its name from the salty, grated biscuits with which it was previously associated. Lobster bisque tastes even better if you start with the shells of live lobsters.

to the boil and season with salt and cayenne pepper to taste. Serve the soup in deep bowls and place 30 g (1 oz) of the reserved lobster flesh per person in the soup.

- 300 g (10½ oz) small turbot
- 300 g (10½ oz) small red snapper
- 500 g (1 lb 2 oz) small redfish
- 500 g (1 lb 2 oz) monkfish
- 130 g (4½ oz) fennel bulb
- 150 g (5½ oz) carrots
- 200 g (7 oz) celery
- 1 sprig fresh rosemary
- 3 sprigs fresh thyme
- 3 bay leaves
- 1 tsp fennel seeds
- 1 tsp black peppercorns
- 100 ml (3½ fl oz) extra virgin olive oil
- 5 garlic cloves
- 10 saffron threads
- 1 tbsp tomato purée
- 100 ml (3½ fl oz) dry vermouth
- 350 ml (12 fl oz) white wine
- 1.5 litres (2½ pints) water
- 1 tsp coarse sea salt

1

Bouillabaisse Stock Base

1. Wash, gut and fillet the fish, then pull out the small bones with fishbone tongs. Cover the fillets and keep them in the refrigerator until you need them for the bouillabaisse. Remove the gills from the fish heads and rinse the heads and bones under running water, until there is no blood residue. Then drain the fish bones and heads well.

2. Peel the vegetables and cut them into 1-cm (½-inch) pieces. Chop the herbs coarsely, then crush the fennel seeds and peppercorns with the flat side of a knife. Cover the fish bones with the vegetables, herbs, 2 tbsp olive oil, crushed garlic cloves and saffron threads, and leave to marinate for about 2 hours.

3. Heat the remaining olive oil in a wide pan, then fry the marinated fish bones and the remaining marinade mix.

4. After 5 minutes, add the tomato purée and pour in the dry vermouth, white wine and the water. Season it with salt. Reduce the temperature to medium heat and let everything simmer for 20 minutes. Remove the foam with a ladle when necessary.

5. Pass the stock through a coarse sieve and press down firmly on the fish bones.

6. Next, pass it through a fine sieve. Set the stock aside and use it later for the bouillabaisse.

Makes about 1.6 litres (2¾ pints).

■ Rouille sauce (see p. 52) goes well with bouillabaisse stock.

*
 * 160
*

200 g (7 oz) red peppers

 200 g (7 oz) green peppers

 200 g (7 oz) carrots

 200 g (7 oz) fennel bulb

 200 g (7 oz) leeks

 Filleted fish, from the Boullabaisse stock base preparation (see p. 178)

 ½ tsp salt

 3 sprigs fresh thyme

 4 tbsp extra virgin olive oil

 12 saffron threads

 2 garlic cloves

 1 pinch of black pepper

 50 ml (1⅔ fl oz) dry vermouth

 100 ml (3½ fl oz) white wine

 1.5 litres (2½ pints) bouillabaisse stock (see p. 178)

 ½ bunch fresh basil

 350 g (12 oz) rouille sauce (see p. 52)

1

Bouillabaisse

1. Wash the red and green peppers and the carrots, peel them and thinly julienne them (see p. 344). Wash the fennel and leeks, cutting them into thin strips as well.

2. Marinate the fish fillets with salt, thyme leaves, 2 tbsp olive oil and half of the saffron threads.

3. Put the rest of the olive oil in a pan and sweat the peeled, finely diced garlic in it until translucent. Then add the vegetables and likewise sweat them for 5 minutes. Add the rest of the saffron and season with salt and pepper.

4. As soon as the vegetables are done, pour in the dry vermouth and white wine and reduce until all the liquid is evaporated. Pour in the finished stock and let it simmer gently for 10 minutes.

5. Now lay the fish fillets in by hand and bring it back to the boil. Rinse the basil, removing any damaged pieces, tear the leaves in thin ribbons and add them to the pan. Serve it with rouille sauce. You can also put some of the sauce directly in the soup to bind it well and make it thicker.

■ Familiar with a different bouillabaisse? There are about 280 variations. You can make this dish however you like it, using other fish, shellfish or mussels as well.

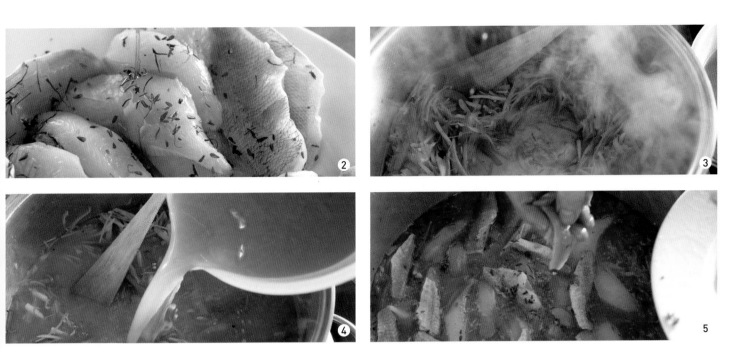

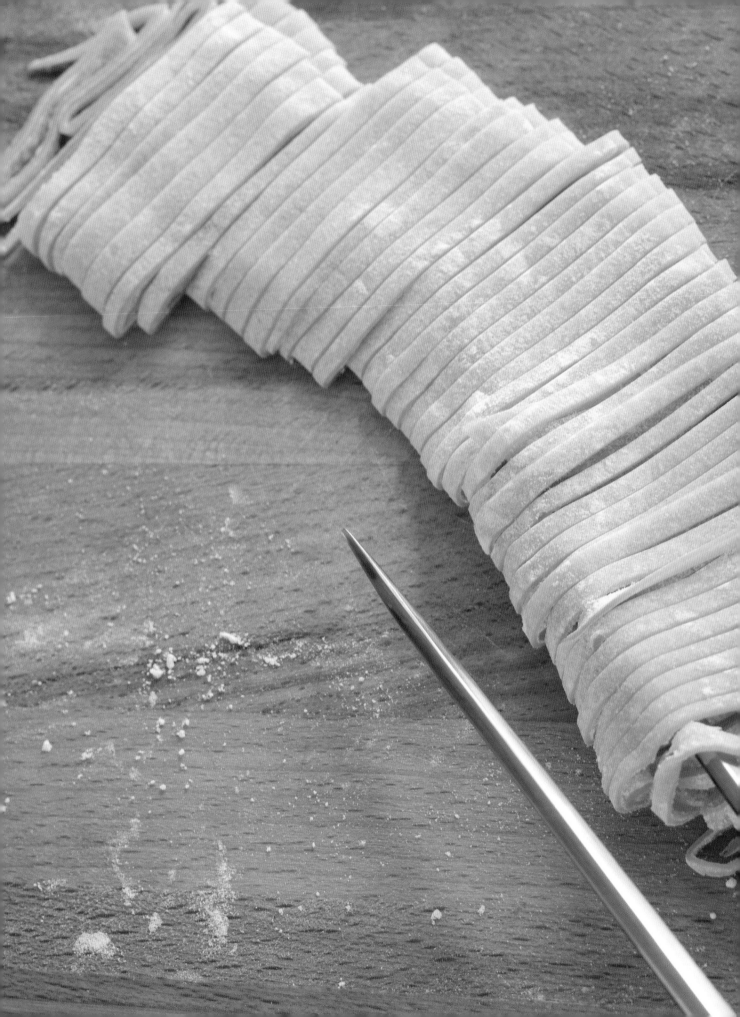

Pasta

Contents

Types of Pasta

Pasta is legendary in Italian cooking, even though many countries have different regional noodle specialities. Spaghetti, tagliolini and tortellini are different shapes of noodle made with semolina. Rice noodles and vermicelli are made with rice flour and water.

They are available in varying sizes and widths. Glass noodles are made from a base of mung bean starch and water. They're thin and almost transparent. There is a variety in Korea made from sweet potato starch.

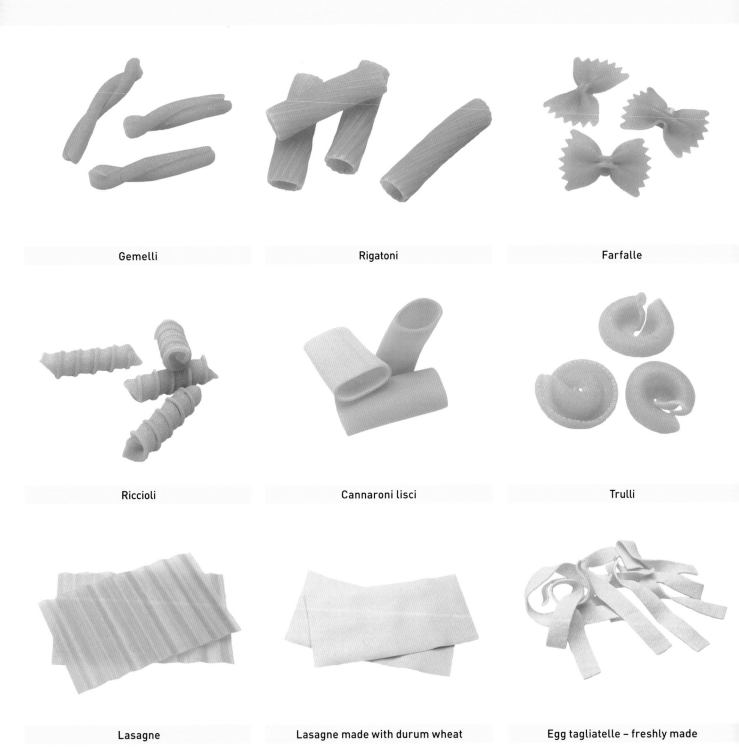

Gemelli	Rigatoni	Farfalle
Riccioli	Cannaroni lisci	Trulli
Lasagne	Lasagne made with durum wheat	Egg tagliatelle – freshly made

Soup Noodles

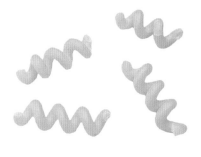

Dinosaur-shaped pasta

Cavatappi or cellentani

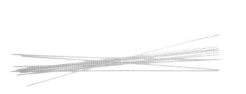

Capellini

Penne

Mafaldine

Thin rice noodles

Spinach tagliolini – freshly made

Black sepia spaghetti

Dried egg tagliatelle

Tagliolini

Wholegrain spiral noodles, eliche or fusilli

 400 g (14 oz) flour

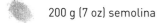 200 g (7 oz) semolina

7 eggs

1 pinch of salt

3 tbsp extra virgin olive oil

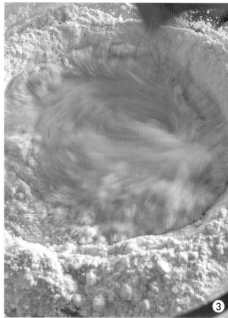

Pasta Dough

1. Mix the flour and semolina in a bowl.

2. Add the eggs and salt.

3. Mix some flour into the eggs using a whisk.

4. Add the olive oil and mix with the eggs and the rest of the flour.

5. Put the dough on a flat work surface and knead it vigorously.

6. Knead the dough until the flour is completely worked in and has a firm consistency. Now the dough can be rolled out as desired using a pasta machine.

■ The pasta dough can be flavoured with tomato purée, puréed spinach, porcini powder, finely chopped rosemary or thyme, or truffle paste.

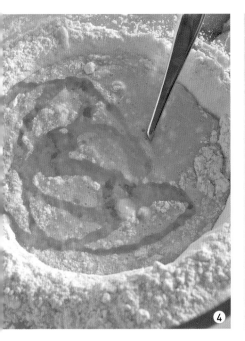

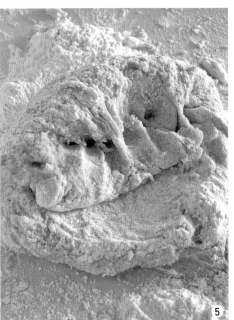

Spinach Pasta Dough

1. Remove **450 g (1 lb) spinach leaves** from their stems and rinse well. Cook for 5 to 8 minutes in plenty of salted water until soft. Pour into a sieve, cool it under cold water and firmly push out the water. Purée the dry spinach in a blender.

2. Separate **6 eggs**. In a bowl, add the **egg yolks, 450 g (1 lb) flour, 200 g (7 oz) semolina, 2 tbsp oil** and **1 pinch of salt**.

3. Add the cooled, puréed spinach.

4. Knead until it makes a smooth dough.

5. Work in more flour as needed to reach the desired consistency. Wrap the spinach pasta dough in cling film and leave it to rest for about 1 hour.

Cooking Pasta

1. Bring plenty of water to the boil in a large pan and add a good amount of salt. Do not add oil to the water, or the pasta will not properly absorb sauces added later.

2. Add the pasta to the boiling water. The ratio of water to pasta should be 5:1. Cook the pasta according to the packet instructions and personal taste.

3. Pour the cooked pasta into a colander and let it drain. If the pasta is going to be eaten immediately, do not rinse in cold water, but put it directly in the sauce.

4. If the pasta is not used until later, rinse it under cold running water. Then let it drain well.

5. Put it in a sealed container. Drizzle some oil and stir through so the pasta does not stick.

Cooking Asian Egg Noodles

1. Asian egg noodles are made from wheat flour and eggs, and resemble thin spaghetti.

2. Put the egg noodles in a pan with plenty of boiling water. Cook the noodles according to the packet instructions.

3. Using a fork, separate the egg noodles while cooking so that they stay loose.

4. Pour into a colander and rinse with cold water.

5. Then either use the noodles immediately as required, or mix with a little oil in a bowl, cover and store in the refrigerator for later use.

Cooking Asian Rice Noodles

1. Rice noodles are made from rice flour and rolled out into thin ribbons. When cooked, they are so tender that they melt in the mouth.

2. Put the rice noodles in plenty of boiling water and cook according to the packet instructions. It is important to follow them because every type of rice noodle has a different constitution and therefore requires a different cooking time.

3. Pour the noodles into a colander and rinse immediately with cold water.

4. Drain well. If the rice noodles are to be stored, mix in a little oil to keep them from sticking together, cover with cling film, and keep in the refrigerator.

350 g (12 oz) flour

 7 eggs

 50 ml (1²/₃ fl oz) water

 1 pinch of salt
1 pinch of white pepper

 1 pinch of nutmeg, freshly grated

Spaetzle Dough

1. Add the flour to a bowl, make a well, and add the eggs, some water, and a pinch each of salt, pepper and nutmeg.

2. Mix the eggs and water and, from the middle outwards, work the flour in a little at a time.

3. Pour in more water as needed – the dough should have a creamy consistency.

4. Whip the spaetzle dough thoroughly, then let it set for 15 minutes until bubbles appear.

5. Bring some water to the boil in a pan. Using a rubber spatula, push the spaetzle dough through a sieve, directly into the water.

6. Boil the spaetzle briefly in the water, until it rises to the surface.

7. Take out the spaetzle with a slotted spoon.

Let it drain in a sieve and as desired, either toss with butter and serve it as a side dish, or make cheese spaetzle – layered in a dish with freshly grated cheese, then baked in the oven.

■ Instead of water, mix the spaetzle dough with 50 g (1¾ oz) spinach or herb purée. This makes the spaetzle a wonderful green and is a feast for the eyes as a side dish with beef or poultry.

* * *

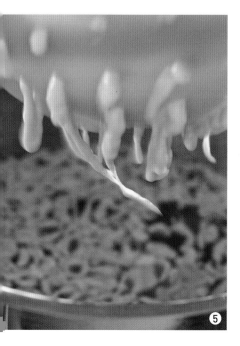

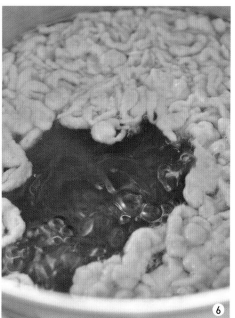

120 g (4½ oz) breadcrumbs

 1½ tsp sweet paprika

 2 tbsp extra virgin olive oil

 800 g (1 lb 12 oz) cooked macaroni or penne

 100 g (3½ oz) Gouda cheese, grated

 100 g (3½ oz) Cheddar cheese, grated

 150 ml (5 fl oz) double cream

 1 pinch of black pepper

 1 tsp butter

Noodle Casserole with Cheese

1. Preheat the oven to 180°C (350°F/Gas Mark 4). Mix the breadcrumbs with the paprika and olive oil.

2. Put the macaroni in a large bowl. Add the grated cheese and cream on top and season with black pepper.

3. Mix the noodles and the cheese well.

4. Place the noodles in a casserole dish greased with butter.

5. Then sprinkle the seasoned breadcrumbs over the macaroni and put in the oven for 30 minutes.

Divide onto plates and serve.

■ Other types of cheese can be used in this dish if desired, but choose varieties that melt during cooking. Gruyère and raclette cheese have an especially full flavour and melt nicely.

8 garlic cloves

 1 bunch fresh parsley

 1 dried pepper

 3 pepperoncini or chillies

 6 tbsp extra virgin olive oil

 500 g (1 lb 2 oz) spaghetti

 1 pinch of salt

Spaghetti with Aglio Olio

1. Peel the garlic and chop it finely. Rinse the parsley, pick the leaves from the stems, removing any damaged pieces, and chop it finely. Cut the pepper and chillies into strips.

2. Heat the olive oil in a pan, add the garlic, and cook until golden yellow. Then add the peppers and chilli strips and sauté them to remove some of the heat from the chilli.

3. Then add some boiling water and salt.

4. Now add more water to the spaghetti and cook it until it has completely absorbed the liquid and is *al dente*.

5. Sprinkle parsley over the pasta and mix. Add salt to taste. Arrange on plates.

■ After cutting chillies, do not touch your eyes – thoroughly wash your hands first. This dish tastes just as good with thinner pasta such as capellini or spaghettini.

½ bunch fresh parsley

 ½ bunch fresh basil

 2 garlic cloves

 200 g (7 oz) cherry tomatoes

 1 kg (2 lb 4 oz) mussels

 5 tbsp extra virgin olive oil

 1 pinch of salt
1 pinch of black pepper

 150 ml (5 fl oz) white wine

500 g (1 lb 2 oz) spaghetti

Spaghetti with Mussels

1. Rinse the parsley and basil, pick the leaves from the stems and chop finely. Peel the garlic and chop finely. Rinse the cherry tomatoes and cut them in half. Rinse and clean the mussels (see p. 480). Heat the olive oil in a pan, add the garlic, and sauté until golden. Then add the cherry tomatoes, salt and pepper and sweat for a minute.

2. Drain the mussels well, then add them to the pan and stir.

3. Add the white wine. Cover and steam the mussels for another 2–3 minutes, until they open.

4. Then uncover. Remove any unopened mussels. They are not suitable for consumption.

5. Meanwhile, cook the spaghetti until *al dente*. Add the basil and parsley, folding them in. Add more salt and pepper, and drizzle a little olive oil on the cooked pasta. Serve the pasta with the mussels in deep bowls.

35

■ The best tasting mussels are small. You can also use them with other molluscs such as clams. If you add cooked octopus or fried calamari to it, you have frutti di mare spaghetti!

600 g (1 lb 5 oz) pasta dough (see p. 186)

 100 g (3½ oz) flour

 100 ml (3½ fl oz) cream

 50 g (1¾ oz) butter

2 tbsp extra virgin olive oil

1 pinch of salt

1 pinch of nutmeg, freshly grated

 20 g (⅔ oz) white truffles

Tagliolini with Truffles

1. Put the pasta dough on a floured surface and, with a rolling pin, roll it out to about 5 mm (¼ inch) thick. Keep turning the dough and sprinkling it with flour.

2. Then fold the outer edges to the middle to make a square. Add more flour and continue rolling it out evenly.

3. Roll the dough thinly enough so you can see the shape of your hands when you pick it up.

4. Now continue to fold both ends towards the middle until it makes a block about 5 cm (2 inches) thick and keep adding flour.

5. Using a sharp knife, cut the pasta dough into thin strips.

6. Pick up the strips of dough with a meat fork, lift them up and shake. This separates the pasta.

7. Put the tagliolini in a pan with plenty of boiling salted water and cook for about 1 minute.

8. In the meantime, bring the cream to the boil in another pan. Add the butter and olive oil. Drain the cooked pasta and add it to the sauce. Season with salt and nutmeg, and mix together. Bring to the boil again so the pasta takes up the sauce well. Then divide it among plates and shave the cleaned white truffles very thinly over the pasta.

30

■ A very good butter is required for this dish. Add a few drops of white truffle oil to the cream to enhance the flavour but use it sparingly, as it has an intense flavour and it is important not to overpower the dish.

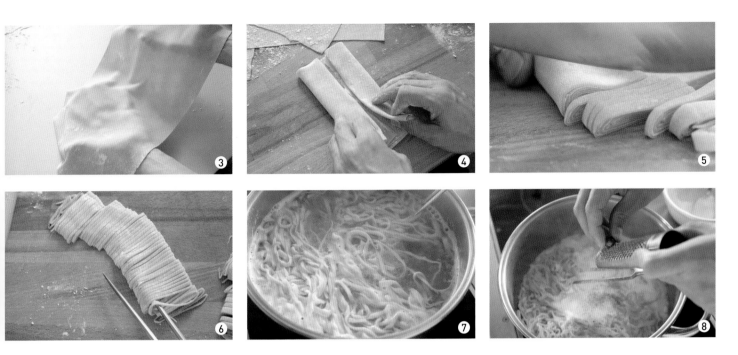

75 g (2½ oz) Gouda cheese

 250 g (9 oz) penne

 500 ml (17 fl oz) béchamel sauce (see p. 156)

 750 g (1 lb 10 oz) Bolognese sauce (see p. 158)

 1 pinch of black pepper

 3 tbsp olive oil

Penne Bolognese

1. Preheat fan oven to 200°C (400°F/Gas Mark 6). Grate the Gouda cheese. Cook the penne until *al dente*. Then refresh it in cold water and drain. Fill the bottom of a casserole dish with the béchamel sauce, put a layer of penne over it, and then spread a layer of Bolognese sauce on top.

2. Spread some more of the béchamel sauce over the Bolognese sauce. Béchamel sauce makes the casserole taste creamy and delicious.

3. Then sprinkle the grated cheese over it and follow with another layer of penne and Bolognese sauce.

4. Cover with the rest of the cheese and pour the béchamel sauce over the top. The cheese will melt better while baking and will combine with the béchamel sauce.

5. Finish by seasoning with pepper, add a drizzle of olive oil and bake in the oven for about 20 minutes. Remove the casserole and serve.

■ This recipe works with other types of pasta such as macaroni, fusilli, farfalle or rigatoni. If starting with cooked pasta, use 500 g (1 lb 2 oz).

30 g (1 oz) butter

 1 litre (1¾ pints) béchamel sauce, thin (see p. 156)

 250 g (9 oz) green lasagne sheets

 750 g (1 lb 10 oz) Bolognese sauce

 1 ball of mozzarella cheese

 100 g (3½ oz) Edam cheese

2 tbsp extra virgin olive oil

Lasagne

1. Preheat the oven to 180°C (350°F/Gas Mark 4). Grease a rectangular casserole dish with butter and spread around a medium-sized ladleful of béchamel sauce.

2. Put down a layer of lasagne sheets and another ladleful of béchamel sauce over it. The pasta will fully absorb the sauce, making the lasagne nice and creamy. Spread a layer of Bolognese sauce on top.

3. Repeat these steps until the casserole dish is full and the top layer of lasagne is covered in béchamel sauce.

4. Cut the mozzarella into small pieces, grate the Edam and sprinkle both over the lasagne. Finish by drizzling olive oil over the top and bake in the oven, for about 50 minutes. To prevent the lasagne from getting too brown on top, cover it with kitchen foil and remove it just 5 minutes before it has finished cooking. Serve the lasagne from the casserole dish.

■ Home-made green lasagne pasta: roll out and cut the lasagne sheets from spinach pasta dough (see p. 188). Use less béchamel sauce in this case, because fresh pasta does not absorb as much liquid and too much sauce would make the lasagne too soft.

250 g (9 oz) ricotta cheese

 3 eggs

 1 tbsp pesto (see p. 60)

 1 pinch of salt
1 pinch of black pepper

 1 pinch of nutmeg, freshly grated

 500 g (1 lb 2 oz) pasta dough
(see p. 186)

 100 g (3½ oz) butter

 1 bunch fresh sage

 50 g (1¾ oz) Parmesan cheese

Spinach and Ricotta Ravioli with Sage Butter

1. Crumble the ricotta cheese into a bowl. Separate 2 eggs and add the yolks. Add the pesto, season with salt, black pepper and nutmeg and mix everything into a smooth filling.

2. Make the pasta dough and use a pasta machine several times to roll it thinly. Before rolling it out each time, keep sprinkling with flour then fold it together. This gives the dough the correct consistency. Using a teaspoon, place hazelnut-sized portions of the ricotta mixture on a sheet of dough, about 5 cm (2 inches) apart from each other.

3. Beat the third egg with 1 tbsp water and brush the edges of the dough with it. Cover the dough and filling with a second sheet of dough, press the edges hard and make indentions with a suitably shaped pastry cutter.

4. Cut out the ravioli with a round pastry cutter about 6 cm (2⅓ inches) wide, a pastry cutting wheel or a smooth knife, and put them on a flour-covered baking tray until ready to use. Cook the ravioli in boiling salted water for about 4 to 5 minutes and then carefully remove them with a slotted spoon. Meanwhile, heat the butter in a pan until golden. Pick the

■ The remaining uncooked ravioli can be stored on a tray in the freezer. They will be easier to remove from the tray later and can be stored in the freezer in a container or freezer bag for a few weeks. When cooking frozen ravioli, be sure to lengthen the cooking time (which depends on the ravioli size) by about 1–2 minutes.

✳✳✳ 90

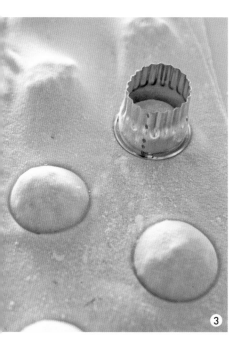

sage leaves from the stems, add them
and remove the pan from the heat. The
butter's temperature is high enough to
make the sage crisp. Lightly salt the
butter. Place the ravioli on plates, pour
sage butter over them and garnish with
Parmesan shavings.

250 g (9 oz) chicken mince

 75 g (2½ oz) raw ham

 ½ tsp salt
1 pinch of black pepper

 1 sprig fresh rosemary

 1 slice of white bread

 100 ml (3½ fl oz) milk

 80 g (2¾ oz) courgette

 20 g (⅔ oz) butter

 1 pinch of nutmeg, freshly grated

 ½ bunch fresh parsley

 2 eggs

 1 kg (2 lb 4 oz) pasta dough
(see p. 186)

 500 ml (17 fl oz) simple tomato
sauce (see p. 144)

 30 g (1 oz) butter

50 g (1¾ oz) Parmesan cheese

½ bunch fresh basil

Chicken and Ham Tortellini in Tomato Basil Sauce with Parmesan Cheese

1. Put the chicken, the ham, cut into pieces, the salt, black pepper and the picked rosemary needles into a food processor and mix everything thoroughly.

2. Put the bread slice into a bowl and pour milk over it to soften it. Meanwhile, wash the courgette and cut into small pieces (see p. 344). Melt the butter in a pan, and add the courgette, salt, pepper and nutmeg. Sweat the courgette, stirring frequently. Rinse the parsley, pick the leaves from the stems and chop finely. Add the courgette and mix. Add 1 egg, beaten, to the bread slice, then the meat and the courgette. Mix everything

well, season to taste, and the pasta filling is done.

3. Using a pasta machine (level 2), roll the pasta dough out, then sprinkle the pasta sheets with flour. Put 1 tsp of filling at a time on the rolled-out noodles.

4. Then cut the pasta dough into 10-cm (4-inch) squares. Separate the second egg and brush the edges of the dough with the white.

5. Fold up the sheets of dough into triangles. Using your fingers, seal the

Kitchen doctor: If the pasta sheets tear while you're rolling them out, simply add a little pasta dough to the torn section and carefully roll it out again in the machine. The pasta dough will repair itself.

3

4

3 tbsp vegetable oil

 100 g (3½ oz) smoked bacon

 600 g (1 lb 5 oz) boiled spaetzle (see p. 192)

 ½ tsp salt
1 pinch of black pepper

2 onions

200 g (7 oz) Cheddar cheese, grated

Cheese Spaetzle with Bacon Strips and Sautéed Onion

1. Cut the bacon into strips. Heat 2 tbsp vegetable oil in a pan and fry the bacon until crispy. Add the spaetzle and season with salt and black pepper. Fry it lightly for about 10 minutes, tossing frequently.

2. Peel the onions, cut them in half and then into thin slices. In a second pan, fry them in 1 tbsp vegetable oil until they are light brown and crispy. Blot the onions on kitchen paper and lightly salt them.

3. Add the Cheddar cheese to the spaetzle and mix well until the cheese has melted.

Serve onto plates and garnish with the sautéed onions. Serve with a green salad or simply with a freshly chilled beer.

■ You can also bake this dish. Preheat the oven to 190°C (375°F/Gas Mark 5). In a casserole dish, alternate layers of the spaetzle and the cheese, then pour in 200 ml (7 fl oz) strong chicken stock and put it in the oven, baking for 15 minutes. In this recipe, put the bacon and onions on top of the spaetzle shortly before serving.

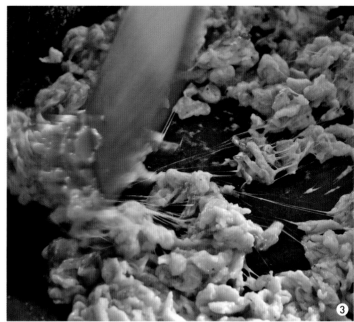

200 g (7 oz) prawns

 2.5-cm (1-inch) piece of ginger

 60 g (2¼ oz) peas

 2 eggs

 15 wonton wrappers

 1 leek

 1.5 litres (2½ pints) vegetable stock

 60 g (2¼ oz) bean sprouts

 2 sprigs fresh coriander

1

Prawn Wontons in Vegetable Stock

1. Peel the prawns and remove the veins. Peel the ginger root, and cut it into thin strips. Put the peas (use frozen, if necessary), peeled prawns and ginger strips in a food processor. Separate the eggs. Add 1 egg white and mix. Then put the mixture in a bowl.

2. Lay out the wonton wrappers on a work surface or chopping board. Put 1 tsp of the puréed prawn mixture in the middle of each wrapper.

3. Using a brush, coat the edges of the wonton wrappers with the remaining egg white. Now close the wonton wrappers so that they form a triangle.

4. Cut the leek into strips (see p. 350). Bring the vegetable stock to the boil, and add the leeks and bean sprouts. Then add the wontons to the vegetable stock and let them simmer for 1 to 2 minutes. Serve in soup bowls and garnish with coriander leaves.

■ Prawn wontons can also be fried in oil instead of boiling them in vegetable stock. You can also use pre-peeled prawns. Serve the fried wontons on a mixed salad with soya dressing.

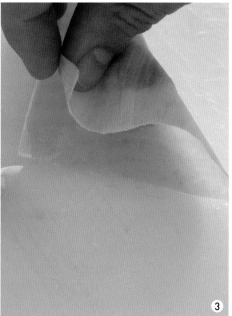

2 limes

 1 red chilli pepper

 2 tbsp soya sauce

 2 tbsp palm sugar

 500 g (1 lb 2 oz) fillet steak

 2 sprigs fresh coriander

 250 g (9 oz) Chinese egg noodles

 6 tbsp vegetable oil

 2 star anise

4 tbsp hoisin sauce

Fried Noodles with Spicy Beef

1. Cut the limes into halves and squeeze them by hand. Cut the chilli pepper into thin rings and add it to the limes, along with the soya sauce and 1 tbsp of the palm sugar, mixing thoroughly.

2. Using a sharp knife, cut the fillet steak into thin strips. In a pan, bring water to the boil and add the beef strips. After just 5 seconds, remove them. The water does not need seasoning, as the lime-chilli marinade will deliver the flavour.

3. Rinse the coriander and chop it finely, including the stems. Add the coriander and beef strips to the lime-chilli marinade and mix together.

4. Cook the egg noodles (see p. 190) and rinse in cold water. Heat the vegetable oil in a wok, crush the star anise with the flat side of a knife and add it along with the rest of the palm sugar.

5. Mix the hoisin sauce with 8 tbsp water in a glass. Add the noodles to the wok, stir and pour the sauce over it. Continue cooking slowly for about 3 minutes, until the noodles have soaked up the liquid. Then serve on plates, putting the marinated beef strips in the middle.

■ The beef strips can also be cooked in a strong beef stock. Then you can serve the dish as a soup with fresh Asian herbs and bean sprouts.

3

4

5

250 g (9 oz) broccoli

 1 green pepper

 1 garlic clove

 250 g (9 oz) rice noodles

 2 large green chilli peppers

 5 tbsp vegetable oil

 2 tbsp Thai fish sauce

 2 tbsp soya sauce

 1 tbsp sugar

 2 eggs

 1 tbsp toasted sesame seeds

Rice Noodles with Broccoli and Green Chillies

1. Rinse the broccoli and cut off the florets. Rinse the green pepper, deseed and cut into thin, 5-cm (2-inch) long strips. Peel the garlic and chop finely.

2. Boil the rice noodles (see p. 191), refresh them under cold water and leave them to drain. Cut the chilli peppers into thin rings.

3. Heat a large wok. Add 3 tbsp vegetable oil and fry the raw broccoli florets for about 5 minutes, stirring frequently. Add the Thai fish sauce. Then remove them and set aside.

4. Add the remaining vegetable oil to the wok and fry first the garlic, then the rice noodles and finally the green pepper. Add the soya sauce and sprinkle sugar over everything.

5. Put the fried broccoli florets back, mixing everything together. Crack the eggs into a bowl and beat them using a whisk. Pour the eggs slowly onto the sides of the wok and stir in. Finish by mixing in the chilli pepper rings. Put in bowls and sprinkle with sesame seeds before serving.

■ Other fresh garnishes and herbs complement this dish as well such as chives, Thai basil, coriander or bean sprouts. Just sprinkle over the finished dish and serve.

2 calamari

250 g (9 oz) cherry tomatoes

1 garlic clove

1 white onion

5 tbsp extra virgin olive oil

1 pinch of salt
1 pinch of black pepper

500 g (1 lb 2 oz) black tagliatelle

½ bunch fresh basil

Black Tagliatelle with Calamari

1. Wash the squid, clean it and let it dry. Cut the bodies into strips, leaving the heads whole.

2. Bring a pan of water to the boil. Add the cherry tomatoes for 5 seconds and immediately use a slotted spoon to lift them into ice cold water. Cut into the tomato skins with a small knife and pull them off. Peel the garlic and the onion, and dice them both finely.

3. Heat 3 tbsp olive oil in a nonstick pan and sear the calamari. Then add the onion and the garlic and continue frying.

Now add the peeled cherry tomatoes and season with salt and pepper. Bring a pan of salted water to the boil and cook the black tagliatelle for about 2 minutes.

4. In the meantime, remove the basil leaves from the stems, rinse and reserve a few leaves for a garnish, cutting the rest into thin ribbons. Drain the black tagliatelle and add to the calamari mixture. Then add the basil strips and the remaining olive oil. Toss everything together briefly, divide onto 4 plates and garnish with basil leaves.

■ **Different-coloured cherry tomatoes make this a bright and appetising dish.**

45

2 tbsp oil

 1 tbsp butter

 80 g (2¾ oz) chopped walnuts

 1–2 garlic cloves, chopped

 100 g (3½ oz) fresh spinach

 200 ml (7 fl oz) cream

 1 pinch of salt
1 pinch of black pepper

 1 pinch of nutmeg, freshly grated

 400 g (14 oz) tagliatelle

 120 g (4½ oz) Gorgonzola cheese

Tagliatelle in Walnut Gorgonzola Sauce

1. Put the oil and butter into a pan and sweat the chopped walnuts and the garlic.

2. Rinse the spinach leaves, removing the stems, add them to the pan and cook briefly.

3. Pour in the cream, stir it in and simmer everything lightly. Season with salt and pepper and nutmeg to taste.

4. Cook the tagliatelle in salted water. Drain them then add to the sauce, mixing well.

5. Shortly before serving, sprinkle small pieces of Gorgonzola cheese over the tagliatelle, letting the cheese melt slightly, then serve immediately.

 **20**

■ To make it milder, substitute mascarpone cheese for half the Gorgonzola cheese. This makes the tagliatelle taste especially creamy.

300 g (10½ oz) egg noodles, cooked weight

 5 tbsp vegetable oil

 6 dried chilli peppers

 2 carrots

 200 g (7 oz) broccoli

 2 skinless chicken breasts

 2 tbsp black bean paste

 100 g (3½ oz) bean sprouts

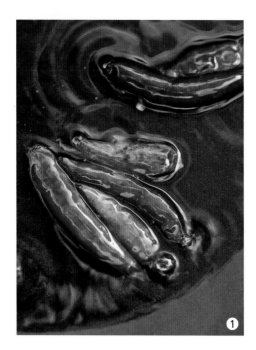

Shanghai-style Fried Egg Noodles with Chicken

1. Cook the egg noodles (see p. 190). Heat the vegetable oil in a wok and lightly brown the chilli peppers. This takes a little of the heat out of them.

2. Peel the carrots, cut in two and slice them on a diagonal line. Cut the broccoli into florets. Add the carrots and broccoli florets to the wok and fry for 3 minutes. Turn them frequently.

3. Cut the chicken breasts into thin strips and add to the wok. Add the black bean paste, mix and continue stirring.

4. Lastly, add the cooked egg noodles and bean sprouts to the wok, stir and continue frying.

Divide onto plates and serve immediately

■ Other vegetables that go well with this dish are green asparagus, peppers and pak choi.

300 g (10½ oz) cooked rice noodles

 1 tbsp vegetable oil

 1 tsp red curry paste

 2 tbsp soya sauce

 400 ml (13½ fl oz) coconut milk

 100 g (3½ oz) cherry tomatoes

 ½ bunch fresh coriander

Rice Noodles in Red Curry Sauce with Coriander

1. Boil the rice noodles (see p. 191). Heat the vegetable oil in a pan and lightly toast the curry paste, until it turns more fluid.

2. Add the soya sauce and let it reduce.

3. Pour in 50 ml (1⅔ fl oz) coconut milk and let it simmer a few minutes.

4. Pour in the remaining coconut milk. Add the cherry tomatoes whole and leave to simmer for 5 minutes.

5. Lastly, heat up the cooked rice noodles in the pan and add the coriander, coarsely chopped.

Serve in soup bowls.

■ You can also try out this dish with the yellow or green curry sauces (see p. 146) and add baby corn, mangetout, water chestnuts or bamboo shoots.

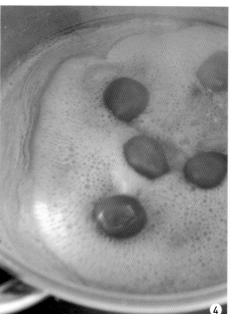

500 g (1 lb 2 oz) strawberries

 10 fresh mint leaves

 ½ tsp green peppercorns

 3 tbsp icing sugar

 600 ml (1 pint) mineral water

 1 litre (1¾ pints) vegetable oil

 250 g (9 oz) fine noodles

Fried Fine Noodles in Strawberry Gazpacho

1. Cut the stems off the strawberries and rinse them briefly. Then cut them in half. Add mint leaves, picked from the stems, as well as the green peppercorns.

2. Now sweeten with 2 tbsp icing sugar.

3. Pour in the cold mineral water and mix, then purée everything in a food processor set on high speed. Pour the purée in a bowl and let it cool thoroughly in the refrigerator for about 1 hour. If desired, the strawberry gazpacho can be flavoured with 20 ml (⅔ fl oz) triple sec.

4. Heat the oil to 160°C (325°F) in a small pan about 20 cm (8 inches) wide. Using scissors, cut the fine noodles into

four and fry them in the pan one batch at a time. The pan should be only half filled with oil, because the noodles will increase their volume fivefold.

5. Frying them takes only a few seconds. Leave the fried noodles to drain on kitchen paper and sprinkle them with the remaining icing sugar while still warm. Pour the strawberry gazpacho in deep, chilled bowls and add the noodles on top. Serve immediately before the fine noodles absorb the liquid, losing their crispiness.

■ Watermelon, flavoured with a little vodka, can be used instead of strawberries

※
※ **120**
※

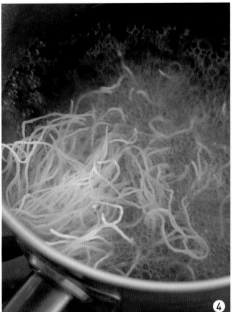

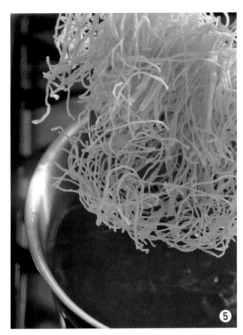

Rice

Contents

Types of Rice

Rice is a staple food in Asia. There are thousands of varieties. They are distinguished in the market according to the size of the grain.

1. Long grain rice/Aromatic rice

Is at least 6 mm (¼ inch) long. It remains granular when cooked. An indigestible casing, or husk, in which the rice grains were enclosed, has been removed in a special mill.

Aromatic rices include Indian basmati and jasmine rice.

2. Partially polished brown rice

Not entirely whole grains of rice. This brown rice is not completely polished, and therefore still has a sliver of protective skin and also contains more vitamins and micronutrients. It has to be cooked somewhat longer than traditional rice.

3. White rice

Loses a lot of nourishment through milling and polishing. It is buffed with a magnesium silicate or a glucose or talc powder to give it more shine.

4. Brown parboiled rice

Processed the same way as white rice, only with the bran and germ retained.

5. Risotto rice

A white, short grain rice. This high-class rice can absorb a lot of water. This is why it is used in risottos.

6. Medium grain rice

Is about 5–6 mm (¼ inch) long with a width of around 1.5–2.5 mm (1/12 inch). It remains granular when cooked, but sticks together when cooled.

7. Short grain rice

Shorter than 5 mm (¼ inch), it usually becomes sticky when cooked.

8. Wild rice

The actual grain is white, only the bran under the husk is black. It has to be boiled for 45 minutes.

9. Black rice

The husk is removed but not the outer layer of the rice grain. It can contain green, unripe grains and is also called 'forbidden rice'. It has a nutty flavour.

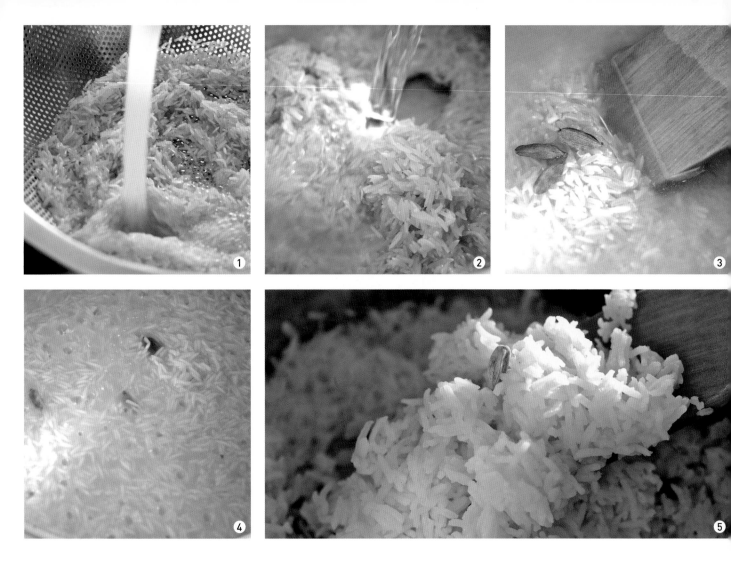

Cooking Basmati or Aromatic Rice

1. Put the rice in a sieve and rinse it well under cold running water, then let it drain.

2. 1 cup rice with 1½ cups water serves 2 people. Add them to a pan.

3. A few cardamom pods elevate the flavour of the rice and lend it an Asian note.

4. Bring the rice to the boil, stirring frequently, then cover the pan. Turn off the heat and let the rice soak for about 15 minutes.

5. Remove the rice with a wooden spoon and serve it with Asian or curry dishes (see Boiled Rice with Turmeric on p. 240).

Cooking Sushi Rice

1. To make sushi, use a Japanese short grain rice, which is unpolished and therefore sticks together.

2. Rinse the rice well under cold running water and let it drain.

3. Add the rice and water in a ratio of 1:2 to a pan and while stirring frequently, bring it slowly to the boil.

4. Boil the rice gently for about 15 minutes, stirring, so it doesn't burn on the bottom of the pan.

5. Put the rice in a bowl, spreading it around so it can cool faster. Depending on whether you want to make savoury or sweet sushi, mix in mirin (rice wine) and vinegar, or ginger syrup and sugar, then let it cool down.

1 cup long grain rice

 20 g (²/₃ oz) butter

 1 bay leaf

 2 cloves

 1 small onion

 1 pinch of salt

Steaming Long Grain and Partially Polished Brown Rice

1. Sweat 1 cup long grain rice in the butter.

2. Take the bay leaf and use the cloves as studs to attach it to the onion. Add the onion to the rice and stir.

3. Pour in 1½ cups water and stir to keep the rice from sticking.

4. Lightly salt the rice and stir.

5. Cover the pan with a lid and turn the temperature to the lowest setting. Steam the rice for about 15 minutes, then fluff it with a fork. Both types of rice go with poultry or fish, or can be used in salads.

■ With rice, it is important to pay special attention to quality. The rice grains should be large, not broken on the ends, and should all have the same shape.

Cooking Partially Polished Brown Rice

1. Heat 2 tbsp olive oil in a pan.

2. Add 1 cup partially polished brown rice and lightly sweat.

3. Since partially polished brown rice takes longer to cook, add 2½ cups water.

4. Salt lightly and stir to keep the rice from sticking to the bottom.

5. Cover with a lid, leaving in a cooking spoon to create a gap, then boil the rice for about 20 minutes. Stir as necessary.

6. The rice is done when all the liquid has evaporated. This rice goes with dishes that have spicy sauces.

Cooking Long Grain Rice

. In a pan, bring plenty of water to the oil and add salt.

. Add the long grain rice to the water nd stir. Add only 300 g (10½ oz) rice to litres (3½ pints) water.

. Boil the rice over a medium heat for bout 15 minutes.

4. Pour the rice into a sieve.

5. Rinse the rice under cold running water and store it in a bowl for later use.

1. Boiled Rice with Turmeric

Add **1 tsp turmeric** and **1 tsp curry powder** to a pan with **10 g (¼ oz) melted butter**, stir, and season with **1 pinch of salt** and **1 pinch of black pepper**. Mix in **400 g (14 oz) boiled rice** and heat up.

■ Serve this rice with Indian curries, vegetable dishes or lamb stews.

2. Boiled Rice with Spinach

Add **2 tbsp creamed spinach** (see p. 362) to a pan with **10 g (¼ oz) melted butter**, stir, and season with **1 pinch of salt** and **1 pinch of black pepper**. Mix in **400 g (14 oz) boiled rice** and heat up.

■ This rice goes well with practically every fish dish, but also with roasted poultry breast in a mushroom sauce, or with rabbit in a mustard cream sauce.

3. Boiled Rice with Tomatoes

Add **1 tbsp tomato purée** and **100 ml (3½ fl oz) tomato juice** to a pan with **10 g (¼ oz) melted butter**, stir, and season with **1 pinch of salt** and **1 pinch of black pepper**. Mix in **400 g (14 oz) boiled rice** and heat up.

4. Boiled Rice with Herbs

Rinse **½ bunch chives** and **½ bunch parsley**, removing any damaged pieces, and chop finely. Melt **10 g (¼ oz) butter** in a pan, add **400 g (14 oz) boiled rice**, add the herbs and stir. Season with **1 pinch of salt** and **1 pinch of black pepper** to taste, and heat up.

■ Serve this rice with chicken fricassee, sautéed fish or other dishes with a lot of sauce.

5. Boiled Rice with Paprika

Add **1 tbsp sweet paprika** to a pan with **10 g (¼ oz) melted butter**, stir, and season with **1 pinch of salt** and **1 pinch of black pepper**. Mix in **400 g (14 oz) boiled rice** and heat up.

■ Paprika rice can be improved with a finely diced pepper, sweated in butter. It goes well with roast beef, roast chicken and Hungarian dishes.

300 g (10½ oz) sushi rice

 380 ml (13 fl oz) water

 4 tbsp rice vinegar

 1 tbsp sugar

 1 pinch of salt

 100 g (3½ oz) surimi

 1 cucumber

 4 nori sheets

 1 tsp wasabi

 4 tsp mayonnaise

 8 tbsp soya sauce

2 tbsp sliced pickled ginger

Nigiri Sushi

1. Soak the rice in cold water for half an hour. Then rinse it in a sieve and let it drain well. Add the rice and the water to a pan and, while stirring carefully, bring to the boil. Cover with a lid, turn off the heat and let the rice cook with the residual heat for 15 minutes. Fill a wide bowl with the rice and pour in rice vinegar.

2. Sprinkle with the sugar and salt and stir carefully using a wooden spatula so the grains do not get damaged. Then let the rice cool.

3. Cut the surimi, a very popular imitation crabmeat from Japan made of pure fish flesh, in half lengthways. Peel the cucumber, cut off both ends, and cut into quarters. Then cut out the cores.

4. Lay a sheet of nori on a bamboo mat. Spread about 3 tbsp sushi rice over the bottom third, and add a layer of wasabi on top of it.

5. Then lay two surimi halves on top and spread 1 tsp mayonnaise along the surimi.

6. Cut the cucumber pieces to fit and add them.

7. Lift the nori leaves from the bottom end to envelop the rice around the filling

8. Using the bamboo mat, form a roll and squeeze it together lightly to keep it from unravelling later.

■ Use Nishiki rice if possible, a superior-quality rice that is exceptionally white and flavourful. Nigiri sushi can also be made without nori, but then it should be rolled in sesame seeds or fish roe before cutting. This variety is called a California roll.

Cut each roll into six slices and put
them on serving plates or on Japanese
plates. Serve with soya sauce, wasabi
and pickled ginger.

750 g (1 lb 10 oz) fresh pea pods

 2 red peppers

 2 green peppers

 5 tbsp extra virgin olive oil

 1 kg (2 lb 4 oz) short grain rice

 200 ml (7 fl oz) white wine

 1 pinch of salt
1 pinch of pepper

 1 dash of ground saffron

 2 kg (4 lb 8 oz) fish and seafood

 2 litres (3½ pints) chicken stock

1

2

Spanish Paella

1. Pressing down on the centre, open the pea pods and slide out the peas. Dice the peppers.

2. Heat the oil in a paella pan and sweat the diced peppers and the rice. Add the white wine and season with salt and pepper. Sprinkle with ground saffron.

3. Add the cleaned and rinsed fish and seafood to the rice.

4. Pour in the stock, add the peas and cook the paella for about 20 minutes. Serve direct from the paella pan.

This paella is enough for 6–8 people.

■ Use Spanish short grain rice for best results. Italian short grain rice could make the dish overly thick and become too rich. Other seafoods, shellfish, chicken or rabbit meat can also be used.

1 shallot

 ½ garlic clove

 80 g (2¾ oz) butter

 1 tbsp olive oil

 250 g (9 oz) Arborio rice

 1 pinch of salt
1 pinch of black pepper

 150 ml (5 fl oz) white wine

 750 ml (1¼ pints) chicken stock

 90 g (3¼ oz) Parmesan cheese

 1 tsp fresh parsley

1 tbsp cream, whipped

Parmesan Risotto

1. Peel the shallot and garlic and chop finely. Cut 60 g (2¼ oz) butter into thin slices and put it in the refrigerator. Heat the remaining 20 g (²⁄₃ oz) butter and the olive oil in a nonstick pan until it foams. Add the garlic and shallot and sweat them for about 1 minute, until translucent.

2. Add the Arborio rice, sweat briefly, and add white wine. Add salt and pepper to taste.

3. Let the white wine cook away, and stir the rice with a wooden spoon.

4. Add plenty of hot stock to keep the rice covered in liquid. At this stage the risotto should no longer be stirred with a wooden spoon, but should only be tossed to achieve a creamier texture.

5. Cook the risotto for about 15 to 18 minutes regularly adding hot stock a little bit at a time. Grate the Parmesan cheese, and toss with the butter from the refrigerator in the risotto. Finish by chopping the parsley finely, add it to the rice as well as the whipped cream and mix well. Serve the risotto on plates and as a side dish, or as a main dish with Parmesan shavings.

■ Making saffron risotto follows the basic risotto recipe, except that 1 g saffron or 12 threads are added to the sweating shallots and garlic. Saffron risotto is traditionally served with osso bucco. In this case, bone marrow can be substituted for olive oil.

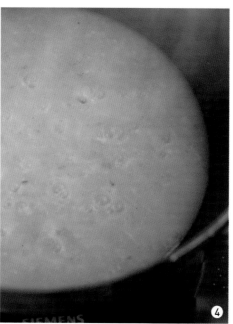

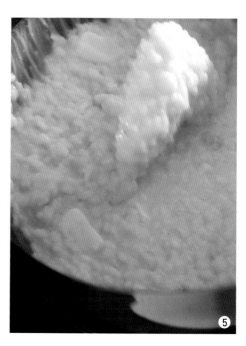

30 g (1 oz) bacon rashers

 250 g (9 oz) tomatoes

 1 garlic clove

 1 shallot

 6 medium artichokes

 80 g (2¾ oz) butter

 4 tbsp olive oil

 1 pinch of sugar

 1 pinch of salt
1 pinch of black pepper

 250 g (9 oz) Arborio rice

 750 ml (1¼ pints) chicken stock

 2 sprigs fresh rosemary

90 g (3¼ oz) Parmesan cheese

1 sprig fresh flat parsley

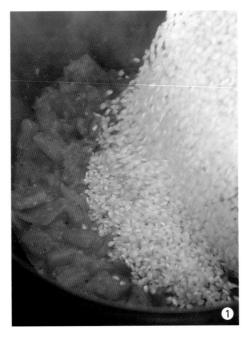

Tomato and Artichoke Risotto

1. Cut the bacon into 1-cm (½-inch) wide strips. Peel the tomatoes (see p. 346) and cut them into 1-cm (½-inch) pieces. Peel the garlic and shallot and chop finely. Rinse and clean the artichokes (see p. 356).

Heat 20 g (⅔ oz) butter and 2 tbsp olive oil in a nonstick pan until it foams, then add the shallot and garlic and sweat them until translucent. Add the tomatoes, sugar, salt and pepper then slowly simmer for about 2 minutes.

2. Add the rice and stir with a wooden spoon, then add the chicken stock until the rice is just covered. The risotto should only be tossed from now on, not stirred (see Parmesan Risotto on p. 246). Simmer the risotto for about 15 to 18 minutes, continually adding hot stock.

3. Meanwhile, cut the artichoke into sixths. Heat the remaining olive oil in a nonstick pan, add the artichokes, rosemary, salt and pepper, and slowly sauté for about 5 minutes. Toss them back and forth.

4. Add the bacon, frying until it is nice and crisp. Then remove the sprigs of rosemary, and add the artichokes and the bacon to the risotto. Finish by tossing in the grated Parmesan cheese and the remaining butter. Serve on plates and garnish with parsley.

■ **Mushroom risotto:** Clean 250 g (9 oz) mushrooms and depending on the size, cut into quarters or sixths. Heat 2 tbsp olive oil in a nonstick pan, add the mushrooms and sauté for 5 minutes until light brown. Add salt and pepper. Peel ½ garlic clove, chop finely and add to the mushrooms. Rinse ½ bunch parsley, pick off the leaves and chop finely. Add them to the garlic and mushrooms. Drizzle the juice of ½ a lemon and then toss into the Parmesan risotto.

350 g (12 oz) pumpkin

 ½ onion

 4 tbsp extra virgin olive oil

 1 tbsp butter

 1 litre (1¾ pints) vegetable stock

 200 g (7 oz) partially polished brown rice

 1 lime

 1 pinch of salt
1 pinch of black pepper

 1 pinch of nutmeg, freshly grated

 120 g (4½ oz) Parmesan cheese, grated

Brown Risotto with Pumpkin and Lime

1. Dice the pumpkin and cut the onion into strips, then sweat them in the oil and butter.

2. Pour in some stock and let simmer.

3. Add the partially polished brown rice to the pan with the lime, cut into slices and stir. Season with the salt, pepper and nutmeg.

4. Add some stock and let it reduce, stirring frequently. Keep adding stock a little at a time and let it reduce. Stop stirring now and just toss the risotto occasionally.

5. The rice is done when it has a creamy consistency, but still has some bite to it. Stir in the grated Parmesan cheese.

Divide onto plates and serve.

■ Before making the risotto, wash the limes well with hot water so the risotto has no unpleasant bitter taste. Carrots and peppers can add to the pumpkin flavour.

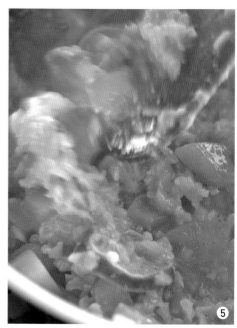

150 g (5½ oz) onion

 400 g (14 oz) beef, top round

 4 tbsp vegetable oil

 1 dried pepper

 1 pinch of salt
1 pinch of black pepper

 3 tbsp sweet paprika

 1 tbsp tomato purée

 300 g (10½ oz) long grain rice

 150 g (5½ oz) tinned sweetcorn

Hungarian Paprikash with Corn

1. Peel the onion, cut it in half, and then into thin slices (see p. 349). First slice the meat, then cut it into strips. Heat the vegetable oil in a pan over medium heat, add the onions and sweat until translucent. Add the pepper whole.

2. Add the meat, salt and pepper, sprinkle with paprika and sauté it lightly. Push it to the side of the pan, add the tomato purée in the middle and likewise sauté it lightly, to reduce the acidity.

3. Add the rice, mix well and sweat lightly.

4. Drain the sweetcorn in a sieve and add it to the rice. Add plenty of water, bring it to the boil, cover and let it cook for about 25 minutes over medium heat. Stir occasionally, adding more liquid as necessary.

5. The dish is finished when the rice has completely absorbed the liquids. Arrange on plates and sprinkle with paprika.

■ Beef stock can be used as a substitute for water, giving the dish more flavour. Red and yellow peppers, cut into strips, can also be added.

1 kg (2 lb 4 oz) lamb shoulder

 1 pinch of salt
1 pinch of black pepper

 5 garlic cloves

 350 g (12 oz) onions

 50 ml (1⅔ fl oz) vegetable oil

 2 cinnamon sticks

 6 star anise

 ½ tsp curry powder

 1 tsp ground cumin

 2 tbsp tomato purée

 600 g (1 lb 5 oz) tinned, peeled tomatoes

 250 g (9 oz) basmati rice

 1 g saffron (12 threads)

Biryani Rice with Lamb

1. Cut the lamb into 3-cm (1¼-inch) cubes, then add salt and pepper. Peel the garlic and cut into thin slices. Peel the onion, cut it in half and then into thin slices (see p. 349). Heat the vegetable oil in a wide pan. Add the garlic, cinnamon sticks, star anise and onions, sweating them for 5 minutes until translucent. Season with salt.

2. Add the lamb, browning it, then sprinkle the lamb with the curry powder and cumin. Continue to brown lightly for 10 minutes, making sure the spices don't toast too long as they can get bitter.

3. After 5 minutes push the meat to the sides of the pan and put the tomato purée in the middle, sautéing it briefly. Then add the tomatoes along with the juice, bring

to the boil, cover and cook for about 40 minutes over medium heat. Steam the rice (see p. 236).

4. Use a fork to test whether the lamb is done. Now remove the cinnamon sticks and the star anise and reserve for decoration.

5. Let the saffron threads soak in 50 ml (1⅔ fl oz) water and then reduce the liquid down to half the volume. Spread the rice over the lamb ragout, drizzle the water-soaked saffron over it, cover and heat for 5 minutes.

■ Sprinkle it with freshly cut mint and serve with natural yogurt. Indian restaurants sometimes lay a few pieces of gold leaf on top of this dish.

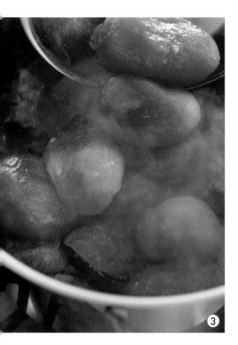

500 g (1 lb 2 oz) long grain rice

 200 g (7 oz) leeks, green parts only

 3 eggs

 3 tbsp soya sauce

 1 tsp curry powder

 3 tbsp vegetable oil

Fried Rice Curry with Leeks

1. Steam the rice (see p. 236). Cut the leeks lengthways into strips.

2. Beat the eggs in a bowl with soya sauce and curry powder.

3. In a wok, heat 3 tbsp vegetable oil and fry the leeks in it.

4. Add the rice and fry it with the leeks. Push them to the sides of the wok and add the eggs to the middle.

5. Mix the eggs with the rice and let them solidify.

Divide into bowls and sprinkle with a little curry powder.

■ This dish tastes even more authentic with steamed basmati or aromatic rice. Mix in other vegetables, such as spinach, pak choi, spring onions or carrot strips, and finely chopped meat or leftover chicken.

250 g (9 oz) chicken legs

 1 bunch fresh coriander

 100 g (3½ oz) green pepper

 100 g (3½ oz) red pepper

 80 g (2¾ oz) leek

 4 garlic cloves

 400 g (14 oz) long grain rice

 5 tbsp vegetable oil

 1 tbsp sugar

 4 tbsp soya sauce

 2 tbsp brown rice vinegar

 100 g (3½ oz) prawns

 2 eggs

(1)

(2)

Fried Rice

1. Using a knife, remove the bones from the chicken and cut the meat, with the skin, into strips. Rinse the coriander and chop it coarsely, reserving a little for garnishing. Deseed the peppers, rinse and cut them in quarters. Cut the leek in thin strips lengthways. Peel the garlic and cut into thin slices. Boil the long grain rice (see p. 239). Heat the oil in a wok, add the chicken strips and brown. As soon as it takes on a nice brown colour, remove it from the wok, but leave the oil in.

2. Add the garlic to the wok, sauté until golden, add the pepper, mix well and let it sweat for 2 to 3 minutes.

3. Add the leek and chicken, season with the sugar, soya sauce and rice vinegar and mix well. Cook everything for 1 minute, stirring continuously.

4. Add the rice and prawns, and fry them in the wok for 3 minutes.

5. Beat the eggs in a bowl with a fork. Push the rice to the sides of the wok. Put the eggs in the middle of the wok and let them set like scrambled eggs, carefully stirring as they solidify.

6. Add the coriander and mix it thoroughly with the rice. Finish by drizzling brown rice vinegar over the rice. Serve the finished dish on plates or shallow bowls and garnish with more coriander.

■ Basmati rice can be used instead of long grain rice. Other good vegetables for this dish are bean sprouts, small broccoli florets, mangetout, baby corn and pak choi.

30 g (1 oz) butter

 10 green cardamom pods

 5 cloves

 50 g (1¾ oz) raisins

 70 g (2½ oz) flaked almonds

 1 cinnamon stick

 1 tsp curry powder

 ½ tsp ground turmeric

 250 g (9 oz) basmati rice

 1 pinch of salt

 600 ml (1 pint) water

 About 50 ml (1⅔ fl oz) sunflower oil

 100 g (3½ oz) yogurt

 1 sprig fresh mint

Indian Curry Rice with Raisins and Cardamom

1. Let 30 g (1 oz) butter foam up in a pan over medium heat. Add the cardamom pods, cloves, raisins, almonds, cinnamon, curry and turmeric, and toast them, stirring continuously.

2. After a minute, add the rinsed basmati rice and salt, then sweat briefly.

3. Add water, bring to the boil and cover then leave it to simmer for 12 minutes over a low heat.

4. In another pan, heat the sunflower oil over a high heat and immediately pour it over the rice. The rice should hiss during this step. This gives it an intense nutty flavour. Serve the rice in a bowl and garnish with yogurt and mint leaves.

■ This rice is outstanding with Indian curries, roasted lamb cutlets or grilled fish steaks.

50 g (1¾ oz) almonds, shelled

 1 rabbit (800 g/1 lb 12 oz)

 1 pinch of salt
1 tsp black pepper, coarsely ground

 4 tbsp vegetable oil

 4 spicy chorizo sausages

 4 tbsp black bean paste

 220 g (8 oz) long grain rice

 800 ml (1½ pints) rabbit or chicken stock

 30 g (1 oz) plain chocolate

Mexican Brown Rice

1. Put the almonds in a food processor and grind finely. Cut the rabbit meat into pieces and sprinkle with the salt and pepper. Heat the oil in a pan, add the meat and brown all sides for about 5 minutes.

2. Cut the chorizo sausages in half and add to the pan. Brown for another 5 minutes. Then sprinkle the almond over the rabbit meat, mix everything together and continue browning until the almond is also golden brown.

3. Add the black bean paste on top of the meat, and coat the meat with it. Continue

cooking, making sure the almonds and black bean paste don't brown too much as this would give the dish a bitter note.

4. Spread the long grain rice evenly ove the meat, adding rabbit or chicken stock

5. Bring it to the boil and, over a low heat, cover and leave it to simmer for about 25 minutes. Serve the finished ric on plates and sprinkle with the coarsely grated chocolate.

* * *
80

■ After the liquids have completely cooked away, leave the rice to sit briefly on the hob The rice cooks a little further at the bottom, intensifying the flavour.

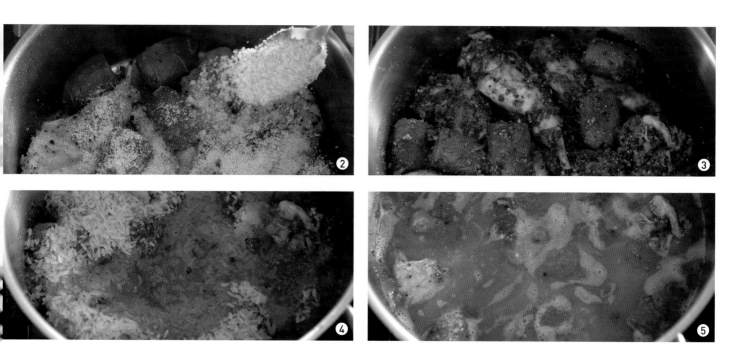

1 orange

 1 lemon

 1 litre (1¾ pints) milk

 4 tbsp sugar

 ½ cinnamon stick

 220 g (8 oz) pudding rice

Rice Pudding with Cinnamon

1. Wash the citrus fruits. Using a vegetable peeler, peel 1 thin layer of rind from both the orange and the lemon.

2. Pour the milk into a pan.

3. Pour in the sugar.

4. Add the cinnamon, as well as the orange and lemon rinds, to the milk.

5. Pour in the pudding rice and bring to a slow boil.

6. Stir the rice continuously to keep it from burning. Let it simmer gently for about 20 minutes.

Remove the lemon and orange peels, as well as the cinnamon stick before serving.

■ Rice pudding tastes best when served warm with a few butter flakes and sprinkled with cinnamon sugar. Serving it with apricot or cherry compote makes an exciting dessert for kids.

Grains & Legumes

Contents

Types of Grain & Legume

Grains and legumes are staple foods in many parts of the world. In Europe and the United States, however, they have been sidelined by corn and potatoes.

Cooking Chart

Product	Amount	Liquid Amount	Temperature	Time	Notes
Couscous	1 unit	2.4 units of liquid	Pour over boiling water	Let it absorb for 30 minutes	Pre-cooked couscous needs only 5 minutes
Bulgur	1 unit	2 units of liquid	Pour over boiling water	Let it absorb for 1 hour	
Green lentils	1 unit	4 units of water	Medium heat	6–8 minutes	Soak for 1 hour in cold water before cooking
Green lentils	1 unit	5 units of water	Medium heat	15 minutes	No soaking
Brown lentils	1 unit	4 units of water	Low heat	10 minutes	Rinse under water first
Long grain rice	1 unit	4 units of water	Low heat	15–18 minutes	Boil
Millet	1 unit	2.5 units of water	Low heat	Let it absorb for 35 minutes	Cover and steam
Quinoa	1 unit	2.2 units of water	Low heat	20 minutes	Wash off with lukewarm water
White beans	1 unit	3 units of water	Low heat	1 hour	Soak for 2 hours in cold water
Borlotti beans	1 unit	3 units of water	Low heat	45 minutes	Soak for 2 hours in cold water
Partially polished brown rice	1 unit	2.5 units of water	Low heat	20–25 minutes	Cover and steam
Azuki beans	1 unit	3 units of water	Low heat	25–30 minutes	Soak for 1 hour in cold water
Chickpeas	1 unit	3 units of water	Medium heat	25–30 minutes	Soak for 2 hours in cold water
Polenta	1 unit	2.8 units of liquid	Boil	10 minutes	Firm polenta for grilling
Polenta	1 unit	3.5 units of liquid	Boil	30 minutes	Moist polenta as a dish

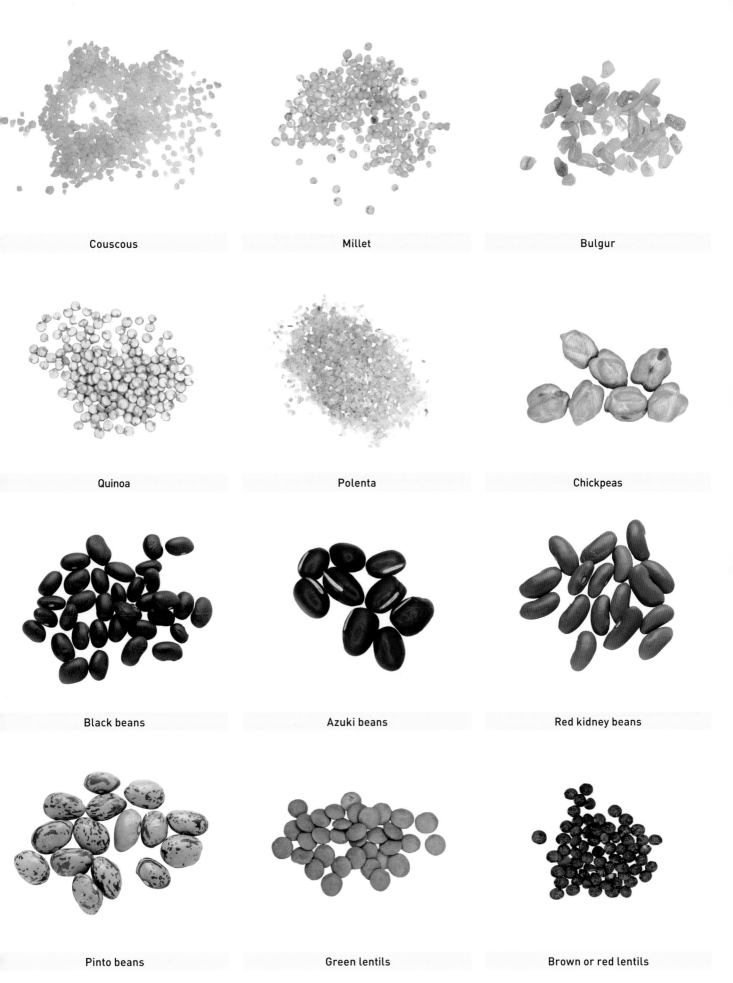

Couscous

Millet

Bulgur

Quinoa

Polenta

Chickpeas

Black beans

Azuki beans

Red kidney beans

Pinto beans

Green lentils

Brown or red lentils

269

Making Couscous

1. Pour **600 ml (1 pint)** boiling **vegetable stock** over **250 g (9 oz) couscous**. Season with **salt** and **black pepper**.

2. Sprinkle with a few **saffron threads** and mix them into the couscous. Leave it to soak for about 30 minutes. Stir frequently.

3. Lastly, round it off with **2 tbsp olive oil** and **1 tsp butter** and serve warm as a side dish with beef or fish. Use cold for salads.

Making Bulgur

Bring **500 ml (17 fl oz) vegetable stock** and **3 tbsp olive oil** to the boil.

Put **250 g (9 oz) bulgur** in a bowl and pour the hot vegetable stock over it.

3. Stir well and leave it to soak for 1 to 2 hours. Personal tastes determines whether the bulgur should be crunchy or soft.

4. Use the bulgur for salads, as a side dish or in fillings.

Cooking Green Lentils

1. The tablespoon on the left holds the traditional green lentils, seen here with a light colour; on the right are the smaller and darker brown lentils. They have a more aromatic flavour.

2. Stud an **onion** or a **shallot** by taking **1 bay leaf** and fixing it to the onion or shallot using **2 cloves**.

3. Bring plenty of water to the boil and add **salt**. Add **1 carrot, 1 unpeeled garlic clove** cut in half, and the studded shallot, and sprinkle in **500 g (1 lb 2 oz) green lentils**.

4. Bring the water with the lentils back to the boil and cook for about 15 minutes. Cooking time depends on lentil size.

5. Lentils are done when they begin to split open a little at the edges.

6. Drain the lentils in a sieve and rinse briefly with cold water. Let them drain and use in salads, lentil patties or in soups.

Cooking Brown Lentils

Bring plenty of water to the boil and dd **salt**. Rinse **500 g (1 lb 2 oz) brown ntils** in cold water and then add them to e boiling water.

Bring the water with the lentils back the boil.

Now add **1 sprig rosemary** and **bay leaf** and cook the lentils for about minutes.

4. Pour into a sieve and refresh with cold water.

5. Store in the refrigerator for later use. Add the lentils to dishes like salad, or serve as a vegetable lentil stew with fish.

Cooking Millet

1. Heat **2 tbsp vegetable oil** in a pan and sweat **250 g (9 oz) millet**.

2. You will need **650 ml (22 fl oz) water** in total. At first, pour in only a quarter of the water until the millet is just covered.

3. Let the water reduce almost completely. Repeat this step three times, then the millet is done. This takes about 35 minutes in total.

4. Finish by stirring **1 tbsp butter** into the millet. Serve it as a side dish with hot meals, in salads, or use it in patties.

Cooking Quinoa

1. Quinoa is rich in magnesium, iron and, notably, unsaturated fatty acids.

2. Rinse **250 g (9 oz) quinoa** under running water, add it to the pan without any fats and toast until dry, stirring frequently.

3. You will need **600 ml (20 fl oz) water** in total. At first, add some cold water so that the quinoa is just covered.

4. Add **1 star anise** and simmer gently for about 20 minutes, stirring frequently.

5. Add water repeatedly to keep the quinoa just covered.

6. The quinoa is done when the grains are slightly translucent and a white dot is easily visible in the middle of each.

2 ripe tomatoes

 1 white onion

 ½ bunch fresh mint leaves

 1 tsp fresh parsley

 300 g (10½ oz) cooked bulgur

 Juice of 1 lemon

 125g (4½ oz) yogurt

 1 pinch of salt
1 pinch of black pepper

 4 tbsp olive oil

Bulgur Mint Salad with Yogurt and Tomatoes

1. Dice the tomatoes and the onion.

2. Add the tomatoes and onions, the mint cut in ribbons, reserving a few leaves as garnish, and the parsley to the cooked bulgur (see p. 271). Squeeze the lemon over it through a sieve.

3. Add the yogurt to the salad.

4. Add the salt, pepper and the olive oil.

5. Now carefully combine everything and let it marinate for 30 minutes for bes results. Then serve, garnishing with the reserved mint leaves.

■ This recipe can also be made with couscous. Mix in fresh salad cucumbers and a few cooked chickpeas. Lastly, season with a pinch of curry powder and some ground cumin. This variation can also be served as a side dish with Indian curries.

3 ripe tomatoes

 1 onion

 ½ garlic clove

 2 avocados

 1 pinch of salt
1 pinch of white pepper

 Juice of 1 lime

 3 tbsp oil

 1tbsp vinegar

 ½ bunch fresh mint

 200 g (7 oz) cooked couscous

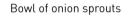 Bowl of onion sprouts

Couscous Salad on Guacamole and Tomatoes

1. Rinse clean and finely dice the tomatoes. Peel and dice the onion. Peel and finely chop the garlic.

2. Use a spoon to scoop out the avocados from their skins.

3. Season the avocado flesh with salt and pepper and drizzle the lime juice over it.

4. Using a fork, mash it together until thoroughly mixed.

5. Put the tomatoes, onions and garlic in a bowl and dress with oil, vinegar, pepper and salt. Mix in plenty of finely chopped mint leaves.

Put the tomato salad on plates, adding guacamole on top, and crown it with a couscous peak. Serve with onion sprouts as a garnish.

■ Cut the avocados in half, separate the halves from each other with a slight twist, and remove the stone.

*
*
* 25

½ bunch fresh coriander

 1 orange

 300 g (10½ oz) cooked millet

 1 egg

 120 ml (4 fl oz) cream

 2 tbsp breadcrumbs

 1 pinch of salt

 1 pinch of white pepper

 2 tbsp olive oil

1

Millet Patties with Coriander and Orange Zest

1. Rinse the coriander and chop coarsely. Using a vegetable peeler, peel off two strips from the orange and add it to boiling salted water for 1 minute. Rinse the strips and cut them into thin slices.

2. Fill a bowl with the cooked millet (see p. 274). Add the egg, cream and breadcrumbs to the millet.

3. Now add the orange peel and the coriander. Season with salt and pepper to taste.

4. Carefully mix the ingredients together and, with moist hands, form small patties. Press them together well so they don't fall apart when frying.

5. In a pan with a little olive oil, fry them on both sides until golden brown.

Put on plates and serve with salad leaves and orange slices.

■ Couscous or quinoa can be used instead of millet. Grate the orange peel and add some fresh ginger to the mix. Then form the patties and fry as described above.

Cooking White Beans

1. Soak **500 g (1 lb 2 oz)** white beans
in a covered pan with water for at least
2 hours, though overnight is best. Then
strain the water.

2. In a pan, sweat **1 slice of smoked
bacon** and **1 pressed garlic clove** in some
oil, then add the beans.

3. Sweat the beans a little, adding **salt**
and **pepper**. Cover in water and let them
simmer gently for about 1 hour.

Cooking Pinto Beans

. Soak **500 g (1 lb 2 oz) pinto beans** in
  covered pan with water for at least
  hours, though overnight is best. Then
  train the water.

. In a pan, heat some **olive oil** and
  sprig rosemary and the drained beans.
  weat briefly, adding **salt** and **pepper**.

. Pour **1.5 litres (2½ pints) water** or
  tock over the beans – the stock gives
  hem more flavour. Simmer them for
  bout 45 minutes, making sure that the
  eans are always covered with liquid.

10 spicy lamb sausages

 2 tbsp vegetable oil

 1 garlic clove, peeled and sliced

 2 onions

 2 sprigs fresh rosemary

 2 bay leaves

 300 g (10½ oz) white beans, soaked overnight

 1 tsp tomato purée

 400 g (14 oz) tinned, peeled tomatoes

1 pinch of salt
1 pinch of black pepper

Tomato Bean Stew with Spicy Lamb Sausage

1. In a pan, brown the lamb sausages on all sides in the vegetable oil. Add the sliced garlic.

2. After the garlic is toasted, remove the sausages and set them aside. Peel and cut the onion in half, then slice and sweat in the pan with the rosemary and bay leaves until translucent. Push them to the side of the pan.

3. Put the soaked beans in a sieve, drain well, then add them to the pan.

4. Add the tomato purée and the tomatoes to the pan and break them down with a wooden spoon. Add salt and black pepper to taste.

5. Pour cold water over the beans until they are covered. Put the sausages back in, cover and simmer gently for 1 hour. Stir frequently and add water as necessary to keep the beans just covered so they can cook completely.

Fill a plate with the bean stew and place the lamb sausages on top.

+ 12 hours soaking time

■ Stew 2 fried duck legs, 1 piece of bacon and a few pieces of lamb with the beans and you have a wonderful cassoulet!

500 g (1 lb 2 oz) chilli beans, soaked

 400 g (14 oz) tinned, peeled tomatoes

 200 g (7 oz) onions

 4 garlic cloves

 3 dried peppers

 4 tbsp vegetable oil

 1 tsp salt
1 pinch of black pepper

 2 tbsp soft brown sugar

 1 tbsp tomato purée

 2 chipotle (smoked japaleño) peppers in adobo (marinade)

 1 litre (1¾ pints) chicken stock

Mexican Chilli with Chipotle Peppers

1. Soak the chilli beans in cold water for at least 2 hours. Chop the tomatoes finely. Peel the onions and dice them finely. Peel the garlic and chop finely. Remove the stem from the dried peppers and cut them into thin strips.

2. In a pan, heat the vegetable oil over medium heat, add the onions and garlic, sweating until translucent. Add the dried peppers, salt, pepper and sugar and sweat for 5 minutes.

3. Push the onions and peppers to the sides of the pan, add the tomato purée in the middle and sauté to reduce the acidity.

4. Drain the beans and add them. Mix everything together and sauté it lightly for 5 minutes.

5. Add the whole chipotle peppers to the beans. For a milder version of this recipe serve the chipotle peppers separately. For an especially spicy dish, chop the chipotle peppers and mix them in.

6. Add the tomatoes, pour the chicken stock over everything, cover, and leave it to simmer gently over medium heat for 1½ hours. Stir as necessary to keep the beans from burning at the bottom of the pan. Put the beans on plates and serve with sunny-side up eggs (see p. 108).

+ 2 hours of soaking time

120

■ It is best to soak the beans overnight – they will keep their shape better when cooking. This dish goes well with grilled meat such as pork chops, spare ribs and fried chicken legs. In Central and South America, it is served for breakfast with sunny-side up eggs and bacon.

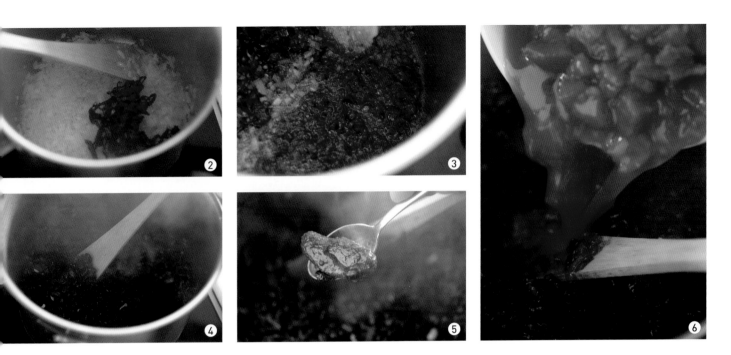

500 g (1 lb 2 oz) pinto beans, soaked

 80 g (2¾ oz) carrots

 80 g (2¾ oz) celeriac

 2 garlic cloves

 80 g (2¾ oz) onions

 2 tbsp olive oil

 4 sprigs fresh rosemary

 3 bay leaves

 1 tsp fennel seeds

 1 tbsp tomato purée

 200 ml (7 fl oz) white wine

 1 pinch of salt
1 pinch of black pepper

 2 litres (3½ pints) chicken stock

 2 duck breasts

1

Pinto Bean Ragout with Roast Duck Breast

1. Soak the beans for at least 2 hours. Peel the carrots and celeriac and cut into 5-mm (¼-inch) pieces. Press the garlic cloves into a bowl, then peel and dice the onions. In a shallow pan, heat 2 tbsp olive oil, add the onions, carrots and celeriac, and sweat them slowly for 10 minutes.

2. Add the rosemary, bay leaves, chopped fennel seeds and pressed garlic, and sauté them lightly.

3. Push the vegetables to one side of the pan. Add the tomato purée to the middle so it loses acidity. Add white wine, allowing the liquid to reduce. Strain the beans in a sieve.

4. Now add the beans to the pan, and sauté for 2 minutes. Add salt and pepper, pour in chicken stock and let it simmer gently for 50 minutes. Stir as necessary to keep the beans from burning at the bottom of the pan. Stir the beans carefully so as not to crush them. Add water if necessary.

Cook the duck breasts (see p. 534). Serve the beans on the plate. Cut the duck breasts into slices and arrange on top of the beans.

+ 2 hours soaking time

✳
✳
✳
80

■ Fennel seeds are easier to chop if you drizzle them with a little oil beforehand to keep them from jumping. The pinto bean ragout also goes well with sausages or stuffed pigs' trotters.

500 g (1 lb 2 oz) chickpeas

 220 g (8 oz) onions

 200 g (7 oz) aubergine

 3 garlic cloves

 200 g (7 oz) tomatoes

 5 tbsp sunflower oil

 1 tbsp anise seeds

 6 cardamom pods

 8 cloves

 1 cinnamon stick

 1 pinch of salt
1 pinch of black pepper

 1 tsp ground coriander

 1 tsp ground turmeric

 1.5 litres (2½ pints) water or vegetable stock

 200 g (7 oz) natural yogurt

 1 dash of ground cinnamon

 A few drops of lemon juice

 2 sprigs fresh mint

Indian Chickpea Curry with Cinnamon Yogurt and Mint

1. Soak the chickpeas in cold water for at least 2 hours. Peel the onions, cut them in half and dice finely. Cut the aubergine into 2-cm (¾-inch) pieces. Peel the garlic and cut into thin slices. Skin the tomatoes and cut them into quarters (see p. 347). Heat the oil in a pan over medium heat, add the garlic, sweating until golden brown. Add the anise seeds, cardamom pods, cloves and cinnamon stick, and sauté them together for a more intense flavour.

2. Add the onions, sweat until translucent, and push them to the sides of the pan. Put the aubergine in the middle. Add salt and pepper and fry for 5 minutes.

3. Sprinkle with ground coriander and turmeric and sweat for 5 minutes until the onion and aubergine are slightly mushy. Pour the soaked chickpeas in a sieve to drain.

4. Add the chickpeas and briefly sweat everything together. Then add the tomatoes, and the water or vegetable stock.

5. Cover with a lid, and simmer in the pan over medium heat for 70 minutes. The chickpeas should remain covered in liquid. Finish by mixing the yogurt with the cinnamon, lemon juice, and mint leaves cut into ribbons. Put the chickpeas on plates and add the yogurt mix on top.

+ 2 hours soaking time

 100

■ If possible, soak the chickpeas the day before, or overnight. This makes them soften faster while cooking. This dish can also be served with roast beef or fried eggs.

500 g (1 lb 2 oz) small lentils

 75 g (2½ oz) carrots

 75 g (2½ oz) celery

 50 g (1¾ oz) smoked bacon

 85 g (3 oz) leek

 2 shallots

 2 garlic cloves

 20 g (⅔ oz) butter

 6 tbsp olive oil

 1 sprig fresh rosemary

 2 bay leaves

 1 pinch of salt
1 pinch of black pepper

 1 tbsp tomato purée

 2 cloves

 200 ml (7 fl oz) red wine

 1 litre (1¾ pints) chicken stock

 1 bunch fresh parsley

 2 tbsp medium-hot mustard

 ½ tsp lemon zest

 ½ tsp orange zest

1 tsp balsamic vinegar

 8 Italian sausages

50

Vegetable Lentil Stew with Italian Sausage

1. Add the lentils to boiling salted water and bring back to the boil. Then shake them into a sieve, cool under cold running water and drain.

2. Finely dice the carrots, celery, bacon, leek and the shallots. Press the garlic in its skin. Heat the butter and 4 tbsp oil in a pan over medium heat. Add the shallots and bacon and brown for about 2 minutes. Add the celery, carrots, leek, garlic, rosemary, bay leaves, salt and pepper, and sweat until translucent – about 5 minutes.

3. Push the vegetables to the sides of the pan. Add the tomato purée to the middle and sauté so it loses acidity. Mix everything together and continue sautéing briefly.

4. Add the drained lentils and the cloves and sauté them for 2 to 3 minutes.

5. Add red wine and cook until the liquid has evaporated, stirring frequently.

6. Add the stock, making sure the lentils are covered in liquid.

■ Lentils can also be seasoned with the following ingredients: fresh marjoram, freshly grated nutmeg, whipped cream, finely chopped anchovies, finely chopped capers or pickle juice.

Add a bunch of parsley tied with kitchen twine. Bring the lentils to the boil and let them simmer gently for [0] minutes. Stir carefully.

Finish by seasoning with mustard, grated lemon and orange zest, and a splash of balsamic vinegar.

Heat the remaining oil in a nonstick pan over a medium heat and fry the sausages for 5 minutes on both sides. Put the lentils on plates, lay the sausages on top, and pour a little of the frying juices over everything.

1 carrot

 2 celery stalks

 1 leek

 1 onion

 2 tbsp oil

 1 tbsp butter

 1 tbsp tomato purée

 250 g (9 oz) red lentils

 150 ml (5 fl oz) white wine

 500 ml (17 fl oz) stock

 1 pinch of salt
1 pinch of black pepper

 ½ tsp dried marjoram

 2 tbsp vinegar

 2 tsp Dijon mustard

 2 sprigs fresh parsley, to garnish

Sour Vegetable and Lentil Stew

1. Rinse and clean the carrots, celery stalks and the leek and dice them finely. Reserve a few celery leaves for garnishing. Peel the onion and dice it too.

2. Sauté the vegetables in hot oil and butter, then add the tomato purée and stir.

3. Add the rinsed lentils to the vegetables and sauté.

4. Add white wine and bring to the boil. Add the stock and simmer for about 20 minutes.

5. Lastly, add salt and pepper to taste, and stir in the marjoram. Season with vinegar and mustard.

Serve sprinkled with parsley and celery leaves.

■ This is an outstanding side dish with grilled fish or roasted whole pigeon, or serve it with just a few crispy strips of bacon. The lentils can also be rounded off with finely chopped anchovies, capers, pickles or even a little whipped cream.

Cooking Polenta

1. Add **250 ml (8½ fl oz) water** and **500 ml (17 fl oz) milk** to a pan and bring it to the boil.

2. Add **1 tbsp butter**, **salt** and a **pinch of freshly grated nutmeg**.

3. Stir in **180 g (6 oz) polenta** to the boiling liquid, then reduce the heat by half.

4. Continue cooking, stirring frequently.

5. After 30–45 minutes, the polenta becomes thick. Stir vigorously to keep it from burning in the pan.

6. Put the polenta on a surface covered with baking paper, scraping the pan well.

7. Spread the polenta to about 3 cm (1¼ inches) thick.

8. Cover with baking paper to keep the polenta from drying out, and leave it to cool down. Then the polenta can be cut into pieces for grilling or for using in oven-baked dishes.

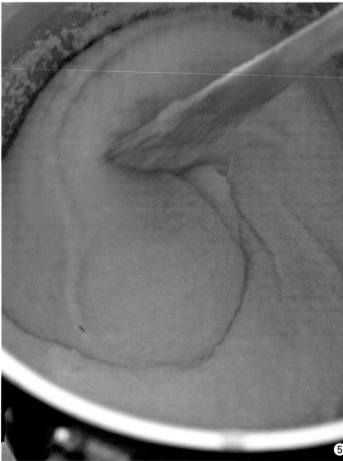

Potatoes

Contents

Types of Potato

There are numerous varieties of potato available for every conceivable purpose – from chips to soups, casseroles and salads. Although the colour and shape may vary, we should avoid potatoes that feel soft or that have been damaged by harvesting equipment. Their skins should be clean and smooth, and not too dry.

There are about 3,000 potato varieties in total. At least 100–150 varieties still reach our markets. They are classified according to when they are harvested. Potatoes must always be cooked before they are consumed and are very versatile. They can be boiled, mashed, steamed, baked, deep-fried or even microwaved.

With so many varieties on offer, it is important to understand the potatoes' characteristics to choose the appropriate one for your dish: floury varieties like

Bintje are very starchy and are best suited to soups, stews, mash, hash browns or dumplings. BF 15 potatoes are quite dry. They are suitable for cooking in their skins, for roasting and for chips. Waxy varieties such as Ballerina are firm, but moist. They are well suited for cooking in their skins, for roasting and for potato salads.

Potatoes from the supermarket should be taken out of their plastic bag. Otherwise, they will quickly become mouldy and rotten. For best results, store potatoes in a wooden box or a basket in a cool, dark, dry environment.

Cooking Chart

Product	Form	Method	Temperature	Time	Comment
Potatoes	Whole	Saucepan	Boiling	20 minutes	
Potatoes	In quarters	Saucepan	Boiling	12–14 minutes	
Potatoes	Chips	Saucepan	Deep-fry at 180°C (350°F)	3 minutes	Precook or deep-fry in advance
Potatoes, raw	Sliced	Frying pan	Low to medium heat	15–20 minutes	
Potatoes, cooked	Whole	Frying pan	Medium heat	8–10 minutes	
Sweet potatoes	Whole	Saucepan	Medium heat	25 minutes	
Sweet potatoes	Sliced	Frying pan	Medium heat	20 minutes	

Kennebec   Charlotte   Monalisa

BF 15   Bintje   Agria

Black Asparges   King Edward   Red

Roseval   Sweet potato   Vitelotte

Potato Cuts

Thin potato discs are used for potatoes au gratin or potatoes boulangère. The latter are layered in an ovenproof dish like potatoes au gratin, sprinkled with gently sautéed onion slices and covered with stock. They are cooked in the same way as potatoes au gratin.

Turned potatoes are potatoes that are cut (turned) into a specific shape. Thus, they are evenly sized and can be used for parsley potatoes or stewed potatoes.

Soufflé potatoes are 1-mm (1/16-inch) thick potato discs that are used to make crisps. First, they are deep-fried in hot fat at a temperature of 140°C (275°F) and then once more at 180°C (350°F), so they rise like a soufflé. Soufflé potatoes go well with roast meat and poultry.

For **cubed potatoes**, cut potatoes into 1-cm (½-inch) pieces, briefly plunge them into boiling water, cool them by immersing them in cold water and let them drain. Fry them in a frying pan with a generous amount of oil until they are golden. Then discard the oil, fry the cubes in butter, and season them with salt. They are delicious on corn salad or with steak, rose veal kidney or liver.

Potatoes à la Lyonnaise consist of approximately 3-mm (⅛-inch) thick discs and are prepared like fried potatoes. They are placed raw in a nonstick frying pan, browned slowly and evenly on all sides, and finally mixed with diced onion.

Chips are approximately 6 cm (2½ inches) long and 5 mm (¼ inch) thick. This is how the classic 'fry' looks.

Matchstick potatoes – their name refers to their shape and size. They are prepared like chips and are nice when added to salads as a crisp ingredient. Formerly, matchstick potatoes were a classic accompaniment to Parisian pepper steak, but they are not easy to eat with a fork!

Straw potatoes are even finer than matchstick potatoes. Like chips, they are cooked until golden and are mostly used to garnish large roasts or other pieces of meat. Try them also with carrots, celery or leeks.

Pont Neuf potatoes are approximately 8 cm (3¼ inches) long and 2 cm (¾ inch) thick. Cook them first in salted water for 2 minutes, then chill them in cold water and put them on a baking tray. Brush them with melted butter and bake them for 20 minutes in the oven. Shortly before they are done, brush them with veal sauce. They can be served with roast meats, roast poultry or T-bone steaks.

Parisian potatoes are small and round and shaped with a special scoop or potato baller. They can be boiled or sautéed in a frying pan until golden.

The leftover potato can be used for soup or potato cakes.

Potato wedges are small or new potatoes that are not peeled, just washed well and cut lengthways into sixths. Put them into a casserole dish, season them with salt and pepper, and drizzle them with olive oil. Bake them in the oven for approximately 20 minutes at 200°C (400°F/Gas Mark 6), until they are golden. They can also be mixed with crushed garlic cloves and baked; this method will add a French touch to the potatoes! They are delicious with roast chicken.

Cooking Gnocchi

1. Add the potato gnocchi to salted water.

2. Simmer gently for approximately 1 minute.

3. Stir them carefully with a slotted spoon and loosen any gnocchi that are sticking to the bottom of the saucepan.

4. Strain them carefully in a colander.

5. Rinse the gnocchi with cold water, until they are cold. Let them drain well and use them as desired.

Cooking Potatoes in Their Jackets

1. Wash starchy potatoes well and place them in a saucepan with a large quantity of salted water.

2. Add 1 tsp caraway seeds to the water and bring it to the boil.

3. Cook the potatoes for approximately 25 minutes, depending on their size.

4. Check that they are done by pricking the potatoes with a fork. You can also tell that they are done if their skins come off easily.

Cooking Sweet Potatoes

1. Wash the sweet potatoes and cover them with water in a saucepan. Add salt and 2–3 cloves and bring to the boil.

2. Let the sweet potatoes cook for approximately 30 minutes and check that they are done by pricking them with a fork.

3. Strain the sweet potatoes and leave them in the pan for 10 more minutes to allow the moisture to evaporate.

4. Then peel them carefully and remove brown sections with a knife. Leave them to cool until they are needed.

Caraway Potatoes

. For this recipe, you will need **800 g (1 lb 12 oz) small, golden, yellow-skinned potatoes**. Wash them well and clean off any dirt with a brush. Cut the potatoes in half and put them in a bowl. Combine them with **1 tsp of salt, a pinch of black pepper, 1 tsp of caraway seeds** and **3 tbsp of vegetable oil**.

. Put the potatoes in a nonstick roasting tin and bake them in the oven at 180°C (350°F/Gas Mark 4) for approximately 35 minutes until golden. Turn them frequently so that they don't stick. Shortly before they are done, add **20 g (2/3 oz) of butter** and continue to roast them. Serve the caraway potatoes with roast pork or simply with buttermilk for a light evening meal.

■ The most suitable potato varieties for this recipe are Yellow Finn, Yukon Gold, La Ratte, Sieglinde and Nicola.

500 g (1 lb 2 oz) potatoes in their skins

 2 litres (3½ pints) vegetable oil for deep-frying

 3 garlic cloves

 1 tsp salt

Deep-fried Potatoes

1. Peel the boiled potatoes (see p. 307) and cut into 2-cm (¾-inch) pieces.

2. Add the oil to a large saucepan, heat it to 160ºC (325ºF) and deep-fry the unpeeled garlic.

3. Add the potato pieces to the hot oil and fry them for approximately

3 minutes, until they are golden. Lift the potatoes out with a slotted spoon.

4. Put them on kitchen paper to drain and season with salt. Arrange them on plates and serve them with a spicy tomato sauce (salsa brava) for dipping.

■ They are delicious as a snack with wine or beer.

4 large potatoes

 1 tsp caraway seeds

 1 pinch of salt

 20 g (²/₃ oz) butter

 400 g (14 oz) quark (20% fat)

 1 bunch mixed fresh herbs

 1 spring onion

 1 pinch of black pepper

3 tbsp olive oil

Juice of ½ lemon

Potatoes en Papillote with Fresh Herb Quark

1. Preheat the oven to 200°C (400°F/Gas Mark 6). Wash the potatoes and cook them with the caraway seeds in salted water for 10 minutes. Then strain the potatoes and let some of the moisture evaporate.

2. Cut a sheet of kitchen foil into pieces large enough to wrap around a potato, and use a brush to coat these with butter. Season them with salt, and sprinkle with some caraway seeds.

3. Wrap each potato in foil and bake them for 50 minutes, turning the potatoes occasionally.

4. In the meantime, mix the quark with the cleaned, finely chopped herbs, diced spring onion, salt, black pepper and olive oil. Season to taste with lemon juice. Open the foil envelopes, cut halfway through the potatoes and spoon the quark mixture on top.

■ These potatoes are just as tasty when they are cooked under the grill instead of in the oven. In that case, however, turn them more often.

250 g (9 oz) cream

 250 ml (8½ fl oz) milk

 1½ tsp salt
1 pinch of black pepper

 1 pinch of nutmeg, freshly grated

 2 garlic cloves

 850 g (1 lb 14 oz) potatoes

10 g (¼ oz) butter

Potatoes au Gratin

1. Preheat the fan oven to 190°C (375°F/ Gas Mark 5). Put the cream and milk in a saucepan to boil and season with salt, pepper and nutmeg. Add the unpeeled, crushed garlic cloves and let them steep for 10 minutes.Then, pass the mixture through a fine sieve.

2. Cut the potatoes into 1-mm (¹/₁₆-inch) slices or use a vegetable slicer or a mandoline. Butter a casserole dish.

3. Spread the potatoes in layers in the casserole dish and pour the cream/milk mixture over them.

4. Dot the top evenly with butter.

5. Cover the dish with kitchen foil and use the tip of a knife to poke small holes in it. Bake the dish in the oven for approximately 20 minutes. Uncover the dish for the last 10 minutes, so that the gratin cooks to a golden colour. You can also use Gruyère or raclette cheese in this dish.

■ For a potato and leek gratin, gently saut 200 g (7 oz) leek strips (see p. 350) in 20 g (²/₃ oz) butter. Butter the casserole dish and put a layer of leeks on the bottom. Then follow the instructions for the potatoes au gratin.

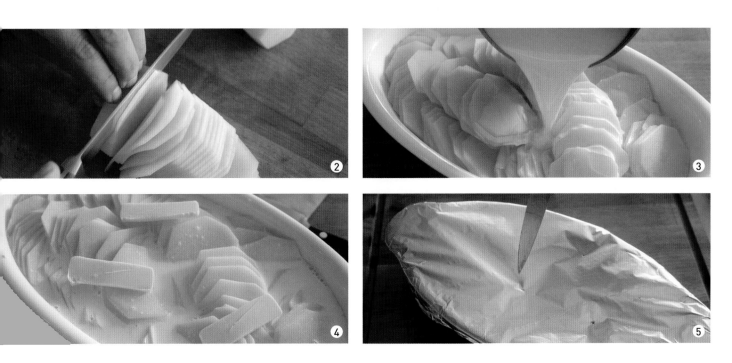

-  800 g (1 lb 12 oz) starchy potatoes
- 150 g (5½ oz) all-purpose flour
- 120 g (4½ oz) durum wheat semolina
- 1 egg
- 1 pinch of salt
- 1 pinch of nutmeg, freshly grated
- 1 tbsp oil

Potato Gnocchi

1. Cook the potatoes, let them cool down, and grate them finely.

2. Spread the grated potatoes out on a work surface. Sprinkle with the flour and semolina. Add the egg and season with the salt and nutmeg.

3. Knead the potato mixture with your hands to form a dough.

4. Divide the dough into 200-g (7-oz) pieces, dust with flour and roll out into 1-cm (½-inch) thick logs. Cut the logs into 1-cm (½-inch) long pieces with a knife. Cook them in salted water (see p. 306) and let them cool in cold water. Drain them and drizzle a little oil on them. Store them in the refrigerator for future use.

■ You can either lightly press on the gnocchi with the tines of a fork, or shape them into finger noodles by rolling them in your hands.

500 g (1 lb 2 oz) potato gnocchi (see p. 316)

 200 g (7 oz) cherry tomatoes

 2 garlic cloves

 3 tbsp olive oil

 1 pinch of salt
1 pinch of black pepper

 1 pinch of sugar

 ½ bunch rocket

Potato Gnocchi with Cherry Tomatoes and Rocket

1. Cook the gnocchi in a large amount of water (see p. 306). Halve the cherry tomatoes; peel the garlic and slice it thinly.

2. In a frying pan, sauté the sliced garlic in the olive oil.

3. Add the cherry tomatoes, and sprinkle them with salt, pepper and a little sugar. Toss them in the frying pan for 2–3 minutes, until they soften slightly.

4. Add the cooked potato gnocchi and mix them with the tomatoes.

5. Add the clean, washed rocket to the gnocchi.

6. Toss the mixture in the frying pan, until the rocket is slightly wilted.

Arrange it on plates and serve immediately. Garnish the dish with some fresh rocket leaves.

■ This is also delicious if you use yellow cherry tomatoes or sliced large tomatoes. Mix them with fresh basil or baby spinach.

25

400 g (14 oz) potato gnocchi (see p. 316)

 350 g (12 oz) low-fat yogurt

 2 tsp tandoori seasoning

 Juice of ½ lemon

 1 pinch of salt
1 pinch of black pepper

 250 ml (8½ fl oz) milk

 1 tbsp butter

 100 g (3½ oz) feta cheese (drained weight)

 3 sprigs fresh coriander, to garnish

Baked Gnocchi in Tandoori Yogurt Sauce

1. Preheat the oven to 180°C (350°F/Gas Mark 4). Cook the gnocchi (see p. 306). Put the yogurt into a tall container and sprinkle it with the tandoori seasoning.

2. Add the lemon juice to the yogurt.

3. Season with salt and black pepper.

4. Pour in the milk and stir well with a fork.

5. Arrange the gnocchi in the bottom of a buttered casserole dish and cover them with the tandoori sauce.

6. Sprinkle them evenly with crumbled feta cheese.

7. Bake for approximately 25 minutes. The gnocchi are done when the cheese has turned a light golden colour.

Serve them from the casserole dish, garnished with the coriander leaves.

■ Curry or garam masala spices can be used instead of tandoori seasoning.

400 g (14 oz) gnocchi dough
(see p. 316)

 1 pinch of salt

 1 tbsp butter

 ½ bunch fresh sage

 100 g (3½ oz) hot salami

 1 pinch of black pepper

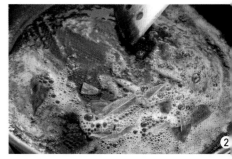

Potato Finger Noodles with Sage and Salami

1. Make small finger noodles with the gnocchi dough and boil them in salted water, until they rise to the top (see p. 306).

2. Melt the butter in a frying pan until it foams, and then add the plucked sage leaves.

3. Slice the salami, add it to the frying pan and sauté gently, so that the flavour can develop.

4. Put the drained finger noodles into th frying pan and sauté them.

5. Continue sautéing for another 5 minutes and season with salt and blac pepper.

Arrange them on plates and serve.

■ This dish can also be made with gnocchi or store-bought finger noodles. Sauerkraut and bacon can also be added.

1.5 kg (3 lb 5 oz) potatoes

 3 litres (5¼ pints) vegetable oil

 1 tsp salt

Chips

1. Peel the potatoes and cut into large wedges. Remove the corners in order to even out the sides. Cut the wedges into 1-cm (½-inch) thick strips

2. Wash them thoroughly in cold water to remove the starch. This makes the chips nice and crisp.

3. Dry the potato strips with kitchen paper before deep-frying them. If the strips are damp, the oil will bubble up and splash.

4. Pre-fry the chips in vegetable oil at 140°C (275°F) for about 1 minute without browning them.

5. Remove the pre-fried chips from the pan with a slotted spoon and leave them to cool on a baking tray.

6. Then fry the chips for a second time at 180°C (350°F), until they are crisp and golden yellow.

7. Remove the chips from the oil and leave them to drain on kitchen paper. Season them with salt and serve them o a plate as a side dish.

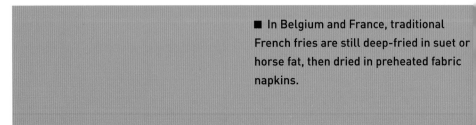

■ In Belgium and France, traditional French fries are still deep-fried in suet or horse fat, then dried in preheated fabric napkins.

1. Golden Potato Cakes

Peel **800 g (1 lb 12 oz) starchy potatoes**, grate coarsely into a bowl, and season with **1 pinch of salt** and **1 pinch of black pepper**. Then use your hands to squeeze the excess water out of the grated potatoes. Heat **2 tbsp vegetable oil** in a nonstick frying pan. Add the potato mixture and fry for approximately 10 minutes, stirring occasionally. Flatten the potato mix and shape it into a pancake. Add another **2 tsp vegetable oil** to the side of the frying pan and cook it for 10 minutes longer. Transfer the potato cake onto a plate and, with the browned side facing upwards, slide it back into the frying pan. Fry it for another 10 minutes, until it is golden brown. Turn it out onto a plate, cut it as you would a cake and arrange the slices on plates.

■ Serve golden potato cakes with roast duck, cold-cured salmon or fresh steak tartare.

2. Grilled Potatoes

Preheat the oven to 200°C (400°F/Gas Mark 6). Peel **600 g (1 lb 5 oz) waxy potatoes**. Cut them in half lengthways, then into eighths and boil in salted water for 2 minutes. Crush **4 unpeeled garlic cloves**. Put the potatoes and the garlic into a casserole dish and season with **1 pinch of salt** and **1 pinch of black pepper**. Roast them in the oven for approximately 20 minutes. Just 5 minutes before the end of cooking, pluck off the needles from **a sprig of rosemary** and add them. Do not add them any earlier, otherwise they will burn.

■ Serve grilled potatoes as an accompaniment to cutlets, steaks, burgers or buttered sole.

3. Hash Browns

Peel **500 g (1 lb 2 oz) starchy potatoes**, add **½ garlic clove** and finely grate the potatoes into a bowl. Add **1 egg** and **1 tbsp flour** and rub in **½ tsp dried marjoram** by hand. Season with **1 pinch of salt** and **1 pinch of black pepper** and combine everything to form a dough. Heat **4 tsp vegetable oil** in a frying pan. Use a small ladle to transfer the potato mixture to the frying pan and to form it into small hash browns. Fry on each side for at least 3 minutes, until they are golden.

■ Serve hash browns with roast duck, cold-cured salmon or fresh steak tartare. Variation: Omit the marjoram and garlic and serve them with apple sauce.

800 g (1 lb 12 oz) potatoes in their jackets

 60 g (2¼ oz) onion

 ½ bunch fresh parsley

 3 tbsp vegetable oil

 1 pinch of salt
1 pinch of black pepper

 20 g (⅔ oz) butter

Fried Potatoes

1. Cook the potatoes in their jackets (see p. 307), peel them with a knife and slice them into 5-mm (¼-inch) thick discs. Peel the onion and dice it finely. Wash the parsley, pick the leaves and chop them finely.

2. Heat the oil in a nonstick frying pan and add the potato discs.

3. Season with salt and pepper. Fry them at medium heat for approximately 10 minutes, tossing frequently and taking care to keep the potatoes as intact as possible.

4. As soon as the potato discs are golden brown, and nice and crisp, add the butter and continue to cook them. This will help to bring out their flavour.

5. Add the diced onion and cook for 1 minute more, tossing frequently.

6. Add the finely chopped parsley, toss thoroughly once more, and serve immediately. These potatoes go well with cutlets, or alongside creamed spinach with a fried egg. They are also delicious if you top them with strong cheese and bake them in the oven.

■ Fried potatoes are even tastier if they are cooked in goose fat and seasoned with caraway seeds, cooked bacon strips or chives.

750 g (1 lb 10 oz) starchy potatoes

 1 bunch fresh chives

 1 egg

 1 tbsp crème fraîche

 1 pinch of nutmeg, freshly grated

 20 g (²/₃ oz) butter

 1 pinch of salt

 5 tbsp cornflour

 40 g (1½ oz) flour

1 tbsp vegetable oil

①

Macaire Potatoes

1. Peel the potatoes, cook them for 20 minutes in salted water, and then press them through a potato ricer. Wash the chives, remove any damaged pieces, and chop finely with a sharp knife.

2. Form a little well in the centre of the potatoes. Separate the egg and put the egg yolk, along with the crème fraîche, nutmeg, chives, butter, salt and cornflour, into the well.

3. Mix with your hands, and shape the mixture into an elongated roll. As you

work, dust the roll with flour so that it doesn't stick to your hands.

4. Use a floured knife to slice the dough into 1.5-cm (⅝-inch) thick discs.

5. Briefly toss the discs in flour and shape them into evenly sized cakes.

6. Use kitchen paper to oil a nonstick frying pan, then brown the potato cakes for approximately 3 minutes on each side

■ Crisp roasted cubes of ham can be added to the potato mixture. Macaire potatoes go well with roast saddle of venison, haunch of venison, or veal medallions with cream sauce.

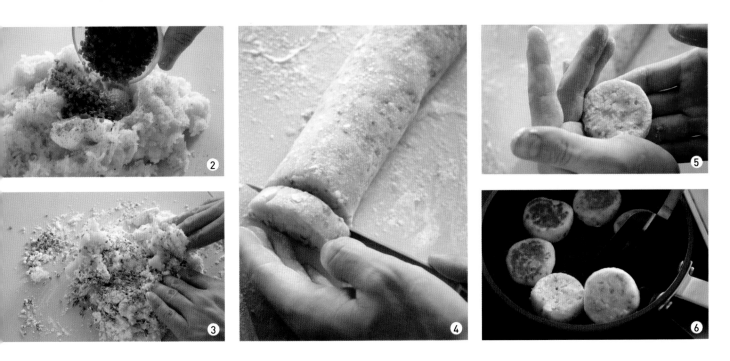

1 garlic clove

 600 g (1 lb 5 oz) waxy potatoes

 2.5-cm (1-inch) piece ginger

 3 tbsp vegetable oil

 1 tsp fennel seeds

 ½ tsp ground turmeric

 1 pinch of nutmeg, freshly grated

 1 pinch of salt

 20 saffron threads

 400 ml (13½ fl oz) coconut milk

 1 sprig fresh mint

Indian Saffron Potatoes in Coconut Milk

1. Peel the garlic and chop it finely. Peel the potatoes, cut them into 3-cm (1¼-inch) cubes and set them aside in cold water, so that they don't turn brown. Peel the ginger and cut it into fine julienne strips. Heat the vegetable oil in a deep saucepan, add the garlic, ginger, fennel seeds and turmeric, and sauté gently for a short time.

2. Add the potato cubes, season them with nutmeg and salt, and sauté them gently for approximately 1 minute.

3. Then add the saffron threads and sauté gently for a short time.

4. Pour in the coconut milk, cover the pan and let the mixture simmer slowly for approximately 20 minutes. Stir occasionally, adding some water if necessary, so that the potatoes don't stick to the pan. Finally, arrange the potatoes in a bowl and sprinkle them with mint leaves.

■ You can also use garam masala, the Indian spice mixture, instead of the various spices listed. Garam masala incorporates many flavours and is very versatile. Alternatively, half the potatoes can be replaced by cooked chickpeas. The addition of fresh spring onions makes this variation especially delicious.

500 g (1 lb 2 oz) sweet potatoes

 100 g (3½ oz) cooked basmati rice

 1 egg yolk

 2 tbsp flour

 ½ tsp cumin seeds

 ½ bunch fresh coriander

 1 pinch of salt
1 pinch of black pepper

 4 tbsp breadcrumbs

 1 litre (1¾ pints) vegetable oil for deep-frying

1

Sweet Potato Balls with Crisp Basmati Rice Coating

1. Cook the sweet potatoes (see p. 308), let the moisture evaporate, then grate them finely and put them in a bowl. Cook the basmati rice (see p. 234) and leave it to cool.

2. Add the egg yolk, flour and cumin seeds to the sweet potatoes. Wash the coriander, remove any withered leaves, and finely chop the remaining leaves and stems. Add the coriander to the bowl and season the mixture with salt and pepper.

3. Add the breadcrumbs and work the mixture into a dough. Add more breadcrumbs, as needed, so that a homogenous mixture is created.

4. Moisten your hands, and shape the dough into small balls.

5. Roll the balls in the cooked rice and deep-fry in the heated oil at 180°C (350°F), until they are crisp. Remove the balls with a slotted spoon and leave them to drain on kitchen paper.

These sweet potato balls go well with chicken strips and vegetables.

■ Serve the sweet potato balls as a snack with wine, accompanied by a spicy yogurt dip.

1 kg (2 lb 4 oz) starchy potatoes

 1 tbsp salt

 150 g (5½ oz) butter

 300 ml (10 fl oz) milk

1 pinch of nutmeg, freshly grated

Home-made Mashed Potatoes

1. Peel and halve the potatoes. Put them in a saucepan with salted water and bring them to the boil. Cook the potatoes for approximately 25 minutes, until they are completely soft.

2. Discard the water, and return the potatoes to the saucepan. Heat them on the hob for as long as it takes to boil away any remaining liquid and for the potatoes to become very starchy.

3. Mash the soft potatoes with a wooden spoon.

4. Work the potatoes with the wooden spoon until you have an almost glossy mass.

5. Add the sliced, cold butter, and work i in with the aid of the wooden spoon.

6. The butter must be fully absorbed by the mashed potatoes.

7. Heat the milk, and gradually stir it int the mash.

8. Finally, season with nutmeg and salt.

9. Use a wooden spoon, not a wire whisk to mix everything together – the whisk will make the mashed potatoes tough.

■ Olive oil can be used instead of butter to smooth the mashed potatoes. However, in that case, be sure to use good-quality virgin olive oil.

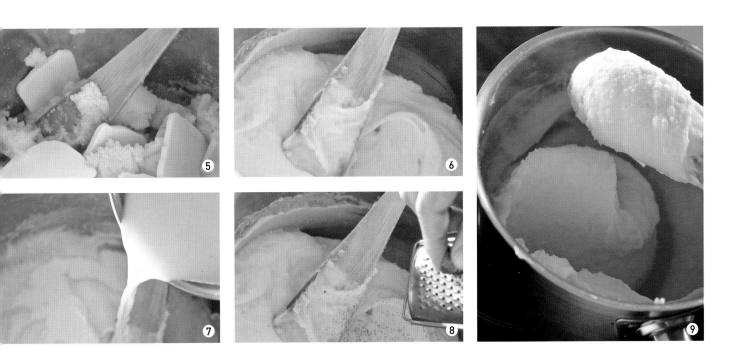

500 g (1 lb 2 oz) potatoes

 1 bunch fresh chives

 1 tbsp vinegar

1 litre (1¾ pints) béchamel sauce
(see p. 156)

Swedish Potatoes with Chives

1. Peel the potatoes with a vegetable peeler and cook whole for 25 minutes.

2. Wash the chives, shake them dry and chop them finely with a knife.

3. Drizzle some vinegar onto the cooked potatoes.

4. Pour the hot béchamel sauce over the potatoes.

5. To finish, sprinkle them with chives and arrange them on a plate.

* * * 40

■ For best results, use small yellow potatoes. Chervil or dill may be mixed with the potatoes instead of chives. Serve as an accompaniment to boiled fish or meatloaf.

Vegetables

Contents

Types of Vegetable

Choosing vegetables used to be simple: they had to be crisp and ripe. Unfortunately, now *all* vegetables seem to be crisp, sometimes for weeks or even months. Sadly, this characteristic no longer stands for taste. Dehydration is the natural enemy of any vegetable. Vegetable varieties with excessively dry stalks or leaves are to be avoided. The other rule is that vegetables should be washed in lemon water. This removes pesticides and fungicides effectively.

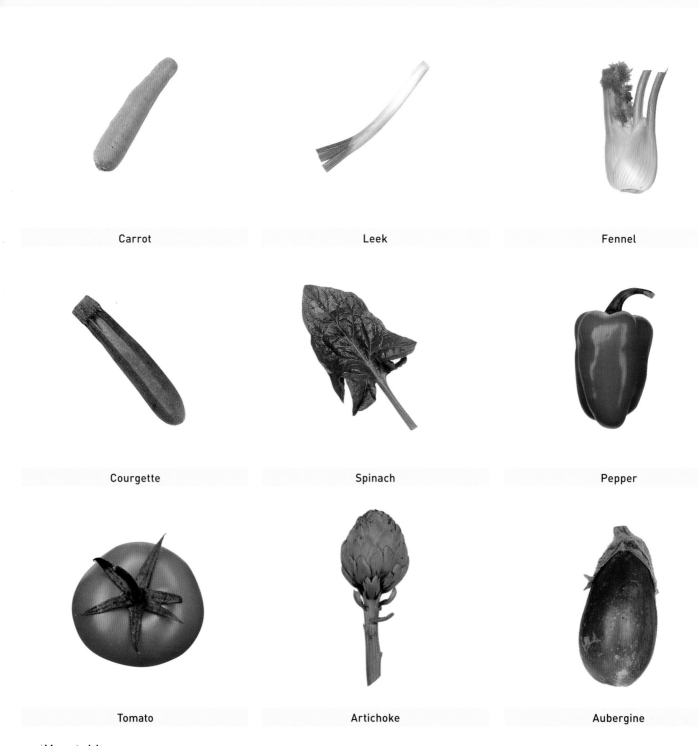

Carrot	Leek	Fennel
Courgette	Spinach	Pepper
Tomato	Artichoke	Aubergine

Peas

Broad beans

French beans

Garlic

Broccoli

Cabbage

Asparagus

Cucumber

Button mushrooms

Morel

Chanterelle

Porcino

Vegetable Cuts

Bâtonnets: Broad strips, approximately 1 cm (½ inch) wide and 5 cm (2 inches) long, are used as a garnish for sauces and also as an accompaniment to poached fish dishes.

Julienne: Thin vegetable strips that are approximately 1 mm (1⁄16 inch) thick and 5–7 cm (2–2¾ inch) long, and are suitable for potato dishes, for poaching with fish, or as a garnish for soups and sauces.

Brunoise: Delicate 1-mm (1⁄16-inch) cubes that are used for salad dressings, as a garnish for fish sauces, for dishes with beans and lentils, and for stews, or they can be poached with whole vegetables.

Small dice 5-mm (¼-inch) cubes that are suitable for soups and stews, and cook in approximately 15 minutes.

Medium dice 1-cm (½-inch) cubes that are suitable ingredients for sauces that are not cooked for too long. Ratatouille ingredients can also be diced in this manner, as well as vegetables for rustic soups and stews.

Large dice 2–3-cm (¾-1¼-inch) cubes that are braised with roasts and stews or gently fried and added to gravies.

Soup vegetables refers to vegetables that are just cut into quarters or thirds. They are added to soups or stocks that have to cook for a long time and don't cook down as fast as the other vegetable cuts.

Small mirepoix: Cut the vegetables into medium-sized cubes. Cut unpeeled garlic cloves in half. Use 2 parts of onions/shallots to 1 part of each of the remaining root vegetables (celery, carrots, celeriac or Hamburg parsley). Small mirepoix is used as an addition to shellfish and poultry sauces.

Large mirepoix: Peel the vegetables and cut them into coarse pieces or cubes, measuring approximately 3 cm (1¼ inches). Cut unpeeled garlic cloves in half. The same proportions of vegetables are used for both small and large mirepoix. The large mirepoix is used for meat sauces or vegetable stocks, or in marinades for wild game.

Cooking Chart

Product	Form	Method	Temperature	Time
Artichokes	Whole	In water	Boiling	35 minutes
Artichokes	Slices	Frying pan	Medium heat	8 minutes
Artichokes	Quarters	Frying pan	Medium heat	12 minutes
Asparagus, green	Whole	In water	Boiling	6 minutes
Asparagus, green	Pieces	Frying pan	Medium heat	5 minutes
Asparagus, white	Pieces	Frying pan	Medium heat	8 minutes
Asparagus, white	Whole	In water	Boiling	10 minutes
Aubergines	Slices	Griddle	High heat	10 minutes
Aubergines	Large cubes	Frying pan	Medium heat	8 minutes
Broad beans	Whole	In water	Boiling	2 minutes
Broccoli	Florets	Frying pan	Medium heat	15 minutes
Broccoli	Whole	In water	Boiling	20 minutes
Button mushrooms	Slices	Frying pan	High heat	4 minutes
Cabbage	Quarters	Oven	160°C (325°F)	45 minutes
Cabbage	Slices	Saucepan with lid	Medium heat	35 minutes
Cabbage	Slices	Frying pan	High heat	10 minutes
Carrots	Julienne strips	In water	Boiling	10 seconds
Carrots	Slices	Frying pan	Medium heat	6 minutes
Carrots	Small cubes	In water	Boiling	5 seconds
Cauliflower	Whole	In water	Boiling	25 minutes
Cauliflower	Florets	Frying pan	Medium heat	15 minutes
Chanterelles	Whole	Frying pan	High heat	3 minutes
Chard	Leaf	Frying pan	Medium heat	5 minutes
Chard	Stalk	Frying pan	Medium heat	8 minutes
Courgettes	Slices	Frying pan	Medium heat	6 minutes
Courgettes	Julienne strips	In water	Boiling	10 seconds
Courgettes	Bâtonnets	In water	Boiling	15 seconds
Courgettes	Small cubes	Frying pan	Medium heat	15 seconds
Cucumber	Slices	Frying pan	Medium heat	6 minutes
Cucumber	Whole	Oven	160°C (325°F/Gas Mark 3)	20 minutes
Fennel	Whole	Oven	160°C (325°F/Gas Mark 3)	50 minutes
Fennel	Bâtonnets	Frying pan	Medium heat	2 minutes
Fennel	Small cubes	Frying pan	Medium heat	1 minute
Green beans	Whole	In water	Boiling	2 minutes
Leeks	Julienne strips	Frying pan	Medium heat	1 minute
Leeks	Slices	Frying pan	Medium heat	2 minutes
Leeks	In thirds or quarters	In water	Boiling	20 minutes
Morels	Whole	Frying pan	Medium heat	6 minutes
Pea pods	Whole	Frying pan	Medium heat	1 minute
Peas	Shelled	In water	Boiling	2 minutes
Peppers	Bâtonnets	Frying pan	Medium heat	10 minutes
Peppers	Small cubes	Frying pan	Medium heat	3 minutes
Porcini	Slices	Frying pan	High heat	5 minutes
Spinach	Whole	Frying pan	Medium heat	5 minutes
Tomatoes	Whole	Oven	160°C (325°F/Gas Mark 3)	25 minutes
Tomatoes	Small cubes	Frying pan	Medium heat	1 minute

Peeling and Coring Tomatoes the Quick Way

1. Cut out the stem of the tomato with a sharp knife.

2. Cut the tomato into quarters.

3. Cut out the core with a knife and scrape out the remaining seeds.

4. Using a sharp knife, cut the flesh off the skins. While you are doing this, tilt the knife at a slight downward angle, so that all of the flesh is loosened from the skin.

5. Cut the tomato quarters into small cubes and use them for sauces, salads or fillings. The tomato quarters can also be used to garnish fish fillets or can be stuffed with quark and herbs, or with olive paste.

5

Peeling and Coring Tomatoes the Proper Way

Cut out the stem of the tomato with a sharp knife. Score the tomato skin crosswise. Bring water to the boil and place the tomatoes in it for 5–10 seconds.

As soon as the skin starts to loosen, remove the tomatoes from the water.

Put them into a bowl of iced water immediately, to interrupt the cooking process.

4. Carefully remove the skin with a small knife.

5. Then cut the tomatoes into quarters, cut out the core with a sharp knife and use the flesh as needed.

 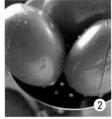   

Deseeding Tomatoes

Cut the seeds out of the tomatoes, as they make salads or sauces watery. The tomato flesh can be cut into cubes or strips and used as a topping for bruschetta or pasta dishes, or for salads.

Use the seeds in the preparation of sauces or soups.

Dicing Onions

  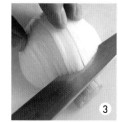   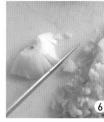

1. Cut the peeled onion in half lengthways.

2. With a sharp knife, cut the onion halves into slices lengthways. You should not cut completely through the slices at the stem, so that they hold together and the onion doesn't fall apart.

3. At a right angle to the slices, make a horizontal cut into the lower third of the onion half, almost to the end.

4. Make another cut into the upper third of the onion half.

5. Now cut the onion half vertically to dice it finely. By cutting through the onion half twice, as described above, fine dice will be created.

6. The stem end, which held the slices together, will be left over.

7. Cut as much onion as possible from the stem end to avoid excessive waste.

Preparing Spring Onions with Green Tops

1. Depending on the size of the onions, a bunch may consist of three to five onions.

2. Cut off the upper third of the green tops and discard.

3. Cut off the root base.

4. Cut off the remaining green part at the top, which will be used later.

5. Remove the outer onion skin.

6. Cut off any bad parts of the stem base.

7. Cut the green tops into fine slices and use them for soup or as a garnish for salads.

8. The white part is best used raw, as young onions are not that hot, but are very flavourful nonetheless.

   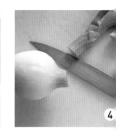

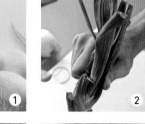  

Avoiding Blunt Knives When You Work with Onions

If your knife is blunt, the onions will be more crushed than cut, as you can't really cut thin slices.

The onion will disintegrate when it is cut and the danger of cutting yourself will be much greater than when you are using a sharp knife.

Furthermore, if a blunt knife is used, the result is very irregular, squashed dice and far too much waste is created.

The onion on the left was cut with a blunt knife: the edges are translucent; the onion was crushed and is probably bitter. The onion on the right was cut with a sharp knife: the cut is smooth and the onion is still juicy.

Cutting Onions into Strips

Cut the onion in half lengthways.

Cut the stem and the root ends off on a slight inward slant.

Cut the onion half into thin strips lengthways. These strips are ideal for stews, as they cook better in this form and are a good way of thickening sauces.

Preparing and Washing Leeks

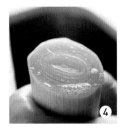

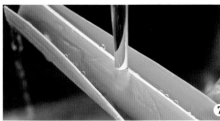

1. Cut approximately 1 cm (½ inch) off the root base.

2. Cut through the stalks at the top.

3. Tear the outer leaves off the leek.

4. You can determine whether the leek is fresh by piercing the stalk. Juice will ooze out at the point of the cut if the leek is fresh. Otherwise, it will be dry and woody.

5. Peel off the outer leaves of the green part of the leek and use only the white leaves.

6. Rinse the white and light green part of the leek under running water so that all of the dirt will be washed away.

7. Wash out the bright green parts of the leek under cold water as well.

Preparing and Washing Young Leeks

1. Cut the upper green leaves off the young leeks.

2. Cut off the root base and remove the first leek leaf, as it is usually limp.

3. Wash the leeks well under running water, as earth usually clings to the leaves.

4. Let them drain well after washing, and either use them immediately or put them in containers, cover and store in the refrigerator.

Chard – Separating the Leaves and the Stalks

- Trim the bottom end of the stalk.

- Cut the leaves off the stalks.

- Chop the leaves coarsely and prepare the chard like leaf spinach.

- Cut the stalks into 5 1-cm (2 ½-inch) pieces. Steam the stalks or use them in stews.

Washing and Sorting Spinach

- Wash the spinach leaves well in copious amounts of water, several times. Remove any yellow, wilted leaves.

- Separate the leaves from the stems and keep the spinach leaves in a bowl covered with a damp cloth if they are not to be used immediately.

Cutting Pumpkin into Cubes

1. Halve the pumpkin, scrape out the seeds with a spoon and set them aside.

2. Cut the pumpkin halves into quarters and slice them into smaller segments. Use a knife to remove the skin.

3. Use a knife to remove a thin layer of the inner part of the pumpkin.

4. Cut the pieces into even thinner segments. These segments are suitable for coating in breadcrumbs or for baking in a batter.

5. Cut the pumpkin segments into 1-cm (½-inch) cubes and use them for soups, stews or gratins.

6. Clean the pumpkin seeds and roast them in the oven for approximately 30 minutes at 160°C (325°F/Gas Mark 3), sprinkle them with salt, and munch on them instead of crisps!

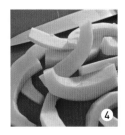

Preparing Courgettes for Stuffing

1. Cut off the stem ends and the tips of the courgettes.

2. Cut the courgettes into 3-cm (1¼-inch) pieces.

3. Hollow out the courgette pieces with a small spoon.

4. Scoop out the courgette flesh, leaving a 1-cm (½-inch) thick base, and fill the cavity with meat, cheese or Bolognese sauce.

Preparing Carrots

Cut off both ends of the carrots with a knife.

Peel the carrots lengthways, then cut them into slices, grate them or use them for soup.

Peeling and Deseeding Cucumbers

Wash the cucumber and peel it with a vegetable peeler.

Cut the cucumber in half lengthways and then either cut it into slices and use it whole for salads, or remove the seeds with a teaspoon. Cucumbers can be stuffed with meat or fish, or simply braised as a vegetable in butter and herbs.

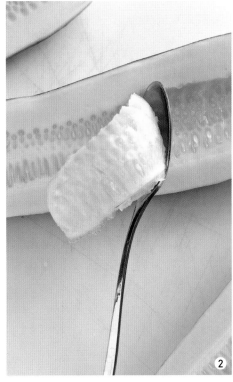

Runner Beans

1. Top and tail the beans with a knife.

2. Remove any bruised or brown spots with a small knife.

3. Cut the beans into 2-mm (⅛-inch) thick, diagonal strips and use them for a delicate bean side dish or for fermented beans with dill.

4. Another variation: cut the beans into approximately 5-cm (2-inch) pieces, cook them in salted water and sauté them with onions and bacon.

Celery Stalks

1. Cut 1 cm (½ inch) off the stump and the tops of the stalks.

2. Wash the celery stalks well under running water.

3. Divide the head into outer stalks, middle stalks, and the innermost heart stalks. Cut the heart stalks into pieces 8 cm (3¼ inches) long. Serve them with various dips or add them to salads.

4. Remove the fibres from the middle stalks in the lower part of the head.

5. Then cut the sticks diagonally into thin slices and use them for meat and vegetable dishes.

6. Use a knife to remove the brown parts from the outer sticks.

7. Then cut them into 5-cm (2-inch) pieces and use these for meat or vegetable stocks.

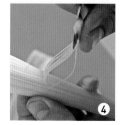
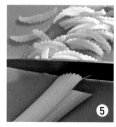
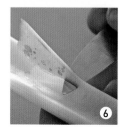

Preparing Fennel Bulb

Wash the fennel bulb well under running water.

Cut off the base.

Peel away the outer layer of the fennel bulb to remove any brown spots.

Cut 1 cm (½ inch) off the stalk to remove any brown parts.

Remove any remaining brown spots and blemishes under running water.

The prepared bulb is snow white and can now be used in the preparation of various dishes. Store the green fennel fronds in water or chop them immediately and add them to sauces or soups. Use the cut-off stalks for soup or stock.

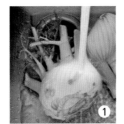

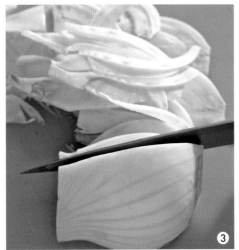

Cutting Fennel Bulb into Cubes or Strips

Cut the fennel bulb in half from the stalk base down to the bottom.

Cut it into segments and sauté them or braise them with other vegetables.

Cut the fennel bulb into thin slices, marinate these in oil and lemon juice and serve them as a salad.

Dice the fennel bulb and use it in stews and soups, or as an ingredient in vegetable dishes.

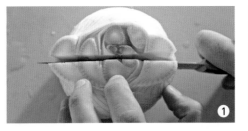
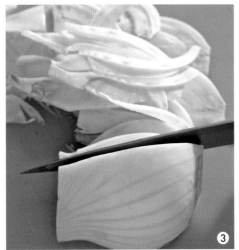

Preparing Artichokes

1. Cut the artichoke stem down to 3 cm (1¼ inches). Cut off approximately two-thirds of the upper part of the artichoke.

2. Peel off the outer petals until the bright green part is revealed.

3. Then peel off the stem and the remaining dark green parts with a small knife.

4. Scrape out the so-called 'choke' (the fibrous core) with a scoop or a small spoon.

5. Store the prepared artichoke bottoms in lemon water to prevent browning.

Marinating Raw Artichoke Bottoms

1. Cut the artichoke bottoms into thin slices.

2. Mix lemon juice, salt, ground fennel seeds and extra virgin olive oil in a bowl and marinate the artichoke slices for approximately 10 minutes.

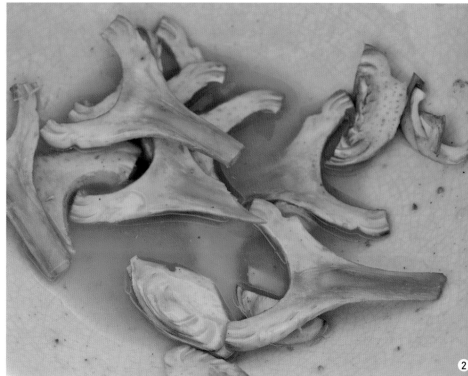

Cooking Artichokes Whole

. Remove the stem at the base and cut
ff the top half with a serrated knife.

. Put a slice of lemon on the cut surface
nd fasten it in place with kitchen twine.

. In general, only larger artichokes
hould be used in this kind of preparation,
s only then is this way of cooking them
vorth the effort.

. Cook the artichokes with some white
vine, peppercorns, a bay leaf and salt
or approximately 35 minutes, and serve
ukewarm with a herb sauce.

Frying Artichokes

. Cut the artichoke bottoms into small
egments.

. Heat some olive oil in a frying pan and
dd unpeeled garlic cloves, thyme and
he artichoke pieces.

. Season them with salt and pepper,
ry them until they are golden, and serve
hem with salad or with fish dishes.

Slicing Aubergines

1. Wash the aubergine and cut off the stem with a knife.

2. Remove brown tips or any other bruised spots.

3. Cut the aubergine into thin slices lengthways.

4. Lay the last slice flat on the chopping board and make one last horizontal cut. Aubergine slices are suitable for grilling or for coating with a herb, cheese and breadcrumb mixture.

Deseeding Peppers

1. Wash the pepper and cut it in half lengthways from the stem to the tip.

2. Open the pepper.

3. Twist the green stem out and cut the pepper into quarters.

4. Cut out the white membranes and use the pepper quarters as desired.

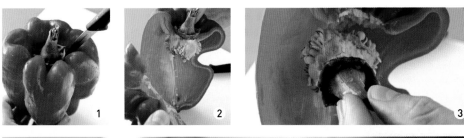

Preparing Chilli Peppers for Stuffing

1. Cut out a cone-shaped section to remove the green stem.

2. Cut out the white membranes and the seeds by inserting a knife as far as you can into the pepper. Then wash the pepper and use it as desired.

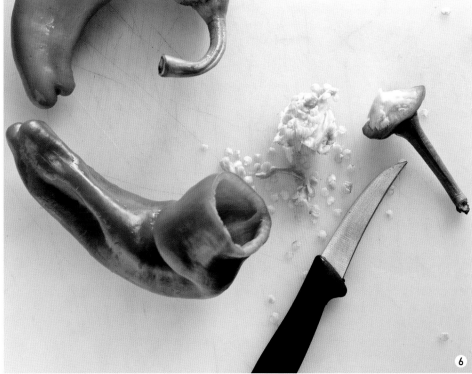

Button Mushrooms

1. Cut off the stalk along with any soil residue.

2. Rub the cap with kitchen paper and clean it carefully.

3. Put the clean mushrooms into a dry bowl.

4. For sauces or omelettes, use a long knife to cut the mushrooms into thin slices.

5. The mushroom gills must be light brown and the caps must be tightly closed. These mushrooms have the best flavour.

6. Cut the caps into quarters if you want to marinate them as a starter or use them for mushroom ragout.

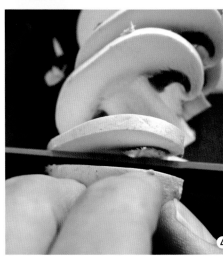

Oyster Mushrooms

Cut off the stalk of the oyster mushroom level with the cap.

Never cut oyster mushrooms, but always tear them by hand along the gills into chunks of the desired size.

Store oyster mushrooms in a cool place and use them as quickly as possible.

Oyster mushrooms can be grilled whole or breaded like cutlets.

Shiitake Mushrooms

Cover dried shiitake mushrooms with cold water.

Let them soften in cold water for hours. Smaller shiitake mushrooms will take less time.

3. Cut off the stalks of the shiitake mushrooms, as these remain hard. Cut the caps into slices and use for stuffing and for Asian dishes.

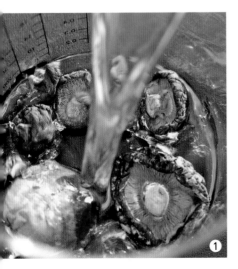

2 shallots

500 g (1 lb 2 oz) spinach leaves

40 g (1½ oz) butter

1 pinch of salt
1 pinch of black pepper

1 pinch of nutmeg, freshly grated

1 garlic clove

Steamed Spinach Leaves

1. Peel the shallots and dice them finely. Clean the spinach leaves and remove the stems (see p. 351). Melt the butter in a saucepan, add the shallots, and sweat them briefly.

2. Add the spinach leaves and season with salt, pepper and nutmeg. Steam them for approximately 3 minutes until the liquid is reduced.

3. Spear the peeled garlic clove with a fork and stir the spinach leaves with it, so that they acquire a light, subtle garlic flavour. Serve the spinach leaves as an accompaniment to prime boiled beef, grilled sole or other saltwater fish.

■ Creamed spinach: Pour 100 ml (3½ fl oz) cream onto the spinach and let it reduce. Blend the cream and spinach with a hand-held blender until smooth. Serve the creamed spinach with fried potatoes, fried eggs, prime boiled beef, roasted veal medallions, or as an accompaniment to potatoes en papillote (see p. 312) with roast beef.

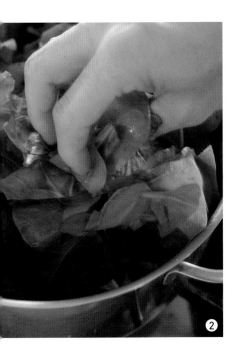

350 g (12 oz) flour

 2 tsp baking powder

 3 eggs

 400 ml (13½ fl oz) beer

 150 ml (5 fl oz) vegetable oil

 ½ tsp salt

 3 courgettes

 4 sprigs fresh thyme

 200 g (7 oz) yogurt

 Juice of 1 lemon

 1 pinch of salt
1 pinch of black pepper

 2 litres (3½ pints) groundnut oil

①

Courgettes in a Thyme-flavoured Batter with Yogurt Sauce

1. Put the flour and the baking powder into a bowl and mix them. Separate the eggs, and add the egg yolks. Pour the beer in slowly and mix everything with a wire whisk until a smooth batter is created. Then, stir in the vegetable oil, so that the batter will become nice and crisp. Beat the egg whites with salt until semi-stiff peaks form, and fold them into the batter.

2. Wash the courgettes and cut into 1-cm (½-inch) thick slices. Pluck the thyme leaves from the stems and coat them and the courgette slices with batter. Put the yogurt into a bowl and season to taste with the lemon juice, salt and pepper, and stir the mixture until it's smooth.

3. Heat the groundnut oil to 160°C (325°F) in a wide saucepan and fry the batter-coated courgette slices until golden on both sides. Then let them drain on kitchen paper and sprinkle them lightly with salt. Serve the courgette slices on a platter with the yogurt dip.

■ The batter can also be prepared with white wine or mineral water. Batter-coated fried basil or sage leaves provide a delicious snack with an aperitif.

250 g (9 oz) mixed meat mince

 150 g (5½ oz) goat's cheese

 1 egg

 2 tbsp breadcrumbs

 3 spring onions

 1 tbsp basil strips

 ½ tsp salt
1 pinch of black pepper

 1 tsp dried oregano

 2 large aubergines

 4 tbsp olive oil

 500 ml (17 fl oz) tomato juice

 1 tbsp sugar

Stuffed Aubergines with Goat's Cheese and Oregano

1. Preheat the oven to 180°C (350°F/ Gas Mark 4). Put the minced meat, the coarsely mashed goat's cheese, the egg, the breadcrumbs, the sliced spring onion rings, the basil strips, salt, black pepper and oregano into a large bowl.

2. Mix the filling by hand. Do not knead it, however, as the pieces of cheese will need to be distinguishable in the finished dish.

3. Cut off the stems of the aubergines and cut them in half lengthways, cutting off some of the curved base, so they will be more stable and less likely to tip over.

4. Scoop out the inside of the aubergine with a teaspoon.

5. Grease a casserole dish with olive oil and put the aubergine halves into it. Fill them with the meat mixture, put them into the oven, and bake them for approximately 45 minutes. Add water once in a while and baste them with the juice produced. Mix the tomato juice with the sugar, salt and black pepper, and pour it over the aubergine halves. Bake for 15 minutes longer.

Arrange an aubergine half with sauce on each plate to serve.

* * * 80

■ Stuff courgettes, peppers or cucumbers with the same mixture and braise them in the oven.

1 garlic clove

 4 tbsp extra virgin olive oil

 1 pinch of salt
1 pinch of black pepper

 450 g (1 lb) tomatoes

 1 sprig fresh rosemary

 125 g (4½ oz) mozzarella cheese

 2 slices of toast

Tomatoes au Gratin with Rosemary and Mozzarella Cheese

1. Preheat the oven to 190°C (375°F/ Gas Mark 5). Rub a casserole dish with the garlic clove, drizzle it with 1 tbsp of the olive oil and season it with salt and pepper.

2. Peel the tomatoes (see p. 347) and cut them into 5-mm (¼-inch) thick discs. Put them into a casserole dish in layers and season them with salt and pepper.

3. Remove the rosemary needles from the stem and chop them finely. Halve the mozzarella and cut it into discs. Cut the crusts off the bread and grate it or put it into the blender to make fine breadcrumbs. Distribute the mozzarella evenly between the tomato

slices and sprinkle everything with rosemary.

4. Sprinkle the breadcrumbs on the gratin and drizzle it with the remaining olive oil. Bake the casserole for approximately 30 minutes in the oven. The tomatoes are ready when the cheese has a brilliant golden hue. Serve from the casserole dish.

50

■ This tomato casserole goes very well with fried veal cutlets, spring chicken, or a grilled chicken breast fillet. It can also be served as a main course with toasted garli bread and a green salad. If you are serving it as a main course, double the quantities the ingredients.

2

3

4

40 g (1½ oz) cooked ham

 1 young onion

 20 g (⅔ oz) butter

 150 g (5½ oz) mangetout

 450 g (1 lb) peas

 1 pinch of salt

 1 pinch of sugar

 1 pinch of white pepper

 150 ml (5 fl oz) chicken stock

½ head of lettuce

2 sprigs fresh mint

20 g (⅔ oz) chilled butter

Mangetout Stewed with Lettuce and Ham Strips

1. Cut the cooked ham into thin strips. Peel the onion and finely dice it. Let the butter foam in a saucepan, add the cooked ham and the onion, and sauté them gently.

2. Clean the mangetout, remove the stems, and cut the pods diagonally, twice. Add the pods to the ham with the peas, mix them, and season them with the salt, sugar and white pepper.

3. Pour in the chicken stock, cover the pan, and stew for approximately 5 minutes.

4. Wash the lettuce and cut it into strips Likewise, chop the mint into fine strips. Add the lettuce and the mint to the peas and mix in the chilled butter. Season them to taste and serve them in bowls.

■ Fresh peas are the most delicious kind for this recipe. To get 450 g (1 lb) shelled peas, you will need at least double the amount of pea pods. This dish is very nice when served as an accompaniment to poultry such as pigeon or Bresse chicken and is also delicious with roast veal.

2 shallots

 1 bunch fresh parsley

 1 garlic clove

 600 g (1 lb 5 oz) shelled broad beans

 40 g (1½ oz) butter

 1 pinch of salt
1 pinch of black pepper

 1 pinch of nutmeg, freshly grated

Shelled Beans with Garlic and Onions

1. Peel the shallots and chop them finely. Wash the parsley, pluck the leaves, and chop them finely. Peel the garlic and chop it finely as well. Bring water to the boil in a saucepan, add the beans, and cook them for 1 minute. Put the beans in a colander and rinse them under cold water.

2. Remove the white pod from the beans with your fingers. Very small beans can also be cooked in their pods.

3. Let the butter foam up in a frying pan, add the shallots and garlic and sauté them gently until they are translucent.

4. Add the shelled beans and season them with salt, pepper and nutmeg.

5. Let them sauté gently for 2 to 3 minutes more, then add the parsley, mix and arrange the beans on plates to serve.

■ For 600 g (1 lb 5 oz) beans, you will need 3 kg (6 lb 8 oz) fresh broad beans. This dish can also be prepared with wax beans, or a combination of various kinds. However, the beans should be cooked in salted water first until they are *al dente*.

2 red peppers

 1 green pepper

 3 young onions

 500 g (1 lb 2 oz) potatoes

 2 garlic cloves

 Rind of 1 lemon

 ½ tsp caraway seeds

 3 tbsp vegetable oil

 2 tsp ground sweet paprika

 1 pinch of salt
1 pinch of black pepper

 1.2 litres (2 pints) vegetable stock

Vegetable Goulash

1. Halve, deseed and clean the red and green peppers. Then cut them into approximately 2-cm (¾-inch) pieces. Peel, halve and dice the onions coarsely. Peel the potatoes, cut them into 2-cm (¾-inch) pieces and store them covered with cold water, so that they don't go brown. Peel the garlic cloves and chop finely with the lemon rind. Prepare the caraway seeds by drizzling some oil on them and then chopping them.

2. Heat the oil in a stainless steel pan and sauté the onions in it. Then pour the potato pieces into a colander and let them drain well. Add the potatoes to the onions and sauté gently for 5 minutes.

3. Sprinkle the garlic, lemon rind, caraway seeds and paprika on the potatoes and onions, and sweat slightly.

4. Add the red and green peppers, season with salt and pepper, and sauté them gently for a few minutes over medium heat.

5. Pour in the vegetable stock and let the mixture simmer slowly for approximately 25 minutes, stirring occasionally. Ladle the goulash into soup plates and serve with rye bread.

■ Courgettes and whole cherry tomatoes can be used instead of green and red peppers.

55

2 spring onions

 2 sprigs fresh parsley

 400 g (14 oz) flat mushrooms

 1 garlic clove

 3 tbsp vegetable oil

 ½ tsp salt
1 pinch of black pepper

 ½ tsp caraway seeds

 4 slices of brown country bread

Fried Flat Mushrooms on Garlic-Caraway Bread

1. Wash and clean the spring onions and slice them into rings. Wash the parsley, shake it dry and chop finely.

2. Clean the mushrooms, remove the stalks, and put the caps upside down into a frying pan.

3. Peel the garlic clove and chop it finely. Pour the oil over the mushrooms and braise them gently.

4. Sprinkle the spring onions, garlic and parsley on top, and season the mushrooms with salt and pepper. Drizzle some oil on the caraway seeds and chop them, then add them to the frying pan.

Remove the mushrooms from the frying pan with some of the oil and arrange them on the slices of bread.

■ Button mushrooms, oyster mushrooms, shiitake mushrooms or king oyster mushrooms can also be used for this recipe.

377

600 g (1 lb 5 oz) chanterelles

 2 shallots

 40 g (1½ oz) butter

 1 pinch of salt
1 pinch of black pepper

 1 pinch of nutmeg, freshly grated

 ½ bunch fresh parsley

 200 ml (7 fl oz) cream

 2 tbsp crème fraîche

 Juice of 1 lemon

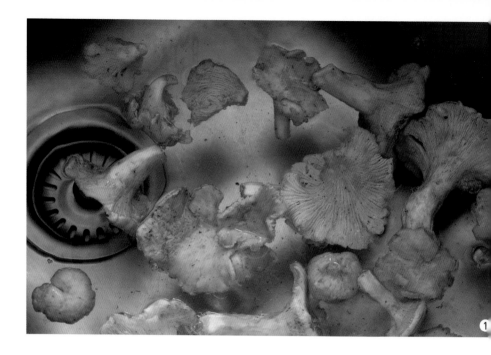

1

Mushroom Ragout with Nutmeg and Parsley

1. Remove the dirt from the chanterelles with a small knife and wash them in cold water – only briefly, so that they do not become saturated. Put them on kitchen paper immediately to drain.

2. Cut the large chanterelles into 5-mm (¼-inch) slices and leave the small ones whole. Peel the shallots and chop them finely.

3. Melt the butter in a wide saucepan and sweat the shallots gently until they are translucent, stirring them constantly with a wooden spoon.

4. Add the chanterelles, season them with salt, pepper and nutmeg, and sweat them for 2 to 3 minutes. Meanwhile, wash the parsley, pluck the leaves and chop them finely.

5. Add the cream and the crème fraîche and simmer the ragout gently for approximately 5 minutes. Finally, season it with the lemon juice, mix with the finely chopped parsley and serve.

■ Other wild mushrooms, such as porcini, bay boletus, birch boletus or morels, can be prepared in the same way. You can also use a mix of different mushrooms, and serve it as a main dish with bread dumplings.

1 medium-sized beetroot, cooked and peeled

 2 eggs

300 g (10½ oz) ricotta cheese

 1 pinch of salt
1 pinch of black pepper

1 pack spring roll wrappers

2 litres (3½ pints) vegetable oil for deep-frying

Deep-fried Beetroot-Ricotta Pockets

1. Finely grate the beetroot.

2. Separate the eggs and add the egg yolks, ricotta cheese, salt and black pepper to the beetroot. Set the egg whites aside.

3. Mix the ingredients well and season to taste.

4. Lay the spring roll wrappers flat on a work surface and fold the right corner to the centre. Brush the outer edge with egg white.

5. Fold the left corner to the centre and place it on top of the right corner. Press it lightly so that the sides stick together.

6. Lift the combined corners to open the pocket created and stuff with 2 tsp of the filling.

7. Continue to press the filling into the corners and paint the upper section with egg white.

»

■ These pockets can be stuffed with any filling you like. However, it must not be too moist, as the pockets would burst open during the deep-frying process.

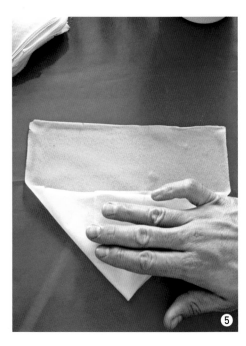

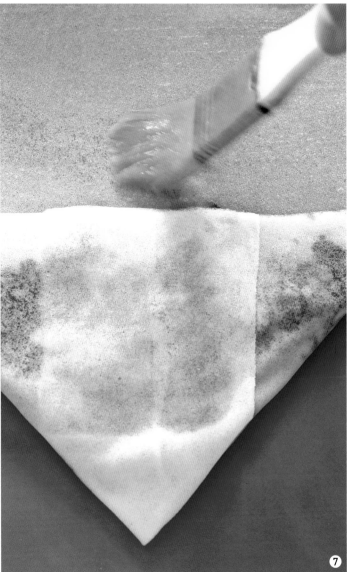

8. Fold the upper half down.

9. Turn the pocket over and paint the protruding corners with egg white.

10. Turn down the ends and seal the pocket well so that the filling cannot come out when the pocket is being deep-fried.

11. Heat the oil to 160°C (325°F) in a saucepan and deep-fry the pockets in it for 3 minutes. Let the pockets drain briefly on kitchen paper.

Serve as a snack with wine.

■ These pockets can also be prepared in advance and stored in the freezer for later use as desired.

180 g (6 oz) carrots

 80 g (2¾ oz) celery

 60 g (2¼ oz) shallots

 600 g (1 lb 5 oz) pumpkin

 2.5-cm (1-inch) piece of ginger

 30 g (1 oz) butter

 20 ml (⅔ fl oz) olive oil

 1 pinch of salt
1 pinch of black pepper

 1 tsp sweet paprika

 1 pinch of curry powder

 40 g (1½ oz) tomato ketchup

 1 bay leaf

 200 ml (7 fl oz) chicken stock

 250 ml (8½ fl oz) cream

 250 ml (8½ fl oz) milk

 1 pinch of nutmeg, freshly grated

 80 g (2¾ oz) Fontina cheese

Pumpkin au Gratin with Fontina Cheese and Paprika

1. Preheat the oven to 190°C (375°F/ Gas Mark 5). Chop the carrots, celery and shallots into 5-mm (¼-inch) cubes and the pumpkin into 2-cm (¾-inch) cubes (see p. 352). Peel the ginger and grate it finely.

2. Let the butter and the olive oil foam up in a wide saucepan. Add the shallots and sauté them until they are translucent and then sauté the diced celery and carrots. Add the pumpkin, season with salt, pepper, grated ginger, paprika and curry powder and brown for 5 minutes.

3. Push the ingredients to the sides of the pan and put the tomato ketchup in the middle. Brown the tomato ketchup slightly and then mix it with the other ingredients.

4. Add the bay leaf and pour in the chicken stock. Let it simmer for approximately 5 minutes, stirring constantly. Then pour in the cream and the milk and bring the mixture to the boil. Let it simmer gently for 5 more minutes.

5. Remove the bay leaf, season the pumpkin with nutmeg and spread it evenly in a casserole dish. Grate the cheese finely and sprinkle it on top of the pumpkin gratin. Put the casserole dish in the oven and bake it for approximately 15 minutes. Cover the dish with kitchen foil if necessary to ensure that the cheese does not brown too much.

■ This gratin can also be served as a main dish; the quantities specified above will serve two people.

1 tbsp butter

 1 small onion

 ½ medium-sized cauliflower

 1 pinch of salt
1 pinch of black pepper

 1 pinch of nutmeg, freshly grated

 250 ml (8½ fl oz) vegetable or
chicken stock

 400 ml (13½ fl oz) cream

Fluffy Cauliflower Purée

1. Melt the butter in a saucepan, chop the peeled onion into strips, and sauté it gently in the butter until it is translucent. Cut the cauliflower into florets first, wash it well, then cut the florets into slices. Sauté the cauliflower gently for approximately 3 minutes, seasoning it with salt, black pepper and nutmeg.

2. Pour in the stock, cover the pan and cook the cauliflower for 10 minutes.

3. Add the cream and bring the mixture to the boil. Remove the lid and simmer the mixture gently for 5 minutes longer.

4. Put the mixture in a blender and purée it finely. Season it to taste once again.

5. Fill a siphon three-quarters full with the mixture and close it. Twist a nitrogen capsule onto the siphon and shake it gently a few times.

Spray the foam into a bowl and serve it immediately as a side dish. It's wonderfully light and delicious.

■ Serve the cauliflower purée with roast poultry or fish. It's also delicious with boiled potatoes.

*
* 40
*
*

1 onion

 700 g (1 lb 9 oz) cauliflower

 ½ bunch fresh coriander

 6 tbsp vegetable oil

 1 tsp cumin seeds

 6 star anise

 1 pinch of salt
1 pinch of black pepper

 150 ml (5 fl oz) water

 180 g (6 oz) cherry tomatoes

1

Ayurvedic Cauliflower with Tomatoes and Cumin

1. Peel the onion and chop finely. Divide the cauliflower into small florets. Wash the coriander and chop it coarsely.

2. Heat 4 tsp of the vegetable oil in a long-handled saucepan. Lightly brown the cumin seeds and the star anise in the oil but do not cook them for too long, or the spices will burn and become bitter or lose some of their flavour.

3. Add the cauliflower and sauté it gently for approximately 5 minutes. Add salt and pepper to taste, then add the water and cook for 5 minutes more with the lid closed until the liquid is reduced.

4. Next, add the whole cherry tomatoes and fry them gently for 5 minutes. Heat up the remaining oil in a frying pan and fry the onions until they are golden. Arrange the cauliflower on plates and p▪ the onion and the coriander on top.

■ Serve the cauliflower with a cool, light yogurt-cinnamon sauce. Instead of cauliflower, you can add a choice of broccoli, kohlrabi or carrots. When they are prepared in this way, vegetables taste quite different and are particularly spicy.

600 g (1 lb 5 oz) carrots

 3 tbsp olive oil

 1 pinch of salt

 1½ tbsp sugar

 1 pinch of black pepper

 2 tbsp balsamic vinegar

Glazed Carrots

1. Peel the carrots, halve them lengthways and cut them diagonally into 1-cm (½-inch) wide strips.

2. Heat the olive oil in a frying pan, add the carrots, season them with the salt, sugar and pepper and sauté them gently, constantly stirring them. The sugar will brown slightly when you are doing this. If the frying pan becomes too hot, you can add some water.

3. Finally, sprinkle the carrots with the balsamic vinegar. This provides a nice balance for the sugar and lends the carrots a sweet-and-sour character.

■ Glazed carrots can also be served cold with roasted pine nuts and finely chopped basil as an antipasto. They are a delicious accompaniment to roast chicken or grilled lamb chops. It is important not to fry them at an excessively high temperature, or the sugar will become too dark.

600 g (1 lb 5 oz) carrots

 30 g (1 oz) butter

 1 pinch of sugar

 1 pinch of white pepper

 200 ml (7 fl oz) Vichy mineral water

Vichy Carrots

1. Peel the carrots and cut them into thin slices. The most suitable carrots for this recipe are young carrots with green tops, as they taste fresh and sweet.

2. Let the butter foam up in a saucepan, add the carrot slices, season them with the sugar and pepper, and sauté them briefly. Add the mineral water, just covering the carrots in liquid, and then bring them to the boil.

3. Steam the carrots for approximately 10 minutes with a closed lid, until almost all of the liquid has evaporated. Continue to stir the carrots occasionally so that they cook evenly.

■ In this recipe, Vichy mineral water is used as a substitute for salted water. If you like your carrots a little saltier, salt can be added to taste. It's important to use young carrots with green tops as they have a very delicate taste. Serve as an accompaniment to small veal cutlets or a roast.

200 g (7 oz) flour

 140 g (5 oz) butter

 ½ tsp salt

 4 eggs

 1 tbsp water

 250 g (9 oz) leeks

 100 g (3½ oz) bacon rashers

 1 pinch of black pepper

 150 ml (5 fl oz) cream

 1 pinch of nutmeg, freshly grated

 200 g (7 oz) Gruyère cheese

Quiche Lorraine with Leeks

1. Sift the flour onto a work surface. By hand, work half of the chilled butter and the salt into the flour. Then add 1 egg and the water, and knead the mixture quickly into a smooth dough, so that the butter doesn't become too warm and the dough doesn't puff up when it's baked. Wrap it in cling film and leave it to rest in the refrigerator for 30 minutes. Then put the dough on a floured surface and roll it out evenly with a rolling pin until it is approximately 3 mm (⅛ inch) thick. Dust the dough with flour, so that it doesn't stick to the work surface.

2. Place an oval flan dish on the rolled-out dough to check that the dough is large enough. Roll the dough around the rolling pin.

3. Coat the flan dish with 10 g (¼ oz) butter, and unroll the dough, fitting it into the dish so that it doesn't tear.

4. Press the dough into the edges of the dish and cut off the surplus projecting over the sides. Then prick the dough with a fork so that it doesn't puff up during baking but bakes evenly. Put the dish in the refrigerator until it is needed.

5. Preheat the oven to 180°C (350°F/Gas Mark 4). Clean the leeks, remove the outer leaves, and cut the stalks into rings. Wash them under running water and let them drain well. Cut the bacon rashers into fine strips. Let the rest of the butter foam up in a frying pan, gently sauté the bacon strips in it briefly, and

+ 30 minutes resting time

✳
✳ 45
✳

■ Instead of leeks, you can use button or oyster mushrooms. This quiche is also delicious with ratatouille or fennel bulb and peppers.

add the leeks. Season the mixture to taste with salt and pepper and sauté it gently for approximately 5 minutes, until the leeks have wilted and the liquid has reduced.

6. Whisk the cream with the remaining eggs, salt, pepper and nutmeg in a container. Grate the cheese finely and set it aside.

7. Remove the oval flan dish from the refrigerator and spread the leek-bacon filling in the bottom.

8. Spread the grated cheese on top of the filling and cover it with the cream-egg mixture. Bake in the oven for 15–20 minutes. Then let it rest briefly, cut it into portions, and arrange them on plates to serve.

Boiled White Asparagus

Peel **500 g (1 lb 2 oz) white asparagus spears** evenly from the tip downwards, and cut approximately 1 cm (½ inch) off the base. Bring **2 litres (3½ pints) water** to the boil in a large saucepan and add **1 tbsp salt, 1½ tbsp sugar** and the juice of **½ lemon**. Add the asparagus to the boiling water and cook it for approximately 6–8 minutes, depending on the size and thickness of the spears. Melt **40 g (1½ oz) butter** in a frying pan. Remove the asparagus from the water, toss it carefully in the frying pan and serve it with chopped parsley.

■ You can use the water in which the asparagus was cooked as asparagus stock, or you can save it to use as the basis for asparagus soup.

Boiled Green Asparagus

Peel the lower half of **500 g (1 lb 2 oz) green asparagus spears** and cut approximately 1 cm (½ inch) off the base. Add **1½ tbsp salt** to **2 litres (3½ pints) water** in a large saucepan and bring to the boil. Add the asparagus and cook for approximately 5 minutes, depending on the size and thickness of the spears. You can use the tip of a knife to check whether the end of the spears are already soft enough. Grind **2 slices of white bread** in a food processor. Let **50 g (1¾ oz) butter** melt in a frying pan, add the breadcrumbs and brown them slowly, stirring continuously to prevent their becoming too dark. Then place the asparagus onto plates and serve them with the toasted breadcrumbs arranged on top.

Stir-fried White Asparagus

Peel **500 g (1 lb 2 oz) white asparagus spears** evenly from the tip downwards, and cut approximately 1 cm (½ inch) off the base. Cut the spears diagonally into 5-cm (2-inch) lengths. Heat **2 tbsp sunflower oil** in a frying pan and add the asparagus. Season it with **1 pinch of salt, 1 pinch of black pepper** and **1 tbsp sugar**, and sauté it gently. Wash **2 oranges**, peel off strips of rinds with a vegetable peeler, and cut them into very narrow strips with a sharp knife. Sprinkle these strips on the asparagus spears. Squeeze the oranges and strain the juice through a fine sieve to remove the pulp. Pour the orange juice on the asparagus spears and cook them for 6–8 minutes. This dish is ready when the orange juice has reduced and the asparagus is golden yellow.

■ This side dish goes very well with roast breast of duck, baked salmon fillet, or veal medallions with Hollandaise sauce (see p. 152).

300 g (10½ oz) onions

 2 tbsp sugar

 100 ml (3½ fl oz) water

 60 g (2¼ oz) smoked streaky bacon

 3 tbsp vegetable oil

 2 bay leaves

 3 cloves

 1 garlic clove

 10 black peppercorns

 5 juniper berries

 150 ml (5 fl oz) white wine

 800 g (1 lb 12 oz) fresh sauerkraut

 750 ml (1¼ pints) chicken stock

 ½ tsp salt

 ½ potato

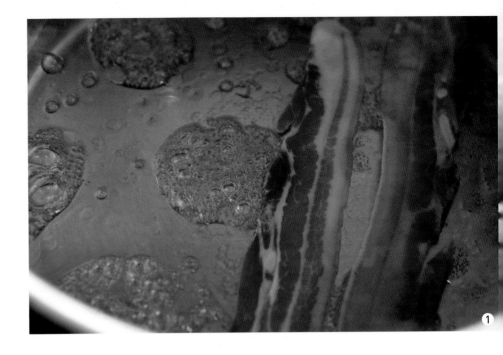

Sauerkraut with Bacon

1. Peel and halve the onions and cut them into thin strips. Boil the sugar in a saucepan with the water and heat it until it turns a bright golden colour and caramelises. Place the bacon in the caramel, add the vegetable oil, and brown them slightly.

2. Turn the bacon after a few minutes and add the onions.

3. Add the bay leaves, cloves, garlic, peppercorns and juniper berries, and sauté them gently until the onions are translucent.

4. As soon as the onions are translucent, add the white wine and let it boil away completely. Loosen the scrapings with a wooden spoon.

5. Add the sauerkraut and spread it evenly in the pan, pour in the chicken stock, and season it with salt. Cover the pan and let the mixture simmer gently over moderate heat for approximately 40 minutes. About 5 minutes before the end of cooking, grate the potato finely and mix it with the sauerkraut. The potato starch will bind the sauerkraut, so that it is nice and shiny at the end. Remove the peppercorns before serving the sauerkraut.

■ Sauerkraut goes well with loin ribs and smoked sausages. Depending on the use, you can add goose or pork fat instead of oil. The spices are easier to remove from the sauerkraut later if you put them into a little sachet before adding them.

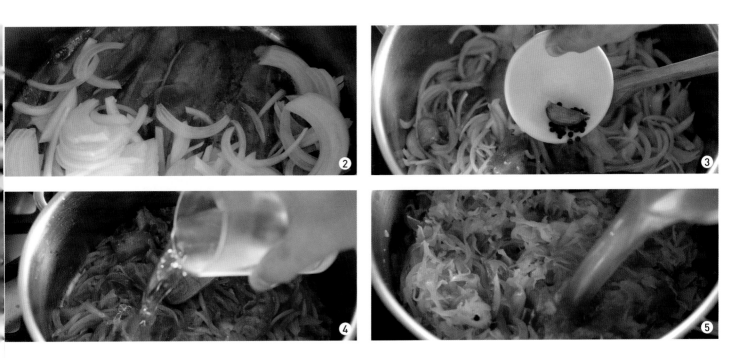

Plant Proteins

Contents

Types of Plant Protein

If you have never explored vegetarian cuisine, you may never have been concerned with plant proteins. Some of the most important basic ingredients in a vegetarian diet are tofu, soya milk, seitan, tempeh and yuba. Most of these exotic-sounding ingredients originate from Asia.

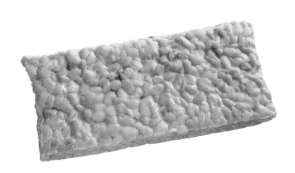

Tempeh

Tempeh probably originated in Indonesia. It is made by a fermentation process that binds soya beans. However, there are varieties that are made of kidney beans or peanuts. It has a strong flavour. Don't worry about grey or black speckles: these are normal. However, beware of tempeh that is speckled pink, yellow or blue and may have a foul odour – this is an indication that it was not fermented properly.

Seitan

Seitan is made from gluten-rich wheat flour and water. Its texture is very similar to that of meat. It is believed to have originated in Chinese cuisine, and is a popular meat substitute used in many parts of Asia.

Yuba pockets

Yuba is a meat substitute from Japan with a nutty flavour. Yuba is the skin that forms when soya milk is boiled. Despite its strong flavour, soya milk is used just like cow's milk. Yuba is a by-product of the tofu-making process.

Miso

Miso is a seasoning produced by fermenting soya beans. Dark miso is typically more salty and the lighter kind is sweeter in flavour.

Tofu

Tofu is basically solidified soya milk. It has very little flavour of its own,
so it can be used with a variety of ingredients. Smoked tofu and tofu
flavoured with herbs are also available.

100 g (3½ oz) spinach leaves

 80 g (2¾ oz) tofu

 1 litre (1¾ pints) water

 1 sheet dried kombu seaweed

 1 tbsp miso paste

1 tbsp sesame oil

Miso Soup with Spinach and Tofu

1. Wash the spinach leaves and separate them. Cut into 5-mm (¼-inch) wide strips. Cut the tofu, which should be soft and fresh, into 1-cm (½-inch) large cubes and set aside for later.

2. Put the water, the kombu and the miso paste together in a saucepan and simmer slowly for about 10 minutes.

3. Remove the kombu.

4. Add the spinach strips and tofu cubes and bring to the boil. Serve in soup bowls. If you like, sprinkle some sesame oil over it.

■ The high glutamic acid content of the miso paste enhances the soup's flavour and provides just the right amount of tastiness.

1 red pepper

 200 g (7 oz) yogurt

 1 pinch of salt
1 pinch of black pepper

 Juice of ½ a lemon

 1 tsp miso paste

 70 g (2½ oz) sugar

 100 ml (3½ oz) red wine vinegar

 400 g (14 oz) tempeh

 1 litre (1¾ pints) groundnut oil

1

Fried Tempeh with Various Dips

1. Cut the red pepper into quarters, deseed it and purée it using a food processor.

2. Put the yogurt in a bowl. Mix with the salt, pepper, lemon juice and miso paste. Cover and place in the refrigerator until ready to use. Put the sugar and red wine vinegar in a small saucepan and bring to the boil.

3. Then add the puréed pepper and slowly simmer for about 15 minutes until it thickens to a paste-like consistency. Cool, transfer to serving bowls and set aside.

4. Cut the tempeh into 4-cm (1½-inch) cubes, and fry for about 3 minutes in groundnut oil preheated to 170°C (340°F). This gives the tempeh a strong, nutty flavour.

5. Remove the tempeh from the oil with a slotted spoon and let it drain on kitchen paper. Divide between small bowls and serve as a starter alongside the yogurt and pepper dips.

■ Fried tempeh is also delicious on a salad of bean sprouts and carrots with various spicy sauces.

250 g (9 oz) red cherry tomatoes

 50 g (1¾ oz) yellow cherry tomatoes

 500 g (1 lb 2 oz) tofu

 ½ bunch fresh Thai basil

 150 g (5½ oz) baby corn

 2 tbsp groundnut oil

 1 tbsp soft brown sugar

 1 tsp red curry paste

 600 ml (1 pint) coconut milk

 3 tbsp soya sauce

Tofu in Hot Curry Sauce with Thai Basil and Baby Corn

1. Wash the cherry tomatoes. Cut the tofu into 3-cm (1¼-inch) cubes. Wash the Thai basil and pluck the leaves. Wash the baby corn and cut twice diagonally.

2. Heat the oil in a saucepan. Caramelise the sugar and red curry paste, and then add the coconut milk. Season with the soya sauce and simmer for an additional 3 minutes.

3. Add the tofu cubes, cherry tomatoes and baby corn, and simmer for another 3 minutes while stirring.

4. Mix in the basil leaves, left whole, reserving a few. Serve the curry in bowls and garnish with the reserved basil leaves.

■ For anyone who enjoys a more fruity curry, adding fresh pineapple or mango cut into small cubes does the trick. You can also replace the Thai basil with fresh coriander. For additional ingredients, try beans and aubergines.

400 g (14 oz) tofu

 2 garlic cloves

 10 anchovies

 500 g (1 lb 2 oz) cauliflower

 3 tbsp oil

 1 pinch of salt
1 pinch of black pepper

 500g (1 lb 2 oz) cooked corn
fusilli pasta

 2 tbsp parsley leaf

Corn Fusilli Pasta with Cauliflower and Anchovies

1. Cut the tofu into cubes; peel and slice the garlic cloves. Remove the anchovies from the oil and drain. Wash the cauliflower and separate it into florets.

2. Sauté the tofu, garlic, anchovies and cauliflower in the oil.

3. Season with salt and pepper, and continue sautéeing while stirring until the anchovies develop a creamy consistency.

4. Add the corn fusilli pasta and stir into the tofu and vegetables.

5. Mix well; reheat until the pasta is hot.

Serve on plates and garnish with washed and chopped parsley leaves.

■ This dish is very tasty with smoked tofu or seitan roasted over a medium heat. To add a splash of colour, mix the cauliflower with broccoli or romanesco. The broccoli has a more assertive flavour. This dish is also delicious with other kinds of pasta such as penne, farfalle or rigatoni.

30

1 red chilli pepper

 1 bunch fresh mint

 200 g (7 oz) Chinese cabbage

 4 tbsp Thai fish sauce

 4 tbsp sweet soya sauce
(or Ketjap Manis)

 12 fried yuba pockets

Yuba Pockets Filled with Chinese Cabbage and Sweet Soya Sauce

1. Finely slice the red chilli pepper. Wash the mint, pluck the leaves, and finely chop them. Wash the Chinese cabbage, drain and finely slice it.

2. Pour the Thai fish sauce into a bowl. First add the chilli, and then the sliced Chinese cabbage. Marinate for about 5 minutes.

3. Add the mint and 2 tbsp sweet soya sauce and mix well.

4. Carefully open the fried yuba pockets and fill with the Chinese cabbage salad. Then arrange them on plates and sprinkle with a few drops of sweet soya sauce. Serve as a starter with chilled beer.

■ You can find fried yuba pockets in any well-stocked Asian speciality store. Yuba is rich in protein and has a creamy, nutty and sweet flavour when fried.

½ tsp caraway seeds

 4½ tbsp oil

 500 g (1 lb 2 oz) seitan

 1 garlic clove

 1 tsp fresh marjoram

 1 pinch of salt
1 pinch of black pepper

 3 onions

 500 g (1 lb 2 oz) starchy potatoes
such as Russet, peeled and cubed

 2 tbsp sweet paprika

1 litre (1¾ pints) vegetable stock

1 tsp fresh chives

Vegetarian Goulash with Potatoes and Paprika

1. Drizzle the caraway seeds with some oil and chop them finely. The oil helps the caraway seeds to stay on the chopping board while chopping.

2. Cut the seitan into cubes and marinate for 10 minutes with the chopped garlic, caraway seeds, the washed and chopped marjoram, and the salt and pepper.

3. Peel the onions and cut into strips; sauté in 4 tbsp oil. Add the peeled and cubed potatoes.

4. Dust with the paprika and stir well.

5. Add the marinated cubes of seitan to the potatoes and mix.

6. Add the stock and let it all simmer together for about 30 minutes.

Place on plates and sprinkle with washed and snipped chives.

■ Adding other vegetables such as red and yellow peppers, courgettes and pieces of tomato adds additional zest to the goulash. This gives it a fruitier and fresher flavour. Seitan is a tasty substitute for beef or pork. If you like goulash really hot, then replace half the sweet paprika with hot paprika.

½ tsp red curry paste

 2 tbsp oyster sauce

 250 g (9 oz) seitan

 250 g (9 oz) green asparagus

 500 g (1 lb 2 oz) broccoli

 3 tbsp oil

Broccoli with Asparagus and Seitan

1. Place the curry paste in a small bowl and mix with the oyster sauce to make a marinade.

2. Cut the seitan into finger-sized strips. Wash the asparagus, cut off the ends and cut the spears into 5-cm (2-inch) long pieces. Clean the broccoli, wash it and cut into small florets.

3. Marinate the seitan for about 15 minutes.

4. Heat the oil in a frying pan. First sauté the broccoli, then add the asparagus pieces and sauté together.

5. Finally add the marinated seitan strips and mix well in the pan.

Serve in small bowls.

■ This dish is also delicious with chard, bean sprouts, leeks, spring onions and various Asian herbs. Thai basil and coriander go especially well together. In addition, many varieties of rice can accompany this dish.

Freshwater Fish

Contents

Types of Freshwater Fish

If you are looking for excellent quality fish, you should buy it whole at a fish market or fishmonger. There, they will gut, descale and fillet the fish. It is best to eat the fish within the next two hours or at least on the day of purchase, otherwise it will oxidise and become unsavoury. Fish can be frozen; however, in most cases, the fish loses flavour noticeably when deep-frozen.

Carp: They live in rivers, lakes and ponds, and often taste a bit musty. However, if you place the gutted and descaled carp in water with some added vinegar for 1–2 hours, the taste will improve. The water must be changed frequently. It is difficult to remove the scales from a carp: scaling is a lot easier if you briefly place the fish in boiling water first. You can use nearly every part of a carp. Even its tongue, lips and cheeks are said to be delicious.

Tilapia: A type of cichlid fish, tilapias generally come from fish farms. The quality of the flesh varies greatly depending on the farming conditions.

Salmon: The Atlantic salmon or ouananiche is a type of salmon found in lakes and rivers. It is smaller than other salmon and can be prepared like trout.

Trout: They live in lakes, rivers and also the sea. Species of trout include salmon trout, rainbow trout, Arctic char and grayling. The various species of trout vary in size and flavour. Trout from clear water tastes best; if the water quality is poor, they can taste a bit brackish. Trout need no descaling, and filleting is easy.

Catfish: They are either net- or line-caught, and are served fried or baked.

Cooking Chart

Product	Weight	Method	Temperature	Time	Notes
Trout	250–300 g (9–10½ oz)	Pan	Medium heat	10–14 minutes	
Pike	250 g (9 oz)	Oven	160°C (325°F/Gas Mark 3)	20–25 minutes	
Carp	200 g (7 oz)	Pan	Medium heat	8 minutes	
Salmon (frozen)	200 g (7 oz)	Oven	85°C (185°F)	45 minutes	
Salmon steak	200 g (7 oz)	Pan	Medium heat	6 minutes	
Tilapia	160 g (5¾ oz)	Pan	Medium heat	6 minutes	
Catfish	Approx. 150 g (5½ oz)	Saucepan	Medium heat	8–10 minutes	In root vegetable stoc
Zander or Pike-perch fillet	300 g (10½ oz)	Pan	Medium heat	8–10 minutes	Skin-side down

Carp

Tilapia

Salmon

Trout

Grayling

Pike-perch

Eel

Pike

Catfish

Cleaning and Descaling Fish

It is best to ask the fishmonger to gut the fish and cut the gills. If you do it yourself, follow the instructions for sea bass (see p. 444).

Take sharp kitchen scissors and cut off the pectoral fins.

Cut off the pelvic fins with scissors.

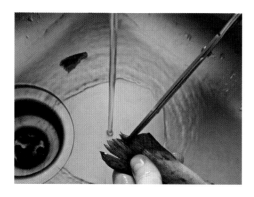

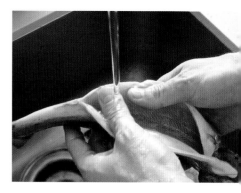

Trim the tail fin by half, otherwise it could burn during pan-frying.

Use a small kitchen knife to scale the fish.

Rinse well under running water and wash off any blood and pieces of skin.

If you descale the fish under running water, the scales will be rinsed off by the water rather than flying all over the kitchen.

Remove the excess water by hand.

Then put the fish on kitchen paper and make a small slit in the skin from the head to the tail fin. It is easier to get the knife under the flesh to fillet the fish this way, and it prevents the skin from tearing irregularly during frying.

How to Fillet Fish

ace the fish on a chopping board to fillet it.
sing a knife, cut at an angle from the head to
e backbone.

Turn the blade towards the tail fin and make
a small cut.

Push the knife along the backbone and cut off
the fillet. Ensure that the top fillet is always
stretched as this makes the job easier.

move the fillet with the knife all the way to
e tail fin. Turn the fish over and remove the
ttom fillet.

Remove the rib cage without cutting away too
much flesh and put the cuttings aside.

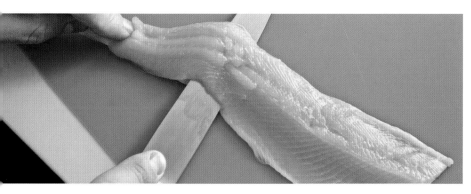

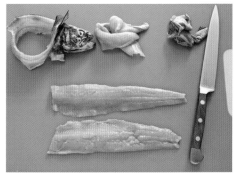

en separate the fillet from the skin. Hold the
in with your left hand and with the other hand
move the fillet with your knife.

Then remove the small bones with fish pliers.

The leftovers from filleting can be used
to prepare fish stock later. Stock from
freshwater fish is sometimes a bit cloudy
and does not have the distinctive taste of
saltwater fish stock.

4 trout (250 g/9 oz per person)

1 pinch of salt

50 g (1¾ oz) flour

4 tbsp vegetable oil

80 g (2¾ oz) butter

1 bunch fresh parsley

Juice of 1 lemon

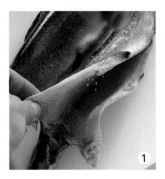

* * * **35**

Trout Meunière

1. Gut the trout and descale, clean and drain them (see p. 424). Season both the insides and outsides of the fish with salt and dust them lightly with flour.

2. Heat the oil in an oval frying pan; place the trout in the pan and pan-fry for about 5–7 minutes on each side. When each trout is golden brown in colour on both sides, remove the oil from the pan using a tablespoon.

3. Then add the butter, sprinkle with washed, finely chopped parsley, and sauté. Finally, add the lemon juice, put the fish on a serving plate, and serve with parsley potatoes.

4 trout (250 g/9 oz) per person

1 pinch of salt

50 g (1¾ oz) flour

4 tbsp vegetable oil

80 g (2¾ oz) butter

60 g (2¼ oz) flaked almonds

Juice of 1 lemon

* * * **35**

Trout Amandine

1. Gut the trout and descale, clean and drain them (see p. 424). Season both the insides and outsides of the fish with salt and dust them lightly with flour.

2. Heat the oil in an oval frying pan; place the trout in the pan and pan-fry for about 5–7 minutes on each side. When each trout is golden brown in colour on both sides, remove the oil from the pan using a tablespoon.

3. Add the butter and the flaked almond to the pan and sauté. The almonds shou be light golden brown in colour. Then add the juice of a lemon, put the fish on a serving plate and serve with parsley potatoes.

① ② ③

Ingredients

 4 catfish fillets, 140–160 g (5–5¾ oz) each

 80 g (2¾ oz) leeks

 80 g (2¾ oz) carrots

 ¼ celeriac

 750 ml (1¼ pints) water

 3 tbsp salt

 3 tbsp white vine or cider vinegar

 1 onion

 1 bay leaf

 1 clove

 150 ml (5 fl oz) fish stock

 50 g (1¾ oz) butter

 ½ bunch fresh chives

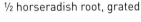 ½ horseradish root, grated

Catfish in Root Vegetable Stock

1. With a knife, trim the skinned catfish fillets and cut them in half. Slice the leeks, carrots and celeriac into long thin strips (julienne-style, see p. 344). Fill a pan with the water and add 2 tbsp salt and the vinegar. Stud the onion with the bay leaf and clove, and place it in the pan. Bring to the boil and let it simmer for 5 minutes. Place the catfish in this stock, take it off the hob, and leave it to stand for 8–10 minutes. In the meantime, cook the julienned vegetables in salted water for about 1 minute, and then refresh them with cold water.

2. Combine the fish stock with 200 ml (7 fl oz) of the cooking stock, strain into a saucepan and reduce the liquid for 5 minutes. Then add the cold butter using a wire whisk to blend the stock more easily. Wash the chives and finely chop them.

3. Place the julienned vegetables and the catfish fillets in the stock and bring to the boil. Then serve in soup plates and sprinkle the chives and horseradish over the dish as a garnish. Serve with vegetable rice or parsley potatoes.

■ Cod fillets can be prepared the same way. However, increase the cooking time to 8 minutes and add 1 tsp mustard to the stock. This gives the dish more flavour.

45

① ②

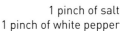

4 catfish fillets, 140–160 g
(5–5½ oz) each

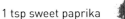

Juice of 1 lemon

1 pinch of salt
1 pinch of white pepper

1 tsp sweet paprika

1 tbsp extra virgin olive oil

750 ml (1¼ pints) paprika cream
sauce (see p. 150)

2 tbsp double cream, whipped

Catfish in Paprika Sauce

. With a knife, trim the skinned catfish
fillets and cut into 2-cm (¾-inch) long
strips. Place in a bowl and sprinkle with
the lemon juice. Season to taste with salt,
pepper and paprika. Next, add the olive oil
and mix. Marinate for about 10 minutes.

2. Pour the paprika cream sauce into
a saucepan and bring to the boil. Place
the marinated strips of catfish in it and
reheat slowly for about 3 minutes. Do not
boil it. This would make the fillets tough.
Then mix in the whipped cream and
arrange on plates. Serve with parsley
potatoes or steamed rice.

■ Catfish is typically associated with
traditional deep-South American cooking.
Pan-fried, grilled or baked catfish with
blackening seasoning is known as catfish
creole, Cajun-style or blackened catfish.
In addition, catfish is, next to cornmeal,
the ingredient for hush puppies. Catfish
gumbo (okra, tomatoes and seasonings)
is another traditional deep-South
American dish.

20 *
**
*

1 bunch fresh dill

 3 cucumbers

 800 g (1 lb 12 oz) salmon fillets, skinned

 ½ horseradish root

 1 lemon

 60 g (2¼ oz) butter

 1 pinch of salt
1 pinch of white pepper

 1 pinch of sugar

 200 ml (7 fl oz) fish stock

 100 ml (3½ fl oz) double cream

 100 g (3½ oz) crème fraîche

2 tbsp double cream, whipped

Salmon Fillets with Horseradish Butter and Dill Pickles

1. Wash the dill, then set it aside. Peel the cucumbers, halve them lengthways, and remove the seeds with a small spoon. Then cut the cucumbers diagonally into 1-cm (½-inch) thick slices.

2. Skin and clean the salmon, remove any bones with fish pliers, and cut the fillets into four equal portions. Then marinate the fillets with freshly grated horseradish and the juice of half a lemon. Cut the other half of the lemon into thin slices.

3. Melt 20 g (⅔ oz) butter in a wide pan and add the cucumber slices. Season with salt, white pepper and sugar, and sauté briefly. Add the fish stock and simmer for about 5 minutes until it is reduced by half.

4. Then add the cream and the crème fraîche and let it simmer for 1 minute. Finely chop the dill, combine with the whipped cream, and add the mixture to the cucumbers.

5. In the meantime, melt the remaining butter in a nonstick frying pan. Season the marinated salmon steaks and place in the frying pan. Sauté slowly on both sides for about 3 minutes, while pouring the butter from the frying pan over it. Arrange the cooked cucumbers on plates, place one piece of salmon on each plate and garnish with a slice of lemon.

■ You can prepare a horseradish crust for the salmon pieces by beating 60 g (2¼ oz) butter until creamy then adding 2 egg yolks, 2 tbsp grated horseradish and 80 g (2¾ oz) white breadcrumbs. Mix the ingredients and season with salt and pepper to taste. Pour the mixture over the raw pieces of salmon and place them in a buttered soufflé dish. Pour 100 ml (3½ fl oz) white wine over it and bake for 15 minutes at 170°C (340°F/Gas Mark 3½) until golden brown.

50

4 tbsp salt

 3 bay leaves

 1 tsp anise seeds

 1 tbsp black peppercorns

 1 tbsp juniper berries

 1 tsp fennel seeds

 5 tbsp sugar

 1 bunch fresh dill

 1 lemon

 1 orange

 1 kg (2 lb 4 oz) salmon

 12 golden potato cakes (see p. 326)

Potato Cakes with Marinated Salmon

1. In the food processor, grind the salt, bay leaves, anise seeds, peppercorns, juniper berries and fennel seeds. Then put the herbal mixture in a bowl, add the sugar and mix.

2. Wash the dill and chop it, reserving some for garnish. Peel the lemon and orange with a paring knife and slice them in fine strips. Clean the salmon and place it in a soufflé dish, skin-side down. Arrange the dill and the orange and lemon rind over the salmon, distributing them evenly.

3. Then sprinkle the salt-sugar-herb mixture over the top and pat down lightly. Cover with cling film and refrigerate in the marinade for about 24 hours.

4. After 12 hours, turn the salmon over and put it back in the refrigerator for an additional 12 hours, covered in cling film. Then remove the salmon from the marinade and cut it into thin, diagonal slices with a long sharp kitchen knife. Place them on the finished potato cakes and garnish with dill and lemon slices.

+ 24 hours to marinate

■ Serve crème fraîche with a little lemon juice or a mustard-dill sauce as a dip.

433

2 carp fillets

  1 pinch of salt
1 pinch of black pepper

 2 lemons

 2 eggs

 100 g (3½ oz) flour

 500 g (1 lb 2 oz) breadcrumbs

4 tbsp oil

60 g (2¼ oz) butter

Carp Fried in a Batter

1. Descale the carp fillets and clean with kitchen paper. Hold the fish with one hand while carefully removing the bones with fish pliers.

2. Cut the fillets into 3-cm (1¼-inch) wide strips and feel with your fingers for any remaining bones. If necessary, use the fish pliers again.

3. Season the carp strips with salt and pepper, and rub the fillet on both sides with a halved lemon. Slice the other lemon into small wedges and save for garnishing.

4. Beat the eggs in a shallow dish. Dip the carp strips first into the flour on both sides, then in the egg mixture. Last, coat them with the breadcrumbs. Gently pat the batter in place.

5. In a large frying pan, melt the oil and butter and fry the carp pieces on both sides for about 8 minutes, until golden brown. Then place them on kitchen paper to drain. Serve on plates with the lemon wedges

Potato and vegetable salad is a good side dish for this meal.

90

■ Carp is predominately used in 'gefilte fish', or stuffed fish, which is a traditional Jewish dish. If you use a large carp, remove the skin with a long sharp kitchen knife to avoid the dish from becoming too fatty. It is best to use a carp that weighs approximately 1–1.5 kg (2 lb 4 oz–3 lb 5 oz)

435

150 g (5½ oz) butter

 2 tbsp fresh dill

 1 tbsp fresh parsley

 1 egg yolk

 1 pinch of salt
1 pinch of white pepper

 2 tbsp breadcrumbs

 4 portions of salmon, 200 g (7 oz) each, skinned

 100 ml (3½ fl oz) dry white wine

1 lemon

Slow Roast Salmon

1. Preheat the oven to 85°C (185°F). Use a small mixing bowl to beat the butter until creamy. Wash and finely chop the dill and the parsley. Separate the egg white from the yolk and mix the yolk with the butter and the herbs. Season to taste with salt and pepper. Carefully mix in the breadcrumbs and season to taste again.

2. Season the drained and cleaned salmon portions with salt, place them in a buttered soufflé dish, and brush on the herb butter.

3. Pour the wine over. Slice the lemon and add 1 slice to each portion.

4. Cook the salmon in the oven for about 45 minutes. Remove and serve with white bread or rice. Cooking at such a low temperature makes the fish flesh very tender and the herb butter makes it juicy.

■ Vary this salmon dish by chopping the herbs together with 1 tbsp ginger and 1 bunch fresh coriander and adding the butter. Then continue as described above.

250 ml (8½ fl oz) red wine

 100 ml (3½ fl oz) port

 1 pinch of sugar

 150 ml (5 fl oz) double cream

 1 pinch of salt
1 pinch of black pepper

 100 g (3½ oz) butter

 400 g (14 oz) spinach leaves

 1 pinch of nutmeg, freshly grated

 4 tilapia fillets, 140–160 g
(5–5¾ oz) each

 Juice of ½ lemon

 2 tbsp vegetable oil

 8 sprigs fresh lemon thyme

Poached Tilapia in a Red Wine and Butter Sauce

1. Combine the red wine and port with the sugar in a saucepan and reduce the liquid to about a sixth of its volume.

2. Then add 50 ml (1⅔ fl oz) double cream and bring it to the boil. Season with salt and pepper.

3. Cut 60 g (2¼ oz) of the butter into thin slices and place in the red wine reduction to bind it. Set the sauce aside.

4. Thoroughly drain the washed spinach leaves. Melt 20 g (⅔ oz) of the butter in a saucepan until it foams, add the spinach leaves and leave them to sweat. Season with salt, pepper and nutmeg to taste.

Then, add the remaining double cream and slowly simmer for an additional 2 minutes.

5. With a kitchen knife, cut the tilapia fillets into nice shapes, sprinkle the lemon juice over them, and season with salt on both sides. Heat the remaining butter and the oil in a nonstick saucepan. Place the fillets in it and top each with a sprig of lemon thyme. Pour some butter over them occasionally and sauté slowly for about 3 minutes on each side until lightly coloured. Arrange some spinach in the middle of a plate; place one sautéed tilapia fillet on top and garnish with a sprig of lemon thyme.

■ A good-quality red wine is an absolute must for a flavourful red wine and butter sauce. This recipe can also be prepared using turbot, haddock, flounder or pike instead of the tilapia. Leeks or chard can be substituted for spinach.

Saltwater Fish

Contents

Types of Saltwater Fish

Fish must be fresh to be enjoyed at its best. Despite this, fish are sometimes as much as 14 days old when they are sold at the market, especially if they were not caught close to the coast. Large fishing boats can stay out at sea for a week or more. Then the fish is delivered to the fish market, where wholesalers buy it. The wholesalers in turn sell it to small fishmongers or seafood markets.

In general, a fish should always have bright, often protruding eyes. Its flesh must be firm to the touch and its gills bright pink or red. When you buy at a fishmonger or market, get them to gut, descale and fillet the fish. It is best to use the fish within the next two hours, or at least on the same day. Otherwise, the fish oxidises and becomes bland.

Cooking Chart

Product	Weight	Method	Temperature	Time	Notes
Plaice fillet	120–140 g (4½–5 oz)	Pan	Medium heat	4 minutes	
Bream	600–800 g (1 lb 5 oz–1 lb 12 oz)	Oven	230°C (450°F/Gas Mark 8)	35 minutes	Bake
Tuna	200 g (7 oz)	Griddle pan	High heat	4 minutes	Grill
Monkfish	50 g (1¾ oz) medallions	Pan	High heat	3 minutes	Stir fry
Turbot	200 g (7 oz) piece	Pan	Medium heat	10 minutes	Fry
Sole	500 g (1 lb 2 oz)	Pan	Medium heat	10 minutes	Fry
Flounder	150 g (5½ oz) piece	Oven	160°C (325°F/Gas Mark 3)	12 minutes	Poach
Hake	150 g (5½ oz) piece	Saucepan	Low heat	10 minutes	In stock or spiced milk
Sea bass	600–800 g (1 lb 5 oz–1 lb 12 oz)	Pan	Medium heat	16–18 minutes	Fry
Sardines	500 g (1 lb 2 oz)	Saucepan	High heat	2 minutes	Fry in oil
Salmon	200 g (7 oz) piece	Pan	Medium heat	12 minutes	Pan-fry or fry in batter for 5 minutes

Sardine

Monkfish

John Dory

Sole

Bream

Sea bass

Turbot

Hake

Hake roe

Tuna

Rosefish

Gurnard (soup fish)

Gutting and Preparing Sea Bass

Slit open the underside from the anus to the gills carefully so as not to damage the organs.

Carefully remove the innards.

Then wash the fish thoroughly under running water.

In order to prevent injury during the preparation of the fish, use scissors to cut off all fins.

The dorsal fin is especially sharp and dangerous.

First, cut into the sides of the gills with scissors.

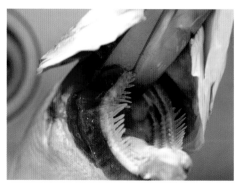

Then remove them from the inside and cut them out. Wash the fish thoroughly.

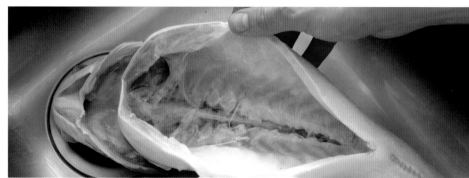

Then take a knife and slit the underside of the backbone under running water and remove the blood residues with a small spoon or wash it out. The result is a completely gutted and cleaned sea bass.

You can check the freshness of fish by its protruding eyes. When the fish is fresh, it can be kept in the refrigerator for 3–4 days.

The gills must be bright red and, if possible, without slime. You can quickly smell whether a fish is fresh! It is fresh if it smells like the sea or has a relatively neutral odour.

Kitchen doctor: Innards and gills are the first parts of the fish to emit odours. By removing them, you can increase the fish's shelf life.

When storing fish, it is important to gut them and not to store them in water. It is best to place them on kitchen paper in a storage container and cover it with cling film. Keep it refrigerated at about 4°C (39°F).

How to Prepare Turbot

1. Wash the turbot, remove the innards from its underside, and pat the fish dry with kitchen paper.

2. With kitchen scissors, cut off the tail fin, the ventral fins and the dorsal fins.

3. Use a sharp knife to cut above the backbone.

4. Then make a cut underneath the backbone. Turn the turbot over to repeat this step.

5. Next, cut out the fillets along the centre bone using a serrated knife.

6. Use the head including the centre bone for fish stock. Turbot fillets are fried whole with the bones. This improves flavour and moistness.

How to Prepare Sole

1. With a knife, make a slit in the skin at the centre of the tail fin and lightly peel in order to get a better grip.

2. Hold the skin with kitchen paper, so it doesn't slip out of your hands.

3. Pull off only the dark skin until over the head. Leave the white skin and descale.

4. With kitchen scissors, cut off the fin rays.

5. Make a cut along its underside and remove the innards and the blood residues.

6. Wash the sole under running water and pat dry with kitchen paper. Keep covered in the refrigerator until ready to use. Either pan-fry the fish whole or remove the fillets with a knife.

1 sea bass 2kg (4 lb 8 oz)

 350 g (12 oz) prawns

 ½ bunch fresh dill

 3 eggs

 2 tbsp double cream

 1 tsp salt

 150 g (5½ oz) crème fraîche

 1 pinch of cayenne pepper

 Juice of ½ lemon

 2 tbsp flour

 750 g (1 lb 10 oz) puff pastry

 500 ml (17 fl oz) shellfish cream sauce (see p. 143)

1

Sea Bass Baked in Puff Pastry

1. Gut the sea bass, clean and pat dry. Peel the prawns, remove the veins and refrigerate them. Wash the dill, then chop it. Separate 2 eggs and combine the yolks with the double cream. Refrigerate the egg-cream mixture until ready to use. With a sharp, long thin knife, cut open the fish, starting at the backbone. Cut off the tail fin. Turn the fish over and repeat the previous step, so that the fillets are connected only at the head. With scissors, remove the entire backbone and cut the bones away close to the underside. Remove any remaining bones with fish pliers.

2. With a knife, cut the skin from the fillet. Hold the blade diagonally towards the bottom skin and separate it from the fillet, starting at the tail. With your other hand, hold the skin, applying light tension. Then refrigerate the sea bass.

3. Mix the prawns with the remaining egg and ½ tsp salt in a food processor for 1 minute and then pour the mixture in a bowl.

4. Add the minced dill, crème fraîche and cayenne pepper to the prawn mixture. Mix with the lemon juice, and put it in the refrigerator for later use.

5. Season the sea bass with salt, carefully turning it over. Then spread the prawn mixture on top of the bottom fillet and place the top fillet over it. Press down lightly to avoid any air spaces.
»

■ Take your time when preparing the fish, especially when deboning.

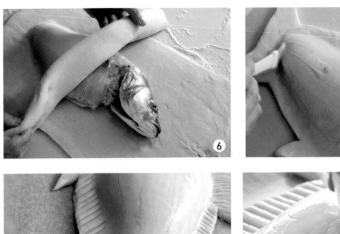

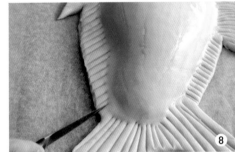

6. Dust the work surface with flour, halve the pastry dough, and roll each half out to a thickness of about 5 mm (¼ inch). Brush some of the egg-cream mixture on the dough. This helps to seal the puff pastry cover. Place the stuffed fish carefully on top of the dough and cover with the second portion of the dough.

7. Press the dough along the edges, so it sticks together better. Take a knife and cut out the shape of a fish and set aside the remaining dough. Brush the egg-cream mixture on the dough fish.

8. Then place the dough fish on a baking tray covered with baking paper and with the back of the knife blade create a fin pattern in the dough.

9. Then take a round object such as a grappa glass and mimic the scales. Add a strip of dough to mark the head. Then brush on the egg-cream mixture.

10. Cut a small hole in the pastry at the head to prevent enclosed air from tearin the dough during baking.

11. Preheat the oven to 180°C (350°F/Ga Mark 4), place the fish in it, and bake for about 40 minutes. After a few minutes, cover the head, tail and the edges with kitchen foil, to prevent the puff pastry from burning. After 20 minutes, reduce the temperature to 160°C (325°F/Gas Mark 3).

12. Remove the baked sea bass from the oven, take a serrated knife and cut it into 3-cm (1¼-inch) portions. In the meantime, arrange the reheated shellfis cream sauce on the serving plates and carefully place one portion of sea bass on it.

■ This dish can also be prepared with frozen puff pastry dough. This recipe is excellen for special occasions. The fillings can vary; you can use spinach and vegetables, or lobster and truffles. There are no boundaries to creativity! Serve with well-chilled vintage Champagne.

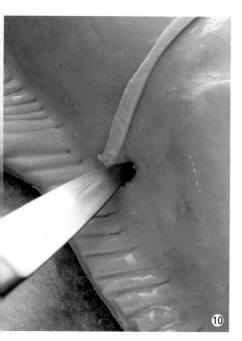

300 g (10½ oz) salmon fillet

 1 pinch of salt

 60 ml (2¼ fl oz) double cream

 1 egg

 Juice of ½ lemon

 1 pinch of cayenne pepper

 40 ml (1⅓ fl oz) dry vermouth

 8 chard leaves

 600 g (1 lb 5 oz) flounder fillets

 20 g (⅔ oz) butter

 3 tbsp extra virgin olive oil

 2 tbsp pesto (see p. 60)

 400 ml (13½ fl oz) simple tomato sauce (see p. 144)

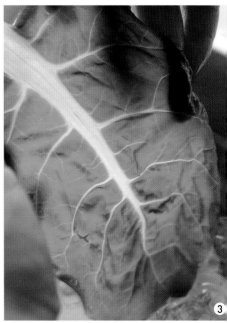

Flounder Steamed in Chard Leaves Served in Tomato Sauce with Pesto Oil

1. Skin the salmon fillet, then cut into 2-cm (¾-inch) pieces and put them in a food processor. Add 3 crushed ice cubes. Season with salt and add the double cream. Separate the egg and add the egg white.

2. Mix well for about 1 minute. Then season with the lemon juice, cayenne pepper and some vermouth. Use a rubber spatula to push the mixture through a fine sieve into a bowl, cover, and refrigerate for later use.

3. Boil water in a pan, season with salt and add the chard leaves. Cook for only 15 seconds. Then place in a bowl with water and ice cubes to chill, stopping the cooking process. Remove the chard leaves and place them on kitchen paper to drain.

4. Place 2 chard leaves on top of each other and brush 1 tbsp of salmon mixtur on top. Cut the flounder fillets into 4 equal portions, season with salt, and place in the centre of the chard leaves. Wrap the sides and roll up like a parcel.

■ Cut off the chard stem, so the leaves roll up more easily. Other types of fish such as turbot, salmon, haddock or pike also taste delicious when wrapped in chard.

* * * **50**

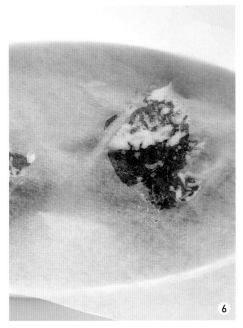

5. Coat a soufflé dish with butter and pour in the remaining vermouth. Brush a little butter on the top side of the parcel and season with salt. Preheat the oven to 160°C (325°F/Gas Mark 3). Mix the olive oil with the pesto and heat the tomato sauce in a saucepan.

6. Cover the soufflé dish with baking paper and cook in the oven for about 12 minutes. Arrange the tomato sauce on the serving plates. Cut the chard parcels in half and place them with the cut side up on the tomato sauce. Sprinkle with pesto oil and serve.

2 turbots, about 800 g (1 lb 12 oz) each

 1 pinch of salt
1 pinch of white pepper

 30 g (1 oz) flour

 4 tbsp vegetable oil

 60 g (2¼ oz) butter

 ½ bunch fresh parsley

 Juice of 1 lemon

①

Turbot Fillet Fried on the Bone

1. Fillet the turbot along the backbone (see p. 446). Season both sides of the turbot fillets with salt and pepper and lightly dust with flour. Remove any excess flour. Heat the oil in a large oval frying pan. Pan-fry the turbot for 5 minutes, on the dark-skinned side, continually basting the fish with oil from the pan. Turn the fish over and fry for another 5 minutes.

2. Then, with a spoon, remove the oil from the pan, add the butter, and slowly sauté the turbot at low heat for 2 minutes. Make sure the butter is not getting too brown.

3. While the turbot is in the pan, remove the dark skin. It is easily removed now that the turbot is cooked. Season with salt to taste.

4. Rinse, clean and chop the parsley and add the lemon juice. Slightly tilt the pan and continually baste butter from the pan over the turbot. Place the turbot on a serving plate and pour the parsley butter over it. Serve with home-made mashed potatoes (see p. 336).

■ As an alternative, you can prepare one 300 g (10½ oz) turbot fillet per person. Tarragon, basil and chives can be substituted for the parsley.

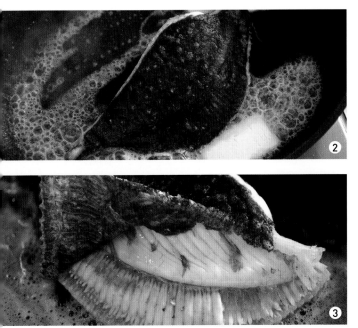

½ bunch fresh sage

 1 bunch fresh parsley

 500 g (1 lb 2 oz) small potatoes, low in starch, such as white potatoes

 4 soles

 1 pinch of salt

 1 lemon

 4 tbsp flour

 125 ml (4 fl oz) safflower oil

 100 g (3½ oz) butter

Sole in Sage Butter

1. Wash the sage and set aside the leaves. Wash the parsley and chop. Peel the potatoes and cook in salted water. Slit the fish on both sides along the backbone. This makes it easier to remove the bones later. Season with salt and sprinkle some lemon juice over it. Dust with flour, removing any excess flour. Heat an oval frying pan over medium heat, add the safflower oil, and fry the fish for 5 minutes, on the white-skinned side, until golden brown. Then turn it over and fry for another 5 minutes. Spoon out the oil and add 80 g (2¾ oz) butter and let it foam.

2. Re-fry the fish in the butter and baste occasionally. Drain the potatoes. Use the remaining butter and the parsley for the potatoes, mix and season with salt to taste.

3. Add the sage leaves and continue to pour butter over the sole until the sage leaves are crisp. Arrange the potatoes on serving plates. Place the whole fish on the plate and pour the sage butter over it.

■ The bones of a fried sole can be carefully removed with a spoon. Serve sole with fresh spinach or white wine sauce.

2 soles

 1 pinch of salt

 200 g (7 oz) white fish fillet, such as cod

 50 ml (1⅔ fl oz) double cream

 1 pinch of cayenne pepper

 1 bunch fresh parsley

 10 fresh basil leaves

 2 sprigs fresh tarragon

 ½ bunch fresh chives

 300 g (10½ oz) potatoes

150 ml (5 fl oz) butter, clarified (see p. 34)

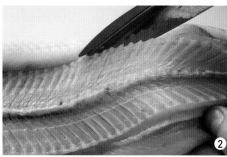

Stuffed Sole Garnished with Potato Scales

1. Use a sharp flexible knife to cut the prepared soles (see p. 447) along their backbone. Slowly loosen the fillet until the centre bone is clearly visible, but the fillets are still attached to the sole.

2. Then separate the outside of the centre bone starting from the fish's tail, using kitchen scissors.

3. With the knife, cut along the centre bone to loosen it.

4. Then bend the centre bone, which is now only attached at one point, from the tail end up and gradually pull out. Season the sole on the inside and outside with salt.

5. Cut the white fish fillet into cubes and place in the freezer for 5 minutes. Place the refrigerated fish cubes in a food processor, add the double cream and mix until smooth. Season with salt and cayenne pepper. Wash the herbs, clean and chop them, and add to the mixture. Spread the filling on the open sole.

6. Close the fillets. This brings your sole back to its original shape.

7. Peel the potatoes and slice paper thin Place three slices on top of each other and cut out 2-cm (¾-inch) circles.

■ You can also prepare the herb filling with watercress or dill. In addition, you can coat the unfilled sole with breadcrumbs, like Wiener schnitzel, and bake it in butter and oil until golden brown. Then put the herb or tomato butter inside and let it melt.

5 **6**

7 **8** **9**

8. Place the potato slices in a scale-like pattern on the sole and generously brush on the clarified butter, then season with salt.

9. Place the sole for 3 minutes in the freezer, so the butter solidifies and the sole can be placed in a frying pan without the potato scales moving around. Use a nonstick frying pan over a medium heat and slowly sauté the fish with the scales on the bottom. Tilt the pan occasionally and use the liquid in the pan to pour over the sole with a spoon. Carefully turn it over after 5 minutes and sauté for another 5 minutes.

- 2 kg (4 lb 8 oz) coarse sea salt
- 1 bream, about 1 kg (2 lb 4 oz), unscaled
- 1 slice of fennel
- 1 slice of lime
- 10 white peppercorns
- 1 sprig fresh rosemary
- Some fennel greens

Bream Baked in a Salt Crust

1. Preheat the oven to 230°C (450°F/Gas Mark 8). Moisten the coarse sea salt with a little water and mix.

2. Fill the prepared but unscaled bream with the fennel, lime, the white peppercorns, the rosemary sprig and the fennel greens. Then close the fish up, so that no salt crust can get inside the fish.

3. Place baking paper on a baking tray and add a 1-cm (½-inch) thick layer of salt. Place the bream on top and cover with the rest of the salt.

4. Pat down the salt around the fish to form the shape of a fish.

5. Put the fish in the oven and cook for about 35 minutes. Then break open the salt crust to free the fish from the salt.

6. Cut the skin along the backbone, and then use a spoon and a knife to skin the fish.

7. Carefully remove the fillets. Make sure the fish does not come into contact with the salt crust. Place the fillets on a serving plate and reassemble them. Serve with fresh bread or rosemary potatoes.

■ Prepare a light vinaigrette using diced tomatoes, olive oil, lemon juice, fennel greens, salt and pepper. Then drizzle it over the fish fillets.

* * * 50

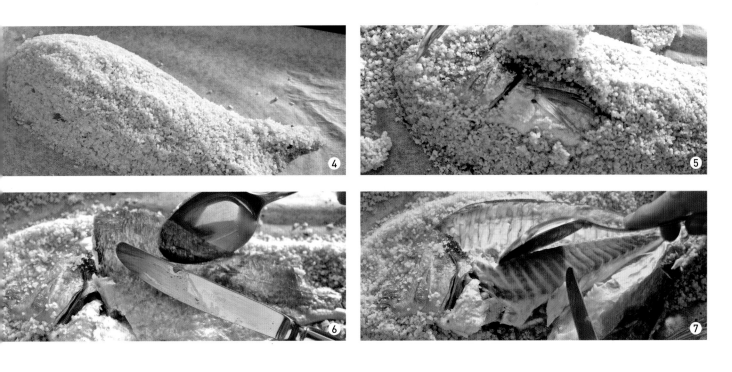

461

½ leek

 5 button mushrooms

 40 g (1½ oz) butter

 4 bream fillets, 180 g (6 oz) each

 1 pinch of salt

 1 pinch of white pepper

 40 ml (1⅓ fl oz) vermouth

 150 ml (5 fl oz) good-quality white wine

 1 tbsp fresh basil leaves

Sautéed Bream Fillets in White Wine with Button Mushrooms

1. Cut the leek lengthways in half and slice into thin strips. Clean the button mushrooms and cut into thin slices. Brown both in the pan with 2 tbsp foaming butter and season with a little salt.

2. Pat the bream fillets dry with kitchen paper and season with salt and white pepper. Put the fish on top of the vegetables in the frying pan.

3. Add the vermouth and the white wine. Reduce the heat to about one-third.

4. Sprinkle with basil leaves and cover with a lid. Steam for about 5 minutes. Then add the remaining cold butter.

Serve with potatoes or rice.

■ Try this dish with sea bass, turbot or halibut fillets instead of the bream and serve with white wine or butter sauce.

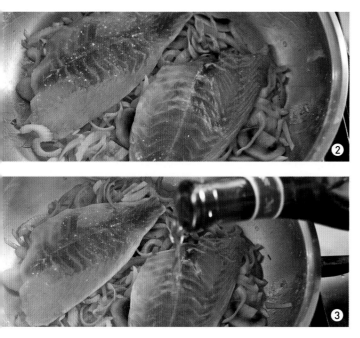

3 eggs

 300 g (10½ oz) flour

 1 tsp baking powder

 1 tsp salt

 360 ml (12½ fl oz) beer

 600 g (1 lb 5 oz) salmon fillet

 1 pinch of white pepper

Juice of ½ a lemon

 2 litres (3½ pints) vegetable oil for frying

Fish in a Batter

1. Separate the eggs and refrigerate the egg whites. Pour the flour in a mixing bowl. Add the egg yolks, the baking powder and 1 pinch of salt.

2. Gradually add the beer, beating until the batter is smooth.

3. Add some vegetable oil. It will make the batter nice and crispy. Then beat the egg whites with 1 pinch of salt until half-firm, and carefully fold into the batter.

4. Cut the salmon fillets into 40-g (1½-oz) pieces, season with salt and pepper, sprinkle some lemon juice over them and carefully dip them in the batter.

5. Place the salmon pieces in the oil heated to 160°C (325°F), fry for about 5 minutes and turn them. Drain on kitchen paper.

Serve with chips or potato salad and garnish with lemon wedges.

※
※   35
※

■ To prevent the fat splattering, it is best to use a high-sided pan.

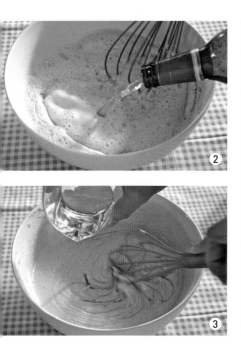

 250 g (9 oz) sardines

2 tbsp flour

2 litres (3½ pints) vegetable oil
for frying

½ tsp salt

1 lemon

①

Fried Sardines

1. Clean the sardines under running water. Slowly break away the head towards the top and pull out the innards at the same time.

2. Open the stomach with your thumb and wash it thoroughly. In addition, after removing the head you can loosen the backbone and remove it completely.

3. Place the sardines or sardine fillets in a sieve, pat dry, and sprinkle with flour.

4. Then place the sieve over the sink to shake off any excess flour.

5. Heat the oil in a wide pan to 170°C (340°F). Fry whole sardines for 2 minutes, sardine fillets for 1 minute. Remove from the oil and drain on kitchen paper. Season with salt to taste. Serve with a lemon wedge as a snack with beer.

■ 'Italian-style' sardines are marinated in balsamic vinegar and olive oil and served cold with white bread.

1 aubergine

 1 pinch of salt

 6 tbsp extra virgin olive oil

 1 tsp tandoori powder

 2 red onions

 3 tomatoes, peeled (see p. 346)

 10 fresh basil leaves

 2.5-cm (1-inch) piece of ginger

 4 limes

 1 pinch of black pepper

 800 g (1 lb 12 oz) tuna fillet

Tuna Steaks

1. Cut the aubergine into 1-cm (½-inch) thick slices, season with salt to taste, and sauté on both sides in a frying pan using 2 tbsp olive oil. Mix the tandoori powder with 2 tbsp olive oil in a small bowl and season lightly with salt.

2. Peel and dice the onions. Deseed the peeled tomatoes (see p. 347). Chop the basil leaves, peel the ginger and finely grate it. Combine all the ingredients in a bowl with the juice of 2 limes. Season with salt and pepper.

3. Cut the tuna fillet into 3-cm (1¼-inch) thick steaks, spread the remainder of the olive oil over them and season with salt. Cut the remaining limes in half.

4. Cook the tuna steaks in a nonstick griddle pan for 2 minutes on each side. Pour the tomato-onion mixture on the serving plates and arrange the fried aubergine slices and tuna steaks over it. Garnish with the tandoori oil and the lime halves, and serve.

■ Tuna remains fresh longer if sliced shortly before processing.

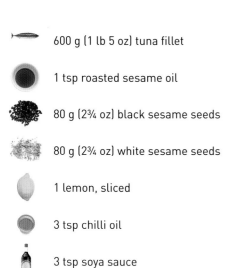

600 g (1 lb 5 oz) tuna fillet

1 tsp roasted sesame oil

80 g (2¾ oz) black sesame seeds

80 g (2¾ oz) white sesame seeds

1 lemon, sliced

3 tsp chilli oil

3 tsp soya sauce

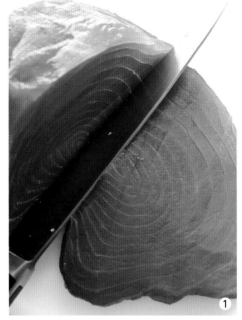

Sesame-coated Tuna Sticks

1. Pat dry the tuna fillet, remove any tendons, and cut into 1-cm (½-inch) thick slices.

2. Cut the slices into 2-cm (¾-inch) thick strips.

3. Sprinkle the roasted sesame oil over the strips and turn them in so that they are evenly coated.

4. Place the tuna pieces on a tray with the mixed black and white sesame seeds, turning the fish over to coat them on all sides with the seeds.

5. Fry them in a nonstick pan without oil for about 1 minute. The tuna should be slightly raw on the inside. If you like the fish well done, then double the cooking time.

Arrange the fish sticks on a serving plate, add the lemon slices, sprinkle a bit of chilli oil over them and serve with soya sauce.

Serve cooked rice or steamed spinach as a side dish.

＊
＊
＊
15

■ The sesame seeds can be mixed with chopped fennel seeds, coriander seeds or a few Szechuan peppercorns. This gives the tuna sticks more zest and aroma.

2 shallots

 750 g (1 lb 10 oz) cherry tomatoes of various colours

 1 tbsp capers

 1 garlic clove

 ½ bunch fresh basil

 1.5 kg (3 lb 5 oz) monkfish

 1 sprig fresh thyme

 30 g (1 oz) butter

 2 tbsp extra virgin olive oil

 1 pinch of salt

 1 tsp sugar

 1 pinch of black pepper

 500 ml (17 fl oz) fish stock

2 tbsp safflower oil

1 pinch of sea salt

1 tbsp coarse mustard

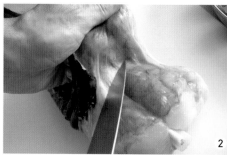

Monkfish Medallions on a Ragout of Tomatoes with Capers

1. Peel and dice the shallots. Wash and skin the cherry tomatoes. Chop the capers. Peel and dice the garlic. Wash the basil and chop into fine strips.

2. Prepare the monkfish. First, remove the outer skin by holding it taut with the left hand and cutting it with the tip of the knife. Just pull off the last 10 cm (4 inches) of the skin.

3. Cut off the dorsal and ventral fins with scissors.

4. Remove the top layer of the skin and all bloody skin layers carefully with a sharp knife. Cut the fish into 3-cm (1¼-inch) thick slices.

5. Sprinkle the thyme leaves over the monkfish.

6. Melt 10 g (¼ oz) butter with olive oil in a saucepan at medium heat and brown the garlic with the shallots. Add the cherry tomatoes and season with salt, sugar and black pepper. Reduce the temperature to low. Pour in the fish stock and simmer for 7 minutes.

★ ★ ★ 50

■ The range of tomatoes adds a variety of both colours and flavours to the ragout.

7. Pour the safflower oil into a frying pan and sauté the monkfish on both sides for 2–3 minutes at medium to high heat. Season with sea salt.

8. Add the capers, the basil, the mustard and 20 g (⅔ oz) butter to the tomatoes and lightly toss in the pan. Arrange the finished tomato ragout on serving plates and place the sautéed monkfish medallions on top of it.

1.2 kg (2 lb 12 oz) hake

 600 g (1 lb 5 oz) steamed rice (see p. 236)

 2 tbsp safflower oil

 1 tsp hot paprika

 2 litres (3½ pints) milk

 4 shallots

 5 garlic cloves

 1 tbsp salt

 3 bay leaves

 3 sprigs fresh thyme

 3 dried jalapeño peppers

 5 cloves

 10 juniper berries

 1 tsp fennel seeds

 ½ tsp white peppercorns

 4 tsp paprika oil

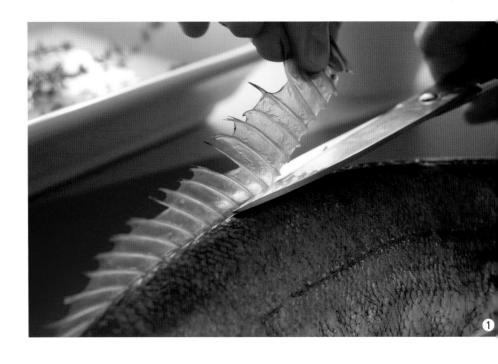

Hake Poached in Spiced Milk

1. Prepare the hake like a sea bass (see p. 444) and gut. Then cut off the dorsal, ventral and pectoral fins.

2. Cut out the skin of the abdominal cavity and rinse the fish thoroughly. Then descale the hake and rinse again.

3. Cut into 4-cm (1½-inch) thick portions and set aside. Prepare the steamed rice. Mix the safflower oil with the paprika.

4. Pour the milk into a wide cooking pan. Slice the shallots, crush the garlic cloves in their skin, and add them with the salt and all of the herbs and spices. Bring to the boil and reduce the heat.

5. Place the hake pieces in the spiced milk and leave them to simmer for about 10 minutes. Arrange the rice on the serving plates and place the hake directly from the spiced milk on top of the rice. Then sprinkle with some hot paprika oil and serve.

■ Small whiting and hake can be cooked whole in milk. They make a delicious meal.

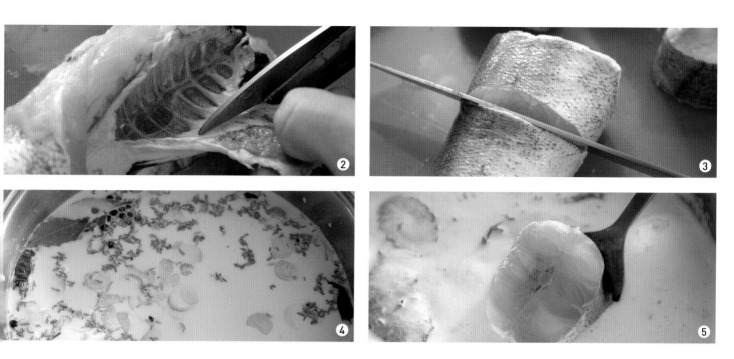

Crustaceans & Shellfish

Contents

Types of Crustacean and Shellfish

Whether lobster or crayfish, crustaceans should be bought alive and consumed on the same day. The so-called noble crustaceans such as lobster and crayfish have little taste when frozen. Don't buy precooked crustaceans. You don't really know how long they lived in the tank or whether the dealer cooked them correctly. Two additional rules make it a little easier to shop for lobsters and crayfish: as with fish, crustaceans from tropical waters are less noble than their cousins from the cold Arctic seas. And as with poultry, beef, pork or venison, female animals taste better than their male counterparts. If you don't feel good about placing a live lobster in a cooking pan, let it rest in the refrigerator for a few hours: then the lobster is a bit dazed or is sleeping deeply.

Mussels should also be bought fresh. Mussels that open easily and without resistance should not be eaten. Wrap clam shells firmly with a moist towel to prevent them from opening.

Cooking Chart

Product	Weight or size	Method	Temperature	Time	Notes
Crayfish	1 kg (2 lb 4 oz)	Large pan	Boil	3 minutes	
Oysters	Belon 00 or Fines de Claire	Oven	220°C (425°F/Gas Mark 7)	2–3 minutes	Bake with sauce
Lobsters	550 g (1 lb 4 oz)	Large pan	Low heat	10 minutes	Put the lobster in boiling water to kill it, then let it simmer and cook until the shell has turned red
Prawns	Medium-sized without shell	Saucepan	Medium heat	2 minutes	
Octopus	Approx. 1 lb 4oz (600 g)	Large pan	Medium heat	40 minutes	
Mussels		Large pan	High heat	3–5 minutes	Depending on size
Razor shells		Oven	220°C (425°F/Gas Mark 7)	8 minutes	Baked
Scallops	Muscle only	Pan	High heat	1–2 minutes	Taste delicious when eaten raw or only fried on one side
Cuttlefish	Approx. 150 g (5½ oz)	Griddle pan	High heat	4–6 minutes	

Prawn

Lobster

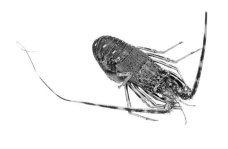

Spiny lobster

Langoustine, Norway lobster

Mussel

Scallop

Oyster

Clams

Crayfish

Cuttlefish

Squid

Octopus

Cleaning Mussels

1. Wash the mussels carefully under cold running water.

2. Remove any outer soil by hand and remove the 'beard' or byssal threads, which come off easily after wiggling them back and forth a bit.

3. As you clean, sort out any open mussels. They are no longer alive and should not be eaten.

How to Open an Oyster

1. Clean the outside of the oyster under running cold water and rub the shell with a brush. Do not place the oysters in water, unless it is seawater.

2. Hold the oyster in a tea towel with the rear sticking out. The towel prevents the oyster from moving while opening. Stick the tip of the oyster knife in the small opening on the back and insert the knife by moving it back and forth.

3. Now crack the oyster with a twist. Use the oyster knife to detach the muscle that clings to the top shell and open the oyster carefully, so you don't lose the liquid inside. Remove any remaining shell pieces with a small brush dipped in saltwater.

How to Open Razor Shells/Razor Clams

1. Thoroughly wash the razor shells with cold water.

2. To open the shell, place a small knife at the top edge.

3. Press the shells lightly apart. Carefully cut along the underside with the knife and loosen the muscle.

4. Discard any cracked shells.

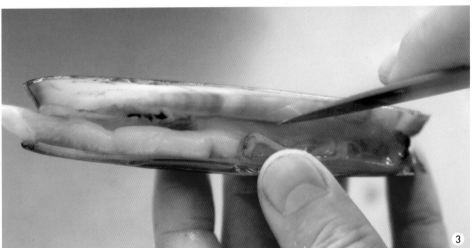

Cracking a Cooked Lobster

1. First twist the claws towards the inside to separate them from the body.

2. Then separate the tail from the body.

3. Turn the lobster and hold its back. Then, break away its head towards the top.

4. Use a small spoon to remove the tomalley. You can eat it just as it is or use it in lobster sauce, soup or lobster butter. Crack the head further, remove and discard the stomach.

5. Push with both hands on the shell to break it.

6. Then break the shell apart with both hands. The flesh will remain intact.

7. Break the joints of the pincers by hand.

8. Even the joints contain meat. To crack them open and remove the meat, just tap the shell a few times with a knife handle.

9. Cut along the side of the joints with kitchen scissors to get the flesh.

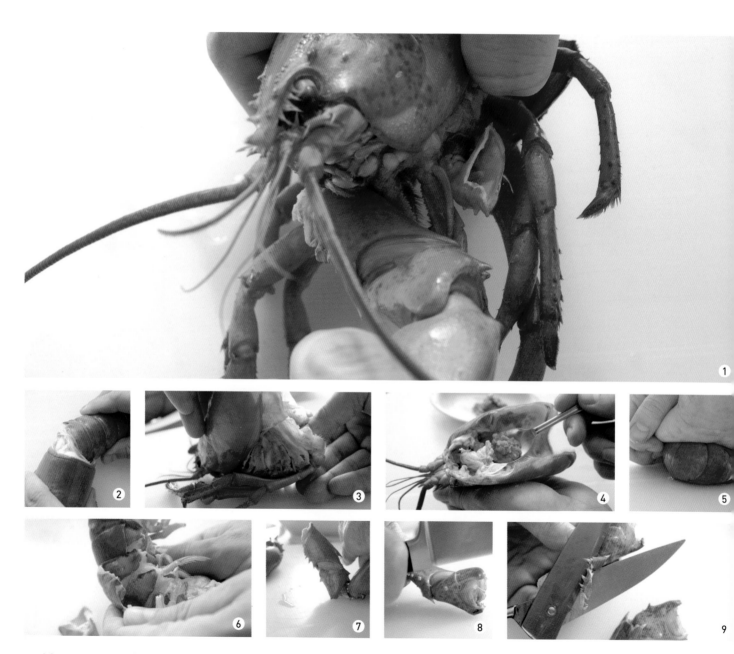

10. Then open it with your thumb and pull out the flesh. Clean off the white protein parts by hand, but do not rinse them off.

11. Tap the pincers on the chopping board to loosen the meat inside. Push the smaller part of the pincer once downwards and once upwards.

12. Then carefully remove the pincer so that both tendons come out.

13. Crack the underneath of the pincer with the back of the knife. Repeat this step for the top side.

14. Then tap from the side, so that the front part comes loose.

15. Use the lobster shells for soups, sauces or stock. The lobster is now completely cracked open.

10

11

12

13

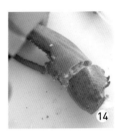
14

15

Peeling Prawns

1. Gently twist the head off the body. The heads and shells can be used to prepare soups, stock and sauces.

2. Then simply remove the shell. Leave the last piece attached at the tail if you want to fry the prawns whole. If you are using the prawn to prepare a sauce or ragout, remove the shell entirely.

3. Make a shallow cut along the length of the back with a knife.

4. Get under the vein with the tip of the knife.

5. Remove the vein in one piece. The fresher the prawn, the easier it will be to remove the vein.

6. You can also determine the freshness of prawns by their colour pattern. Their colour bleaches after some time and the shell becomes grey.

Defrosting Crustaceans and Shellfish

1. It is best to defrost peeled prawns in the refrigerator. Drain the water from defrosting, place the prawns on kitchen paper to drain, and then prepare them. Frozen crustaceans can be defrosted gently and quickly by placing them in a watertight bag in cold water. Do not place them directly in water, because they would swiftly leach out.

2. The frozen prawn on the right is covered with a layer of ice to prevent freezer burn. The frozen prawn on the left has freezer burn. Freezer burn is not unhealthy. However, the prawns become blander and the flesh tough.

3. A dark discoloration on the head means that the prawn is not very fresh.

4. It is best to defrost unpeeled prawns slowly over the course of 2 hours by placing them side by side on a tray or baking tray.

5. For faster defrosting results, put unpeeled prawns directly into cold water. Their shell protects the protein-rich flesh from leaching.

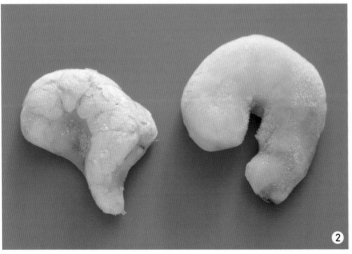

1 small pineapple

 500 g (1 lb 2 oz) cooked prawns

 300 ml (10 fl oz) cocktail sauce

 4 slices of oranges

 4 celery leaves

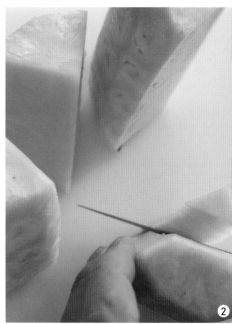

Prawn Cocktail with Cocktail Sauce

1. Cut off the pineapple skin with a knife.

2. Cut the pineapple into quarters lengthways and cut out the core and brown 'eyes' (see p. 654).

3. Cut the pineapple in 5-mm (¼-inch) cubes, so they are about the size of the prawns.

4. Place the prawns and the pineapple in a bowl, add the cocktail sauce and mix. Serve the cocktail in small bowls and garnish with a slice of orange and celery leaves.

■ Wash knives and chopping boards carefully. The flavours of vegetables, onions and garlic can be passed on to fruit.

Add cooked pieces of asparagus (white and green), sautéed button mushrooms or slices of ripe peaches for another delicious version on the prawn cocktail. It is best to decorate the cocktail dishes first with finely cut salad leaves and serve with a glass of Champagne.

500 g (1 lb 2 oz) peeled prawns

 1 egg

 1 tbsp soya sauce

 2 tbsp unpeeled sesame seeds

 1 tbsp black sesame seeds

 1 tsp Szechuan pepper

 ½ bunch watercress

 4 tbsp soya vinaigrette with coriander (see p. 63)

1

2

Sautéed Sesame-coated Prawns

1. Devein the peeled prawns (see p. 484). Separate the yolk from the egg white and combine the egg white with the soya sauce in a bowl and beat.

2. Marinate the prawns for about 10 minutes in the egg white and soya mixture.

3. Mix the sesame seeds with Szechuan pepper in a bowl and turn the prawns in this mixture.

4. Heat the oil in a nonstick frying pan and sauté the prawns for about 2 minute on both sides. Then wash the watercress drain, and arrange it on the serving plates. Add the prawns to the plates and sprinkle the soya vinaigrette over them.

■ Prawns in a crust of spices taste delicious on rocket, tomato or marinated asparagus salad.

***
35

8 garlic cloves

 ½ bunch fresh parsley

 2 dried jalapeño peppers

 1 kg (2 lb 4 oz) raw prawns

 150 ml (5 fl oz) extra virgin olive oil

 ½ tsp coarse sea salt

A few drops of lemon juice

Garlic Prawns

1. Peel the garlic and cut into thin slices. Wash the parsley, then chop. Lightly press down on the jalapeño peppers. Peel the prawns.

2. Heat the oil in a frying pan over medium heat, add the jalapeño peppers and the garlic and brown slightly.

3. After about 1 minute add the prawns and sauté for another 2 minutes. Then add the parsley. Season with salt and a few drops of lemon juice to taste.

Serve with fresh white bread or rice.

■ Mix some chopped spaghetti and a few cubes of tomatoes into the garlic prawns. Add a few spoons of cooking water, so that the oil binds better with the pasta.

4 sweetcorn cobs

 4 lobsters

 2 tbsp coarse sea salt

 1 pinch of cayenne pepper

 100 g (3½ oz) butter

 1 tsp fine sea salt

①

Boiled Lobster with Sweetcorn and Melted Butter

1. Remove the leaves and silks from the cobs, and cut off the stalks. Add water in a pan large enough for 4 corn cobs and bring to the boil. Do not add salt – it could make the corn tough.

2. Place the corn in the boiling water and simmer for 8 minutes.

3. With a knife, remove the elastic bands from the lobster's pincers. Use another pan with 5 litres (8¾ pints) water and bring to the boil. Season with sea salt and cayenne pepper.

4. Quickly put the lobster head-first into the boiling water and return the water to the boil. Then turn off the heat and let the lobster simmer for 10 minutes.

5. Melt the butter. Arrange the lobster on the serving plates. Add one corn cob to each plate, drizzle with the melted butter and sprinkle some fine sea salt on it. Serve with lobster pliers to crack open the lobster.

■ There are many companies that will deliver fresh Cornish lobster to your door.

100 g (3½ oz) white bread

 300 g (10½ oz) crabmeat

 ½ bunch fresh coriander

 2 tbsp crème fraîche

 3 eggs

 1 pinch of salt

 1 pinch of black pepper

 2 tbsp vegetable oil

Crispy Crab Cakes

1. Cut away the bread crust and finely chop the bread in a food processor. Put the crabmeat in a mixing bowl and crush with a fork, so it will be easier to mix it with the other ingredients.

2. Wash the coriander and chop finely. Add the crème fraîche to the crabmeat. Separate two eggs and add the two yolks as well as the remaining whole egg, season with salt and pepper, and mix in the coriander.

3. Then add half of the breadcrumbs and mix. Cover and place in the refrigerator

for 15 minutes. The mixture is easier to work with when cold.

4. With a tablespoon, take some mixture and shape into cakes by hand. Dip into the remaining breadcrumbs.

5. Heat the oil in a nonstick frying pan. Fry the cakes on both sides for 2–3 minutes until golden brown. Turn them over carefully. Then arrange them on plates and serve with a dip.

■ Dip recommendation: Pour 200 g (7 oz) tomato ketchup in a mixing bowl, add 1 tsp finely grated ginger and mix in a few drops of Tabasco sauce. The cakes can also be prepared with raw, chopped prawns or with leftovers of other cooked crustaceans instead of the crabmeat.

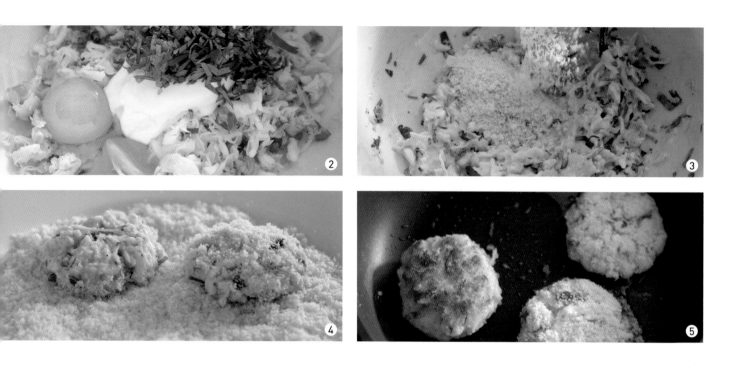

2 kg (4 lb 8 oz) live crayfish

 3 carrots

 3 spring onions

 3 shallots

 2 leeks

 4 celery stalks

 1 garlic clove

 1 bunch fresh dill

 5 cloves

 1 tsp black peppercorn

 3 bay leaves

 1 dried jalapeño pepper

 500 ml (17 fl oz) white wine

 2 tbsp coarse sea salt

 150 g (5½ oz) mayonnaise (see p. 50)

Crayfish in Dill Stock

1. First check that the crayfish are still moving; if not, discard. Peel the carrots, the spring onions and shallots. Cut the leeks in half and wash. Cut the celery and other vegetables into 5-mm (¼-inch) slices. Crush the garlic clove in its skin. Wash the dill and chop.

2. Pour 5 litres (8¾ pints) water in a large pan with the cloves, peppercorns, bay leaves, jalapeño pepper, white wine and sea salt and bring to the boil. Then add the vegetables and the dill and simmer for 3 minutes.

3. Place half of the crayfish in the simmering stock. Cover with a lid and immediately bring back to the boil. When the crayfish have turned red, remove them using a large skimming ladle. Then cook the other half. Break away the tails and arrange the crayfish on a plate with a dash of mayonnaise. Serve with fresh, lightly toasted white bread.

■ Simply serve the crayfish in a large bowl on a table, where everyone can have a bite. Savour the crayfish during the summer months with fresh white wine and cocktail sauce.

40

1 shallot

 5 tbsp red wine vinegar

 1 tbsp water

 24 oysters

Oysters on Ice

1. Peel the shallot and finely chop it. Pour the red wine vinegar into a bowl with some water, add the shallot and mix.

2. Crack the oysters with an oyster knife (see p. 480).

3. Open the oysters and serve on a platter with crushed ice. Place the sauce in a small bowl in the centre of the platter.

■ Garnish the ice with seaweed and the oysters will taste like the sea. Serve with buttered rye bread cut into small pieces and arranged on a small plate. The photograph shows Belon oysters in size 00. This is a very tasty flat oyster variety, which can also be served in the smaller size 0. Rock oysters such as Fines de Claires, Portugaise, Sylter Spezial or the American Blue Point are true delicacies when eaten raw.

※
※
※
30

24 oysters

2 leeks

2 tsp butter

1 pinch of salt
1 pinch of black pepper

1 pinch of nutmeg, freshly grated

200 ml (7 fl oz) Hollandaise sauce
(see p. 152)

1 kg (2 lb 4 oz) coarse sea salt

Baked Oysters

1. Open the oysters (see p. 480), remove from their shells and place in a sieve. Clean the oyster shells and place for 3 to 5 minutes to dry in a preheated oven. Wash the leeks and slice diagonally into fine strips.

2. Heat the butter until foaming in a pan, add the leeks, season with salt, pepper and nutmeg, and brown. Add 100 ml (3½ fl oz) water and simmer for 2 to 3 minutes until the leeks are done and the liquid reduced. Place the leeks in the dried oyster shells and place the oysters on top.

3. Pour the Hollandaise sauce over the oysters. Grill for 2 to 3 minutes under a preheated grill. Because of the short cooking time, you must ensure that the oysters do not turn brown. Then place the oysters on a plate on top of the coarse sea salt and serve.

■ **Oysters removed from their shells can be baked like fried fish in a beer batter and served with tartar sauce, or fried wrapped in bacon and served on sauerkraut.**

45 ✳
✳
✳

 1 kg (2 lb 4 oz) octopus

2 tbsp coarse sea salt

1 lemon

1 sprig fresh thyme

250 ml (8½ fl oz) white wine

1 tbsp sweet paprika

¼ tsp cayenne pepper

4 tbsp extra virgin olive oil

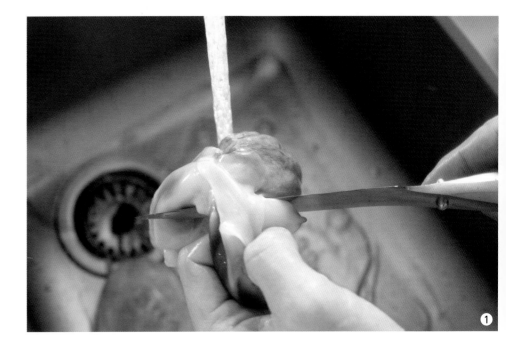

Cooked Octopus with Lukewarm Vinaigrette

1. Thoroughly wash the octopus. Turn the body inside out, pull away the entrails and cut them off with a knife.

2. Rinse thoroughly and remove any remaining skin.

3. Pinch the lower part of the head of the octopus in order to be able to grip the beak and remove it.

4. Bring water to the boil in a deep pan and place the octopus in it with salt, one lemon slice and the thyme sprig.

5. Let it simmer for about 40 minutes. Cut one piece of the octopus to check that it is done. To make the vinaigrette, pour the juice of ½ the lemon in a mixing bowl. Add the paprika and the cayenne pepper. Mix with the olive oil and 1 tbsp of the hot cooking liquid from the octopus. Remove the octopus from the pan, drain and slice into pieces. Arrange on plates and sprinkle some vinaigrette over it.

■ In Spain, cooked octopus is often served on cooked potato slices. It is also delicious when served with fresh garlic sauce or on a mixed bean salad (see p. 88). The cooking time depends largely on the size of the octopus. This is why it should be tasted to check that it is tender.

3 shallots

 60 g (2¼ oz) celery

 1 leek

 1 garlic clove

 30 g (1 oz) butter

 2 bay leaves

 1 sprig fresh thyme

 1 pinch of salt
1 pinch of black pepper

 2 kg (4 lb 8 oz) mussels
(500 g/1 lb 2 oz per person)

 150 ml (5 fl oz) white wine

 ½ bunch fresh parsley

①

Mussels Steamed in White Wine

1. Peel the shallots and cut into fine strips. Then cut the celery and leek into fine strips. Press the garlic clove in its skin. Melt the butter in a pan. First add the garlic and the shallots, then the bay leaves, the thyme, the celery and the leek, and sauté briefly. Season with salt and pepper.

2. Add the washed and cleaned mussels (see p. 480) and mix with the vegetables. Add the white wine, cover the pan with a lid and leave to simmer for 3 to 5 minutes until the mussels open. Wash the parsley, finely chop and sprinkle over the mussels. Mix well and serve.

■ Use an empty mussel shell to eat the others without silverware.

30

2 tomatoes

 2 shallots

 5 fresh basil leaves

 1 bunch fresh parsley

 1 pinch of salt
1 pinch of black pepper

 3 tbsp red wine vinegar

 8 tbsp olive oil

 2 kg (4 lb 8 oz) cooked mussels
(see p. 504)

1

Mussels Served Cold in a Herb Marinade

1. Peel the tomatoes, cut them into quarters, deseed and dice them. Peel and dice the shallots. Chop the basil leaves. Wash and clean the parsley and chop. Combine and mix in a small mixing bowl.

2. Season with salt and pepper and pour the red wine vinegar over it. Add the olive oil and mix.

3. Remove the flesh from the cooked mussels. Place the mussels in the herb marinade, cover with cling film and refrigerate for 30 minutes. Then arrange the mussels on plates and serve with toasted slices of white bread.

✳
✳
✳ **60**

■ This dish is especially delicious made with cockles, clams or cooked sea snails. It is particularly important not to serve them directly from the refrigerator, but at room temperature.

3 slices of white bread

 ½ bunch fresh parsley

 3 sprigs fresh thyme

 1 kg (2 lb 4 oz) razor shells

 2 tbsp soya sauce

3 tbsp extra virgin olive oil

1

Razor Shells with Herbs and Soya Sauce

1. Preheat the oven to 220°C (425°F/ Gas Mark 7). Cut the crust off the white bread and cut the bread into cubes. Wash the parsley and the thyme and remove the leaves from the stalks. Put the bread and herbs in a food processor and grind them.

2. Wash the razor shells, open with a knife and place side-by-side in a soufflé dish. Sprinkle some soya sauce over the razor shells.

3. Spread the herb-bread mixture over the mussels and sprinkle with olive oil. Bake the razor shells for about 10 minutes in the oven. Serve from the soufflé dish.

■ Mussels and clams are also delicious prepared this way.

Poultry

Contents

Types of Poultry

In earlier times, poultry dealers dressed their wares right in front of their customers. The trained eye could gain a lot of insight into the life of a bird by looking at its feet, beak or the size of its stomach. Caged chickens have no claws. Birds that are fed mashed foods daily do not develop large, strong stomachs. The supermarkets do not provide reliable signs of quality. Poultry looks mostly the same under cling film. Sometimes, spots can be seen on the skin if the product was handled too much.

Cooking Chart

Type of Poultry	Weight	Method	Temperature	Time
Chicken	1.2 kg (2 lb 12 oz)	Oven	200°C (400°F/Gas Mark 6)	45 minutes
Chicken leg	120 g (4¼ oz)	Oven	160°C (325°F/Gas Mark 3)	25 minutes
Duck	1.6 kg (3 lb 8 oz)	Oven	160°C (325°F/Gas Mark 3)	90 minutes
Goose	Approx. 4–5 kg (9–11 lb)	Oven	150–160°C (300–325°F/GM 2–3)	150–180 minutes
Goose breast	300 g (10½ oz)	Oven	160°C (325°F/Gas Mark 3)	70 minutes
Goose leg	250 g (9 oz)	Oven	160°C (325°F/Gas Mark 3)	100 minutes
Chicken breast	180–200 g (6–7 oz)	Frying pan	Medium heat	10 minutes
Turkey	Approx. 8 kg (18 lb)	Oven	150°C (300°F/Gas Mark 2)	300 minutes
Duck breast	200–250 g (7–9 oz)	Frying pan	Medium heat	10 minutes
Pigeon	300 g (10½ oz)	Oven	210°C (410°F/Gas Mark 6½)	25 minutes
Cornish hens	450 g (1 lb)	Oven	180°C (350°F/Gas Mark 4)	25 minutes
Pheasant	800 g–1 kg (1 lb 12 oz–2 lb 4 oz)	Oven	180°C (350°F/Gas Mark 4)	40 minutes
Quail	120 g (4½ oz)	Oven	190°C (375°F/Gas Mark 5)	20 minutes
Chicken for soup	1.2 kg (2 lb 12 oz)	Pan	Boil	50 minutes

GM = Gas Mark

Cornish hen

Turkey

Pigeon

Chicken leg

Duck breast

Chicken wing

Foie gras

Duck

Chicken

How to Cut Up Poultry

1. Remove the foot joints with a knife. Place the bird on a clean work surface, legs pointing towards you.

2. Pull the legs away from the body and cut to the bone with a knife.

3. Break the legs off at the joints and turn the bird over.

4. Remove the thumb-size fillets and cut off the drumsticks.

5. Make an incision around the wing, keeping about 3 cm (1¼ inches) away

from the breast, and scrape off the meat to the tip of the wing to expose the bone. Then separate the wing with the rear of the knife.

6. Carefully move the skin up so as not to damage it and loosen the wishbone with the tip of the knife.

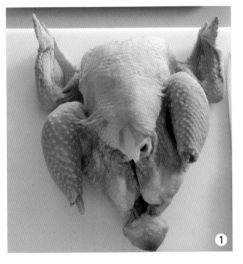

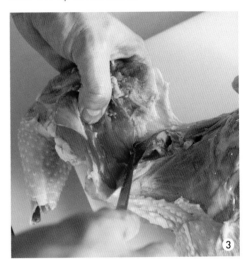

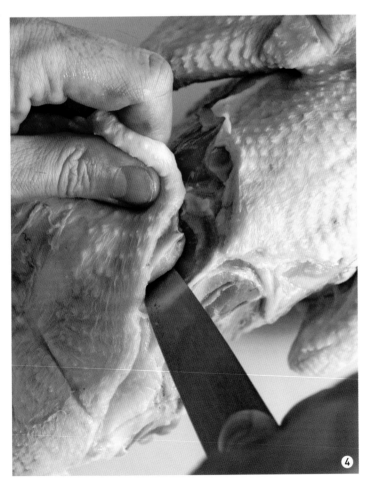

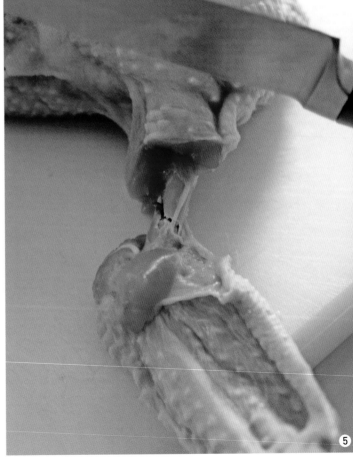

7. Carefully remove the wishbone. This will make it easier to cut out the fillet around the chest. Otherwise, you would have to cut around the wishbone, which takes a lot of practice.

8. Make an incision along the breastbone from where the wishbone was removed

and cut from the abdominal cavity to the neck.

9. Use your hand to pull back the breast fillet and cut in such a way that the wing bone remains attached to the fillet.

10. Continue to process the breast fillet, the drumsticks and wings. Use the bones for soups or sauces.

■ **You can prepare the liver and kidneys separately and serve them, for example, as a starter with lamb's lettuce.**

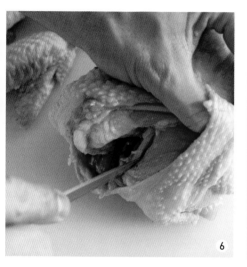

2 kg (4 lb 8 oz) poultry bones

 3 tbsp vegetable oil

 250 g (9 oz) onions

 100 g (3½ oz) shallots

 150 g (5½ oz) carrots

 150 g (5½ oz) celery stick

 1 head of garlic

 1 tsp white peppercorns

 5 cloves

 ½ bunch fresh parsley

 2 sprigs fresh rosemary

 3 sprigs fresh thyme

 5 bay leaves

 1 tsp coarse sea salt

 1 tbsp tomato purée

 100 ml (3½ fl oz) white port

 200 ml (7 fl oz) white wine

 3 litres (5¼ pints) water

Brown Poultry Sauce

1. Cut the poultry bones into walnut-sized pieces with a large meat cleaver or kitchen scissors. Heat the oil in a wide pan and sauté the bones for about 20 minutes until golden brown. Stir frequently.

2. Peel the onions, the shallots and the carrots and slice them and the celery stick into 5-mm (¼-inch) thick slices (see p. 344). Combine and sauté them.

3. Cut the head of garlic diagonally in half and combine with the vegetables. Sauté for another 10 minutes, stirring to prevent the pan scrapings from burning or becoming too dark. Crush the peppercorns and cloves with the flat side of a kitchen knife. Wash the parsley

and pluck the leaves. Add the stems of the rosemary, the thyme, bay leaves, sea salt and the remaining spices to the pan scrapings and sauté at medium heat.

4. Push the sautéed vegetables and herbs to the sides of the pan and put the tomato purée in the middle. Sauté lightly to reduce acidity and to prevent the sauce from becoming too red. Then mix well with the rest of the ingredients and sauté briefly.

5. Add the port, then the white wine to deglaze the pan.

6. Scrape up the bottom of the pan. They will dissolve later in the sauce during cooking and provide a roasted flavour.

* * * **180**

■ You can use the bones of the wings, neck or breast. It is important to leave some skin on the bones, as this provides flavour for the sauce when sautéed. Properly cooked, the sauce gels and retains the bones' flavour, which can be intensified by adding poultry jus. The jus can be served with any poultry dish. It is also easy to freeze for future use.

7. Add sufficient cold water to cover the bones by approximately 1 cm (½ inch). Slowly bring to the boil.

8. After the liquid has boiled, skim the froth and fat from the surface and simmer the sauce for about 2 hours. Add the parsley leaves to the sauce about 20 minutes before the end of the cooking time and continue to simmer.

9. Strain the sauce twice. First, filter the bones through a coarse sieve and gently press down the vegetables. Then strain through a fine sieve. Bring the sauce to the boil once more. Skim the froth and season with salt and pepper to taste.

6–8 chicken legs

 2.5-cm (1-inch) piece ginger

 150 ml (5 fl oz) BBQ sauce (see p. 56)

 2 tbsp vegetable oil

 1 pinch of salt
1 pinch of black pepper

 100 ml (3½ fl oz) water

Chicken Legs in BBQ Sauce

1. Cut the chicken legs into two parts at the joint. Make one or two slits in the skin so that the meat can better soak up the marinade.

2. Peel and slice the ginger. Place the drumsticks in a soufflé dish and pour the BBQ sauce, the oil and the ginger slices over the drumsticks. Cover with cling film and let it marinate for a minimum of 2 hours.

3. Then season the drumsticks with salt and pepper on both sides and roast in a preheated oven at 200°C (400°F/Gas Mark 6) for about 40 minutes. After 20 minutes, deglaze with water and baste regularly with the marinade. Remove the drumsticks from the oven.

Serve with salad, toasted bread or carrots.

■ It is best to marinate the chicken legs one day before use. This allows the meat to absorb the BBQ sauce properly.

 **180**

2 sprigs fresh rosemary

2 sprigs fresh thyme

1 whole chicken

1 pinch of salt
1 pinch of black pepper

1 egg

1 tbsp flour

80 g (2¾ oz) slices of white bread

3 tbsp olive oil

Baked Chicken with Herb Crumbs

. Pluck the rosemary needles and thyme leaves from their stems and finely chop them. Cut up the chicken (see . 518) and put the parts on a chopping oard. Cut the breast twice. Separate he legs at the joint and cut through the pper part along the bone. Season with alt and pepper.

. Beat the egg in a mixing bowl. Add our, rosemary, thyme and salt. Mix vith a fork and work into a batter. Cut ff the crust from the bread slices and nely grind in a food processor. Place the

chicken pieces in the bowl and dip them in the egg mixture. Then add the white breadcrumbs and mix.

3. Place the chicken pieces on an aluminium baking tray and drizzle with some olive oil. Preheat the oven to 200°C (400°F/Gas Mark 6). You may have to cover the chicken with kitchen foil to prevent the herb crumbs from burning.

Arrange the chicken in a serving dish on the table and serve with mashed potatoes and carrots.

70 *
**
*

4 skinless chicken breasts

 1 pinch of salt
1 pinch of black pepper

 4 slices cooked ham

 2 slices of Gouda or Swiss cheese

 100 g (3½ oz) flour

 2 eggs

 200 g (7 oz) breadcrumbs

 6 tbsp vegetable oil

 1 tbsp butter

Chicken Cordon Bleu

1. Cut a pocket lengthways into each chicken breast. Season the breasts on both sides with salt and pepper and fill each pocket with a slice of ham and a slice of cheese.

2. Fold the chicken breast over, enveloping the ham and cheese.

3. Seal any open spots and press the meat down a little.

4. Coat the breasts in the flour, shaking off any excess. Then dip them in the beaten eggs and finally coat with the breadcrumbs.

5. Place the breaded chicken breast in a frying pan with oil and butter. Cook on both sides for about 7 minutes over a medium heat.

■ Alternatively, you can stuff the chicken breast with prosciutto (or Parma ham), Serrano ham, or blue cheeses such as Gorgonzola or Stilton. The cutlets must be thoroughly coated in breadcrumbs to prevent the melting cheese from seeping out during cooking. This dish can also be prepared with veal or pork cutlets. They taste delicious with a spinach filling.

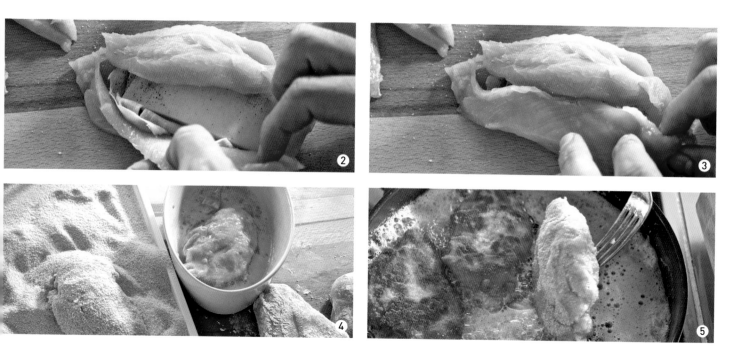

4 skinless chicken breasts

 1 pinch of salt
1 pinch of pepper

 2 eggs

 1 dash mineral water

 100 g (3½ oz) flour

 400 g (14 oz) breadcrumbs,
best bought fresh at a bakery

 6 tbsp oil

 1 tbsp butter

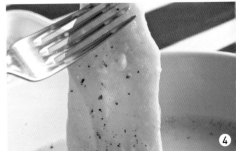

Traditional Chicken Schnitzel

1. Remove any tendons from the chicken breast. Season on both sides with salt and pepper.

2. Season the eggs with pepper and mix with the mineral water using a fork.

3. Dust the chicken breasts with the flour, shaking off any excess.

4. Dip the chicken breasts in the egg until they are completely covered.

5. Coat the breasts in fine breadcrumbs. Don't compress the coating as it would prevent it from becoming nice and fluffy.

6. Heat the oil and butter in a frying pan.

7. Place the schnitzel in the frying pan and sauté in the oil and butter mixture.

8. Shake the frying pan gently so that the fat covers the cutlets. This ensures that the meat gets cooked on the top.

9. After about 5 minutes, turn the schnitzel over and sauté for another 5 minutes. Keep shaking the pan so the batter becomes really crispy.

10. Remove the schnitzel from the frying pan and drain on kitchen paper.

Arrange on serving plates and serve with either parsley potatoes or cucumber salad.

 20

■ To make the meat even more tender and flavourful, marinate the cut chicken breasts for 2 hours in a mixture of yogurt and hot mustard.

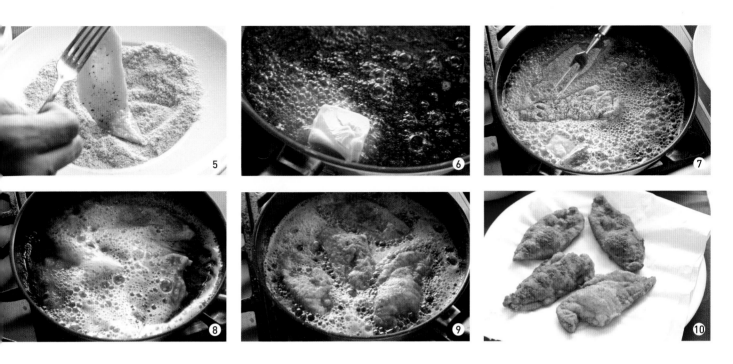

4 skinless chicken breasts

 1 pinch of salt
1 pinch of pepper

 100 g (3½ oz) flour

 2 eggs

 250 g (9 oz) fine coconut flakes

 1 tsp curry powder

 125 ml (4 fl oz) vegetable oil

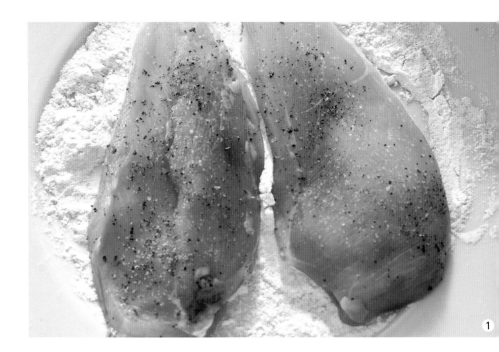

Chicken Schnitzel in Coconut Curry

1. Remove the tendons from the chicken breasts. Season with salt and pepper. Lightly dust with flour, shaking off any excess.

2. Beat the eggs well and coat the flour-dusted chicken breasts with the eggs.

3. Sprinkle the coconut flakes in a wide dish and mix with the curry powder.

4. Coat the chicken breasts in the coconut flakes and curry powder.

5. Heat the oil in a frying pan and sauté the chicken for about 5 minutes over a medium heat.

6. Then turn them and sauté for another 5 minutes.

7. Remove the schnitzel and drain on kitchen paper.

Arrange on serving plates and serve with almond rice and spicy hot spinach leaves

■ You can prepare chicken legs the same way. Debone the legs and lightly pound. Then coat with breadcrumbs and prepare them the same way. The meat from the legs is a bit tougher and must be sautéed for an additional 3 minutes.

4 pigeons

 4 slices of white bread

 1 shallot

 ½ bunch fresh parsley

 100 g (3½ oz) butter

 2 eggs

 1 pinch of salt
1 pinch of pepper

 1 pinch of nutmeg, freshly grated

 8 smoked bacon rashers

 4 garlic cloves

 10 juniper berries

 2 tbsp vegetable oil

 4 sprigs fresh rosemary

1

Stuffed Pigeons Wrapped in Bacon

1. Ask the butcher to prepare the pigeons so they are ready to cook and to pack the heart and liver separately. To make the stuffing, finely cube the heart and liver. Remove the crust from the white bread and cut the bread into 5-mm (¼-inch) cubes. Peel the shallot and chop finely. Wash the parsley, then chop finely. At room temperature, beat the butter in a bowl until it is fluffy. Separate the eggs and add the yolks one by one to the butter. Season with salt and pepper. Add nutmeg and mix with a wire whisk. Then add the shallot and parsley.

2. Add the liver, heart and the white bread cubes, and mix carefully.

3. Rub the inside of the pigeons with kitchen paper and remove any skin and blood residues. Season inside and out with salt and pepper and fill with the stuffing.

4. Wrap each of the pigeons with 2 bacon rashers and tie together with kitchen twine. With the flat side of a knife, crush the unpeeled garlic and the juniper berries.

5. Preheat the oven to 210°C (410°F/ Gas Mark 6½). Heat the oil in a frying pan and place the pigeons, the rosemary, the juniper berries and the garlic in the pan. Sauté back-side up first, then on their backs. Roast the pigeons in the oven for about 25 minutes and baste with the jus continually. Remove the pigeons; take off the kitchen twine, and halve the pigeons lengthways using a sharp knife. Arrange on plates and serve.

■ Place any excess stuffing in a buttered soufflé dish and bake in the oven for about 15 minutes at 200°C (400°F/Gas Mark 6). The butter makes it easier to turn out the stuffing later. Pumpkin gratin and salsify, which is also called vegetable oyster, make wonderful side dishes to complement the pigeon dinner.

2 shallots

 600 g (1 lb 5 oz) poultry liver

 1 sprig fresh oregano

 40 g (1½ oz) butter

 1 pinch of salt
1 pinch of black pepper

 40 g (1½ oz) pine nuts

 30 g (1 oz) raisins

 60 ml (2 fl oz) balsamic vinegar

 100 ml (3½ fl oz) brown poultry sauce (see p. 520)

Sautéed Venetian-style Poultry Liver

1. Peel the shallots and chop finely. Clean the poultry liver, removing any tendons and veins. Pluck the oregano leaves and chop finely. Melt the butter in a frying pan until foamy and add the liver.

2. Then season with salt and pepper and sear.

3. Turn the pieces of liver over carefully. Season the liver in the pan again, otherwise it becomes dry and tough.

4. Add the shallots, pine nuts and raisins and sauté for about 1 minute. Then sprinkle the oregano over them.

5. Add the balsamic vinegar and simmer. Then add the brown poultry sauce. Reheat quickly and serve immediately.

■ This dish tastes delicious when served with mashed potatoes, fried polenta, or salad topped with Parmesan shavings and vinaigrette.

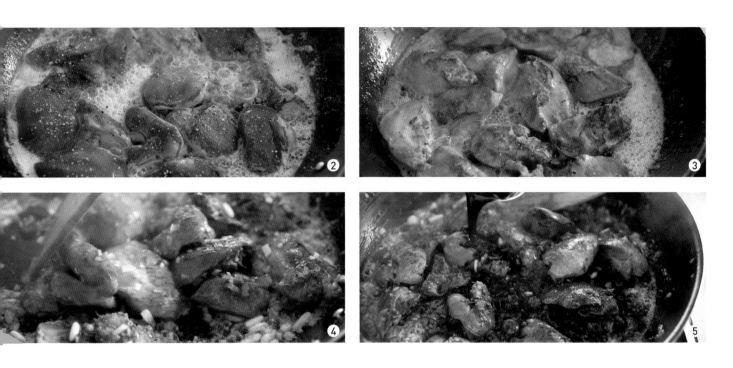

1 head of garlic

 1 lemon

 1 bunch fresh parsley

 4 Cornish hens (approx. 350 g/ 12 oz each)

 1 pinch of salt
1 pinch of pepper

 300 g (10½ oz) small onions

 60 g (2¼ oz) butter

Cornish Hens Roasted with Lemon and Garlic

1. Preheat the oven to 180°C (350°F/Gas Mark 4). Set the head of garlic stem upright on the work surface and press down with the palm of your hand to loosen the garlic cloves. Remove the outer skin and crush the cloves still in their skins. Rinse the lemon under hot water and cut into 5-mm (¼-inch) thin slices. Wash the parsley. Dress the Cornish hens, clean them, and dry the inside with kitchen paper.

2. Season the inside and outside of the hens well with salt and pepper. Stuff with the pressed garlic cloves and the parsley. Reserve some of the parsley for garnishing.

3. Place the stuffed hens on a roasting tray. Wash the onions and remove their skins. Cut off the stalk end. Arrange the onions around the hens. Distribute the butter over the meat.

4. Roast for 25 minutes in the oven. Garnish with the lemon slices. Add 100 ml (3½ fl oz) water and loosen the scrapings. Baste the hens with the jus and roast for an additional 15 minutes. Remove from the oven. Sprinkle the reserved parsley on the hens and serve with the onions and the jus.

✳ ✳ ✳ 80

■ Be careful not to injure the skin when you pluck the remaining pinfeathers with fishbone pliers. The white meat would dry out at these spots. Cornish hens taste just as delicious cold. Serve with any type of potato dish.

541

100 g (3½ oz) sliced lard

 1 tsp juniper berries

 ½ bunch fresh thyme

 5 shallots

 1 pheasant (approx. 1 kg/2 lb 4 oz)

 1 pinch of salt,
1 pinch of black pepper

 5 bay leaves

 150 g (5½ oz) green grapes

 500 g (1 lb 2 oz) sauerkraut with bacon (see p. 398)

 20 g (⅔ oz) butter

 40 ml (1⅓ fl oz) dry vermouth

 30 ml (1 fl oz) vegetable oil

Pheasant on Sauerkraut with Mashed Potatoes

1. Place the lard slices on a plate. Crush the juniper berries with the flat side of a large kitchen knife and chop coarsely. Pluck the thyme leaves from 2 sprigs, combine them with the juniper berries, and sprinkle over the lard slices.

2. Peel the shallots and cut them into quarters. Reserve 3 sprigs of thyme, then chop the remaining sprigs. Clean the pheasant thoroughly inside and out. Remove any remaining pinfeathers and possible pellets. Then season the pheasant inside and out with salt and pepper. Stuff with the shallots, the chopped thyme and two bay leaves. Peel the grapes with a small kitchen knife.

Wrap the pheasant with the seasoned lard. It prevents the meat from drying out during roasting, and provides extra flavour. Place 2 sprigs of thyme and the remaining bay leaves on top of the drumsticks.

3. Tie the pheasant with kitchen twine t keep the lard in place during roasting. Tie the bay leaves and thyme sprigs, too

4. Heat the sauerkraut. Melt the butter in a frying pan until it foams. Add the peeled grapes and toss in the pan. Pour over the vermouth and add the sauerkraut.

■ Lard is bacon fat. It is mostly used to bard or wrap meat. One pheasant serves 4, if a soup is served prior to the main pheasant course or the pheasant is served as a starter. For all other occasions, you should prepare 2 pheasants. Home-made mashe potatoes make a delicious side dish. Serve with 150 ml (5 fl oz) brown poultry sauce o prepare it from the pheasant's carcass.

90

5. Heat the oil in a frying pan. Sauté
the pheasant on both sides for about
5 minutes and baste with the pan
scrapings frequently. Then place it in a
baking dish in a preheated oven at 180°C
(350°F/Gas Mark 4) for about 40 minutes.
Baste the pheasant with its own juices
occasionally. Remove the kitchen twine
after roasting. Carve the breast and
remove the drumsticks and then serve
with wine sauerkraut. Garnish with the
fried lard.

Beef & Veal

Contents

Types of Beef and Veal Cuts

The quality of beef and veal is not easy to detect visually. Lighting at the butcher's counter can be deceptive and conceal the true colour of the meat. The country of origin or breed is not always a guarantee either. You are usually not allowed to touch the product.

In general, female calves and cows taste better than their male counterparts.

The ox is the exception to this rule. It is desirable for the beef to have some layer of fat. This layer is an important carrier of flavour. For example, there is a top-quality variety of beef called Charolais and an inferior-quality variety that is sold under the same name.

Cooking Chart

GM = Gas Mark

Product	Weight	Method	Temperature	Time	Notes
Beef joint	1.8 kg (4 lb)	Oven	160°C (325°F/GM 3)	120 minutes	Cover with lid
Beef, roast	2 kg (4 lb 8 oz)	Oven	200°C (400°F/GM 6)	40 minutes	Sear
Beef sirloin	200 g (7 oz)	Frying pan	Medium heat	6 minutes (medium)	
Beef fillet steak	200 g (7 oz)	Frying pan	Medium heat	5 minutes	
T-bone steak	500 g (1 lb 2 oz)	Griddle pan	High heat	12 minutes (medium)	Grease before
Beef olive	approx. 300 g (10½ oz)	Pan with lid	Low heat	90 minutes	Sear before
Beef tournedos	60 g (2¼ oz)	Frying pan	Medium heat	4 minutes	
Beef sirloin tips	100 g (3½ oz)	Frying pan	High heat	2 minutes	
Beef, boiled	1.6 kg (3 lb 8 oz)	Saucepan	Low heat	80 minutes	
Hamburger	200 g (7 oz)	Frying pan	Medium heat	4 minutes	
Meatloaf	2 kg (4 lb 8 oz)	Oven	190°C (375°F/GM 5)	80 minutes	
Entrecote	250 g (9 oz)	Frying pan	Medium heat	8 minutes (medium)	
Veal leg, deboned and rolled	1.3–1.5 kg (3–3lb 5 oz)	Oven	160°C (325°F/GM 3)	90 minutes	
Veal leg, whole	1.8–2.4 kg (4–5 lb 5 oz)	Oven	170°C (340°F/GM 3½)	120 minutes	
Veal roast, lean Veal roast, lean	2 kg (4 lb 8 oz)	Oven	150°C (300°F/GM 2)	100 minutes	
Veal breast, stuffed	2.5 kg (5 lb 8 oz)	Oven	150°C (300°F/GM 2)	100 minutes	
Veal chops	300 g (10½ oz)	Frying pan	Medium heat	12 minutes	
Veal loin	200 g (7 oz)	Frying pan	Medium heat	10 minutes	
Veal medallions	60 g (2¼ oz)	Frying pan	Medium heat	10 minutes	
Veal roast	1.5 kg (3 lb 5 oz)	Oven	180°C (350°F/GM 4)	90 minutes	
Osso bucco or veal knuckles	400 g (14 oz)	Pan with lid	Medium heat	120 minutes	10 minutes
Veal cheeks	200 g (7 oz)	Pan with lid	Medium heat	120 minutes	Also possible in the oven
Hamburger patties	100 g (3½ oz)	Frying pan	Medium heat	8 minutes	
Veal schnitzel	90 g (3¼ oz)	Frying pan	Medium heat	5 minutes	
Calf liver	100 g (3½ oz) slices	Frying pan	Medium heat	1–2 minutes	
Calf kidneys	In small lobes	Frying pan	High heat	1 minutes	
Calf tongue	500 g (1 lb 2 oz)	Pan	Medium heat	60 minutes	Cook in vegetable stock

Fillet of beef

Beef joint

Roast beef

T-bone steak

Veal roast

Calf bones

Calf kidneys or rognon

Veal cutlet

Whole fillet steak

Beef fillet steak (tournedos)

Veal knuckle

Beef steak

How to Cut and Trim Veal Fillet

1. Carefully remove the outer skin with a medium-sized knife and on one side expose the long cord, which is also called the chain.

2. Carefully separate the chain from the fillet.

3. Cut with the knife under the outer sinew to separate it from the meat.

4. Hold the sinew taut and cut off with the knife. Hold the knife at an angle and slice towards the top to cut off as little meat as possible.

5. Turn the fillet over and remove any remaining small tendons or skin with a knife.

6. The fillet is ready to cook when it is free of sinew and skin.

7. Separate the fillet tip and the head part that is attached to the top of the fillet. Cut the centre into medallions. Cut the tip of the fillet and the upper part into small pieces and use for stews.

8. Use the sinew and skin for sauces. Remove the remaining sinew from the chain and use for fillings or stuffing.

How to Cut and Trim Beef Fillet

Prepare a whole fillet of beef to cut into portions: first separate the meat pieces on the sides (chain) with a knife. Then remove the uppermost white sinew just as for veal (see p. 548). Turn the fillet around and cut off the outermost white sinew and skin. Then trim and use as follows:

1. Use the fillet tips for stews.

2. Cut filet mignon each weighing 40–50 g (1½–1¾ oz) and use for light meals or for stews. Sear fillets briefly on each side.

3. Cut tournedos each weighing about 60–70 g (2¼–2½ oz) and sear them briefly on each side, or poach.

4. Cut fillet steaks from the centre in portions of 200 g (7 oz) or keep as one Chateaubriand weighing 400–600 g (14 oz–1 lb 5 oz). This is really the prime cut of beef.

5. From the fillet head, where the meat is less sinewy, cut fillet steaks each weighing 200–300 g (7–10½ oz).

6. Use the fillet chain for stews or Asian stir-fry pan dishes.

7. Cut 6-cm (2½-inch) pieces from the lower fillet chain and sauté in a frying pan. These flavourful pieces can also be used in stews.

8. Use the cuts from the head of the fillet for Asian stir-fry dishes.

9. Use the end of the fillet head for stews.

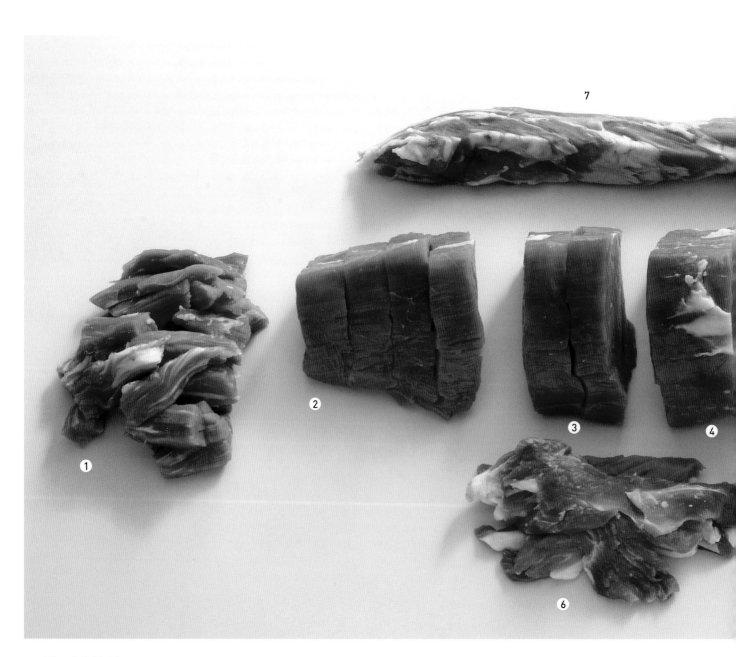

■ Wrap the fillet steak in fatty bacon and tie with some kitchen twine. After roasting you can either discard the bacon or serve and eat.

551

Degrees of Cooking for Beef

Beef fillet steak

Rare/bleu: The meat is sautéed for 1 minute on each side and is raw on the inside.

Medium rare/saignant/bloody: The meat is sautéed for 3 minutes on each side and has a pink centre with a bloody core.

Medium/medium/pink: This is by far the most common degree of cooking. The meat is sautéed for 5 minutes on each side and remains pink on the inside. However, the core is no longer bloody.

Medium well/à point/half-done: The meat is sautéed for 6 minutes on each side and is slightly pink on the inside. However, there are no bloody juices when cut.

Well done/bien cuit: The meat is sautéed for 8 minutes on each side and is well done on the inside. There are no juices when cut.

175 g (6 oz) green peppers

 100 g (3½ oz) red peppers

 3 onions

 2 garlic cloves

 750 g (1 lb 10 oz) lean beef shoulder

 400 g (14 oz) cooked pinto beans

 3 tbsp soft brown sugar

 100 ml (3½ fl oz) white wine vinegar

 4 tbsp vegetable oil

 5 cloves

 2 bay leaves

 1 pinch of salt
1 pinch of black pepper

 1 tbsp sweet paprika

 ½ tbsp flour

 2 chipotle peppers in adobo (marinade)

 500 g (1 lb 2 oz) tinned, peeled tomatoes

 100 ml (3½ fl oz) soured cream

 80 g (2¾ oz) raclette cheese

Chilli con Carne

1. Wash and clean the green and red peppers. Cut into 5-mm (¼-inch) cubes. Peel the onions and the garlic and chop finely. Cut the beef into 5-mm (¼-inch) cubes. Drain the beans in a sieve. Dissolve the sugar in 100 ml (3½ fl oz) water and heat it in a pan until it caramelises. Deglaze with the white wine vinegar and simmer to reduce the liquid. Add the vegetable oil and the garlic and sauté.

2. Crush the cloves with the flat side of a knife. Add the bay leaves, onions and the peppers. Sauté for about 10 minutes.

3. Add the beef. Season with salt and pepper, and sauté slowly for another 10 minutes.

4. Dust with paprika and flour. The flour binds the spices. Add the marinated chipotle peppers and lightly sauté for 5 minutes.

5. Put the tomatoes in a bowl and mix with a hand-held blender. Then add to the meat, cover the pan with a lid, and let it gently simmer for about 1 hour. Stir occasionally. After 45 minutes, add the beans and simmer for 15 minutes. Serve, pour the cream over it and sprinkle with the grated cheese.

■ Chilli con carne can also be prepared using minced beef or kidney beans instead of pinto beans. In addition, you can add fresh sweetcorn or small pieces of corn on the cob.

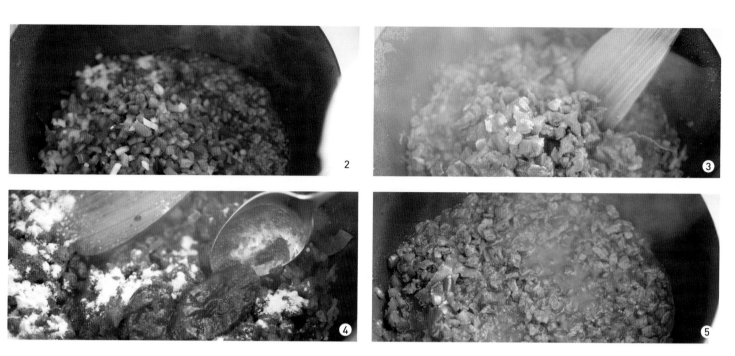

2 slices of white bread

 1.5 kg (3 lb 5 oz) roast beef

 1 tsp sea salt

 1 pinch of black pepper

 3 tbsp vegetable oil

 1 tbsp hot mustard

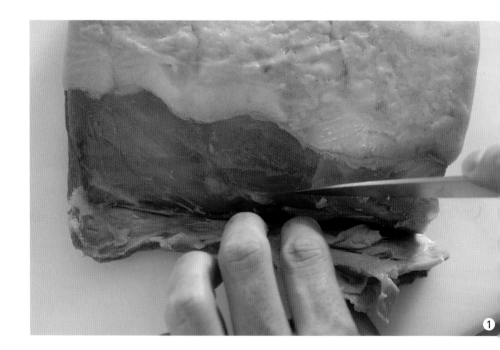

Roast Beef

1. Preheat the oven to 210°C (410°F/ Gas Mark 6½). Remove the crust from the white bread and grind the bread in a food processor. Loosen the outer tendons from the meat. Cut off some of the layer of fat, leaving about 5 mm (¼ inch) on the meat. Turn it over, remove the tendons and skin and trim nicely.

2. Make small incisions in the fat layer at various points so the fat cooks better, making the roast beef wonderfully crispy. It will also make it easier to carve the roast meat.

3. Season the beef with salt and pepper on all sides, gently rubbing in the seasoning.

4. Heat the oil in the frying pan; place the meat in it, and sauté for about 2 minutes on each side.

5. Grease a baking tray with a little oil and place the sautéed meat on it. Brush the mustard on the top side and sprinkle breadcrumbs over it. Place the roast beef in the oven. Roast for about 25 minutes. Remove and arrange on a serving platter and leave it to sit for about 5 minutes before slicing.

■ Serve potato gratin or baked potatoes with roast beef; pepper cream sauce and green beans are other popular and delicious accompaniments. Another option is to serve the roast beef cold in thin slices with fried potatoes and tartare sauce (see p. 52).

5 juniper berries

 5 white peppercorns

 2 onions

 160 g (5¾ oz) carrots

 160 g (5¾ oz) leeks

 160 g (5¾ oz) celery stick

 1 tbsp coarse sea salt

 1 kg (2 lb 4 oz) stewing meat

 2 cloves

 1 bay leaf

 3 sprigs fresh parsley

½ bunch fresh chives

1

Beef Stew with Root Vegetables and Herbs

1. With the flat side of a knife, lightly crush the juniper berries and the peppercorns.

2. Halve the onions with their skin on, but cut off the root ends. Wash the root vegetables. Peel the carrots and halve. Cut the leeks and celery stick into 2 or 3 pieces depending on their size.

3. In a large pan, bring water and salt to the boil and simmer the beef for about 1 hour.

4. Then add the vegetables and spices, and leave to simmer for another hour.

5. Then season with salt and pepper to taste.

Cut the vegetables into bite-sized pieces and arrange them on a serving platter with the beef. Sprinkle some parsley leaves and strips of chives over the dish.

■ Serve with parsley potatoes, fried potatoes or creamed spinach. This dish tastes delicious with tartare sauce.

120

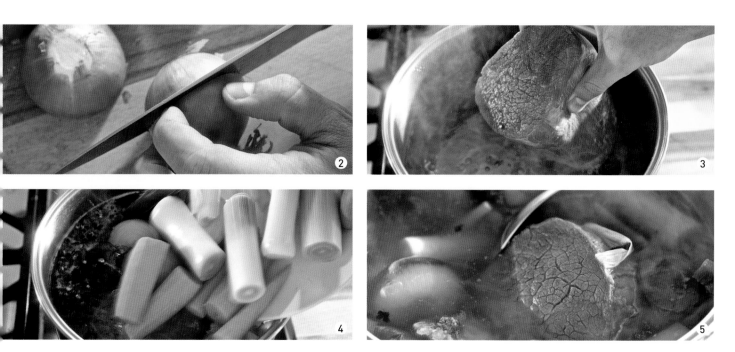

200 g (7 oz) onions

 1 tsp sweet paprika

 1 tbsp flour

 1 litre (1¾ pints) vegetable oil

 3 shallots

 30 g (1 oz) butter

 ½ tsp dried marjoram

 1 tsp tomato purée

 100 ml (3½ fl oz) beer

 250 ml (8½ fl oz) veal stock

 800 g (1 lb 12 oz) fried potatoes

 4 pickles

 1 bunch fresh chives

 4 pieces roast beef (200 g/7 oz) each

 1 pinch of salt
1 pinch of black pepper

①

Onion Roast with Fried Potatoes

1. Peel the onions and finely slice. Dust with the paprika and the flour and mix well.

2. Heat the oil in a pan to 160°C (325ºF), reserving 2 tbsp. Fry the onion rings in two batches until golden brown. Remove and drain them on kitchen paper. Add a dash of salt.

3. Peel the shallots and finely chop them. Heat the butter in a frying pan until it foams and sauté the shallots until golden brown. Then add the dried marjoram and the tomato purée and sauté lightly.

4. Add the beer to the pan scrapings and reduce the liquid. Add the veal stock and reduce the liquid to a quarter of its volume. In the meantime, prepare the fried potatoes. Cut the pickles in half. Wash the chives and chop.

5. Lightly pound the beef and season with salt and pepper. Heat the reserved oil in a frying pan and sauté the meat for about 2 minutes on both sides.

Arrange the fried potatoes and the beef on a serving plate. Pour the sauce over it and garnish with the roasted onions and chives. Serve with a pickle.

■ The onion roast is especially tender and delicious if you use pieces of fillet steak instead of roast beef.

600 g (1 lb 5 oz) fillet steak

 100 g (3½ oz) button mushrooms

 2 pickled gherkins

 160 g (5¾ oz) red beetroots (from a jar)

 2 shallots

 50 g (1¾ oz) butter

 1 pinch of salt
1 pinch of black pepper

 1 tbsp vegetable oil

 4 tbsp pickle juice

 250 ml (8½ fl oz) beef jus (see p. 138)

 200 g (7 oz) crème fraîche

 ½ tsp hot mustard

 1 pinch of sugar

Beef Stroganoff with Pickles and Button Mushrooms

1. Cut the fillet steak into 5-cm (2-inch) long, thin strips. Clean the button mushrooms and slice. Finely slice the gherkins and the red beetroots. Set aside. Peel the shallots and dice.

2. Melt 40 g (1½ oz) butter in a frying pan and add the beef strips. Season with salt and pepper. Fry briefly until light brown on all sides. Remove and place on a plate. Cover with kitchen foil to keep warm.

3. Pour the oil into the same frying pan and brown the shallots. Add the mushrooms, seasoning with salt and pepper. Sauté briefly. Then add the pickle juice and reduce the liquid.

4. Pour the beef jus into the frying pan and bring to the boil. Add the jus of the fillet steak.

5. Add the crème fraiche. Season with pepper.

6. Place the beef strips in the sauce and cover with the pickle slices. Mix the mustard into the sauce, but do not heat.

7. Melt the remaining butter in a pan and sauté the beetroot briefly. Season with salt and sugar.

Arrange the beef strips on plates with the sautéed beetroot on top, and pour the butter over them.

 60

■ This dish is just as tasty with rump steak. It also goes well with soured cream and steamed rice.

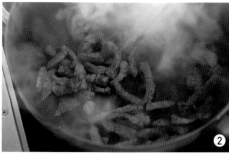

4 onions

 2 tbsp sugar

 1 bay leaf

 1 pinch of salt
1 pinch of black pepper

 100 ml (3½ fl oz) fruit vinegar

 800 g (1 lb 12 oz) lean beef mince

 2 tbsp oil

 8 lettuce leaves

 2 tomatoes

 2 pickles

 4 soft sesame-seed hamburger buns

 4 tsp mayonnaise

 1 tbsp medium-hot mustard

4 tsp tomato ketchup

Traditional Hamburgers with Onion Relish

1. To make the onion relish, peel, halve and thinly slice the onions. Combine them with the sugar, bay leaf, salt, pepper and fruit vinegar, and place in a frying pan. Then add 200 ml (7 fl oz) water and slowly simmer for 25 minutes. The onion relish is ready as soon as the liquid is completely reduced and the mixture has a jam-like consistency.

2. Form 4 hamburger patties of equal size from the minced beef. Heat the oil in a nonstick frying pan and place the hamburgers in it. Season with salt and pepper, and sauté for about 2 minutes.

3. Turn the patties over. Season with salt and pepper again, and sauté for an additional 2 minutes.

4. Wash the lettuce leaves. Slice the tomatoes and pickles. Cut the sesame-seed buns in half and toast them. Put mayonnaise on the bottom half of the buns. Place a lettuce leaf on top and add one patty. Brush the mustard on the patty.

5. Add slices of tomato and top with the onion relish. Place the pickle slices on top, then the tomato ketchup, then put the top part of the bun onto the hamburger patty.

■ Hamburgers are best served with fresh home-made chips. You can use other spicy sauces, cooked bacon rashers or fresh onion rings. If you like, add 1 slice of soft cheese to make a cheeseburger.

45

5 tbsp vegetable oil

 3 cinnamon sticks

 8 black cardamom pods

 1 tbsp black mustard seeds

 ½ tsp star anise seeds

 1 tbsp ground turmeric

 500 g (1 lb 2 oz) onions

 3 garlic cloves

 1 kg (2 lb 4 oz) beef shoulder

 1 tsp salt
1 tsp black pepper

 1 tbsp palm sugar

 400 ml (13½ fl oz) tinned, peeled tomatoes

3 bay leaves

Indian Beef Curry with Black Cardamom and Cinnamon

1. Heat the vegetable oil in a frying pan. Add the cinnamon sticks, cardamom pods, mustard seeds, star anise seeds and turmeric. Lightly toast this mixture to intensify the flavour.

2. Peel the onions and the garlic. Cut the onion into 8 pieces and chop the garlic. Add the mixture to the pan and sauté lightly. Cut the beef into 3-cm (1¼-inch) cubes.

3. Season the beef with the salt, pepper and palm sugar. Place the meat in the pan and sauté for 5 minutes.

4. Add the tomatoes and the bay leaves. Put a lid on the pan and gently simmer for about 50 minutes. Add some water occasionally to get a delicious sauce.

Serve with the spices and with steamed basmati rice.

■ Create an Indian curry paste with the following ingredients: 3 red chilli peppers, 150 g (5½ oz) shallots, 5 garlic cloves, 10 g (¼ oz) galangal, 10 g (¼ oz) fresh ginger, 8 g (¼ oz) fresh turmeric root (or, as an alternative, use 1 tsp ground turmeric), 2 tbsp coriander seeds, ½ tsp anise seeds, 5 cloves, ½ tsp fennel seeds and 1 stalk of lemon grass. First, grind the solid spices in a mortar. Add the other ingredients one by one until paste-like. Use this paste with fish, poultry or vegetables. Store in glass jars or freeze.

750 g (1 lb 10 oz) beef mince

 1 large onion

 4 small day-old rolls

 500 ml (17 fl oz) milk

 2 eggs

 2 tsp sweet paprika

 1 pinch of salt
1 pinch of black pepper

 1 tsp dried marjoram

 1 tbsp English mustard

 1 tsp cornflour, mixed with a little water

Meatloaf with Sauce and Parsley Potatoes

1. Preheat the oven to 190°C (375°F/Gas Mark 5). Place the minced beef in a bowl and add the peeled and finely chopped onion.

2. Soak the buns in a dish containing the milk and an equal quantity of water for 20 minutes.

3. Squeeze the liquid from the buns and combine them with the eggs, paprika, salt, pepper, marjoram and hot mustard, and add this to the minced beef. Mix well and season to taste.

4. Place the meatloaf in a buttered baking dish and smooth with a moistened hand.

5. Roast for about 1 hour in the oven. Occasionally pour some water over the meatloaf. After 1 hour, remove the meatloaf from the baking dish and slice. Bind the sauce with the cornflour and water mix.

Pour the sauce over the slices of meatloaf. Serve with parsley potatoes.

110

■ Add a dash of fresh double cream to your sauce. It tastes delicious and it stretches out the sauce, just in case you get more company for dinner than expected!

2 heads of romanesco

 3 shallots

 2 tomatoes

 1 bunch fresh coriander

 2.5-cm (1-inch) piece of ginger

 400 g (14 oz) beef fillet steak

 4 tbsp oyster sauce

 4 tbsp groundnut oil

 1 garlic clove

 1 pinch of sugar

 Juice of 1 lime

(1)

Vietnamese Beef Stew with Ginger

1. Wash the romanesco and divide it into florets, including the stalk. Peel the shallots and slice them lengthways. Cut the tomatoes into quarters, deseed, and cut each quarter twice. Wash the coriander and chop. Peel the ginger and finely slice. Remove any fat or tendons from the beef fillet steak and cut the meat into strips 2-cm (¾-inch) wide and 3-cm (1¼-inch) long. Place in a bowl, combine with the oyster sauce and marinate for 20 minutes.

2. Slowly sauté the romanesco florets with half of the oil in a nonstick wok for about 3 minutes. Move the florets to the side, then pour in the rest of the oil on the other side of the wok.

3. Peel the garlic clove and chop. Add it to the oil and sauté it. Then add the marinated beef strips and sear for 1 minute while stirring.

4. Add the shallots, ginger and tomato pieces, and toss. Fry only briefly, so the vegetables stay crispy.

5. Then add the coriander, sugar and juice of the lime. Mix it only once and serve.

■ You can mix cooked glass noodles or wide rice noodles into the dish. You need about 200 g (7 oz) cooked noodles for this recipe.

* * * 30

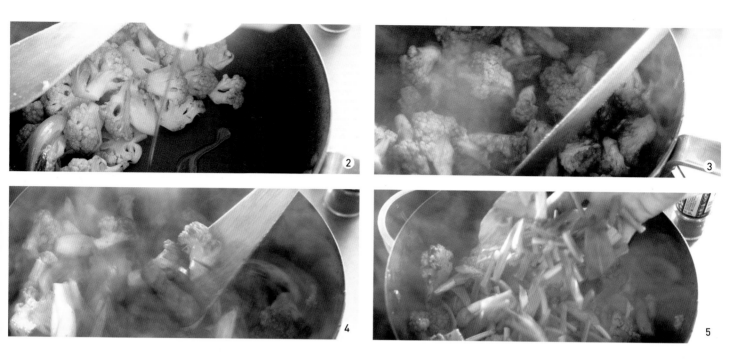

1.5 kg (3 lb 5 oz) veal fillet

 1 tsp salt
1 pinch of white pepper

 5 sprigs fresh rosemary

 1 tbsp flour

 200 g (7 oz) carrots

 300 g (10½ oz) young onions

 150 g (5½ oz) celeriac

 7 cloves

 60 g (2¼ oz) butter

 3 tbsp vegetable oil

 2 bay leaves

 100 ml (3½ fl oz) white wine

 800 g (1 lb 12 oz) small potatoes

Veal Roast with Root Vegetables and Small Potatoes

1. Preheat the oven to 180°C (350°F/Gas Mark 4).Season the meat with salt and pepper. Leave the tendons and fat on the meat; they make the roast juicier. Cover with the rosemary sprigs and the bay leaves, and tie with kitchen twine. Then dust with flour.

2. Peel and chop the carrots, and halve the onions. Peel and chop the celeriac. Place them in an oven dish with the cloves. Dot the butter among them. Season the vegetables lightly with salt and pepper.

3. Heat the oil in a nonstick frying pan and sauté the veal evenly on all sides until golden brown.

4. Then add it to the vegetables and put it in the oven. Roast for 30 minutes and baste frequently. Add 50 ml (1⅔ fl oz) white wine every 10 minutes.

5. In the meantime, peel the potatoes and cook in a pan of salted water for about 10 minutes. Drain and add them to the roast. Cook for an additional hour in the oven at 170°C (340°F/Gas Mark 3½). Baste frequently with the juices and turn the roast and the vegetables over occasionally. Remove from the oven. Arrange the vegetables, the potatoes and the sauce on serving plates. Remove the kitchen twine and the herbs from the roast. Slice the roast and arrange it on the plates.

■ If the meat is too lean, your roast can dry out. Both the neck and shoulder are well suited to this dish. The added vegetables are a wonderful side dish and create a natural sauce that does not need binding.

120

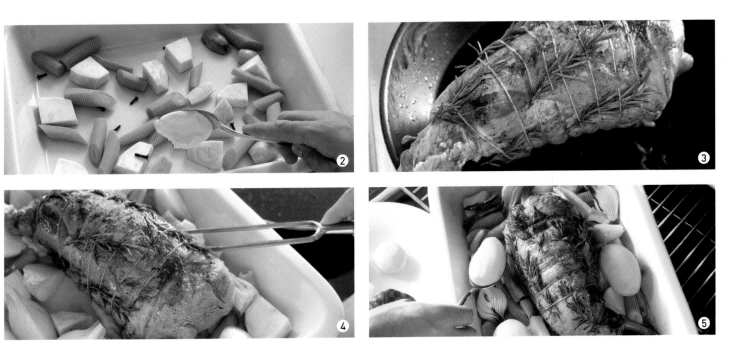

6 veal knuckles, 200–300 g (7–10½ oz) each

 1 tsp salt
1 pinch of black pepper

 2 tbsp flour

 250 g (9 oz) carrots

 150 g (5½ oz) onions

 5 garlic cloves

 100 g (3½ oz) celery stalks

 100 g (3½ oz) leeks

 ½ bunch fresh parsley

 1 orange

 1 lemon

 1 tsp fennel seeds

 90 g (3¼ oz) butter

 3 tbsp olive oil

 1 tbsp tomato purée

 250 ml (8½ fl oz) white wine

 250 g (9 oz) tinned, peeled tomatoes

 500 ml (17 fl oz) veal stock

 1 bay leaf

 2 sprigs fresh thyme

Osso Buco (Braised Veal Knuckles) with Gremolata

1. Dry the veal knuckles with kitchen paper. Season with salt and pepper and dust with flour.

2. Peel the carrots, onions and garlic. Wash the celery stalks and leeks and chop them all finely.

3. For the gremolata, chop the parsley, 2 garlic cloves, the orange and lemon peel, a few celery leaves and the fennel seeds. Mix with 50 g (1¾ oz) butter.

4. Heat the oil in a frying pan that is wide enough to fit all the knuckles in side by side. Slowly sauté the knuckles for 10 minutes on each side.

»

*** 180

■ Don't heat the meat too much. It would cause the knuckles to curve.

582 | **Beef & Veal**

5. Chop the remaining 3 cloves of garlic. Place two knuckles on top of the others and put the remaining butter in the available space. Let it foam up, then sauté the garlic and the tomato purée.

6. Add the diced onions, carrots, leeks and celery (see p. 354) to the pan. Sauté lightly and distribute around the knuckles. Continue to sauté for another 10 minutes and turn the meat over occasionally. Deglaze with the white wine and simmer.

7. Then add the tomatoes, veal stock, bay leaf and thyme sprigs. Cover with a lid and braise the knuckles slowly for about 2 hours. Turn them over occasionally and make sure they are covered with sauce. If necessary, add some water. Then season with salt and pepper to taste and arrange on serving plates. Add the gremolata to the finished sauce, and pour over the knuckles to complete the dish.

Serve with risotto flavoured with saffron.

■ The gremolata can alternatively be prepared with fresh marjoram or fennel. The butter takes on all flavours.

1 kg (2 lb 4 oz) veal fillet

 1 pinch of salt
1 pinch of black pepper

 2 tbsp vegetable oil

 150 g (5½ oz) lean veal

 100 g (3½ oz) cooked ham

 2 eggs

 70 ml (2½ fl oz) double cream

 1 tbsp cognac

 100 g (3½ oz) button mushrooms

 40 g (1½ oz) butter

 1 pinch of nutmeg, freshly grated

 200 ml (7 fl oz) Madeira

 30 g (1 oz) pistachios

 ½ bunch fresh parsley

 250 g (9 oz) puff pastry dough

①

Veal Fillet in Puff Pastry with Herb Stuffing

1. Remove all skin and tendons from the veal fillet steak and cut into 4 equal portions. Season with salt and pepper. Heat the oil in a frying pan and sauté the veal fillet on both sides, so the pores close. Place on a plate to cool. Slice the lean veal and cooked ham into 5-mm (¼-inch) cubes and place in a food processor. Add salt, pepper, 1 of the eggs, 50 ml (1⅔ fl oz) of the double cream and the cognac. Mix for about 1 minute.

2. Wash the button mushrooms and chop finely. Melt the butter in a large frying pan and sauté the mushrooms. Season with salt and pepper and sprinkle with nutmeg. Add the Madeira. Place in

a bowl to cool. Finely chop the pistachios in the food processor and place in a bowl. Wash and chop the parsley. As soon as all ingredients have cooled down, combine the stuffing with the pistachios and parsley and mix well.

3. Spread the mushroom-herb stuffing over the sautéed veal fillet until the meat is completely covered.

4. Preheat the oven to 220°C (425°F/ Gas Mark 7). Roll out the puff pastry dough 5 mm (¼ inch) thick and separate into 4 equal squares. Place the veal fillet in the centre of the dough. Separate the remaining egg and beat the egg yolk with

■ Serve with a truffle sauce (see tournedos rossini, p. 566), a herb or pepper cream sauce (see p. 148), or with fresh chanterelles.

* * * 80

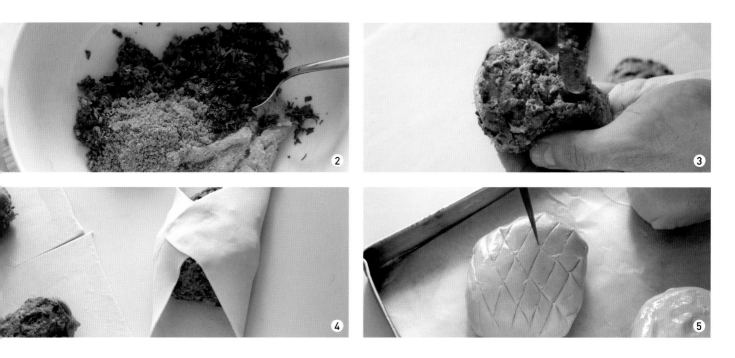

tbsp double cream. Brush this mixture
onto the edges of the puff pastry and
wrap them up into packages. Lightly push
down on the edges to seal them.

6. Place the veal pastries with the
smooth side up on a baking tray lined
with baking paper. Brush the remaining
egg mixture on them and make a
diamond pattern in the dough with the
back of the knife. Cook for about 25
minutes in the oven. Halfway through the
cooking time, reduce the heat to 200°C
(400°F/Gas Mark 6). Arrange the veal
pastries on a serving platter.

800 g (1 lb 12 oz) calf kidneys

 1 shallot

 200 g (7 oz) French beans

 1 tbsp salt

 1 kg (2 lb 4 oz) home-made mashed potatoes (see p. 336)

 2 onions

 4 tbsp vegetable oil

 1 pinch of black pepper

 ½ bunch fresh parsley

 20 g (²/₃ oz) butter

 40 ml (1¹/₃ fl oz) white port

 300 ml (10 fl oz) double cream

 1 tbsp coarse mustard

Kidneys in Mustard Cream Sauce with Mashed Onion Potatoes

1. Separate the kidneys and cut away any fat with a knife. Peel the shallot and finely dice it. Clean the French beans, remove any stems, and cut into 2-cm (¾-inch) pieces. Cook in a pan filled with salted water for about 3 minutes. Then place in water with ice cubes to cool. This helps to preserve the beans' green colour.

2. Peel the onions, halve, cut into strips, and sauté in 2 tbsp oil until golden brown. Then mix into the mashed potatoes. Heat the remaining oil in a nonstick frying pan. Add the kidneys, season with salt and pepper, and sear on all sides.

3. Place the kidneys in a sieve and drain. This avoids making the sauce too intensely flavoured. Wash and clean the parsley and chop it.

4. Heat the butter in a frying pan until foamy and sauté the shallots. Add the port and reduce the liquid. Add the double cream and again reduce the liquid by half.

5. Add the well-drained kidneys and the mustard. Mix and reheat. Then mix in the green beans and the chopped parsley. Arrange on serving plates together with the mashed onion potatoes.

■ You may sear the kidneys with vegetables such as small button mushrooms, whole white onions, small carrot pieces or French beans, and add gin and beef jus.

½ garlic clove

 100 g (3½ oz) cooked ham

 5 tbsp butter

 2 onions

 1 tsp fresh marjoram

 ½ bunch fresh parsley

 500 g (1 lb 2 oz) veal, minced

 4 slices of white bread

 150 ml (5 fl oz) milk

 1 pinch of salt
1 pinch of black pepper

 1 tbsp mustard

 2 eggs

Sautéed Veal Patties

1. Peel the garlic and chop finely. Cut the ham into small cubes.

2. Add 2 tbsp of the butter to a pan and brown the garlic and ham. Peel and dice the onions, and add to the pan, sautéeing them until light brown. Remove from the heat and mix in the marjoram. Wash the parsley and chop.

3. Put the veal in a bowl. Soak the bread in the milk, squeeze dry and add to the bowl.

4. Add the cooled onion-ham mixture. Season with salt and pepper. Add the mustard and the eggs.

5. Mix well – this is best done by hand.

6. Moisten your hands and form patties, each about 50 g (1¾ oz).

7. Carefully sauté the patties in the remaining 3 tbsp butter for about 5 minutes on each side.

8. Baste the patties continuously with the jus. That keeps them juicy.

Arrange on plates and serve with mustard, potato salad or fried potatoes.

■ Instead of cooked ham, you can use finely cubed bacon, which adds additional zest to your patties.

35

4 veal cutlets, 160 g (5¾ oz) each

 1 pinch of salt
1 pinch of pepper

 100 g (3½ oz) flour

 2 eggs

 300 g (10½ oz) breadcrumbs

 100 g (3½ oz) flaked almonds

 5 tbsp vegetable oil

 30 g (1 oz) butter

Veal Cutlets in Almond-Bread Batter

1. Lightly pound the cutlets with the blade of a large kitchen knife.

2. Season with salt and pepper.

3. Coat the cutlets in flour and shake off any excess.

4. Put the eggs into a bowl and beat them. Dip the cutlets in the egg, completely covering the meat.

5. Pour the breadcrumbs and the flaked almonds into a wide dish, mix, and cover the cutlets in the mixture.

6. Put the oil and the butter into a frying pan and heat until foamy. Place the cutlets in the pan and sauté them, turning over after a good 3 minutes.

7. Sauté for another 3 minutes on the other side, continuously basting with the jus.

8. Remove from the pan and leave the cutlets to drain on kitchen paper.

Arrange on plates; serve with parsley potatoes and garnish with lemon slices.

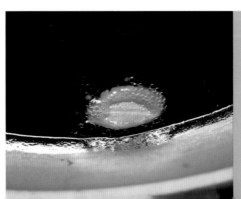

■ Drop a flaked almond into the oil. When it bubbles, the oil is at the right temperature.

8 veal cutlets, thinly sliced (70 g/2½ oz each)

 1 pinch of salt
1 pinch of pepper

 3 sprigs fresh sage

 8 slices of prosciutto

 800 g (1 lb 12 oz) grilled potatoes (see p. 326)

 1 tbsp olive oil

 60 g (2¼ oz) butter

 100 ml (3½ fl oz) Marsala wine

 150 ml (5 fl oz) veal stock

1

Saltimbocca alla Romana with Sage and Prosciutto

1. Lightly pound the veal slices and season with salt and pepper on both sides. Use only a little salt, because the prosciutto is already salty. Then top them with some sage leaves.

2. Place the prosciutto slices on the veal and lightly press on them with your hand. If necessary, use cocktail sticks to hold them in place, even though they prevent the saltimbocca from frying evenly.

3. Heat the olive oil and half of the butter in a frying pan. Place the cutlets with the prosciutto on the bottom into the frying pan and sauté for about 2 minutes over a medium heat. Then turn over and sauté for another 2 minutes.

4. Pour the Marsala over the saltimbocca and remove them from the frying pan. Add the veal stock to the jus and reduce to about half its original volume.

5. Bind the sauce with the remaining butter and put the meat back into the sauce.

Arrange the grilled potatoes and the saltimbocca on serving plates and garnish with oregano.

■ Use cutlets from the loin or top rounds. You can serve this dish with spinach leaves, Vichy carrots or green beans. Instead of Marsala, you can use Madeira or sweet white wine.

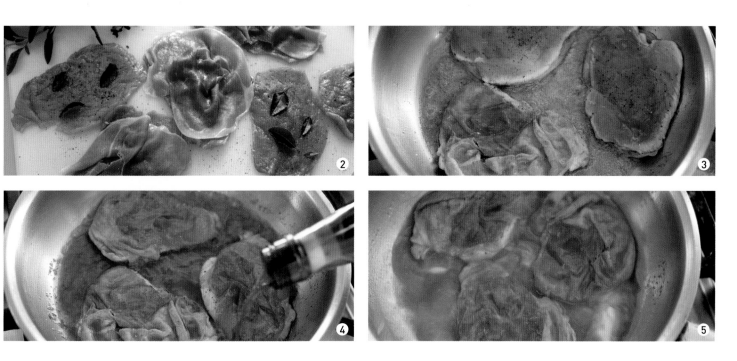

8 slices of top round of veal
(70 g/2½ oz each)

 1 pinch of salt
1 pinch of pepper

 1 kg (2 lb 4 oz) potatoes

 80 g (2¾ oz) butter

 1 bouquet fresh parsley

 80 ml (2¾ oz) vegetable oil

 150 g (5½ oz) pastry flour

 3 eggs

 350 g (12 oz) breadcrumbs

 1 lemon

Wiener Schnitzel

1. Pound the veal on both sides with a meat mallet. Then season with salt and pepper on both sides. Peel the potatoes and halve or quarter them depending on size, then boil in salted water for about 20 minutes. Drain and put 40 g (1½ oz) of the butter over the potatoes. Wash and clean the parsley and set aside.

2. Coat the veal with flour on both sides and shake off any excess. Crack the eggs into a bowl and beat with a fork. Add a small dash of mineral water. This helps the batter rise during frying. Then dip the veal into the beaten egg.

3. Make sure the veal is covered with egg on all sides so that the batter sticks.

4. Place the breadcrumbs in a deep dish. Coat the veal on all sides with the crumbs and gently press down on the crumbs. Do not press too firmly, as this would prevent the coating from expanding while frying.

5. Pour the oil and the remaining butter into a large frying pan and heat until foamy. Then add the schnitzel and fry for 2 minutes.

6. Carefully turn the schnitzel over with a fork and fry for another 3 minutes. Remove and place on kitchen paper to drain. Chop the parsley and add it to the cooked potatoes. Arrange the schnitzel and the potatoes on serving plates and garnish with lemon wedges.

■ After covering the veal in breadcrumbs, place it on a chopping board that has previously been covered with the crumbs. This ensures that the coating does not soak through, even if the schnitzel cannot be cooked straight away as planned. An anchovy fillet stuffed with capers and placed on a slice of lemon is the original garnish for Wiener schnitzel.

Pork

Contents

Types of Pork Cut

The hallmarks of good pork are an almost ivory white, odourless, firm meat without moistness. It's not necessarily a bad sign if a piece of pork has two different colours. This can be due to the fact that a butcher made a cut at a crucial place, or it can indicate the stress levels of the pig before it was slaughtered. Pork tastes best when it comes from free-range farms. This is particularly the case if the animals were fed on acorns and chestnuts.

The meat of intensively factory-farmed pigs ('turbo pigs') proves to be disappointing: their flesh is watery and they have enormous chops and hams. The characteristic fat has been bred out.

There are hardly any reliable signs of quality. Nevertheless, when buying pork, we should make sure that it is dry and is not exuding any liquid. Meat that turns grey quickly also comes from intensively farmed pigs in the industrial sector. For best results, the fat should be removed only after the pork has been roasted or stewed: it's an important flavour enhancer. If the pork has been wrapped in paper by your butcher, it will keep for about two days in your refrigerator at a temperature of 2°C (36°F).

In France, there is a well-known saying: *Tout est bon dans le cochon*; everything on a pig is good. Indeed, expert butchers know how to make full use of this animal. The blood is used in black pudding and the intestines are made into sausage casings. The breast can be smoked or cured. The belly and the neck are far fatter than fillets: that is not a disadvantage. As we have already said, fat is an important flavour enhancer.

Cooking Chart

Product	Weight	Method	Temperature	Time	Note
Roast pork with crackling (cut into the crackling with a razor blade)	1.8 kg (4 lb)	Oven	180°C (350°F/ Gas Mark 4)	100 minutes	
Rolled pork roast	1.5 kg (3 lb 5 oz)	Oven	160°C (325°F/GM 3)	110 minutes	
Smoked pork roast, uncooked	1.6 kg (3 lb 8 oz)	Oven	150°C (300°F/GM 1)	70 minutes	
Pork fillet medallions	60 g (2¼ oz)	Frying pan	Medium heat	8 minutes	
Pork mince	2 kg (4 lb 8 oz)	Oven	160°C (325°F/GM 3)	80 minutes	
Suckling pig leg	2.2–2.5 kg (5–5 lb 8 oz)	Oven	160°C (325°F/GM 3)	90 minutes	
Goulash	Large cubes	Saucepan with lid	Low heat	70 minutes of stewing	20 mins of gentle sautéeing
Knuckle of pork	1.2 kg (2 lb 12 oz)	Oven	180°C (350°F/GM 4)	80 minutes	
Spare ribs	1 kg (2 lb 4 oz)	Oven	160°C (325°F/GM 3)	40 minutes	
Minced pork meatballs	500 g (1 lb 2 oz)	Oven	180°C (350°F/GM 4)	25 minutes	
Pork chops	250 g (9 oz)	Frying pan	Medium heat	6 minutes	
Pork neck steaks	300 g (10½ oz)	Frying pan	Medium heat	10 minutes	

GM = Gas Mark

Pork fillet

Pork chop

Roast pork

Pork neck

Ham hocks

Pork mince

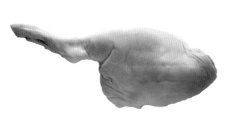

Suckling pig leg

Spare ribs

Pork belly for a rolled pork roast

Ribs

Pig's trotter

Pig's ears

601

1 pork shoulder with rind, about 1 kg (2 lb 4 oz)

 ½ tsp caraway seeds

 2 tbsp vegetable oil

 1 kg (2 lb 4 oz) caraway potatoes (see p. 309)

 2 garlic cloves

 1 pinch of salt
1 pinch of black pepper

 2 carrots

 ¼ celeriac

 4 small onions

 200 ml (7 fl oz) water

 150 ml (5 fl oz) beer

1

Roast Pork with Sauce and Caraway Potatoes

1. Preheat the oven to 160°C (325°F/ Gas Mark 3).Put the pork shoulder on a work surface and, with a very sharp knife or cutter, make approximately 5-mm (¼-inch) deep slits in the rind in a diamond-shaped pattern. Rub in the caraway seeds. Drizzle the meat with the vegetable oil, so that the spices will adhere better to the roast.

2. Peel the garlic cloves and dice them finely. Rub the salt, pepper and garlic gently into the scored pork shoulder. Peel the carrots and the celeriac and cut them into big pieces.

3. Then rub off the loose outer skins of the onions with your hands and cut off the root bases. There is always residual dirt in these areas. Put the unpeeled onions in an oven dish with the pork. Add 200 ml (7 fl oz) water and put the roast into the oven for 40 minutes.

4. Baste the roast repeatedly with the juices. After 40 minutes, put the caraway potatoes into the oven on the bottom rack. Cook the roast and the potatoes for 40 minutes longer. Then pour the beer over the roast and add the vegetables. Increase the temperature

■ Roast pork is also delicious with sauerkraut, red cabbage or Vichy carrots. This recipe can also be prepared with pork neck or pork knuckle.

130

to 180°C (350°F/Gas Mark 4) for the last 10 minutes of cooking and refrain from basting the roast during this time, so that the skin can become nice and crisp. Then remove it from the oven, carve it and serve it with the potatoes and the root vegetables.

1 tsp salt

 1 onion studded with cloves and a bay leaf

 2 carrots, peeled

 100 g (3½ oz) celeriac, peeled

 1–2 suckling pig legs

 1 pineapple

 1 tbsp cloves

 3 tbsp acacia honey

 1 pinch of cinnamon

 2 tbsp vegetable oil

Suckling Pig Leg with Honey and Pineapple

1. Preheat the oven to 160°C (325°F/Gas Mark 3). In a large pan, bring salted water to the boil. Add the onion studded with cloves and the bay leaf, the carrots and the celeriac. Add the pig legs and simmer them for 5 minutes. Remove the legs and let them cool on a chopping board, so that you can handle them easily.

2. Score the skin with a very sharp knife or a cutter every 1 cm (½ inch). Cut the skiin off the pineapple (see p. 654), cut it into 1-cm (½-inch) thick slices and set them aside. Stick the cloves into the meat. This will impart a wonderful flavour to the dish.

3. Put the meat into an oven dish and drizzle it with the honey. Roast it in the oven for 1½ hours. Baste it frequently from the start with water and the pan juices. This way, the skin will become nice and crispy. Season the pineapple slices lightly with salt, dust them with cinnamon and rub them with oil. Sear them on both sides for 1 minute in a nonstick pan. Then arrange them on plates and put the pig legs on top.

180

■ For best results, use small suckling pig legs, each weighing 800 g (1 lb 12 oz). Two legs are needed for four people. Serve them with mashed potatoes, roasted beetroots, grilled sweet potato slices or glazed carrots. The sweet potato slices can also be added to the suckling pig legs half an hour before the end of cooking to absorb the pan juices and so develop even more flavour.

1 pork shoulder, weighing
1 kg (2 lb 4 oz)

 1 tsp salt
1 pinch of black pepper

 2 tbsp sweet paprika

 1 tsp dried marjoram

 1 tbsp flour

 300 g (10½ oz) onions

 3 garlic cloves

 20 g (⅔ oz) fresh parsley stems

 40 g (1½ oz) pork lard

 ½ lemon

 ½ tsp caraway seeds

 20 g (4 tsp) butter

 1 tbsp tomato purée

 500 ml (17 fl oz) chicken or
beef stock

500 g (1 lb 2 oz) fresh tagliolini (see
p. 200)

1 bunch fresh chives

Pork Goulash with Paprika and Butter Noodles

1. Cut the pork shoulder into 4-cm (1½-inch) cubes. Leave the sinew and the fat on the meat, as they will make the goulash tender and juicy. Put the meat into a bowl, season it with the salt, pepper, paprika and marjoram, and dust it with the flour.

2. Mix everything well with your hands. Peel and halve the onions, and cut them into strips. Peel 2 garlic cloves and dice them finely. Tie the parsley stems together with kitchen twine to form a little bouquet.

3. Heat the pork lard in a large pan, and add first the garlic and then the onions to it. Sauté them gently until the onions are translucent. To make the herb butter, finely chop the remaining garlic clove, 1 piece of lemon zest and the caraway seeds, and combine them with the butter brought to room temperature. Then put the herb butter in the refrigerator to chill.

4. Put the meat in the pan and sauté it gently for 10 minutes, being careful not to brown it. Push the meat to the sides of the pan and add the tomato purée in the middle, and brown it slightly. Mix it with the meat, cover the pan and cook for another 10 minutes.

120

■ For a Szegedin goulash, add 500 g (1 lb 2 oz) cooked sauerkraut and mix 150 g (5½ oz) crème fraîche into the goulash. Serve it accompanied by freshly cooked parsley potatoes and bread dumplings.

5. Pour in the stock and cover again. Cook it slowly for 1 hour. Stir occasionally and add some water, if necessary. After 45 minutes, add the parsley bouquet. Remove it 15 minutes later, add the chilled herb butter and mix the goulash well. Arrange the goulash on plates, and serve it with freshly cooked tagliolini tossed in butter and sprinkled with finely snipped chives.

1 kg (2 lb 4 oz) pork spare ribs

 3 litres (5¼ pints) water

 250 ml (8½ fl oz) fruit vinegar

 150 g (5½ oz) sugar

 2 bay leaves

 8 black peppercorns

 3 shallots

 150 ml (5 fl oz) BBQ Sauce (see p. 56)

Spare Ribs Glazed with BBQ Sauce

1. Get your butcher to cut through the spare ribs once lengthways. Bring the water to the boil in a large pan. Add the vinegar, sugar, bay leaves, peppercorns and unpeeled shallots to the pan, and let it simmer for 5 minutes. Add the spare ribs and simmer them gently in the stock for 10 minutes. Then remove the pan from the heat and allow the spare ribs to cool in the stock – overnight, if possible, but for at least 3 hours in the refrigerator. Then remove the spare ribs from the stock and let them drain.

2. Preheat the oven at 160°C (325°F/Gas Mark 3).Brush the spare ribs generously with BBQ sauce and put them on a baking tray. Then roast them in the oven for approximately 40 minutes. Halfway through, turn the spare ribs and coat them with BBQ sauce once more. Due to the honey contained in the sauce, the spare ribs must be cooked at a low temperature to avoid burning them.

You can also prepare the spare ribs in advance and marinate them in the BBQ sauce in the refrigerator. Alternatively, the spare ribs can be grilled and served with roasted or baked potatoes, or with a salad.

+ 3 hours for chilling

■ The BBQ sauce can be used as the basis of a marinade for Szechuan-style spare ribs. To this recipe, add grated ginger root, finely chopped dried chillies, and crushed star anise pods mixed with onion or dill seeds. Serve the ribs with fried rice or fried noodles and vegetables.

1 thumb-sized piece ginger

 ½ tsp red curry paste

 4 tbsp oyster sauce

 3 tbsp vegetable oil

 800 g (1 lb 12 oz) pork belly

1 lime, cut into quarters

Pork Belly Grilled with an Asian Marinade

1. Peel and finely grate the fresh ginger into a bowl.

2. Add the curry paste.

3. Pour in the oyster sauce.

4. Add the vegetable oil and stir the mixture well.

5. Slice the pork belly and put it into a suitable container. Pour the marinade over it and mix it well. For best results, marinate the meat for at least 1 hour, so that the spices can infuse the meat properly. Chargrill the slices on both sides for approximately 5 minutes in a griddle pan.

Sprinkle them with the juice from the quartered lime and serve them with white bread or baked potatoes.

■ You can also marinate pork chops or pork neck in this mixture and then cook them in a griddle pan or under the grill.

500 g (1 lb 2 oz) pork mince

 2 tbsp oyster sauce

 400g (14 oz) tinned coconut milk

 1 tsp red curry paste

 300 g (10½ oz) tinned sweetcorn

2 tbsp flaked almonds

Minced Pork Meatballs Cooked in a Coconut-Curry Sauce

1. Preheat the oven to 180°C (350°F/ Gas Mark 4). Mix the pork with the oyster sauce and shape into small balls. Put them into a shallow casserole dish. Pour the coconut milk into a tall container. Scrape out all the milk from the tin.

2. Add the curry paste to the coconut milk.

3. Using a hand-held blender, blend the mixture briefly, until the curry paste is thoroughly mixed in.

4. Pour the sauce over the pork meatballs. Drain the sweetcorn in a sieve and sprinkle it over the meatballs. Then sprinkle over the flaked almonds and cook for approximately 25 minutes in the oven. Cover with some kitchen foil so that the flaked almonds don't burn. Arrange the meatballs in bowls.

■ Milder yellow curry paste can be used instead of the red curry paste. A few petit pois can be added to the sauce as well.

45

1 small tin or jar Mexican salsa

1 pinch of black pepper

2 sprigs fresh rosemary

8 pork chops, 120 g (4½ oz) each

2 tbsp olive oil

1 pinch of salt

Grilled Pork Chop with a Mexican Marinade

1. Put the salsa in a bowl. If you like it hot, buy a spicy version of the sauce.

2. Add some black pepper and freshly plucked rosemary needles to the sauce.

3. Put the pork chops on a platter and pour the marinade over the meat.

4. Turn the chops and brush the other side with the marinade as well. Drizzle a little olive oil on the chops.

5. Cover the pork chops with cling film and leave them to marinate in the refrigerator for at least 1 hour (but ideally, for 3–4 hours). Chargrill them on both sides for approximately 3 minutes in a griddle pan and season them with salt.

Serve them with peppers, baked potatoes or a tomato salad.

■ Buy a whole saddle of pork and cut it into 3-cm (1¼-inch) cubes. Stick the cubes of pork onto skewers, alternating them with pepper pieces and diced onions, and season them with the marinade. Then grill them slowly or chargrill them in a griddle pan.

615

600 g (1 lb 5 oz) pork neck

 1 pinch of salt
1 pinch of black pepper

 ½ tsp ground cinnamon

 100 g (3½ oz) flour

 2 eggs

 250 g (9 oz) pistachios

 3 tbsp vegetable oil

1 tbsp butter

Pork Neck Steaks Baked in a Pistachio Crust

1. Cut the pork neck into small steaks and season them well on both sides with salt, black pepper and the cinnamon.

2. Dust the meat with flour and shake off any excess. Dip the steaks in the beaten eggs, making sure they are thoroughly coated.

3. Chop the pistachios with a large knife and put them in a dish. Put the egg-dipped steaks onto the pistachios.

4. Coat both sides of the pork steaks with the pistachios and press down on the coating gently.

5. Heat the vegetable oil and butter in a frying pan until it foams, and add the steaks.

6. Brown the steaks on both sides over a medium heat for approximately 5 minutes and let them drain briefly on kitchen paper.

Arrange the steaks on plates and serve them with carrots, cauliflower and couscous.

25

■ Fry small pistachio-coated pork medallions, topped with Gorgonzola cheese, and grill them briefly.

2 ripe pears

 1 tbsp butter

 1 tbsp sugar

 1 pinch of black pepper

 2 sprigs fresh thyme

 4 pork neck steaks, each weighing approx. 130 g (4½ oz) each

 1 pinch of salt

 1 tbsp vegetable oil

 120 g (4½ oz) Gorgonzola cheese

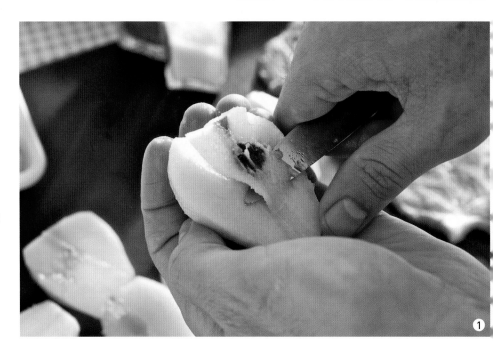

Pork Steaks Baked with Pears and Gorgonzola Cheese

1. Preheat the oven to 180°C (350°F/Gas Mark 4). Peel the pears, cut them in half and cut out the core with a sharp knife. Cut the pears lengthways into segments.

2. Melt the butter with the sugar in a frying pan. Add the pear segments, season them with pepper and add the thyme. Toss everything in the frying pan and allow the mixture to caramelise slightly.

3. Season the pork neck steaks with salt and pepper. Sear the steaks on both sides in vegetable oil in a nonstick frying pan and put them into a baking dish.

4. Put the pear segments on top of the steaks.

5. Lay the Gorgonzola cheese on top and grill for 2–3 minutes.

Arrange the steaks on plates and pour the pan scrapings over them. Serve them with potatoes or pasta.

■ You can use dried fruit such as plums, apples or apricots cooked in red wine instead of pears.

1 ripe mango

 2 oranges

 1 white onion

 60 g (2¼ oz) butter

 1 tbsp honey

 6 green peppercorn clusters

 1 pinch of salt

 600 g (1 lb 5 oz) pork fillet

 2 tbsp vegetable oil

 1 pinch of black pepper

 2 sprigs fresh Thai basil

①

Pork Fillet on a Bed of Mango Sauce with Basil and Green Pepper

1. Peel the mango, remove the fruit from the stone with a knife, and chop it into 5-mm (¼-inch) cubes. Use a vegetable peeler to pare a strip of washed zest from 1 orange and chop it finely. Squeeze the oranges and set the juice aside. Peel the onion and dice it finely. Melt 40 g (1½ oz) of the butter in a long-handled saucepan. Gently sauté the diced onion until it is translucent, and then add the mango cubes.

2. Add the orange zest and the honey, and sauté gently for 5 minutes.

3. Strip the green peppercorns off 2 clusters and reserve the rest for use as a garnish. Add the peppercorns and the orange juice to the sauce, season

it with salt and let it simmer gently for approximately 10 minutes. Meanwhile, cut the clean, trimmed pork fillet into 8 medallions.

4. Let the oil and the remaining butter foam up in a nonstick frying pan. Season the medallions on both sides with salt and pepper and add them to the frying pan. Fry them on both sides for approximately 5 minutes and baste them with the pan juices.

Put portions of mango sauce on plates and lay 2 medallions on top of each portion. Garnish each plate with a green pepper cluster and some Thai basil leaves.

■ You can replace half of the mango with pineapple when you are preparing the mango sauce, which will taste even fruitier. You can also use curry powder, ginger or chilli peppers to season it more intensely.

*
*
*50

Lamb & Wild Game

Contents

Types of Lamb and Wild Game

In order to enjoy really good game, you need to know a hunter. Many consumers don't want lead shot or any authentic taste of the wild in their joint, so 'wild animals' are farm-raised nowadays.

Hare: Female hares taste better than their male counterparts. The males are tougher and more solid. The lighter the colour of the meat, the younger the animal. A red to a reddish-black colour is a sign of an old, tough hare. Young hare is more tender and is suitable for roasting. Older animals are suitable for marinating and for stews.

Venison: Red deer, fallow deer and so on, are mostly farm-raised today. Males have dark, almost brown meat, whereas the meat of females turns out somewhat paler. The colour of fallow deer meat is similar to that of mutton. The smaller the animal, the lighter and more delicate its meat. It is also the case that female animals taste better than their male counterparts.

Lamb: Good lamb is pale pink or almost white with a snowy white, solid layer of fat. This fat layer should be firm to the touch. If you are allowed to touch the meat, warm your hands first before sliding them over the fat layer. If the lamb is too old, your fingers will

subsequently have the distinctive, pungent smell of mutton. A dull red, almost purple, or downright black colour is a bad sign. This kind of meat also comes from older animals and tastes like mutton. You should also be careful with respect to large chops or fillets. A normal lamb weighs between 14 and 15 kg (32 and 35 lb). Anything heavier than 18 kg (40 lb) is classified as mutton. In the case of lamb as well, female animals are tastier than their male counterparts. Lamb can be stored in the chilled compartment of your refrigerator at 0–2°C (32–36°F) for two days.

Cooking Chart

Product	Weight	Method	Temperature	Time	Notes
Leg of lamb	1.5–1.8 kg (3 lb 5 oz–4 lb)	Oven	160°C (320°F/Gas Mark 3)	100 minutes	
Lamb's liver	300 g (10½ oz)	Frying pan	Medium heat	2 minutes	Cut into 1-cm (½-inch) slices
Saddle/rack of lamb	400 g (14 oz)	Oven	160°C (320°F/Gas Mark 3)	20 minutes	
Lamb chop	60 g (2¼ oz)	Griddle pan	Medium heat	5 minutes	Rub the chop with oil in advance, so that it doesn't stick to the griddle pan
Fillet of lamb	40 g (1½ oz)	Frying pan	Medium heat	4 minutes	
Shoulder of lamb	1.3–1.5 kg (3 lb–3 lb 5 oz)	Oven	200°C (390°F/Gas Mark 6)	45 minutes	
Saddle of venison	Whole, 2 kg (4 lb 8 oz)	Oven	180°C (350°F/Gas Mark 4)	35 minutes	Sear on all sides, in advance
Roast venison (female)	1.2–1.5 kg (2 lb 12 oz–3 lb 5 oz)	Oven	160°C (320°F/Gas Mark 3)	45 minutes	
Knuckle of lamb	250–300 g (9–10½ oz)	Oven	160°C (320°F/Gas Mark 3)	90 minutes	
Roast venison (male)	2 kg (4 lb 8 oz)	Oven	160°C (320°F/Gas Mark 3)	70 minutes	
Venison medallion	60 g (2¼ oz)	Frying pan	Medium heat	10 minutes	
Haunch of venison	1 kg (2 lb 4 oz)	Oven	170°C (340°F/Gas Mark 3½)	25 minutes	
Rabbit	1.3 kg (3 lb)	Oven	160°C (320°F/Gas Mark 3)	40 minutes	
Saddle of hare	450 g (1 lb)	Oven	170°C (340°F/Gas Mark 3½)	20 minutes	
Leg of hare	400 g (14 oz)	Saucepan with lid	Medium heat	70 minutes	
Leg of rabbit	250 g (9 oz)	Frying pan with lid	Medium heat	30 minutes	Stew

Leg of venison

Venison medallions

Haunch of venison

Rack of lamb

Lamb chop

Leg of lamb

Saddle of hare

Rabbit

Loin of venison

8 tbsp olive oil

 2 sprigs fresh thyme

 1 sprig fresh rosemary

 1 tsp fennel seeds

 1 pinch of salt
1 pinch of black pepper

 1 leg of lamb, weighing about
1.8 kg (4 lb), plus some lamb bones

 1 head of garlic

Roast Leg of Lamb with Herbs and Garlic

1. Preheat the oven to 200°C (400°F/Gas Mark 6). For the marinade, pour the olive oil in a bowl, pluck the thyme leaves off the sprigs, and add them to the oil.

2. Pluck the rosemary needles, use a knife to roughly chop them and add them with the fennel seeds to the oil. Combine all of the ingredients and season with salt and pepper.

3. Put the leg of lamb into a roasting tin along with the bones, and rub the leg of lamb thoroughly with the herbed oil. Separate the individual garlic cloves from the head, place them in a bowl unpeeled and press down on them lightly with the heel of your hand. Put the garlic cloves on top of the leg of lamb.

4. Put the lamb in the oven and roast it for 30 minutes. Turn the roast frequently and baste it with its juices. Then reduce the temperature to 180°C (350°F/Gas Mark 4) and roast it for another hour. While the lamb is roasting, occasionally add some water to the pan scrapings to create a sauce.

Arrange the leg of lamb on a platter. Remove the bones from the sauce. Pour the sauce over the lamb. Serve the roast leg of lamb with potatoes en papillote or couscous salad.

■ Finely chop parsley, tarragon, marjoram, and lemon and orange zest, and mix them with butter. Let the mixture foam up in a frying pan and pour it over the leg of lamb.

1 leg of lamb, about 1.3 kg (3 lb)

 1 bunch fresh parsley

 1 sprig fresh tarragon

 5 shallots

 150 g (5½ oz) carrots

 3 onions

 1 head young cabbage

 2 garlic cloves

 300 g (10½ oz) potatoes

 2 tbsp vegetable oil

 1 tsp salt
1 pinch of black pepper

 ½ tsp tomato purée

 1 bay leaf

1.2 litres (2 pints) beef stock

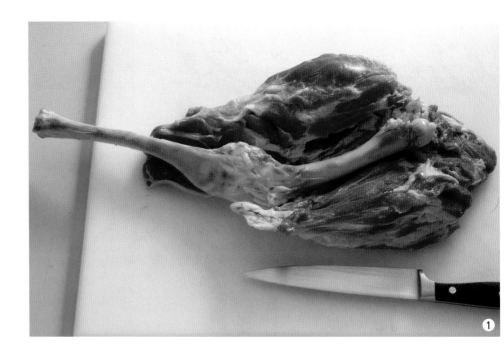

Irish Stew with Young Cabbage and Carrots

1. Cut into the leg of lamb along the bone and remove it carefully from the meat with the tip of your knife. Remove the fat and the gristle from the skin. Cut the meat into 3-cm (1¼-inch) pieces. Wash the parsley and the tarragon, pluck the leaves, and set them aside. They will only be chopped shortly before they are added to the dish, in order to preserve their flavour and their essential oils.

2. Peel and halve the shallots. Peel the carrots and cut them diagonally into 1-cm (½-inch) thick slices. Peel and halve the onions and cut them into strips. Remove the outer leaves from the cabbage, cut

it in half, remove the stalk and wash the head. Cut it into 3-cm (1¼-inches) cubes. Peel the garlic cloves and chop them finely. Peel the potatoes and cut them into 3-cm (1¼-inch) cubes.

3. Heat the oil in a saucepan, add the garlic first and then the onion strips, and cook them until they are translucent. Season the diced meat with salt and pepper, and add it to the pan. Sauté gently for 10 minutes. Push the meat to the sides of the pan, put the tomato purée in the middle and brown it a little, and then mix it with the meat. Add the bay leaf.

■ Lamb shoulder can be used instead of leg of lamb, but it will have to be cooked for 15 minutes longer, as it is more marbled. The quantity of vegetables can be augmented or other vegetables used according to your preference. French beans, celery and Savoy cabbage are every bit as delicious in this stew.

4. Pour the stock over the meat. You can use water as a substitute, but you will need to season the meat more if you do. Bring the stew to the boil and let it simmer for 15 minutes with a lid on.

5. Add the carrots, the shallots and the potatoes and let the stew simmer for 10 more minutes with the lid on. Add the cabbage, mix all of the ingredients thoroughly and simmer the stew for 20 minutes longer. Staggering the times at which the ingredients are added allows all of the ingredients to cook through without becoming overcooked. Finally, chop the parsley and the tarragon finely, stir them into the pan and serve the stew in soup bowls.

2 saddles of lamb, 1–1.2 kg
(2 lb 4 oz–2 lb 12 oz) each

 1 pinch of salt
1 pinch of black pepper

 3 tbsp olive oil

 6 garlic cloves

 2 sprigs fresh rosemary

 30 g (1 oz) butter

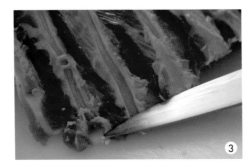

Pink Roast Rack of Lamb with Rosemary

1. Put the saddles of lamb on a chopping board and cut into the skin under the loin fillet at a depth of 1 cm (½ inch).

2. Trim the skin and the meat from the ribs.

3. Shave the skin off the bone with the knife, so that it is easier to remove.

4. Carefully loosen the skin from the bone with your fingers, until the bone is exposed and clean.

5. Then turn it over and cut this part of the skin off.

6. Cut along the backbone and remove the white sinew carefully. Then continue cutting on the back to the ribs.

7. Turn it over again to separate the rack of lamb from the backbone with sharp kitchen shears.

8. Remove small bits of sinew and bones from the separated rack of lamb and season it with salt and pepper on both sides.

■ You can use ready prepared racks of lamb instead of saddle of lamb but you will still need to clean the ribs. The rack of lamb can also be roasted with a pecan-lemon marinade. Chop the pecans coarsely, cut 2 pieces of lemon zest into fine strips and mix them with 1 sprig fresh rosemary, 2 tbsp olive oil and 1 tsp coarse mustard. Roast the lamb with this mixture for the last 5 minutes of cooking. Potatoes au gratin and green beans are very good accompaniments to the rack of lamb.

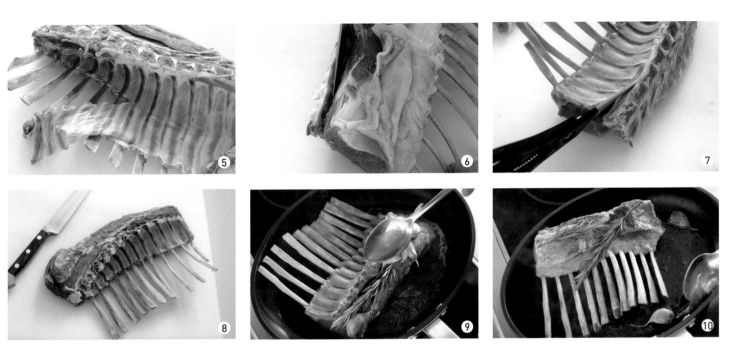

9. Preheat the oven to 180°C (350°F/Gas Mark 4). Heat the oil in a wide ovenproof frying pan and put the rack of lamb in it with its top side facing downwards. Place the garlic cloves, unpeeled, in a bowl and press down on them with the heel of your hand. Add them and the rosemary sprigs to the rack. Baste the lamb with the juices and turn it over after 5 minutes, replacing the rosemary on top of the rack of lamb so that it doesn't burn in the frying pan.

10. Add the butter. Roast the rack of lamb in the oven for approximately 10 minutes, and continue to baste it. Remove it from the oven, cover it with kitchen foil and let it rest for 3 minutes. Finally, cut it up and serve.

1 sprig fresh rosemary

1 sprig fresh thyme

½ bunch fresh parsley

3 garlic cloves

800 g (1 lb 12 oz) lamb chops

4 tbsp olive oil

1 pinch of salt
1 pinch of black pepper

Grilled Marinated Lamb

1. Wash the herbs, remove any damaged parts, pluck the leaves and chop them finely with a sharp kitchen knife.

2. Peel the garlic cloves and use a garlic press to crush them onto the chops.

3. Sprinkle the chopped herbs, olive oil and pepper on the chops and mix everything together. Marinate the chops for approximately 30 minutes.

4. Season the lamb chops with salt, and chargrill them on both sides in a griddle pan or on a barbecue grill, until they are pink in the middle (approximately 2 minutes per side).

Arrange the chops on plates and serve them with garlic bread or grilled vegetables.

45

■ You can use other herbs and spices as a marinade, such as sage, mint and lemon zest, cinnamon, ground cardamom, or curry powder and honey (in which case the lamb chops will have an Asian flavour). Serve these chops with couscous and a yogurt dip.

200 g (7 oz) bacon fat

 2 saddles of hare, around 400 g (1 lb 12 oz)

 4 pears

 1 tsp salt
1 pinch of black pepper

 60 ml (2 fl oz) vegetable oil

 10 juniper berries

 5 bay leaves

 1 sprig fresh rosemary

 40 g (1½ oz) butter

 1 tbsp soft brown sugar

 6 tsp cranberry jelly

①

Larded Saddle of Hare with Cranberry Pears

1. Put the bacon fat in the freezer for half an hour or so. This makes it easier to handle. Remove the skin and the membrane from both saddles of hare. Cut the fat into 5-cm (2-inch) long by 5-mm (¼-inch) thick strips. Grip the strip of fat in the back end of a larding needle.

2. Carefully stick the point of the needle into the meat and guide it through until the bacon fat is evenly distributed in the saddle and slightly protrudes. Repeat this procedure every 2 cm (¾ inch). Larding makes the meat juicier.

3. Peel the pears, cut them in half, and remove the core with a melon baller. Leave the stem on the pear to make it more visually attractive.

4. Preheat the oven to 170°C (340°F/Gas Mark 3½). Season the saddle of hare with salt and pepper. Heat the oil in a frying pan, sear both fillets on one side and then turn them over. Crush the juniper berries, then add them and the bay leaves, and garnish the dish with a rosemary sprig. Then roast the hare slowly in the oven for approximately 20 minutes and baste it frequently with its juices.

 120

■ For best results, use small, red Williams pears. Serve the saddle of hare accompanied by small potato cakes, finger noodles or a mushroom cream sauce (see p. 148).

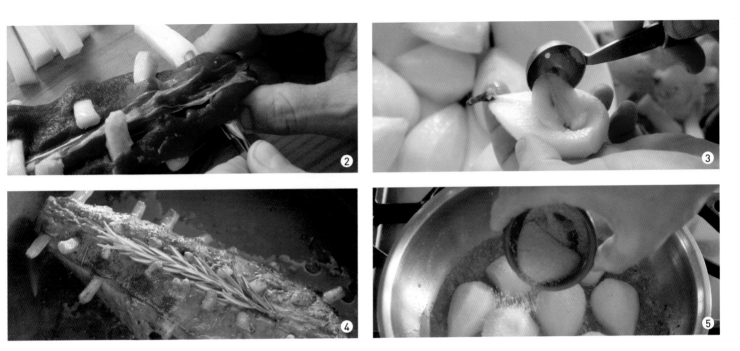

5. Meanwhile, melt the butter in a frying pan and sprinkle in half of the sugar. Lay the pear halves in the frying pan with their cut surface facing down. Sprinkle them with the remaining sugar and sauté them slowly, until they are golden yellow. Turn the pear halves over and fill them with the cranberry jelly. Remove the hare fillets carefully from the saddles with a knife and cut them diagonally into 2-cm (¾-inch) thick slices. Pour the pan juices over the meat, transfer it to a platter and serve it with the pears.

1 head of Savoy cabbage

 2 tbsp salt

 2 shallots

 750 g (1 lb 10 oz) celery

 ½ bunch fresh parsley

 100 g (3½ oz) butter

 1 pinch of black pepper

 1 pinch of nutmeg, freshly grated

 1 tbsp fruit vinegar

 750 ml (1¼ pints) game or chicken stock

 250 g (9 oz) morels

 1 venison backstrap, weighing approximately 750 g (1 lb 10 oz)

 1 sprig fresh rosemary

 2 tbsp oil

 8 juniper berries

 50 ml (1⅔ fl oz) Madeira

 300 ml (10 fl oz) jus (see p. 138)

 250 ml (8½ fl oz) cream

2 tbsp whipped cream

①

Medallions of Venison on a Bed of Savoy Cabbage Purée with Morel Sauce

1. Remove the outer leaves from the cabbage, cut it into quarters and remove the stalk. Wash the quarters and cut them into fine strips, diagonally. Cook the cabbage in boiling, salted water for 10 seconds, remove it and let it cool down in cold water. Then let it drain. Peel the shallots and dice them finely for the celery purée. Peel the celery, cut it into 3-cm (1¼-inch) cubes and cook it in a saucepan with boiling, salted water for approximately 2 minutes. Remove the celery and chill it under cold running water. Wash the parsley, pluck the leaves, and chop them finely.

2. Let 20 g (⅔ oz) of the butter foam up in a long-handled saucepan and gently sauté half of the shallots. Then add the Savoy cabbage and season it with salt, pepper and nutmeg. Pour in half of the stock and leave to simmer gently for 15 minutes, until the cabbage is soft. Meanwhile, heat up another 20 g (⅔ oz) butter in another long-handled saucepan and gently sauté the rest of the diced shallots. Add the celery, season the mixture with nutmeg and add the fruit vinegar. Pour in the remaining stock and gently steam the celery with the lid on until it is soft.

»

■ Brussels sprouts, glazed apples, morel sauce with cream, red cabbage, spaetzle, finger noodles, green beans, various mushrooms or potato cakes with chives go well with these medallions.

*** 150

3. Clean the morels, remove their stalks and wash them briefly in lukewarm water. Remove them immediately and put them on kitchen paper to drain. If mushrooms are left in water for too long, they absorb liquid and release it into the frying pan when they are sautéed.

4. Cut the saddle of venison into 8 medallions and pat them lightly with the heel of your hand. Season them with salt and pepper. Pluck the needles from the rosemary sprig and sprinkle over the medallions.

5. Let the oil foam up with 20 g (²⁄₃ oz) butter in a frying pan and add the medallions. Crush the juniper berries and add them to the meat. Sauté the medallions gently on both sides for approximately 5 minutes and baste them repeatedly with the pan juices.

6. Meanwhile, let the remaining butter foam up in a frying pan, add the well-drained morels, season them with salt and nutmeg, and sauté them quickly. Add the Madeira and reduce it.

7. Then add the beef jus, or a game sauce made from the bones to add a special flavour. Simmer the mushrooms for 5 minutes longer.

8. Pour 100 ml (3½ fl oz) cream onto the Savoy cabbage and stir well. Leave to cook briefly and add the whipped cream and the chopped parsley. Pour the remaining cream on the steamed celery and leave to simmer for 5 minutes longer. Then use a hand-held blender to purée it. Put a mound of puréed celery and a mound of puréed Savoy cabbage on a plate, add 2 medallions, pour some morel sauce over and serve.

■ These medallions go nicely with other side dishes and sauces such as red cabbage, French beans with bacon, glazed apples, salsify or golden pumpkin cakes. Mushrooms such as chanterelles, porcini or shiitakes can also be used for the sauce. You can also add cream and orange liqueur to it.

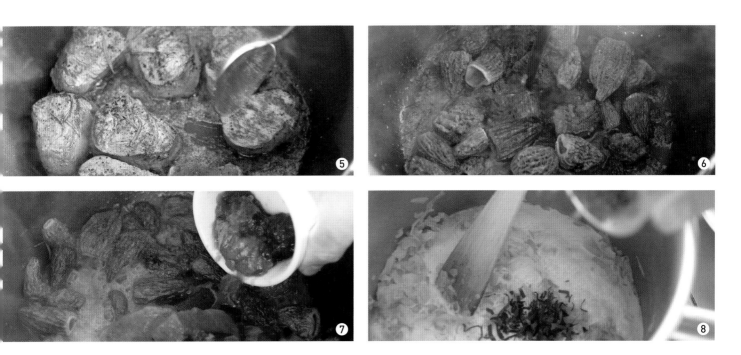

639

50 g (1¾ oz) salt

 2 sprigs fresh rosemary

 2 sprigs fresh thyme

 2 bay leaves

 1 lemon

 1 tsp juniper berries

 10 cloves

 1 tsp black peppercorns

 1 leg of venison, weighing 1 kg (2 lb 4 oz)

 ½ bunch fresh parsley

 5 shallots

 5 slices smoked, marbled bacon

 250 g (9 oz) small porcini mushrooms

 3 tbsp vegetable oil

 40 g (1½ oz) butter

 1 pinch of nutmeg, freshly grated

 40 ml (1½ oz) red port wine

 200 ml (7 fl oz) jus (see p. 138)

 200 ml (7 fl oz) cream

 100 g (3½ oz) crème fraîche

 3 tbsp cranberry jelly

Whole Leg of Venison with a Mushroom Cream Sauce

1. To season the leg of venison, prepare a seasoning mix in the blender using the following ingredients: salt, plucked rosemary needles and thyme leaves, bay leaves, the juice of ½ the lemon, juniper berries, cloves and black peppercorns. Blend everything finely in a food processor.

2. Ask your butcher to remove the leg shank so that you only have the meat to roast. Rub the roast on all sides with the seasoning mix and leave it to rest briefly, so that the flavours seep in. Preheat the oven at 170°C (340°F/Gas Mark 3½. Wash the parsley, pluck the leaves and chop them finely. Peel the shallots, dice two of them finely and cut the rest in quarters lengthways. Cut the bacon into 2-cm (¾-inch) wide strips.

3. Clean the porcini mushrooms to remove any dirt and cut them into 5-mm (¼-inch) slices.

4. Heat the oil in a frying pan and sear the leg of venison on all sides. Then roast it in the oven for 10 minutes.

5. Arrange the quartered shallots and the bacon strips around the leg of venison and roast it at 160°C (325°F/Gas Mark 3) for 20 minutes longer. Baste it frequently with the juices.

■ This dish is delicious when served with handmade spaetzle, crisp potato cakes or finger noodles. Cranberry preserves (home-made if possible), wild mushrooms and a celery purée provide the finishing touches for this feast of wild game.

6. Let the butter foam up in a nonstick frying pan. Gently sauté the porcini mushroom slices and season them with salt and nutmeg. Add the finely diced shallots and continue to sauté them gently until they are translucent. Add the red port wine and reduce the mixture.

7. Add the beef jus and reduce the mixture to one-third of its original volume.

8. Add the cream and crème fraîche to the sauce and bring it back to the boil. Season it to taste, add the cranberry jelly and remove from the heat.

9. It's important not to let the mushrooms disintegrate. They must be nice and firm in the sauce.

Stir the juice from the leg of venison into the porcini mushroom sauce. Pour the sauce onto a platter, and place the leg of venison on top.

4 haunches of rabbit

 1 pinch of salt
1 pinch of black pepper

 3 tsp sweet paprika

 2 small onions

 30 g (1 oz) butter

 500 ml (17 fl oz) chicken or
vegetable stock

 400 ml (13½ fl oz) cream

Stewed Haunch of Rabbit in Paprika Cream Sauce

1. Season the rabbit haunches with salt, pepper and paprika.

2. Peel the onions and dice them finely. Sauté them gently in the butter in a wide saucepan until they are translucent. Add the haunches of rabbit. Brown slightly on both sides.

3. Add the chicken stock and stew it with the lid on for approximately 30 minutes.

4. Turn the haunches of rabbit occasionally. You may have to add water if the liquid evaporates quickly. The bottom of the pan should be always covered with a 1-cm (½-inch) layer of liquid.

5. Add the cream and let the rabbit simmer gently in the sauce. You may need to add more salt and pepper to season the stew.

Serve with bread dumplings or ribbon noodles.

■ A whole jointed rabbit can be prepared in the same manner. If you omit the sweet paprika and add 250 g (9 oz) sliced mushrooms, such as button mushrooms or other wild fungi, after you brown the rabbit, you will obtain a wonderful mushroom sauce.

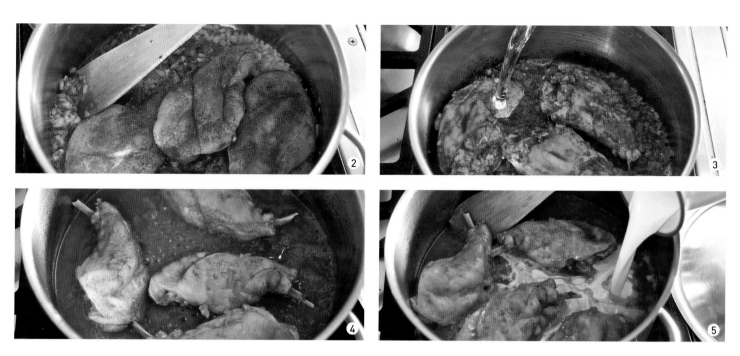

Fruit & Desserts

Contents

Types of Fruit

Unfortunately, beautiful fruit isn't always good fruit. For the most part, shrivelled organic items have more flavour than shiny fruit from the supermarket. Therefore, we can seldom tell the quality of fruit from its appearance alone.

Redcurrants

Raspberries

Strawberry

Red dessert apple

Fuji apple

Golden Delicious apple

Galia melon

Cantaloupe melon

Watermelon

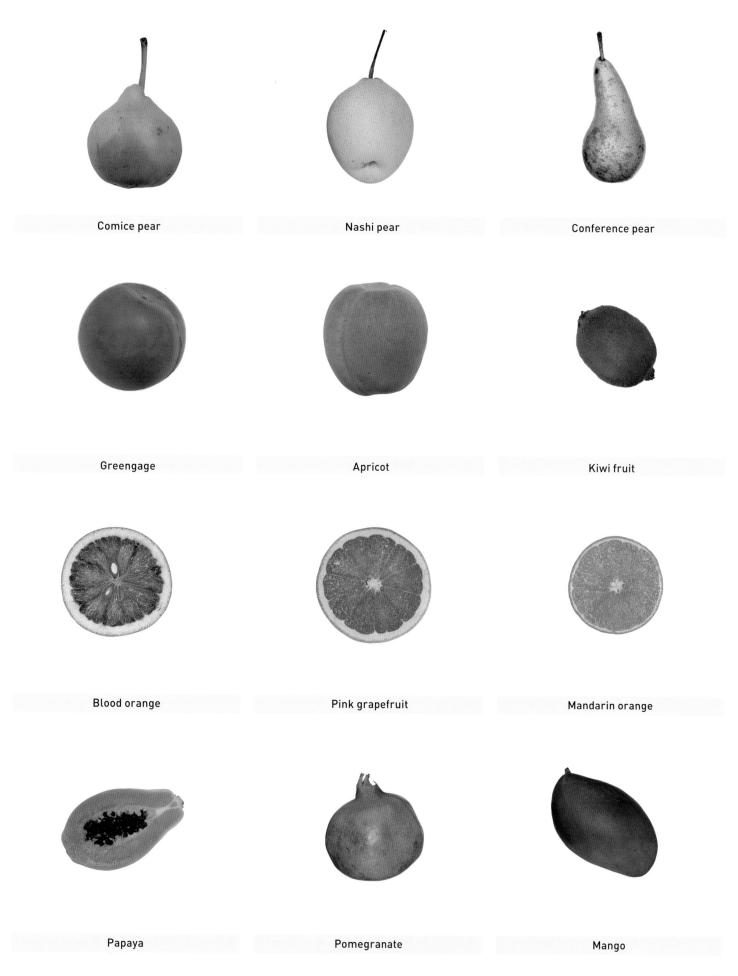

Comice pear

Nashi pear

Conference pear

Greengage

Apricot

Kiwi fruit

Blood orange

Pink grapefruit

Mandarin orange

Papaya

Pomegranate

Mango

Peeling and Stoning Mangoes

1. Remove the mango skin with a small knife or a vegetable peeler.

2. Cut off the flesh of the mango along both sides of the stone.

3. Loosen the flesh that adheres to the stone.

4. Both mango halves and the small pieces of fruit are now ready for use.

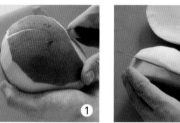

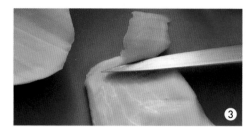

Halving and Stoning Apricots

1. Cut the apricots in half lengthways.

2. Twist the halves with your hands in opposite directions so that one half comes loose from the stone.

3. Remove the stone from the other half with a knife.

4. Use the apricot halves quickly as the cut surface turns brown rapidly.

Stone peaches and nectarines in the same way.

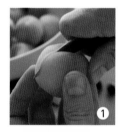

Scraping Out Vanilla Pods, Vanilla Sugar

1. Hold the vanilla pod by one end and use the knife to cut it in half lengthways.

2. Scrape the seeds out of the whole vanilla pod with the tip of the knife.

3. Dark vanilla pods lend desserts and sauces a special aromatic taste.

4. Store the scraped-out vanilla pods with granulated sugar in a preserving jar. If the pod has hardened, put it into a food processor with the sugar, and blend them until you have a fine mixture.

5. In that way, you can create home-made vanilla sugar for the preparation of desserts, cakes and sauces.

Peeling Kiwi Fruit

1. Cut 5 mm (¼ inch) off the bottom and trim the top to the same extent around the core, but do not sever it completely.

2. Then simply fold the top back and the little stalk will also be removed, by twisting the top slightly.

3. Stand the kiwi fruit upright and pare the skin off from top to bottom.

4. Then cut and use the kiwi fruit as you wish.

Cutting Honeydew Melons

1. Cut the melon in half lengthways.

2. Remove the seeds with a small spoon.

3. You can make little boats by dividing the melon halves several times. Then remove the skin leaving a little tag so that the flesh doesn't slip when it is being eaten.

4. Little melon balls can also be scooped out with a melon baller.

5. The scooped-out melon half can be used as a decorative bowl.

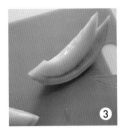
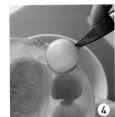

Cutting Pineapple

1. Cut a 3-cm (1¼-inch) thick round off the top and the bottom.

2. Cut the skin off from top to bottom at a thickness of approximately 1 cm (½ inch).

3. Remove the remaining eyes with a V-shaped cut.

4. Cut the flesh into 1-cm (½-inch) thick slices and scoop out the woody centre with a melon baller.

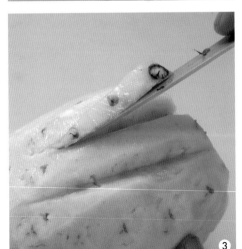

Segmenting Oranges

1. Cut a 1-cm (½-inch) thick round off the top and the bottom.

2. Remove the outer peel and the white pith from top to bottom.

3. Hold the peeled orange in your hand, slice it into segments to the middle of the fruit, and remove them.

Hollowing Out Apples

1. Cut off the top 1.5 cm (½ inch) of the apple.

2. Remove the core with a melon baller.

3. Scoop out the flesh of the apple so that it can be cooked later with a filling.

 ½ honeydew melon

2 bananas

2 apples

3 oranges

250 g (9 oz) red grapes

1 lime

3 tbsp honey

10 fresh mint leaves

Simple Fruit Salad

1. Peel and halve the melon, remove the seeds with a spoon, and cut the flesh into 1.5- × 2-cm (½- × ¾-inch) pieces. Peel the bananas and cut them into 1-cm (½-inch) slices. Peel the apples, remove the core and dice the flesh into 1.5-cm (½-inch) pieces. Slice the oranges.

2. Halve the grapes and remove the seeds with the tip of the knife, as they would add a crunchy, bitter taste.

3. Squeeze the lime through a strainer over the fruit salad, so that none of the pulp is included. The acid will prevent the fruit from discolouring. Finally, add the honey and the chopped mint, mix the ingredients, and chill the fruit salad before serving it.

20

① ② ③

Exotic Fruit Salad

 ½ honeydew melon

1 mango

3 oranges

3 kiwi fruit

2 limes

60 g (2¼ oz) vanilla sugar

4 passion fruits

6 strawberries

1 pinch of lime zest

1 vanilla pod

2 tbsp grated coconut

1. Cut the melon in half, remove the seeds with a spoon, and scoop out balls with a melon baller. Peel the mango and cut it in half, remove the stone and dice the flesh. Peel and segment the oranges. Peel the kiwi fruit, cut them in half and slice them.

2. Wash the limes in hot water. Squeeze them by hand and add them to the salad. The active oils in the zest will add an even more exotic taste to the fruit salad.

3. Add the sugar. Cut the passion fruits in half, scoop out the insides with a spoon and add them to the salad as well. Let the salad marinate for 30 minutes. Remove the limes from the salad. Finally, slice the strawberries thinly lengthways and use them to garnish the fruit salad.

Garnish to taste with lime zest, vanilla pod and grated coconut. Arrange the fruit salad in one of the hollowed-out melon halves.

50 * * *

5 eggs

 130 g (4½ oz) sugar

500 ml (17 fl oz) milk

1 vanilla pod

8 sheets of gelatin

400 ml (13½ fl oz) double cream, whipped

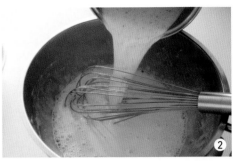

Bavarian Cream

1. Separate the eggs and whisk the egg yolks with the sugar until the mixture is almost white. Prepare a bain-marie on the hob, taking care that the bowl does not touch the water.

2. In another pan, boil the milk with the vanilla pod and the vanilla seeds and, using a wire whisk, stir it gradually into the egg-sugar mixture.

3. Heat the mixture slowly in the bain-marie, stirring it continuously with a

wooden spoon so that the egg doesn't solidify at the edge of the bowl.

4. Stir the mixture until the egg thickens. The mixture is ready when it coats the back of the wooden spoon.

5. Soften the gelatine sheets in cold water, squeeze them and then mix them with the whipped cream. Stir this mixture over a bowl containing iced water until it's cold.

+ 3 hours to chill

✱
✱ 40
✱

■ You can also make a coffee cream, by preparing 4 cups of strong espresso and stirring it into the egg mixture before folding in the cream. Increase the number of gelatine sheets to 9.

6. Carefully fold some of the whipped cream into the egg, sugar and milk mixture until it is homogenous.

7. Then fold in the rest of the cream, turning the whisk with your wrist, just as if you were using a stirring spoon. Pour the cream into dishes or glasses, cover them and leave them to chill in the refrigerator.

Serve the cream with fruit sauce or fresh fruit.

150 g (5½ oz) sugar

 125 ml (4 fl oz) water

 3 eggs

 Seeds from 1 vanilla pod

 10 ml (¼ fl oz) amaretto

 500 ml (17 fl oz) double cream

Vanilla Ice Cream Parfait

1. Add the sugar to the water and heat the resulting syrup to precisely 121°C (250°F). Use a sugar thermometer.

2. Separate the eggs and put the egg yolks into a metal bowl. Mix the syrup little by little with the egg yolks. Stir it continuously with a wire whisk so that the egg doesn't solidify.

3. Mix in the vanilla seeds and the amaretto; whip the mixture with the whisk until it is creamy and stir it over a chilled water bath until it is cold again.

4. Beat the double cream until stiff peaks form and stir in one-third of the cream with a wire whisk at first. Then fold in the rest of the cream carefully, so that the fluffy, airy consistency of the parfait is not diminished by vigorous stirring.

5. Put the mixture into a mould and put it in the freezer compartment for at least 6 hours. Then hold the mould under running hot water briefly and turn out the parfait. Use a hot knife to cut 1-cm (½-inch) thick slices and serve them immediately. Wrap the rest of the parfait in cling film for future use.

Variations on the parfait can be made by adding any of the following ingredients:
1. 200 g (7 oz) strawberry purée
2. 150 g (5½ oz) passion fruit purée, 50 ml (1⅔ fl oz) coconut liqueur
3. 50 g (1¾ oz) roasted almonds, 120 g (4½ oz) coarsely chopped amarena cherries, 20 ml (⅔ fl oz) cherry liqueur
4. 200 g (7 oz) apricot purée with 20 ml (⅔ fl oz) amaretto

+ 6 hours to freeze

* * * 40

■ You can also surprise your guests with an ice cream soufflé by making a collar from baking paper, putting it into a miniature soufflé dish and pouring in some parfait mixture. The parfait creates the effect of a soufflé, but it is made of ice cream.

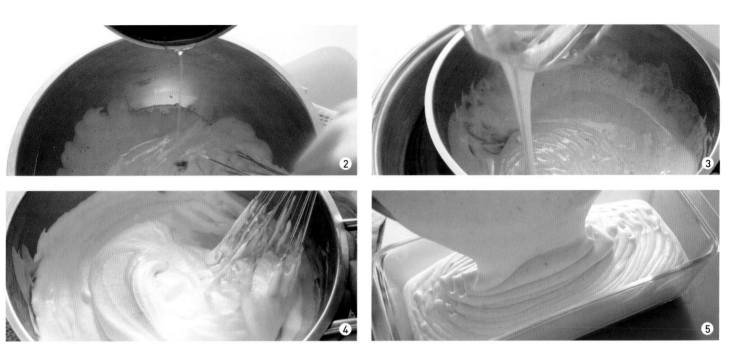

250 ml (8½ fl oz) milk

 80 g (2¾ oz) sugar

 3 eggs

 20 g (⅔ oz) cornflour

 30 g (1 oz) butter

 1 vanilla pod

 250 g (9 oz) puff pastry

 200 g (7 oz) mixed berries

 50 ml (1⅔ fl oz) water

 30 g (1 oz) sugar

 50 ml (1⅔ fl oz) white wine

 1½ sheets of gelatin

 10 g (¼ oz) icing sugar

 1 orange

①

Little Fruit Tarts

1. Preheat the oven to 180°C (350°F/ Gas Mark 4). Mix 60 ml (2 fl oz) of the milk with the sugar, the yolk of 1 egg and the cornflour. Cut the butter into small pieces and chill. Cut the vanilla pod in half lengthways and scrape out the seeds with the back of a knife. Bring the rest of the milk, the vanilla seeds and the scraped pod to the boil. Then pour it through a sieve and put it back on the cooker. Pour the prepared mixture of milk, egg yolk, sugar and cornflour slowly into the milk and let the custard thicken.

2. Stir the custard and the chilled butter over iced water, cover it and let it cool down.

3. Cut the puff pastry into equal triangles and tubes and assemble them as shown in the photograph. Brush them completely with the yolks of the remaining eggs and prick the tart bases with a fork.

4. Bake the little tarts in the oven for 12–15 minutes, and then let them cool. Fill them with the vanilla cream to just below the rim.

5. Top the vanilla cream with fresh fruit. Bring the water, sugar and white wine to the boil, dissolve the softened gelatine in this mixture, and let it cool. Coat the berries with the glaze so that they stay fresh and the little tarts are shiny. Dust them with icing sugar and decorate them with a twist of orange zest, to serve.

■ The little tarts can be topped with any kind of berries you like. A large slice of puff pastry with vanilla cream and fresh strawberries is also a delicious alternative to a cake.

*
*
*
75

1 pineapple

 2 eggs

 1 pinch of salt

 1.5 litres (2½ pints) vegetable oil

 120 g (4¼ oz) flour

 60 g (2¼ oz) sugar

 125 ml (4 fl oz) milk

 40 ml (1⅓ fl oz) dark rum

 30 g (1 oz) coconut flakes

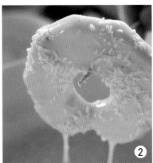
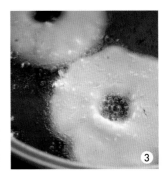

Pineapple Fritters

1. Peel the pineapple and remove the core. Then cut the fruit into ½-cm (¼-inch) thick slices and reserve. Separate the eggs and beat the egg whites with the salt until stiff peaks form. Cover the container and put it into the refrigerator until the egg whites are needed. Put the vegetable oil in a saucepan and heat it to 180°C (350°F). Meanwhile, mix the flour, the sugar, the egg yolks, the milk and the rum, until a smooth batter is obtained. Fold in the egg whites carefully.

2. Dip the pineapple slices in the batter and sprinkle them with coconut flakes.

3. Lower the heat. Fry the pineapple fritters at 160°C (325°F) until they are golden brown. Then drain them well on kitchen paper, sprinkle them with the remaining coconut flakes and serve.

3 eggs

300 g (10½ oz) flour

20g (⅔ oz) baking powder

60 g (2¼ oz) sugar

350 ml (12 fl oz) milk

4 apples

½ lemon

1 pinch of salt

1.5 litres (2½ pints) vegetable oil

1 tbsp vanilla sugar

Apple Fritters

1. Separate the eggs and mix the egg yolks with the flour, the baking powder, the sugar and the milk, until a smooth batter is obtained. Gradually, stir in 160 ml (5½ fl oz) of the vegetable oil. Peel the apples and remove the core with a baller. Cut the apples into 5-mm (¼-inch) thick slices and rub them with the lemon to prevent browning.

2. Beat the egg whites with a pinch of salt until stiff peaks form and fold them into the batter carefully. Put the remainder of the vegetable oil in a saucepan and heat it to 160°C

(325°F). You can check that the correct temperature has been reached by holding a wooden skewer in it – the oil should bubble up.

3. Dip the apples in the batter and put them into the hot oil immediately. Fry the apple fritters until they are golden brown. Let them drain well on kitchen paper, dust them with vanilla sugar and serve them with vanilla sauce (see p. 694).

■ **You can create delicious apple chips by deep-frying apple skins in oil.**

45 ✳ ✳ ✳

8 sponge fingers

 300 g (10½ oz) juicy cherries

 2 tbsp sugar

 ½ tsp ground cinnamon

 20 ml (⅔ fl oz) cherry liqueur

 1 pack spring roll wrappers
(measuring 12 × 12 cm/4¾ × 4¾ inches)

 1 egg white

 2 litres (3½ pints) vegetable oil for
deep-frying

 10 g (¼ oz) icing sugar

Spring Rolls with Cherry Filling

1. By hand, crush the sponge fingers coarsely in a bowl.

2. Wash the cherries, cut them in half and remove the stones. Add the cherries to the sponge fingers.

3. Season with the sugar and the ground cinnamon.

4. Drizzle them with the cherry liqueur and mix them well.

5. Lay the wrappers out on the work surface. Put 2 tbsp of the cherry filling in the centre of each wrapper. Brush the sides with egg white.

6. Fold two opposite corners into the centre and brush the edges with egg white.

7. Fold in the third corner and brush the lower section with egg white.

8. Then fold the lower section onto the filling and press it down lightly. Brush the upper section with egg white and roll the wrap up completely.

9. Put the oil in a large saucepan and heat it to 160°C (325°F). Deep-fry the spring rolls in the pan for approximately 5 minutes, until they are golden.

10. Remove the spring rolls and drain them on kitchen paper.

Arrange them on plates with napkins and sprinkle them with icing sugar.

■ These spring rolls can also be filled with other fruit such as plums, morello cherries, mangoes, bananas or grapes. Fillings with quark or vanilla cream are also an option, although you will need to use some soaked broken sponge fingers to give the filling some kind of structure.

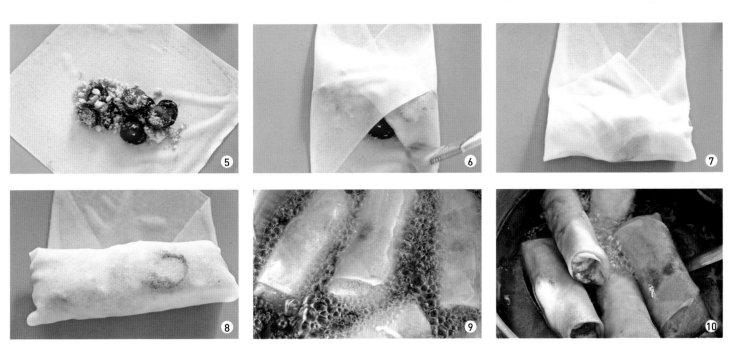

650 ml (22 fl oz) coconut milk

 120 g (4½ oz) coarsely ground tapioca

 60 g (2¼ oz) brown cane sugar

 1 vanilla pod

 1 pinch of salt

 100 ml (3½ fl oz) orange juice

 3 star anise

 1 tbsp sugar

 10 g (¼ oz) cornflour

 20 ml (⅔ fl oz) orange liqueur

 2 oranges

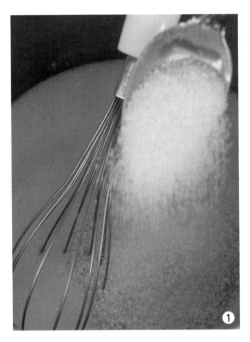

Tapioca-Coconut Pudding

1. Put the coconut milk in a saucepan and bring it to the boil. Sprinkle the tapioca in slowly and stir it in with a wire whisk.

2. Add the brown cane sugar and let the pudding simmer gently for 5 minutes. Scrape out the vanilla pod and add the vanilla seeds and the salt.

3. The pudding is ready once it has a firm, even consistency. Pour it into glasses or bowls, cover them with cling film and let the pudding cool.

4. Bring the orange juice, star anise and sugar to the boil.

5. Mix the cornflour with the orange liqueur and thicken the orange juice with this mixture.

6. Segment two oranges and add the slices to the thickened sauce. Remove the sauce from the heat and let it cool down. Pour it over the tapioca pudding and serve.

■ The coconut milk must not be thickened. If the pudding sticks to the bottom of the pan, stop stirring it and pour it out immediately. Green tea ice cream or stewed papaya is a perfect accompaniment to this pudding.

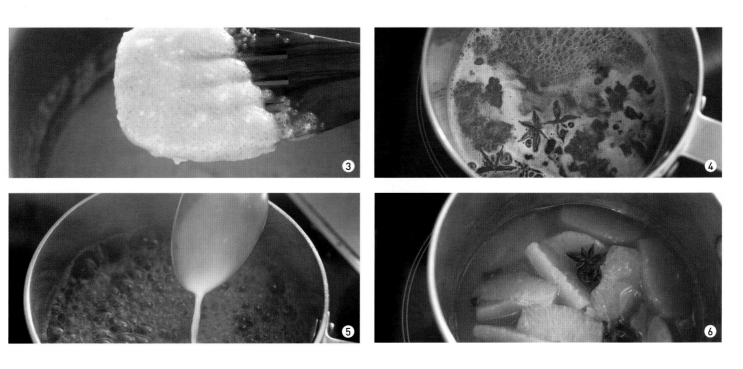

100 g (3½ oz) butter

 100 g (3½ oz) ground almonds

 3 tbsp sugar

 3 tbsp breadcrumbs

 1 tsp ground cinnamon

 500 g (1 lb 2 oz) cooked potato gnocchi (see p. 316)

 10 g (¼ oz) icing sugar

Sweet Gnocchi with Almond Breadcrumbs

1. Melt the butter in a nonstick frying pan and add the ground almonds and the sugar.

2. Add the breadcrumbs to the pan.

3. Sprinkle the cinnamon on the mixture.

4. Gently toast the crumbs in the butter for approximately 5 minutes, stirring frequently.

5. Add the cooked gnocchi to the frying pan and turn them in the breadcrumbs.

6. Cook the gnocchi in the crumbs for 2 minutes more until they are completely coated by the crumbs.

Arrange the gnocchi on plates and sprinkle them with icing sugar.

■ Finger noodles or other gnocchi mixed with pumpkin, poppy seeds or various nuts can also be prepared in this way. It is important to ensure that the almond and the breadcrumbs are well browned and sweetened, and that the gnocchi have a fairly neutral taste. Ground poppy seeds with sugar and butter are also particularly delicious with these gnocchi.

4

5

6

4 eggs

 260 g (9¼ oz) icing sugar

 200 g (7 oz) raspberries

 200 g (7 oz) wild strawberries

 250 ml (8½ fl oz) double cream

 1 vanilla pod

Pavlova with Berries and Vanilla Cream

1. Preheat the oven to 120°C (250°F/ Gas Mark ½). Separate the eggs, add the chilled egg white to the bowl and beat it with the whisk until semi-stiff peaks form. Gradually add the icing sugar and beat the mixture with an egg beater until it is stiff.

2. Use a rubber spatula to put the beaten egg whites into a piping bag.

3. Pipe the egg white mixture into spirals on a baking tray covered with baking paper. Bake them in the oven for

approximately 35 minutes. Then reduce the temperature to 60°C (140°F) and let the meringues dry for 4 hours.

4. Trim the berries, wash them and put them into a bowl.

5. Cut the top off the baked meringue spirals with a sharp, serrated knife. Whip the cream with seeds scraped out of the vanilla pod and put the mixture on the lower halves of the meringue. Put the berries on top of the cream, set the lids on top at an angle, and serve.

+ 4 hours for drying

✳
✳
✳

65

■ Try making a miniature version of these meringue cases. They won't take as long to dry and can be served with afternoon tea. They can also be prepared in advance and filled only just before they are served. You can also use fruit sorbet as a filling instead of fresh fruit.

½ vanilla pod

 500 ml (17 fl oz) cream

 100 g (3½ oz) sugar

 1 tbsp coffee beans

3 sheets of gelatin

Panna Cotta with Coffee

1. Cut the vanilla pod lengthways. Scrape out the seeds with the back of a knife and add them to the cream. Bring the cream with the scraped vanilla pod, the sugar and the coffee beans to the boil. Let the gelatine sheets soften in cold water for approximately 10 minutes.

2. Set the boiled cream mixture aside. Add the softened, squeezed and drained gelatine and dissolve it.

3. Pour the cream through a sieve into a measuring cup.

4. Pour it into glasses and let it chill in the refrigerator for at least 3 hours so that the panna cotta can set. Then put the glasses into hot water briefly and turn out the panna cotta.

■ Sprinkle the panna cotta with crushed almond biscuits or Amarettini and garnish it with amarena cherries. For a lighter panna cotta, use milk as a substitute for half of the cream.

675

1 envelope gelatine powder

700 ml (1¼ pints) milk

100 g (3½ oz) white chocolate

50 ml (1⅔ fl oz) maple syrup

White Chocolate Mousse with Maple Syrup

1. Put the gelatine powder into 4 tbsp cold water, stir it and let it steep for 10 minutes.

2. Heat the milk. Reserve 2 tbsp. Break the chocolate into pieces and dissolve it in the milk.

3. Mix the gelatine with the reserved hot milk and then add it to the chocolate-milk mixture and stir it until it dissolves completely.

4. Pour the chocolate mousse into a siphon with the aid of a funnel.

5. Add the maple syrup and close the siphon when it contains 750 ml (1⅓ pints) of the mixture and shake it well. Let it cool in the refrigerator for approximately 1 hour.

To serve, insert two cartridges and pipe the fluffy mousse into small bowls.

■ The mousse can be prepared in advance using this method. At the last minute, you can serve it fresh in glasses and it will be particularly frothy and taste very fruity. Dark chocolate, nougat or even fruit purées can be added to the milk. However, fruit purées should not be cooked further and the amount of gelatine must be increased by half because of the acid in the fruit. Otherwise, the mousse would be too runny.

677

150 g (5½ oz) plain chocolate

 2 eggs

 3 tbsp sugar

 1 tbsp reduced-fat cocoa powder

 20 ml (⅔ fl oz) cognac

 50 ml (1⅔ fl oz) espresso

 1 pinch of salt

 200 ml (7 fl oz) double cream, whipped

 4 tbsp chocolate shavings

Plain Chocolate Mousse

1. Put the chocolate in a heatproof bowl and set the bowl over a saucepan of barely simmering water to let it melt slowly.

2. Separate the eggs, store the egg white in the refrigerator and whisk the egg yolk with the sugar until it foams up. Stir the cocoa, cognac and espresso into the egg mixture.

3. Add the warm melted chocolate.

4. Stir in the chocolate until everything is mixed well.

5. Beat the egg whites with a pinch of salt until stiff peaks form, and fold them into the chocolate mix with the wire whisk. Then fold in the whipped cream, and let the mousse chill in the refrigerator for at least 2 hours. To serve, scoop out a portion with a spoon and decorate it with some chocolate shavings.

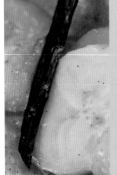

■ Put a ripe banana with two pieces of finely chopped, candied ginger, the juice of half an orange, and half a vanilla pod in a saucepan and bring them to the boil. Add the mixture as an intermediate layer in the chocolate mousse and let it chill. Chocolate and bananas are an excellent combination and will turn the mousse into a wonderful dessert.

250 g (9 oz) strawberries

 400 g (14 oz) sushi rice

 100 g (3½ oz) quinoa

 2 tbsp mango jelly

 20 g (⅔ oz) butter

 2 tbsp soft brown sugar

Sweet Sushi with Strawberries and Toasted Quinoa

1. Wash and clean the strawberries, remove the stems and hulls, and cut the fruit into slices. Cook the sushi rice (see p. 235) and the quinoa (see p. 275).

2. Using two tablespoons, make little sushi shapes out of the sushi rice and put a dab of mango jelly on each one.

3. Decorate each sushi shape with 2 strawberry slices.

4. Heat the butter and the sugar in a frying pan.

5. Add the boiled quinoa and brown it.

Put some toasted quinoa on top of each piece of strawberry sushi and serve them. Serve maple syrup or honey as a dipping sauce.

■ Just like ordinary seafood sushi, this sweet sushi can be served with various thinly sliced fruit. Mangoes, papayas, oranges, melons, plums or cherries are particularly suitable for this.

1 tbsp lemon juice

130 g (4½ oz) low-fat Greek yogurt

130 g (4½ oz) crème fraîche

90 g (3¼ oz) icing sugar

150 g (5½ oz) strawberry purée

4 sheets of gelatin

125 ml (4 fl oz) double cream

2 eggs

30 g (1 oz) sugar

3 strawberries

Strawberry Yogurt Mousse

1. Combine the lemon juice with the yogurt, crème fraîche, icing sugar and two-thirds of the strawberry purée. Soften the gelatine sheets in cold water for 10 minutes, squeeze the moisture out of them and let them dissolve in a small saucepan. Then mix the gelatine with the yogurt mixture.

2. Whip the cream until stiff peaks form, and fold carefully into the mixture with a wire whisk.

3. Separate the eggs. Beat the egg whites and the sugar until stiff peaks form, and fold them into the mixture slowly. Pour the mixture into glasses and put them in the refrigerator to chill for 1 hour. Add a little strawberry purée on top before serving the mousse decorated with strawberry slices.

120

250 g (9 oz) bananas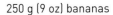

Juice of 2 lemons

50 ml (1⅔ fl oz) banana liqueur

30 g (1 oz) butter

2½ sheets of gelatin

125 ml (4 fl oz) double cream

2 eggs

65 g (2¼ oz) sugar

2 tsp vanilla sugar

4 tbsp chocolate sauce (see p. 694)

Banana Mousse

1. Cut the bananas into thin slices. Drizzle the lemon juice onto the banana slices to prevent browning. Briefly bring the bananas, the banana liqueur and the butter to the boil in a saucepan. Purée the mixture with a hand-held blender and strain it through a sieve. Let the gelatine sheets soften in cold water for approximately 10 minutes, squeeze the moisture out of them, let them dissolve in a small saucepan, and stir the liquid into the banana purée. Then set the mixture aside to cool.

2. Whip the cream until semi-stiff peaks form, and fold carefully into the chilled banana purée.

3. Separate the eggs. Beat the egg whites until they are light and fluffy, and then add the sugar and the vanilla sugar carefully. Beat the egg whites until stiff peaks form, fold them into the mousse, and pour the mousse into individual glasses. Put the glasses in the refrigerator to chill for at least 2 hours. Garnish the mousse with some unpeeled banana slices and drizzle chocolate sauce on top.

■ **You will need approximately 3 bananas to yield 250 g (9 oz) of peeled bananas. You must weigh the bananas precisely for the mousse to be a success.**

160 ✳
✳
✳

6 eggs

 100 g (3½ oz) sugar

 200 ml (7 fl oz) sparkling wine

 50 ml (1⅔ fl oz) dessert wine

 Juice of ½ a lemon

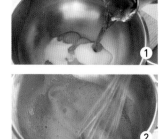
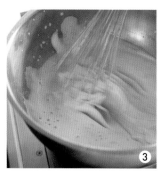

* * * **30**

1. Hot Zabaglione

1. Separate the eggs. Put the egg yolks, sugar, sparkling wine, dessert wine and the juice of lemon juice into a bowl.

2. Beat the mixture over a bain-marie. As you work, take care to whisk evenly, scraping the edges of the bowl to avoid lumps being created.

3. The mixture will become lighter in colour and more viscous, and it will increase in volume.

4. The zabaglione is ready when a creamy, glossy consistency is obtained.

Pour it into glasses and serve immediately.

2. Pistachio Zabaglione

Separate **4 eggs**. Beat the egg yolks with **60 g (2¼ oz) sugar** and **100 ml (3½ fl oz) sparkling wine** in a bain-marie as with the basic zabaglione. Heat **1 sheet of softened gelatin**, dissolve it, and add it to the zabaglione. Stir this mixture over a bowl of iced water until it is cold. Grind **60 g (2¼ oz) pistachio** nuts very finely in a blender until they are almost like a paste and add them to the zabaglione. Then, whip **100 ml (3½ fl oz) cream** until semi-stiff peaks form and fold it in.

Pour the zabaglione into glasses and serve it with fresh raspberries, raspberry sorbet, vanilla ice cream or poached peaches.

3. Campari Zabaglione

Separate **4 eggs**. Beat the egg yolks with **60 g (2½ oz) sugar** and **80 ml (2¾ fl oz) Campari** in a bain-marie like the basic zabaglione. Finely grate some **orange zest** and add it to the zabaglione. Cut **1 orange** in half and squeeze it. Heat **1 sheet of gelatin**e in the orange juice, dissolve it, and add it to the zabaglione. Stir this mixture over a bowl of iced water until it is cold. Then whip **150 ml (5 fl oz) double cream** until semi-stiff peaks form and fold it in.

Pour the zabaglione into glasses and serve it with stewed fruit or pistachio ice cream.

120 g (4¼ oz) butter

 60 g (2¼ oz) soft brown sugar

 3 eggs

 50 g (1¾ oz) flaked almonds

 100 g (3½ oz) white breadcrumbs

 4 peaches

 8 sprigs fresh lavender

 1 vanilla pod

 4 tsp honey

 8 tsp peach liqueur

Baked Peaches with Lavender

1. Preheat the oven to 220°C (425°F/ Gas Mark 7). Beat the butter and the sugar at room temperature until fluffy. Separate the eggs and beat the egg yolks in gradually.

2. Toast the flaked almonds in a frying pan until they are golden, and then let them cool. Add the almonds and the breadcrumbs to the butter-egg mixture and mix them well.

3. Score the peach skins lightly with a knife, and put the fruit into boiling water for approximately 10–15 seconds. Then remove them with a slotted spoon and place them in iced water to cool.

4. Remove the skins from the peaches and cut the peaches in half. Remove the stones and put the peach halves, with the cut side facing upwards, in a dish on top of the lavender sprigs.

5. Fill the peaches with the almond mixture. Cut the vanilla pod in half lengthways and divide it into 3-cm (1¼-inch) lengths. Drizzle the peaches with honey and peach liqueur and bake them in the oven for approximately 20 minutes. Then arrange them on plates, decorate them with the vanilla pods, and serve them with vanilla ice cream or lavender honey, as you prefer.

■ Baked apples with raisin filling: 40 g (1½ oz) fluffy whipped butter, 60 g (2¼ oz) lightly toasted, coarsely chopped almonds, 40 g (1½ oz) raisins (softened in 2 tbsp tea), 50 g (1¾ oz) crustless white bread cubes, 50 g (1¾ oz) marzipan, 8 small, red apples with stems, 1 tbsp butter to grease the baking dish, 1 tbsp sugar, 1 tbsp honey, 5 cloves and 2 cinnamon sticks. Prepare these ingredients in the same way as the above recipe and cook them for the same length of time, too.

687

4 eggs

 80 g (2¾ oz) sugar

 Seeds from ½ vanilla pod

 40 ml (1⅓ fl oz) cognac

 20 ml (⅔ fl oz) Grand Marnier

 500 g (1 lb 2 oz) mascarpone cheese

 150 g (5½ oz) sponge fingers

 200 ml (7 fl oz) espresso

 30 g (1 oz) cocoa powder

Tiramisu

1. Separate the eggs and beat the egg yolks with the sugar and the vanilla seeds until the mixture is fluffy.

2. Add the cognac and the Grand Marnier and stir them in.

3. Use a rubber spatula to add the mascarpone cheese and whisk it into the mixture.

4. Dip the sponge fingers in the espresso for a maximum of 3 seconds, so that they are not completely saturated.

5. Put the ingredients in alternating layers in a bowl. Start with a layer of sponge fingers, then put a layer of the mascarpone cream and repeat the process. Top off the dessert with cream and let it sit in the refrigerator for at least one hour. Then sprinkle it with the unsweetened cocoa and serve.

+ 1 hour to cool

 40

■ Kitchen doctor: If the cream becomes lumpy, you can add some hot milk and beat it in until the mixture is smooth again.

5 eggs

 80 g (2¾ oz) sponge fingers

 40 ml (3 tbsp) Grand Marnier

 50 g (1¾ oz) butter

 1 vanilla pod

 30 g (1 oz) cornflour

 200 ml (7 fl oz) milk

 100 g (3½ oz) sugar

 1 pinch of salt

Vanilla Soufflé

1. Separate the eggs; cover 1 egg white and place it in the refrigerator for future use. Cut the sponge fingers into 5-mm (¼-inch) cubes and marinate them in the Grand Marnier. Let 30 g (1 oz) of the butter soften at room temperature. Cut the vanilla pod in half lengthways and scrape out the seeds with the back of a knife. Beat the 4 remaining egg whites until stiff peaks form, cover them, and leave them to chill in the refrigerator. Mix the cornflour with 40 ml (1⅓ fl oz) of the cold milk. Put the remaining milk in a saucepan, add the rest of the butter, 70 g (2½ oz) of the sugar, the vanilla seeds, the scraped pod and the salt, and bring the mixture to a boil.

2. First use a brush to coat the ramekin moulds evenly with the softened butter. Then put some sugar into one of the moulds and tilt it, as shown in the photograph, so that some sugar coats the inside of the mould and the surplus falls into the bowl. This is called 'lining' in culinary terms. Do the same with the other ramekin moulds.

3. When the milk has come to the boil, add the cold milk and the cornflour, and stir the mixture continuously with a wire whisk for 2 minutes with the heat still on. The cornflour will thicken the milk. Cover the soufflé mixture with cling film and let it cool down. Preheat a fan oven to 180°C (350°F). Line a baking tin with baking paper, pour in water until it has reached a depth of 2 fingers, and put it into the oven until the water starts to boil. The baking paper will ensure that no air bubbles form during baking, which could impair the soufflé's rising.

■ Cover the soufflé with cling film when it is cooling down to prevent a skin from forming.

✳✳✳ 90

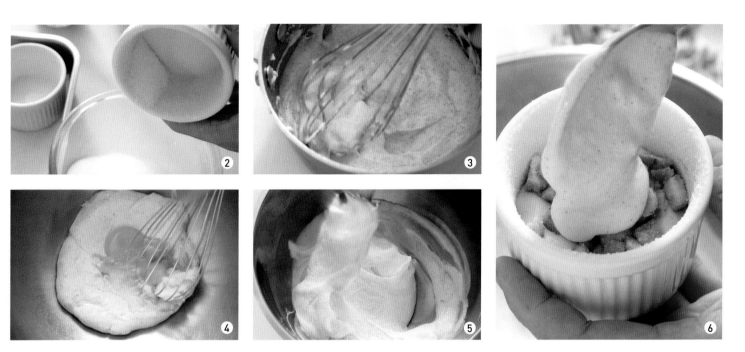

4. Stir the egg yolks into the cooled mixture. It must be cool to prevent the egg from curdling. Then put the mixture through a sieve to remove any lumps, which could affect the soufflé's airy consistency after baking.

5. Fold the stiffly beaten egg whites carefully into the egg yolk mixture with a dough scraper. Stir it gently, so that none of the trapped air will escape. Divide the sponge finger cubes among the ramekin moulds.

6. Spoon the soufflé mixture on top of the sponge finger cubes. Place the ramekin moulds in the water bath in the baking tin and bake the soufflés for 20 minutes. They are ready as soon as they become golden yellow and reach a height of 2–3 cm (¾–1¼ inches) above the rims of the ramekin moulds. Never open the oven while the soufflés are baking, otherwise they will not rise sufficiently. Serve the soufflés as quickly as possible, so that they don't fall. The basic rule is that guests wait for a soufflé, but soufflés don't wait for guests.

50 g (1¾ oz) butter

 20 g (⅔ oz) flour

 1 vanilla pod

 80 g (2¾ oz) walnuts

 20 g (⅔ oz) chocolate

 3 eggs

 80 g (2¾ oz) sugar

 200 ml (7 fl oz) milk

 20 g (⅔ oz) icing sugar

Walnut Soufflé

1. Let 30 g (1 oz) of the butter soften at room temperature and mix it with the flour in a small container until a homogenous mass is created. This is also called beurre manié and is used as a thickener. Cut the vanilla pod in half lengthways and scrape out the seeds with the back of a knife. Use a knife to chop the walnuts and the chocolate coarsely. Separate the eggs. Beat the egg whites until they form soft peaks, cover them, and leave them to chill in the refrigerator. Grease the ramekin moulds with the remaining butter and 'line' the rims with sugar (see the vanilla soufflé recipe, p. 690).

2. Bring the milk mixed with the chopped walnuts, the scraped pod and the vanilla seeds to the boil. After boiling, remove the pods from the milk and stir in the beurre manié.

3. Simmer the mixture for 3 minutes, stirring continuously, until it becomes considerably thicker. Then cover it with cling film and let it cool. Meanwhile, preheat the oven to 200°C (400°F/Gas Mark 6) and prepare a bain-marie for the ramekin moulds. To do this, line a baking tin with baking paper and pour in water until it has reached a depth of 2 fingers. When the mixture has cooled to room temperature, stir in the egg yolks. Remove the beaten egg whites from the refrigerator and fold them in carefully with a rubber spatula. Fill the ramekin moulds two-thirds full with the mixture and bake them in the water bath for 20 minutes, until the soufflés rise to a height of 2 cm (¾ inch) above the ramekin rims. Sprinkle them with icing sugar and serve immediately.

■ You can use this basic recipe to whip up different kinds of soufflés in no time. Just substitute other ingredients for the walnuts. For best results, use hazelnuts, chestnut purée, roasted almonds or grated coconut. However, if you are using coconut, white chocolate should be substituted for the dark chocolate. Otherwise, the dark chocolate would be overpowering.

✳
✳ 90
✳

Vanilla Sauce

Chocolate Sauce

Caramel Sauce

Cut **1 vanilla pod** in half lengthways and scrape out the seeds with the back of a knife. Add the seeds and the pod to **250 ml (8½ fl oz) milk** in a saucepan and bring it to the boil. Meanwhile, separate **6 eggs**, combine the egg yolks with **50 g (1¾ oz) sugar** and stir them until they are fluffy. Bring water to the boil in a long-handled saucepan. As soon as the milk boils, pour it through a sieve so that none of the residue from the vanilla pod is included in the sauce. Add the hot milk gradually to the egg-sugar mixture, stirring continuously. Heat the mixture over the bain-marie and stir it until it has thickened enough to coat the back of a spoon. Finally, stir it over a bowl of iced water until it is cold.

Kitchen doctor: If the sauce becomes too hot, it will curdle. If this happens, pour it through a fine sieve. Stir in 1 tbsp cornflour and 2 tbsp milk, and whisk them into the hot vanilla sauce. Return the sauce to the boil and it will be creamy once again.

Bring **125 ml (4 fl oz) milk**, **100 ml (3½ fl oz) cream** and **½ scraped vanilla pod** to the boil slowly. Chop **100 g (3½ oz) plain chocolate** and **50 g (1¾ oz) milk chocolate** into small pieces with a knife and add them to the milk. Stir the mixture slowly with a whisk and melt the chocolate. Then remove it from the heat, take out the vanilla pod and stir in **10 ml (⅓ fl oz) cognac**, **20 g (⅔ oz) sugar** and **40 ml (1⅓ fl oz) vegetable oil**. Then pour the sauce through a fine sieve and serve it at room temperature, if possible.

■ **Use hazelnut oil in place of the vegetable oil.**

Cook **50 g (1¾ oz) sugar** and **100 ml (3½ fl oz) water** in a small, long-handled saucepan at low heat. Let it simmer until the sugar is golden brown and evenly caramelised. Then add 50 ml (1⅔ fl oz) water to prevent the sugar from browning further. Simmer it again gently, until the water has evaporated (approximately 5 minutes). Then pour in **250 ml (8½ fl oz) milk**. Cut **1 vanilla pod** in half lengthways and scrape out the seeds with the back of a knife. Add the pod and the seeds to the milk and bring the mixture to the boil in a saucepan. Meanwhile, separate **6 eggs**, combine the egg yolks with **30 g (1 oz) sugar** and stir them until they are fluffy. Prepare a bain-marie by putting water in a long-handled saucepan and bring it to the boil. As soon as the milk boils, pour it through a sieve, so that no lumps are included in the sauce. Add the hot milk gradually to the egg-sugar mixture, stirring continuously. Heat the mixture over the bain-marie and stir it until it has thickened enough to coat the back of a spoon. Finally, stir it over a bowl of iced water until it is cold.

Strawberry Sauce

Apricot Sauce

Kiwi Sauce

Wash and clean **250 g (9 oz) strawberries** and remove any rotten spots. Sprinkle **50 g (1¾ oz) icing sugar** on the strawberries, pour **80 ml (2¾ fl oz) mineral water** over them, and purée everything with a hand-held blender to make a thin sauce. Finally, pour it through a fine sieve and serve.

Put **5 apricots** into boiling water for 10 seconds and plunge them into cold water immediately to chill them. Remove the skin with a small knife, cut the fruit in half and remove the stones. Put the apricot halves, the juice of **½ a lemon**, **50 g (1¾ oz) icing sugar** and **80 ml (2¾ fl oz) mineral water** in a bowl, and mix everything with a hand-held blender. Then pour the mixture through a fine sieve and press the fruit pulp through with a spoon or a spatula.

Peel **4 kiwi fruit**, put them in a bowl with **50 g (1¾ oz) icing sugar** and **80 ml (2¾ fl oz) mineral water**, and mix them with a hand-held blender. Then pour the mixture through a fine sieve.

■ **Kiwi fruit cannot be used with any dairy products, as they contain a curdling enzyme (just like pineapples do).**

8 eggs

 200 g (7 oz) sugar

 1 large pinch of ground cinnamon

 800 ml (1⅓ pints) red wine

Wine Chaudeau

1. Separate the eggs and put the egg yolks in a round, stainless steel bowl. Add the sugar and the cinnamon.

2. Pour in the red wine and mix it in with a wire whisk. Put 2 cm (¾ inch) water into a long-handled saucepan and bring it to the boil.

3. Put the stainless steel bowl over the saucepan with the boiling water so that it is heated by the steam.

4. Beat the mixture vigorously, so that its volume is increased threefold and it is rich and creamy as it runs off the whisk. Remove the custard from the heat and pour it into glasses. Serve it hot with some cinnamon sprinkled on top.

■ Hot red wine chaudeau is especially delicious when served with baked pears, peaches or apples. If you substitute Prosecco or Marsala for the red wine, you will produce a mouthwatering zabaglione.

4 eggs

 100 g (3½ oz) sugar

 1 pinch of ground cinnamon

 400 ml (13½ fl oz) red wine

 2 sheets of gelatin

 300 g (10½ oz) cream, whipped

 8 sponge fingers

Cold Wine Cream

1. Make a wine chaudeau from the egg yolks, sugar, cinnamon and 200 ml (7 fl oz) of the red wine (see p. 696). Soften the gelatine sheets in cold water for approximately 10 minutes, then squeeze them and dissolve them in the wine chaudeau. Pour the mixture into a bowl and let it cool.

2. Meanwhile, heat up the remainder of the red wine in a saucepan and let it reduce to a volume of 4 tbsp.

3. Add the whipped cream and almost the entire red wine reduction to the cold wine chaudeau, reserving a little for decoration.

4. Fold the cream and the reduction into the cold wine chaudeau carefully. The red wine reduction will give its colour to the wine chaudeau and will also intensify its flavour.

Break the sponge fingers into pieces and put them in glasses. Add the cream and let it cool for a good hour. To finish, mix some red wine reduction with sugar to taste and drizzle it over the wine cream.

+ 1 hour to cool

■ White wine can also be used for this cold wine cream. If you make a white wine cream, use white wine to make the wine reduction as well. Small, fresh, deseeded white wine grapes can also be added to the sponge fingers. Red grapes go better with the red wine cream. It tastes a little fresher if they are added!

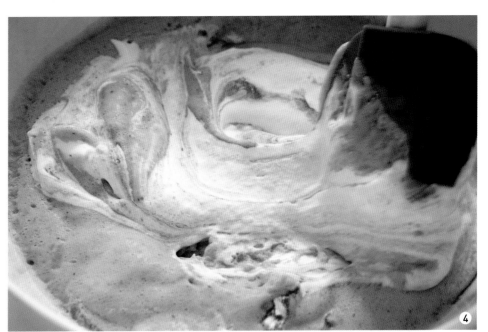

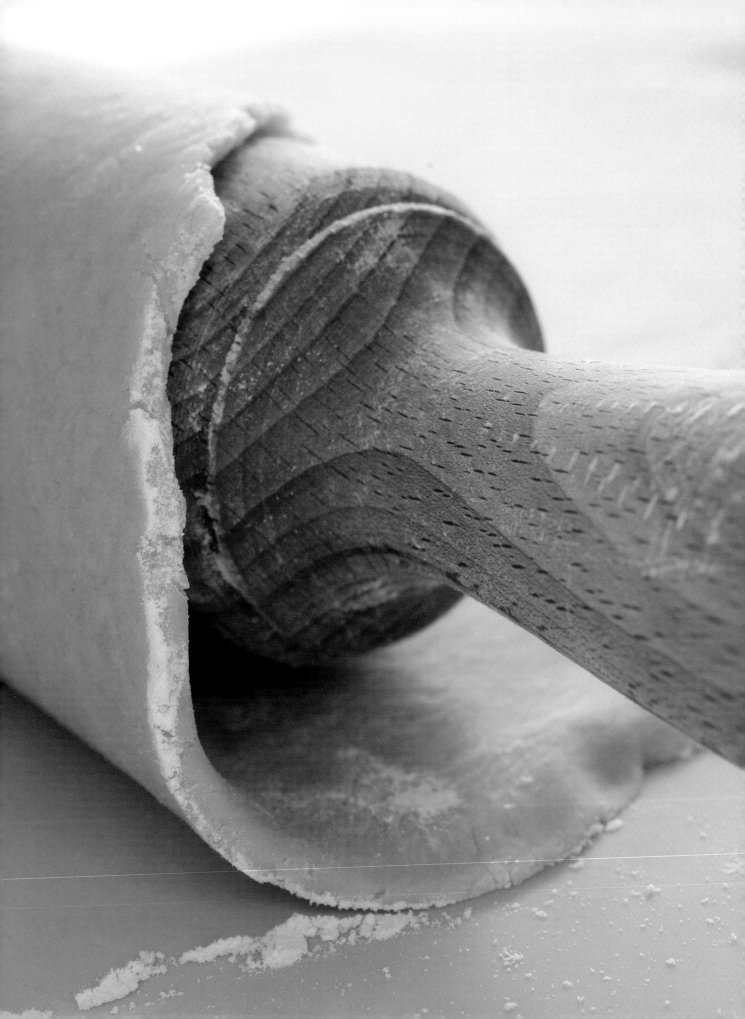

Cakes & Bread

Contents

400 g (14 oz) flour

 200 g (7 oz) unsalted butter,
cut into small pieces and chilled

 100 g (3½ oz) granulated sugar

 1 pinch of salt

 2 eggs

Sweet Shortcrust Dough

1. Place the flour, the chilled butter pieces, the sugar and the salt together on a work surface.

2. Using both hands, quickly rub the butter into the flour. If it is worked too long, the butter will get warm and the dough will crumble later.

3. Next add 1 egg and 1 egg yolk and work them in. Store the remaining egg white in the refrigerator for later use.

4. Knead the dough briskly and thoroughly until it is smooth and has an elastic consistency.

Wrap it in cling film and refrigerate it for at least 1 hour. Then continue working it as desired.

Makes about 750 g (1 lb 10 oz).

75

■ Substitute finely chopped almonds for a quarter of the flour. Then prepare the dough as described, form into biscuits and bake until golden brown.

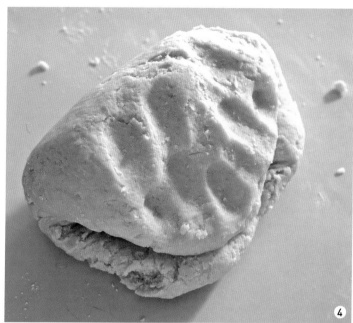

500 g (1 lb 2 oz) sweet shortcrust dough (see p. 702)

2 tbsp flour

100 g (3½ oz) of any fruit jam (e.g. raspberry, redcurrant or apricot)

1 tbsp icing sugar

①

Jam-filled Biscuits

1. Preheat the oven to 200°C (400°F/Gas Mark 6). Roll out the dough on a flour-dusted surface to a thickness of slightly less than 2 mm (⅛ inch). Continually flip the dough as you roll, sprinkling more flour each time so that it doesn't stick to the work surface.

2. Cut out desired shapes from the dough.

3. Put the biscuits on a baking tray lined with baking paper, then bake in the oven.

Keep an eye on the biscuits while baking. Because they are rolled out so thinly, they can quickly get too brown. Baking time is usually around 8–10 minutes.

4. Remove the biscuits from the baking tray using the baking paper and let them cool. Spread jam on half of the biscuits.

5. Place the other halves on top.

Sprinkle with icing sugar and arrange on a plate.

✳
✳ 50
✳

■ If there are no biscuit cutters handy, use the rim of a glass.

8 eggs

 120 g (4¼ oz) granulated sugar

 1 pinch of salt

 60 g (2¼ oz) pastry flour

40 g (1½ oz) cornflour

 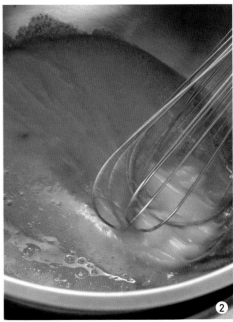

Sponge Cake

1. Preheat the oven to 190°C (375°F/Gas Mark 5). Separate the eggs and add the egg yolks to a mixing bowl. Set aside 4 of the egg whites. Store the remaining egg whites in the refrigerator for later use. Add 60 g (2¼ oz) of the sugar to the egg yolks.

2. Beat the egg yolks and sugar for about 5 minutes, until the mixture is a pale yellow.

3. Slowly beat the 4 egg whites and salt in another bowl. Stir in the remaining sugar a little at a time and beat with a mixer on a medium speed until stiff peaks form, then on the highest speed for 30 seconds. Add the beaten egg whites to the egg yolks and carefully fold them in using a rubber spatula.

4. Sift the flour and cornflour using a fine sieve. This keeps any flour clumps from making it into the sponge cake.

5. Then carefully mix them in using a rubber spatula, without hitting the sides of the bowl. This would 'shock' the sponge cake batter slightly, keeping it from rising properly. To be spongy, the cake must have a lot of air.

6. Line a 30- × 40-cm (12- × 16-inch) baking tray with baking paper, pour the mixture in and smooth it over. Bake the sponge cake in the oven for about 10 minutes, until it is golden yellow. Remove it from the oven and let it cool slightly before working with it further.

■ To make a chocolate sponge cake, fold in 20 g (¾ oz) of preferably low-fat cocoa powder. Then bake as directed. Chocolate sponge cake tastes really delicious as a roll with cherries and cherry marmalade.

1 sponge cake (see p. 706)

 1 tbsp granulated sugar

 200 g (7 oz) strawberries

 200 g (7 oz) strawberry jam

Strawberry Swiss Roll

1. Flip the baked sponge cake, still warm, onto a piece of baking paper sprinkled with sugar. Carefully pull off the top layer of baking paper.

2. Carefully roll up the sponge cake and let it cool. If it is left to cool while rolled up, it won't break later when rolled again – the shape is set in advance, so to speak. In the meantime, clean the strawberries and cut them into thin slices.

3. Unroll the sponge cake and spread the strawberry jam over it. Evenly distribute the sliced strawberries over the jam.

4. Next, roll up the filled sponge cake using both hands, applying a light pressure to keep any hollow spaces out of the roll. Let the finished roll cool off for another 15 minutes and then cut it into slices about 2.5 cm (1 inch) thick.

Arrange on a platter and serve with fresh whipped cream as desired.

■ Rubbing the top sheet of baking paper with moist kitchen paper will make it easier to pull it off the top of the sponge cake after it is flipped out of the tray.

250 g (9 oz) unsalted butter

 450 g (1 lb) granulated sugar

 50 g (1¾ oz) vanilla sugar

 4 eggs

 180 g (6 oz) unsweetened cocoa powder

 250 g (9 oz) flour

 1 tsp baking powder

 1 pinch of salt

 150 g (5½ oz) ground almonds

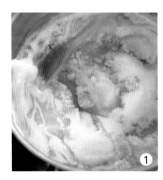

Chocolate Brownies

1. Preheat the oven to 180°C (350°F/ Gas Mark 4). Slowly melt the butter in a wide pan. Mix in the granulated sugar and vanilla sugar. Remove from the heat, and stir in the eggs one at a time.

2. Stir the unsweetened cocoa powder into the butter-sugar mixture using a whisk, then add the sifted flour, baking powder, salt and the ground almonds, mixing everything evenly.

3. Add the mixture to a nonstick baking tray and smooth the surface. Bake the

brownies in the oven for about 35 minutes. Remove the tray from the oven and let it cool. Flip the brownies out of the tray and cut them into 4-cm (1½-inch) squares.

Serve the brownies warm, perhaps with a scoop of vanilla ice cream.

■ **For more chocolate flavour, coarsely chop some bitter chocolate and stir it into the brownie batter, then bake.**

 60

1

2

3

 100 g (3½ oz) soft brown sugar

 250 g (9 oz) unsalted butter

 400 g (14 oz) granulated sugar

 30 g (1 oz) vanilla sugar

 280 g (10 oz) walnuts

 4 eggs

 180 g (6¼ oz) unsweetened cocoa powder

 220 g (7¾ oz) flour

 1 tsp baking powder

1 pinch of salt

Walnut Caramel Brownies

1. Preheat the oven to 180°C (350°F/ Gas Mark 4). In a wide pan over a medium heat, let the soft brown sugar caramelise. Then pour in 100 ml (3½ fl oz) of cold water to dissolve the caramelised sugar. Add the butter, melt it, and remove the pan from the heat. Mix in both sugars. Coarsely chop 200 g (7 oz) of the walnuts and set them aside.

2. Stir in the eggs a little at a time first, then the unsweetened cocoa. Through a fine sieve, sift the flour, baking powder and salt into the mixture. Evenly mix in the coarsely chopped walnuts.

3. Spread the mixture on a nonstick baking tray and smooth the surface. Add the remaining walnuts. Bake the brownies in the oven for about 35 minutes. Remove the tray from the oven and let the brownies cool. Flip the brownies out of the tray and cut them into 4-cm (1½-inch) squares. Serve the brownies warm, perhaps with a scoop of vanilla ice cream and caramel sauce.

■ Brownies also taste good with a variety of other nuts such as macadamias, pecans or Brazil nuts – increase the portion of nuts by half again.

60

✳
✳
✳

350 ml (12 fl oz) milk

 100 g (3½ oz) unsalted butter

 500 g (1 lb 2 oz) flour

 42 g (1½ oz) easy-blend yeast

 1 pinch of salt

 80 g (2¾ oz) granulated sugar

 2 eggs

Yeast Dough

1. Warm the milk and butter until the butter begins to melt. Sift the flour into a bowl and make a well in the middle. Crumble the yeast into the well, and then sprinkle the salt and half of the sugar over the yeast. Pour in a quarter of the warm milk and mix together using a wooden spoon. Keep adding in flour from the sides of the well a little at a time. The starter in the middle should have the consistency of pancake batter as this will best enable the yeast to expand. Cover with a tea towel and leave it to rise in a warm place for about 15 minutes.

2. Crack both eggs and add them. Mix in the remaining sugar and warm milk a little at a time, and incorporate the flour, too.

3. Beat the dough until it no longer sticks to the bowl and its surface is smooth. This means the flour is thoroughly worked in and the dough will rise evenly. Cover the dough with a tea towel again, and let it rise for 30 minutes. After this time, the dough can be worked further.

■ The finished dough can be covered and stored in the refrigerator. This impedes the rising of the dough, so it can be prepared the night before use. However, the dough must be brought back to room temperature and kneaded again before baking.

 **70**

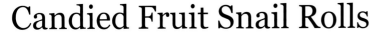

1

2

3

50 g (1¾ oz) flour

1 portion of yeast dough (see opposite page)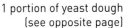

200 g (7 oz) candied fruit

100 g (3½ oz) raisins

30 g (1 oz) dried unsweetened coconut

30 g (1 oz) unsalted butter

50 g (1¾ oz) granulated sugar

200 ml (7 fl oz) cream

1 egg

Candied Fruit Snail Rolls

1. Preheat the oven to 180°C (350°F/Gas Mark 4). Using a rolling pin on a flour-coated surface, roll out the dough to a thickness of slightly less than 1 cm (½ inch). Cut the candied fruit into roughly 2-mm (⅛-inch) pieces, mix them with the raisins and coconut, then distribute over the dough. Next roll up the dough.

2. Grease a baking dish with the butter and coat with the sugar. Cut the dough roll into 3-cm (1¼-inch) thick slices, and place them side by side in the dish. Cover them with a tea towel and leave to rise for 30 minutes.

3. Using a whisk, whip the cream and the egg in a bowl. Pour the mixture over the snail rolls after they have risen. Bake in the oven for about 35 minutes until golden brown. Remove and leave to cool.

Serve with vanilla sauce and whipped cream as desired.

■ **If the dough tears during rolling, simply pull a little dough over the torn area and press it together again using your fingers.**

50

100 g (3½ oz) unsalted butter

 100 g (3½ oz) icing sugar

 80 g (2¾ oz) granulated sugar

 ½ tsp salt

 150 g (5½ oz) pecans

 175 g (6 oz) pastry flour

 1 tsp baking powder

 1 egg

60 g (2¼ oz) flour

Butter Pecan Cookies

1. Rub the butter into the icing sugar, the sugar and the salt with your hands, quickly so the butter doesn't get too warm. Finely grind half the pecans, then coarsely chop the rest.

2. Sift the flour and baking powder over the butter mixture and work it in as with a shortcrust dough. Mix the nuts into the dough.

3. Next add the egg, and knead everything into a uniform dough. Proceed briskly so the butter doesn't get too soft and the dough doesn't get sticky.

4. Roll the dough into a 5-cm (2-inch) roll, cover it in clear cling film, and put it in the refrigerator to chill for 1 hour. This makes the dough much easier to work with.

5. Preheat the oven to 180°C (350°F/Gas Mark 4). Lay a piece of baking paper onto a baking tray. Cut the dough into 2-cm (¾-inch) thick slices and spread them out on the tray, leaving a little space between them. Bake in the oven for about 20 minutes, until golden yellow. Remove the biscuits from the oven and leave them to cool. For best results, store them in a sealable container.

The biscuits taste good with cold milk, fresh coffee or hot chocolate.

■ For chocolate biscuits, work 200 g (7 oz) of coarsely chopped plain or white chocolate and the nuts into the dough. Then bake as directed.

800 g (1 lb 12 oz) quark

 200 ml (7 fl oz) milk

 100 ml (3½ fl oz) cream

 5 eggs

 1 lemon

 50 g (1¾ oz) unsalted butter

 80 g (2¾ oz) vanilla sugar

 90 g (3¼ oz) cornflour

 1 pinch of salt

 120 g (4½ oz) granulated sugar

 250 g (9 oz) sweet shortcrust dough (see p. 702)

German Cheesecake

1. Preheat the oven to 220°C (425°F/Gas Mark 7). Put the quark in a bowl and mix it with the milk and cream until smooth. Separate the eggs and put the egg whites in a covered bowl in the refrigerator. Rinse the lemon with hot water, then finely grate the zest. Cut the lemon in half and squeeze the juice into a bowl. Melt the butter.

2. Add the egg yolk, melted butter, half the vanilla sugar, the lemon juice, lemon zest and cornflour to the quark, and stir everything with a wire whisk until smooth.

3. Beat the cold egg whites with the salt and granulated sugar until creamy peaks form, and then fold them into the quark mixture.

4. Roll out the dough to a thickness of slightly less than 5 mm (¼ inch), and place it in a nonstick springform tin. Cut any excess crust from around the edges with a knife. Fill the crust with the quark mixture and smooth the surface. Put the tin in the oven. After about 5 minutes remove the cake from the oven. Insert a knife by the crust into the skin that develops on top of the cake and make a cut all along the crust. Put the tin back into the oven and bake another 15 minutes. Then take it out again, let the cake sink a little and turn the oven down to 160°C (325°F/Gas Mark 3). Then let the cake bake for another 35 minutes.

5. Remove the cake from the oven, let it cool and take it out of the springform tin. Put it on a cake platter and cut into pieces. Serve it warm with the remaining vanilla sugar sprinkled on top.

■ German cheesecake tastes especially good slightly warm, but it's harder to cut that way – so be careful! Add 50 g (1¾ oz) of rum-soaked raisins to the quark batter if desired.

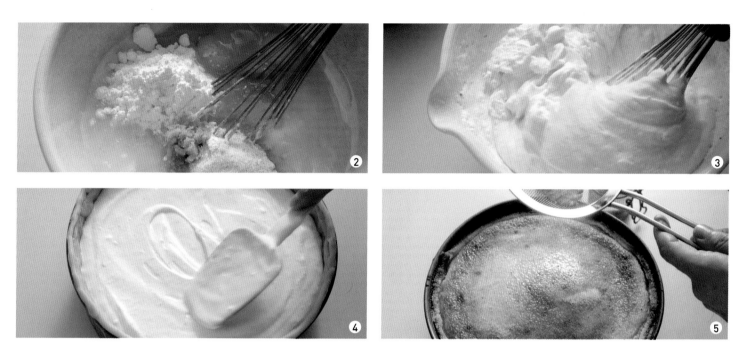

3 eggs

 250 g (9 oz) granulated sugar

 1 tbsp vanilla sugar

 100 ml (3½ fl oz) milk

 120 g (4¼ oz) unsalted butter

 280 g (10 oz) flour

 2 tsp baking powder

 1 pinch of salt

 1 tsp cornflour

 200 g (7 oz) redcurrants

 200 g (7 oz) blueberries

Redcurrant and Blueberry Meringue Cake

1. Preheat the oven to 180°C (350°F/Gas Mark 4). Separate the eggs. Beat the egg yolks with 150 g (5½ oz) of the granulated sugar and the vanilla sugar in a mixing bowl until peaks form. Put the egg whites in a bowl then in the refrigerator. Bring the milk and 100 g (3½ oz) of the butter to the boil, pour it into the sugar-egg mixture and stir well.

2. Sift 250 g (9 oz) of the flour and the baking powder into the bowl and mix everything together.

3. Grease a 28-cm (11-inch) springform tin with butter and coat with the remaining flour. Then fill with the batter and bake in the oven for 18 minutes. Remove the cake from the oven and leave it to cool a bit.

4. Using a mixer, beat the egg whites, a pinch of salt and the remaining sugar until creamy. Add the cornflour and beat on the highest setting for 1 minute, until stiff peaks form. Remove any damaged berries, reserve 1 tbsp of each fruit, and mix the remainder carefully into the egg whites. This makes a fruity meringue.

5. Spread the meringue over the baked cake.

6. Sprinkle the reserved berries over the meringue. Set the oven to grill at 220°C (425°F/Gas Mark 7). Place the cake on the middle rack and bake it again for about 15 minutes. Remove the pan from the oven and let it cool. Finally, cut it into pieces.

■ After the cake has cooled, spread 3-cm (1¼-inch) thick layers of vanilla and chocolate ice cream over it. Cover with the meringue and bake for 5 minutes at 250°C (480°F/Gas Mark 9½). Remove it from the oven and serve immediately. This makes an especially delicious and festive dessert.

250 g (9 oz) rye flour

 500 g (1 lb 2 oz) plain flour

 600 ml (1 pint) lukewarm water

 1 tsp sea salt

 20 g (⅔ oz) easy-blend yeast

 1 tsp granulated sugar

 20 g (⅔ oz) unsalted butter

 1 tbsp oil

 50 g (1¾ oz) flour

1

Home-made Bread with Sea Salt

1. Sift 150 g (5½ oz) of the rye flour and 150 g (5½ oz) of the plain flour into a bowl. Stir in 500 ml (17 fl oz) of the water and the sea salt, then let the dough sit for 1 hour.

2. Stir the yeast and the sugar into the rest of the water, then let it rise for 15 minutes.

3. Add the yeast mixture, the room-temperature butter and the oil to the dough, and mix everything together.

4. Add the remaining all-purpose and rye flours a little at a time, and mix everything into a smooth dough. In a food processor fitted with a dough hook, knead the dough for 5 minutes.

5. Cover it with a tea towel and let it rise for at least 1 hour.

6. Preheat the oven to 210°C (410°F/Gas Mark 6½). Place the dough on a floured surface, shape into a long loaf and lay it on a baking tray. Sprinkle more flour over it, cover it with a tea towel and let it rise for 15 minutes.

7. Using a knife, gently cut into the top of the dough. Bake it in the oven for about 50 minutes. Remove the bread from the oven and let it cool.

Slice the bread and spread butter over it.

+ 2¾ hours rising time

■ For a beautiful crust, pour an espresso cup full of water on the hot oven floor, and then quickly close the oven door again.

500 g (1 lb 2 oz) wholemeal flour

 42 g (1½ oz) easy-blend yeast

 1 tsp granulated sugar

 ½ tsp salt

 80 g (2¾ oz) unsalted butter

 300 ml (10 fl oz) lukewarm water

 100 g (3½ oz) poppy seeds

Sunday Rolls with Poppy Seeds

1. Sift the flour into a bowl and make a well in the middle. Crumble the yeast into it, add the sugar and salt, then the butter and 100 ml (3½ fl oz) of the water. Stir it to form a dough starter. Cover with a tea towel, and let it rise for 15 minutes. Stir the remaining water into the dough and knead the dough for 5 minutes in a food processor fitted with a dough hook. Cover with a tea towel again, and let it rise in a warm place for 30 minutes.

2. Roll out the dough on a floured surface and cut it into 50-g (1¾-oz) pieces.

3. Knead each piece once, from the outside inwards.

4. Preheat the oven at 220°C (425°F/Gas Mark 7). Form each into a round roll with your hands.

5. Brush a little water over the tops and roll them in the poppy seeds.

6. Put the rolls on a baking tray lined with baking paper, and cut crosses into the tops with scissors. Then cover the rolls with a tea towel and let them rise for another 20 minutes. Next, put them on the middle rack of the oven. Pour an espresso cup full of water onto the oven floor and close the door again quickly. The steam makes the rolls nice and crispy. Bake the rolls for about 20 minutes or until golden. Then remove them from the oven and serve warm.

Makes 18 rolls.

+ 65 minutes rising time

* * *
45

■ Top the Sunday rolls with different ingredients as desired – for example, chopped pistachios, sunflower seeds, sesame seeds, green pumpkin seeds, chopped hazelnuts or walnuts.

Cheese

Contents

Where Does Cheese Come From?

Cheese is one of the oldest foods made by human beings. Research suggests that it already existed in Neolithic times, at the end of the fifth and the beginning of the fourth centuries BC. The Code of the Babylonian King Hammurabi already mentions cheese, bread and beer in 1750 BC. The Romans discovered tasty varieties of cheese in Gaul (France), which were in great demand in Rome, although not all of them survived the trip. The more detailed the historical chronicles were for an era, the more extensively the historians wrote on cheese.

Actual cheese production is simple: warm milk curdles on its own. If you let the whey, which mainly consists of water, drain off, you will be left with cheese, even if it is only a very sour cream cheese. The milk will curdle more dependably if you add rennet – a natural substance, which is found not only in the stomachs of calves, sheep and other mammals, but also in many plants. It was known to shepherds and nomads who often stored their milk in pouches made from the stomachs of goats or sheep, whose natural rennet accelerated cheese production. Cheese was produced not just for reasons of taste: large quantities of milk could be preserved quickly as cheese.

Of course, cheese was always made from the milk that was available at the time. We still see cheese made from the milk of cows, sheep and goats on our menus today. The milk of water buffalo is traditionally used to make Italian mozzarella, even though a lot of mozzarella is made from cow's milk today.

A Finnish cheese called Ilves is traditionally made from reindeer's milk. In Jordan, herdsmen use the milk of sheep, goats, cows and camels for their labaneh (yogurt cheese).

Cheese is still produced today using the same basic principles: letting the milk curdle first, draining the whey, and then salting, washing and finally ageing the cheese.

Proper storage and ageing of the cheese are important. Only fresh cheese needs practically no time to mature. Depending on the type, the storage time for cheese can amount to several years, as is the case with Parmesan, which is used dried over various dishes, and requires ample time to mature.

Cheese Categories

Fresh cheese: For this kind of cheese, rennet is usually simply stirred into the milk and allowed to stand. Fresh cheese has a high moisture content and is not pressed, but salt is rubbed onto or into it. It is mild and has a milky taste.

Pressed cheese that is not reheated: Also known as 'semi-firm cheese'. This category includes Pecorino Romano, Edam, Gouda, Reblochon, Cheddar and Cantal, among others.

The curds are skimmed off, crushed and put into moulds. The whey is pressed out. The 'raw cheese' is then removed from the mould and put into a salt bath. While it is ripening, it is regularly salted, turned and brushed. The brushing process imparts an even colour to the rind.

Pressed cheese that is reheated: This category includes Gruyère, Emmental, Parmesan, Comté and Beaufort. They are traditionally made with 'evening milk' (milk which is taken from the cow in the evening) that is left to rest overnight and then mixed with morning milk on the following day. Then rennet is added to the cheese at 33°C (91°F) and the mixture is heated up to 53°C (127°F) (this process is also called 'cooking'). The season is also important. Cheese made with 'summer milk', when cows are eating grass and wild herbs in mountain pastures, is more flavourful than 'winter milk', which comes from animals that are fed with hay.

Cheese with edible mould: Camembert, Brillat-Savarin and Brie de Meaux are examples of this category. They are neither pressed nor cooked, but salted after thickening and sprayed with *Penicillium candidum*. This allows the fine, fur-like growth of mould to sprout.

Cheese with a washed rind: Such as Époisses, Maroilles, Livarot, Münster, Remoudou, Langres and Limburger. They have a strong smell but they range from surprisingly mild to hearty in taste. This type of cheese is washed regularly with a weak saline solution and turned over.

Cheese with a natural rind: Cheese such as Chabichou de Poitou, Saint-Maure de Touraine and Crottin de Chavignol belong to this category.

They are mostly sheep's and goat's cheeses from the Loire Valley, Spain or Italy. The milk is first heated to 30°C (86°F), then the curd is cut and ladled into containers.

Blue cheese: This category includes Stilton, Gorgonzola, Fourme d'Ambert and Roquefort.

Most varieties of blue cheese are produced from cow's milk. The most prominent representative of this category is among the exceptions: sheep's milk is used to make Roquefort, France's first cheese to receive an AOC (Appellation of Guaranteed Origin). Rennet for blue cheese is added to milk at temperatures of around 30°C (86°F). Then, later on, the curd is poured into a mould that is lined with cloth. Even after the cheese is taken out of the mould, it remains in the cloth initially and is turned regularly to allow the whey to drain. Then the wheel is salted and injected with *Penicillium roqueforti* or *Penicillium gorgonzola*.

Processed cheese: The Swiss sapsago variety falls into this category.

It is created by melting down pressed cheese. Then, butter, cream, milk and often flavouring agents are added.

Raw milk cheese: This is made from unpasteurised milk and the taste is thus better preserved. Raw milk cheese can also taste different in the summer than in winter, as cows eat different food, depending on the season. Due to long maturing times and a lot of manual work such as washing the cheese with marc (brandy distilled from grape skins and seeds), such delicacies are also substantially more expensive than cheese made from pasteurised milk. If you are lucky, you'll find them on the cheese trolleys of better restaurants or in gourmet cheese stores.

Some countries such as the United States completely prohibit the import of raw milk cheese. One reason for prohibitions of this kind is hygiene regulations. During pasteurisation, milk is rapidly heated up to 90°C (194°F), and harmful germs such as malignant listeriosis bacteria, which also lurk in sausage, raw meat mince or smoked fish, are effectively killed. Getting ill from cheese can be serious and the legal requirements for raw milk cheese are strict: animals must not have any diseases that are transferable by means of milk, and the germ content must not exceed a certain limit. Last but not least, even in small, artisanal, working cheese dairies, all procedures must follow specific hygiene standards. Dim, mould-covered cellars have been replaced by stainless steel, and computers monitor the temperature and air humidity.

Storing cheese properly: Cheese is always palatable and attractive if you keep it under a glass dome, and this sight is also sure to please your guests. Cheese domes were useful when cheese was stored in cool cellars, but nowadays they are nothing more than expensive fly protection. Most cheese varieties will do well at temperatures of 8–10°C (46–50°F) and with 80–90 per cent air humidity. Modern cheese makers have sophisticated ageing cellars where the air humidity and temperature are strictly monitored.

At home, you can confidently store cheese in the salad drawer of your refrigerator, provided you remember to take it out some time before eating it. Cold cheese doesn't develop its full flavour, and for discerning palates it is as interesting as cold coffee.

Seals of quality: DOC, DO and AOC? Like good wine, good cheese also has its seals of quality. This guarantees that the cheese was produced using traditional methods.

It is very important to make sure that your cheese has received a seal of quality. A name like Camembert or Gorgonzola alone

has not stood for traditional production for a long time. Many cheese names are not legally protected. The supposedly original cheese can be produced quite legally in any country.

Distinctions

AOC (Appellation d'Origine Contrôlée): Appellation of Guaranteed Origin, France.
Label Rouge: Red label, France.
DOC (Denominazione di Origine Controllata): Controlled Denomination of Origin, Italy.

DO (Denominación de Origen): Denomination of Origin, Spain.

British Cheese Awards: A kind of 'taste Olympics' for cheese dairies and producers in the 'fresh cheese', 'soft cheese' and 'blue cheese' sectors. The very best cheeses are awarded the title of 'Supreme Champion'.

PDO and PGI: These are distinctions awarded at European level, on the model of the French AOC. The Protected Designation of Origin (PDO) and the Protected

Geographical Indication (PGI) indicate that the product must be produced, processed and manufactured in a specific geographical area in accordance with a recognised, specific process.

200 g (7 oz) Gruyère

 200 g (7 oz) Appenzell

 350 g (12 oz) raclette cheese

 250 ml (8½ fl oz) white wine

 1 garlic clove

 1 pinch of nutmeg, freshly grated

 1 pinch of black pepper

20 g (⅔ oz) cornflour

Cheese Fondue

1. Cut the rind off the Gruyère, the Appenzell and the raclette cheese, and grate the cheese coarsely.

2. Put the white wine, the peeled garlic clove and the nutmeg into a saucepan and bring the mixture to the boil.

3. Add the cheese and season with black pepper.

4. Stir the mixture constantly with a wire whisk, until the cheese melts and combines with the liquid.

5. Stir the cornflour into 3 tbsp water until no lumps remain and pour this mixture slowly into the cheese fondue, stirring it constantly.

6. Then let it come to the boil again until the cornflour thickens the cheese fondue. Pour the mixture into a fondue pot and serve it with a generous amount of white bread cut into pieces, small unpeeled potatoes, pickled vegetables and fresh black pepper.

■ At the end, mix 40 ml (1½ fl oz) of kirsch (cherry brandy) into the cheese fondue or serve the kirsch in chilled glasses as an accompaniment to the fondue. If you leave the cheese rind on, the fondue will have a stronger flavour.

Wine

Contents

Champagne

Champagne: Whenever we hear the word 'Champagne', we associate this region less with Chagall and Joan of Arc than we do with Dom Pérignon, the monk who supposedly discovered the Champagne method in 1688.

Unlike wine, Champagne is purposefully oriented and attuned to a clientele. Raw wines from various locations and up to ten varied vintages are combined by the cellarmaster to create the desired taste, and are sweetened with a greater or smaller dose of sugar. That sounds like adulteration, but it is real alchemy. Brut Champagne (very dry Champagne) always tastes the same, no matter where it comes from or its age. The classification above Brut is called 'Champagne millésimé'– a vintage Champagne that is only produced in particularly good years.

Its well-known competitors are Winzersekt, Cava, Crémant or Spumante, and come from Germany, the United States, Spain, France and Italy. Bottles of those wines are less expensive than 'authentic Champagne', but they are not second rate, by any means. Although Champagne may only be produced in the Champagne region, the production process is used all over the world and many wine merchants produce their sparkling wines in exactly the same way as the more expensive competition.

Many sparkling wines do not undergo a second round of fermentation in the bottle, as Champagne does, but are fermented in huge pressurised tanks, in accordance with the Charmat method. This does not necessarily detract from the quality – in the opinion of oenologists, the quality of the raw wine is more important than the fermentation process. Californian sparkling wines, for example, are regularly awarded prizes.

The Grape Varieties:

Pinot Meunier: A red grape variety. It produces fruity wines with little acidity and is often used during the blending process to make Champagne more mellow or to blend the other grape varieties better. It is planted on approximately 48 per cent of the cultivated area.

Pinot Noir: A red grape variety. It makes Champagne more potent and is planted on approximately 28 per cent of the cultivated area. A wine made from Pinot Noir, Pinot Meunier or a blend of the two Pinots is called 'blanc de noirs' (white wine from red grapes).

Chardonnay: A white grape variety, cultivated on 24 per cent of the area. It adds freshness, delicacy and lightness to Champagne and makes it more sparkling. Champagne made entirely from Chardonnay grapes is called 'blanc de blancs' (white wine from white grapes).

'Terroirs' and 'crus': Grand cru sites are located in the Côte des Blancs and Montagne de Reims growing areas.

Rosé: There are two approved methods for the production of rosé Champagne. Either a rosé wine is subjected to the classic *méthode champenoise* (Champagne method), or white Champagne is blended with a small amount of red wine (10–15 per cent). The calculation 'red + white = rosé" is allowed by French law exclusively in the region of Champagne.

Mysterious abbreviations: Two tiny letters beside the name of the producer provide information about the true origin of their Champagne:

CM: *Coopérative de manipulation* – Champagne from a cooperative.
MA: *Marque auxiliaire* (subsidiary brand), *Marque d'acheteur* (buyer's brand) – A Champagne bottler's subsidiary brand. It can be bottled specially for consumption in restaurants and it's rarely good if it's a supermarket brand.
NM: *Négociant manipulant* – Champagne from a Champagne company.
RC: *Récoltant coopérateur* – Champagne from a wine grower who is a member of a cooperative.

RM: *Récoltant manipulant* – Champagne from a grower.
SR: *Société de récoltants* – Product of an association of growers.

Tips for Enjoying Champagne

– Storage conditions greatly affect Champagne. Champagne does not like harsh neon light, high temperatures or fluctuating temperatures. It is best if stored at approximately 13°C (55°F) in the dark.

– Young Champagnes and most blancs de blancs are served very cold (at approximately 7°C/45°F); vintage and robust Champagnes may be somewhat warmer (approximately 9–10°C/48–50°F).

– It is only on advertising posters from the *Belle Époque* that Champagne is drunk out of goblets. To enjoy Champagne at its best, you need flutes or tulip-shaped glasses.

– Don't hesitate to store some bottles of good vintages. Champagne does not 'die', i.e. does not turn into vinegar when stored properly, although it loses some of its sparkle over time, becomes mellower and more full-bodied, and sometimes takes on a hint of Madeira.

Sweet Wines

In 1847, Marquis Romain-Bertrand de Lur-Saluces gave the employees at his vineyard instructions that the grape harvest should not begin until his return from a hunting trip to Russia. However, the nobleman's trip lasted longer than anticipated and the grapes had fallen prey to a fungus by the time he returned home. This did not deter him from harvesting them and this proved a blessing in disguise, as the outcome was an excellent sweet wine with an incomparable taste: Château d'Yquem. So goes the legend. Curiously enough, almost the same anecdote is told in the neighboring Château Suduiraut. The only differences are the gender of the main character and the century. Actually, a document dated 4 October 1866, discovered in the regional archives of the Département of the Gironde, proved that the delayed grape harvest was already a long-standing tradition in the region.

Botrytis cinerea is the name of the fungus that still affects grapes in the environs of Sauternes and in Germany's best wine locations. Wine merchants also call it 'noble rot', which is almost a contradiction in itself from a linguistic point of view. When the fungus seems to be destroying the grape, it is actually improving it. Spores penetrate the skin of the berries and promote the evaporation of water in the fruit pulp. The grapes dry out and the concentration of sugar and fruit substances is increased. In addition, the glycerine content increases, making the wine 'oilier' and smoother. Its flavour is similar to honey, and when it is swirled in the glass, it leaves streaks. The rare vintages have been praised in the highest terms by wine critics who have used terms such as 'drinkable light' and 'liquid gold'.

Sweet wines of this kind are a nice accompaniment to foie gras, but they also taste first class with chicken salad, sweetbreads in a cream sauce, duck à l'orange, or with blue cheese such as Roquefort. A classic culinary masterpiece is turbot in Sauternes.

Incidentally, the wines with the honey bouquet are among the most expensive wines in the world. The wines of Egon Müllers Scharzhof in Wiltingen regularly break records for prices at auctions, fetching 2,350 euros (£2,200) for a bottle of *Trockenbeerenauslese* (a wine made with late harvest grapes affected by *Botrytis cinerea*) – a record for a 'young' wine. The 7 hectares (17 acres) at the best locations of the Scharzhofberg vineyard, which have been family owned since 1797, are well known to Asian and American wine connoisseurs. Currently, 50,000 bottles leave this prestigious winery every year, and the Trockenbeerenauslese and ice wines are absolute collectors' items. Yquem still competes with them due to the carefully tended legend. 'The summers of the past burn in the bottles of Yquem,' wrote François Mauriac, winner of the Nobel Prize for Literature. Even Lenin considered growing these grape vines in Russian soil. However, grapes and the right climate alone are not enough. To make really good use of the effect of the noble rot, each individual grape must be picked at its ideal stage of ripeness.

The grape pickers go through the vines at least five times and select the grapes one by one each time. The harvest will take about 45 days, as long as it is not stopped by the first drops of rain. The juice alone is so valuable that the wooden collection baskets are sealed with wax.

MALAGA
VIRGEN

SIRVASE FRIO

Pedro Ximen

Su inconfundible
sabor a uva de
Málaga se realza
al beberlo frío.
¡Disfrútelo!
V.L.C.P.R.D.
— Añada 2002 —

López Hermanos, S.A.
Canadá 10 - Málaga

Alc. 17% Vol.   R.E. 410-MA   75 cl. e

What Is on the Label?

Spain

DO (Denominación de Origen): Denomination of Guaranteed Origin. The Spanish equivalent of the DOC and the AOC.

Vino de la tierra: Country wine.

France

AOC (Appellation d'Origine Contrôlée): Denomination of Guaranteed Origin for better wines.

VDQS (Vin Délimité de Qualité Supérieure): A superior-quality wine with an indication of its origin.

Vin de pays: Country wine.

Vin de table: Table wine. At its worst, it's blended with wines from other EU countries.

First to Fifth Growth (*cru classé*): For Médoc or Sauterne wines. This classification originated in 1855 and was modified only once, in 1973, when Mouton-Rothschild moved up into the top category.

Of course, discerning wine-lovers will select wine bottled by the producer, which can be recognised by the notation 'Mis(e) en bouteille(s) au château' (bottled at the castle) or 'Mis(e) en bouteilles à la propriété' (bottled at the estate). The name and address of the bottler are also required, as well as the quantity and specification of the country of origin for export.

Inscriptions such as 'bottled in the region' or 'Mis(e) en bouteille(s) dans la région' usually mean that the bottle contains a blend of wines from several wine merchants.

Italy

DOCG (Denominazione di Origine Controllata e Garantita): Controlled and Guaranteed Denomination of Origin. For top wines such as Barolo, Barbaresco and Brunello di Montalschino.

DOC (Denominazione di Origine Controllata): Denomination of Guaranteed Origin.

Vini da tavola: Table wines.

Germany

Label

- Production area for choice wines (e.g. Pfalz, Rheingau or Nahe)
- Name of the winery
- Vintage
- Bottled by the producer – means that the wine was bottled right at the winery. Other possible bottlers include distributors and importers.
- Information about the vineyard
- Grape variety (e.g. Riesling, Grey Burgundy and Late Burgundy)
- Information about the quality level of German wines (e.g. Quality wine with distinction)
- Alcohol content of the wine as a percentage of the volume
- Contents of the bottle in litres
- Official control number – contains information about the inspection centre
- Year of inspection and the producer
- Country of origin: in the case of wines for export.

Classification

Tafelwein: Table wine. Simple, not particularly high-quality wine, which must be enhanced with added sugar before fermentation. It can be a blend of wines from various countries.

Landwein: Country wine. May not contain more than 18 g/l (¾ oz/quart) of residual sugar, so it is often dryer than table wine. From a purely theoretical point of view, it is somewhat better than table wine, but far from being a great vintage.

Quality wine from specific growing areas (Q.b.A.): This wine must originate completely from the stipulated region, it must be produced from approved grape varieties, and have a specific must weight that can vary from region to region. That is why it does not offer any guarantee of quality.

Quality wine with distinction (Q.m.P.): From a purely theoretical perspective, this is Germany's top category of wine. As for the previous category, added sugar (chaptalisation) is prohibited and official inspection is required. There are five subcategories, which are based on the must weight. Just like in the case of the 'Quality wine from specific growing area', the quality can vary greatly.

Designations such as 'Grand Vin' (great wine) or 'Reserve' have no legal basis and often emanate from the wine merchant's imagination alone. In addition, imprints with medals and awards do not always vouch for quality. Make sure that the year of the award matches the vintage you are buying.

United States

Front label

- Producer (it's not always the wine merchant who grew the grapes)
- Grape variety
- AVA (American Viticultural Area)
- Vineyard
- Vintage
- Alcohol content (from 7 to 13.9%)
- Proportion of sulphites
- Filtered/unfiltered
- Contents of the bottle (sometimes on the back label).

Back label

- Description of the wine
- Mandatory government warning.

Australia

- Winery, brand or trade name
- Grape variety or style of wine (such as a dry, red wine). The simple word 'wine' is also sufficient
- Region of origin (optional)
- Vintage (optional)
- Bottle size
- Alcohol content
- Standard drinks content (in numbers: for example, 'A bottle contains 7.4 standard drinks')
- A list of allergenic substances (such as sulphites)
- Name and address
- Country of origin.

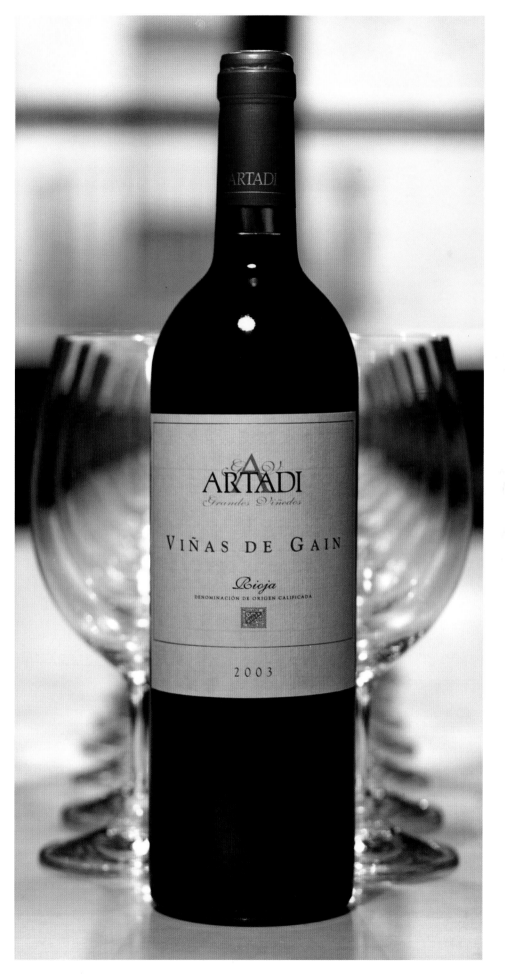

Enjoying Wine

Glasses: Elaborately polished or coloured glasses are not recommended. Although they sometimes look decorative, they hide the colour of the wine. You do not need a different glass for each wine. The professionals from the French INAO (Institut National des Appellations d'Origine), who oversee the testing of wine bottled by producers, use just two: one red wine glass and one white wine glass.

As a general rule, do not drink wine out of glasses made of moulded glass. Avoid quaint designer shapes (square wine glasses have driven even connoisseurs to desperation). Glasses that are customarily used in a region are usually best suited to the local wines.

White wine glasses are smaller and tulip-shaped, and curve inwards. Their shape keeps the flavour in the glass better. Red wine glasses are round bodied as oxygen is good for red wine. The glass can easily be bigger because red wine, which is drunk warmer, does not increase in temperature as quickly.

Temperature: The ineradicable rule that wine is to be enjoyed at room temperature originates from the time before the invention of central heating. Today, wine is served at the following temperatures:

Around 8–9°C (46–48°F) for Champagne, sparkling wines and light whites
10–11°C (50–52°F) for heavier whites such as Rieslings
12–13°C (53–55°F) for great white wines such as noble Chardonnays
14–15°C (57–59°F) for light Beaujolais-style reds
16–17°C (61–63°F) for young reds, and 18–19°C (64–66°F) for heavy, full-bodied red wines such as Barolo and the great Bordeaux wines. In case of doubt, serve the wine preferably a degree too cold. It will eventually warm up on its own.

Corkscrews: There are many types of corkscrews. Some of them promise to remove corks without any effort, or attempt to impress us with particularly nice shapes. Basically, all you need is a solid, traditional corkscrew. It will remove the cork reliably without sticking through it, as this often causes pieces of cork to fall into the wine.

Decanting: Decanting, pouring a wine into a carafe prior to consumption, adds oxygen to a wine and relieves older bottles of sediment (deposits). Many young wines are improved by the addition of oxygen, but you have to be careful with old wines. Many a seasoned old wine has been transformed into a cloudy, lightly alcoholic liquid when decanted hours before drinking. Sommeliers recommend that rare wines should only be decanted shortly before being consumed. However, as with any other rule, there are exceptions. Some old wines are markedly improved by being decanted hours before consumption.

Wine-tasting: If you want to taste several wines one after the other, some basic rules should be followed, no matter whether you are at home or in a restaurant:

· Serve young, light wines first, then follow them with older ones. Otherwise, the young ones will be overwhelmed by the rich taste of the older ones.

· Drink dry wines before sweet ones. Otherwise, the residual sugar will numb your tongue.

· Drink better wines after the less complex ones. In that way, the flavour will increase.

A tasting sip: At first glance, is the colour right? Does the wine seem hazy, dusty or cloudy? Or, on the contrary, is it clear and luminous? Professionals can recognise grape varieties and tell the age of the wine from its colour. To better appreciate whether the red has a slight, rather purple shimmer (a sign of a young wine), or its colour is reminiscent of mahogany (usually a sign of maturity), you should drink by daylight as artificial light can distort the colour. Also, you should hold the glass by its stem, not as you would hold a brandy snifter.

Then let the wine swirl in the glass. If there are hardly any streaks of wine on the edge of the glass, it's light. If you can see several narrow streaks, it is a heavy wine with a high alcoholic content.

Then the nose test: what does the wine smell like? Earth, underbrush, wild cherries? Particularly important: watch out for the smell of musty cork. A pervasive smell of cork is always a cause for alarm. It's often due to flawed corks that let too much oxygen in and inflict their taste on the wine through oxidation. How can we recognise the notorious cork smell? Go ahead and take the time to smell a cork: you will find exactly the same odour and taste in the wine. In short, corked wine is flawed and you would be entitled to send it back in a restaurant. A weak, characterless bouquet is not a good sign either.

Apart from that, it's true that perfume and taste are somewhat subjective. Of course, professionals can recognise immediately whether wine tastes like wild cherries or underbrush, or whether it is nervous, acidic or rich in tannins.

Finally, the actual tasting sip: is the wine at the right temperature? What does it taste like? Here, as well, the taste of cork is once again a sign of a flawed wine. Does the wine have a long finish? That means, does the taste stay in your mouth for a long time after you have swallowed it? That is an excellent characteristic.

And do you like it? Obviously, you have the right not to like a wine, even if it was expensive or comes from a famous *château*. From the perspective of other wine-drinkers, this doesn't mean that you have no taste. You have your own taste.

Buying Wine

Anyone who wants to buy wine on-site from the wine merchant should be aware that the bottles could be damaged on the way home when they are being transported in the boot of a car, due to severe fluctuations in temperature. External aromas can even penetrate into the bottle via the cork – bags of onions or leaking petrol canisters are not ideal companions for a good vintage. After the trip, the wine must first get some rest. Whites should be laid down for approximately four weeks, whereas reds should be left for approximately eight weeks.

Buying wine from the internet

You can find almost any wine on the internet, whether from a mail order hobby business in a garage or a professionally organised range, including everything from inexpensive to rare wines.

Supermarkets

Even if you frequent it every day to buy frozen food or carrots, your supermarket is not a good place for getting the most out of your wine. Months of standing upright under neon lights, at temperatures of around 22°C (72°F) is torture, which only the cheapest, everyday wines can withstand. Gourmet centres are still to be found in reputable stores and the selection there is fitting. Even great Bordeaux wines and Champagnes can be purchased there occasionally at a decent price. The only thing that is left to chance is the advice you receive.

Speciality retailers

A knowledgeable wine merchant is the best person to approach when you are buying wine. Many merchants select their wines personally, know the wine merchants, and can make well-founded recommendations. Most of them store wine correctly and carefully. However, this service means that wines from a speciality retailer are sometimes a little more expensive.

Glossary

Alcohol: Wines have between 8.5 and 15% alcohol by volume.

AOC (Appellation d'Origine Contrôlée): Denomination of Guaranteed Origin. The distinction awarded to first-class French wines.

Assemblage: Blending (mixing) of various grape varieties (such as for Bordeaux wine), or blending of the same wine from several vats.

Astringent: A wine with a high tannin content.

Barrique: An oak barrel with a capacity of 225 litres (59½ gallons).

Botrytis cinerea: Rotten grapes do not always lead to lower-quality wine. *Botrytis cinerea* is a fungus that affects grapes in the area around Sauternes and in Germany's best wine locations. The spores of the fungus penetrate the skin of the grapes and promote the evaporation of water in the flesh of the fruit. The grapes dry out and the concentration of sugar and fruit substances is thus increased. The glycerine content rises; the wine seems 'oilier' and smoother. Its flavour and fragrance are honey-like. Sweet wines of this kind go very well with foie gras or blue cheese.

Bottle fermentation: The second fermentation for Champagnes and other sparkling wines that are produced in a traditional manner. As the name implies, this process happens in the bottle.

Brut: French for very dry.

Cava: Spanish sparkling wine.

Cave: Wine cellar.

Champagne method: Fermentation of Champagne in bottle. In addition to Champagne, wines that are produced in the same way, bear the inscription 'Méthode classique' or 'Méthode traditionelle'.

Chaptalisation: Enriching must with sugar.

Crémant: Sparkling wine.

Cru: French for a good grape-growing area.

Cuvée: A blend of raw wines from different varieties of grape or different vintages.

Decanting: Pouring wine into a carafe.

Development: Ripening of the wine, mostly in steel tanks or wooden barrels.

DO: Spanish and Italian for controlled denomination of origin.

DOCG: The highest distinction for Italian wines, which is currently applied to only 16 wines (Barolo, Barbaresco, Chianti, etc...).

Dry: Wine with less than 9 g (¼ oz) of residual sugar per litre (1¾ pints).

Egg white: Is used to clarify red wine and also binds with yeast and agents, causing cloudiness.

Finish: The flavour impression left by wine after it is swallowed.

Fortification: Adding alcohol or brandy to wine. This is done in the production of liqueur wines such as port.

Gran Reserva: Spanish red wines which have aged for at least six years. A Gran Reserva wine spends two years in a wooden barrel.

Grand Cru: A designation for the best locations and wines in French wine-growing areas.

Ice wine: The grapes are picked at a temperature of -8°C (18°F) or colder, and pressed in a frozen state. It is of at least as high a quality as a sweet wine.

Location: Place and vineyard where the wine was grown.

Liqueur wine: Dessert wine with at least 15% alcohol per volume (e.g. sherry, port, Banyuls and Madeira).

Magnum: A bottle with a capacity of 1.5 litres (2½ pints).

Mature: When a wine has reached the right age to be served.

Must weight: A unit of measurement of the sugar content (and so the potential alcohol content of the wine) on the Öchsle scale.

Noble rot: See *Botrytis cinerea.*

Nose: The aroma and bouquet of the wine.

Oxidation: Occurs when the wine is exposed to oxygen for an extended period of time. This is beneficial to some wines, but can lead to negative effects such as a dull colour and a musty aroma in other wines.

Phylloxera: The scientific name for vine pest.

Sediment: Suspended particles, which are not necessarily a sign of a flawed wine.

Semi-dry: White wines with a residual sugar content of 10–18 g (¼–⅔ oz) per litre (1¾ pints).

Sommelier: A wine waiter or cellarmaster who is in charge of procuring and storing wines for a restaurant and helps restaurant patrons to select a wine which will complement their meals.

Sulphur: Is added to the wine to preserve it and protects it against oxidation.

Sweet wine: A wine made from grapes with *Botrytis cinerea.*

Tannin: It is mostly present in red wine due to the fermentation of the grape skins and their ageing in oak barrels.

Tartar: Acidic deposits in white wines. It's intrinsically harmless and not an indication of poor quality.

Tastevin: A silver tasting cup that is purely decorative nowadays.

Trockenbeerenauslese: A German sweet wine.

Vinification: Winemaking.

Vintage: The year a wine was made.